"Excellent . . . I only wish it could have been available when [my child] was born almost 14 years ago. Because of this book, families who are faced with the near overwhelming task of raising a child with disabilities will now have a short cut to obtaining needed services, supports, and the means to pay for them."

—**Karen A. Shannon,** parent,
Founder, SKIP (Sick Kids [Need] Involved People, Inc.)

"This book represents an excellent overview of programs, resources, and services available for families and children with chronic illness and disability. . . . It is the kind of book that a family can use as a reference book, reading those sections that pertain to a particular time period or need. . . . a wonderful resource for health and other professionals to use and to make available to families."

—**Nancy A. Okinow, M.S.W.,** Executive Director,
National Center for Youth with Disabilities

"a much-needed resource to guide [parents] through the morass of federal programs, private insurance requirements, and other potential sources of help. . . . a valuable road map for those struggling to meet the costs of care for children with special health needs."

—**Marian Wright Edelman,** Founder and President,
Children's Defense Fund

"This book is a valuable and practical guide for families of children with chronic medical problems. The information [presented] has been shown to change behaviors of families concerning both financial management and acquisition for their children of needed services (*Developmental Medicine and Child Neurology*, 1991, Vol. 33, pp. 679–689). In other words, Dr. Rosenfeld's methods have been proven to work."

—**Gordon Worley, M.D.,** Assistant Professor,
Department of Pediatrics, Duke University
Medical Center

*Your Child
and Health Care*

Your Child and Health Care

A "Dollars & Sense" Guide for Families with Special Needs

by

Lynn Robinson Rosenfeld, L.C.S.W., Ph.D.

Private Consultant
Birmingham, Alabama

·P·A·U·L·H·
BROOKES
PUBLISHING C?

Baltimore • London • Toronto • Sydney

Foreword

Lynn Robinson Rosenfeld has done something quite audacious. In *Your Child and Health Care: A "Dollars & Sense" Guide for Families with Special Needs*, she has put the discussion of money on the table. By doing so she removes the stigma that so often accompanies families in their quest for care—and reimbursement.

As the parents of a young child with significant disabilities, my husband and I missed out on some of the insurance benefits to which we were actually entitled. Why? Because we didn't understand that much of the care for our son, who has a high level of paralysis but had none of the colds, fevers, or illnesses we associated with the word "sick," met the requirements of the "prolonged illness" clause in our insurance policy. We didn't think of our son as "sick"! That was 25 years ago; as Lynn Robinson Rosenfeld so aptly states in this book, "the good news and the bad news is that you will get the opportunity for plenty of practice [as advocates for your child]."

Learning words and concepts new to us was one part—perhaps the easy part—of advocating for our son. Understanding what our roles should or could be was quite another matter. No blueprint or guide for families existed. For instance, even though we had talked frequently with our employer, a major university, and our insurers, none of them ever mentioned our eligibility for the "prolonged illness" program. When we learned that our son did qualify for this program, we were surprised and baffled that no one had told us sooner. Over time we learned to read the small print and to ask for what wasn't even in print. We learned to work with other families and health care providers. Above all, we learned to be persistent in our beliefs that there had to be some way to get and pay for the care our son needed and deserved.

At the Federation for Children with Special Needs, we hear daily from families, caregivers, and advocates about the issues families face as they try to get the care their children need—and the means to pay for it. Over the years many exciting and positive changes have occurred, resulting in a proliferation of services, programs, and entitlements. But there is not yet a unified and comprehensive system of care and services; rather, there is a patchwork with many missing pieces. In a statewide survey done several years ago (Project Serve, 1985), families identified that their first need was to obtain information about rights and entitlements for their children. Quite telling though was their second need—help in getting needed services once they had been identified! Actually gaining access to care and services has become a major challenge. Whether intentional or not, the obstacles presented by many systems serve to "ration" care that appears on paper to be available. Perhaps nowhere has this been more true than in the area of health insurance as yearly companies and programs seem to cut back on benefits, increase premiums, and add steps (read *hurdles*) to obtain services.

Throughout this volume, the author outlines for families the kinds of roles they will need to assume, and she offers a wealth of resources and reinforcement for help in doing it. Information, communication, collaboration, and advocacy are the basics, with clear descriptions of the mechanisms and strategies to use. Suggestions to organize home files, methods to keep track of telephone calls, and sample letters are included. Extensive information about parent and other advocacy organizations is provided, which will assist the beginning advocate as well as those with longtime experience. Many of the suggestions for pursuing information and following through can be used in a variety of systems throughout a child's life.

Your Child and Health Care: A "Dollars & Sense" Guide for Families with Special Needs articulately and comprehensively describes the many systems and programs that families are likely to use in ways that they will understand, appreciate, and act on.

In addition to sections on resources and creative ways to obtain care, there are frank discussions of budgeting, managing money, and even how to handle bill collectors. The section about taxes offers substantive information useful in filing federal income tax returns, as well as a state-by-state guide to tax deductions, exemptions, and credits.

Families and other advocates will find this an eminently useful and empowering tool, one that anticipates many of the changes we know are coming in the evolution of care for children with special needs and their families. An outstanding book!

Betsy Anderson
Parent and
Director
CAPP/National Parent Resource Center
Federation for Children with Special Needs
Boston, Massachusetts

REFERENCE

Project Serve. (1985). *New directions: Serving children with special health care needs in Massachusetts.* Boston: Author.

Preface

I f you are raising a child with a disability or chronic illness, this book is for you. If you are a "natural helper"—a pediatrician or therapist, social worker, teacher, or clergy of such a family, this book is for you, too. The purpose of *Your Child and Health Care* is to show you the full range of services and benefits available to children with special health care needs and their families in home- and community-based settings and to suggest the most effective ways to obtain high-quality services at affordable prices.

In my social work practice with families, professionals who worked with families, and the complex organizations with which both must interact, I realized the need for the following:

1. *Information on the broad range of services* that are available in most communities or states for children and youth with disabilities and/or chronic illnesses and their families to enhance well-being
2. *Information on the varied sources of financial assistance*— both public and private, formal and informal—to help the families of such children and youth pay for medical bills and other basic needs of living (e.g., housing, food, clothing)
3. *Strategies to obtain services and financial assistance of all kinds,* including collecting the informed opinions of other parents experienced with these tasks, of professionals, and of relevant national, regional, and state organizations
4. *An understanding that problem-solving of this kind can be time consuming and frustrating, but that persistence pays*
5. *The conviction that children with disabilities or chronic illnesses have the basic rights to obtain the services they need to function maximally and to be as fully included in society as possible.*

This book is an attempt to satisfy these needs.

This book also contains specific national, state, and regional resources to help the parents of children and youth with special health care needs and others who work with them. Information about resources is provided throughout the text and in Appendix B at the end of the book. Each specific resource is accompanied by a description of the resources and suggestions for its use by families. Resource and factual information in the book is based on research done between March 1991 and January 1994.

Each organization listed in this book was contacted regarding the services it offers, current addresses, and telephone numbers including Text Type (TT) services where available. The *Internal Revenue Service (IRS) and 50 State Departments of Revenue* were surveyed in 1991–1992 regarding reductions in personal income taxes available for children with disabilities or chronic illnesses and/or their families. Each *State Department of Insurance* was surveyed regarding its role(s) in helping families obtain health insurance for their children and in resolving disputes families had with health insurance companies over unpaid or underpaid claims. All *national disease- and disability-related organizations* listed in Appendix B were contacted regarding their ability to provide financial assistance to families with children who have special health care needs for medical care and related needs. In addition, *legislation* discussed throughout the book was reviewed by consulting Public Laws, regulations, and critiques of both.

Nine professionals in the field of developmental disability and child development, Medicaid, and disability law—including three parents—read and commented on parts or all of chapter drafts of the book. Many other parents and professionals were contacted by letter or telephone to clarify questions about programs or to get opinions about the best recommendations to make in particular areas.

The idea for this book stemmed from work conducted in Durham, North Carolina, between January 1986 and December 1987 with pediatrician Gordon Worley, M.D., economist Joseph Lipscomb, Ph.D., and the Spina Bifida Association of North Carolina. I was hired to develop and conduct a financial counseling and family advocacy program for the parents of children with spina bifida at the Duke University Medical Center and The University of North Carolina Hospitals. The success of that project and the widespread need for information about resources and strategies led Paul H. Brookes Publishing Co. to approach me to develop this book.

It is my hope that this book will serve the needs of parents, caregivers, and professionals and promote the well-being of children and youth with disabilities and chronic illnesses in communities across the United States.

Acknowledgments

S pecial mention is due to those who helped make this book possible. A number of individuals and organizations provided factual information and general background beyond that readily available: Tom Josephs of the National Association of Counties, Jeanine Breyl of the National Governor's Association, Jeff Smedsrud of Communicating for Agriculture, staff of the Health Insurance Association of America, Barbara Huff and other staff of the Federation for Children's Mental Health, Andrea Meditch of *Kiplinger's Personal Finance Magazine,* Janet Bronstein of the School of Public Health of the University of Alabama, Val Bradley of Human Services Research Institute, Jo Shackelford and Joan Donaher of NEC★TAS, Anita Farel of The University of North Carolina School of Public Health, Henry Ireys of The Johns Hopkins University School of Public Health, Mike Fiore, Mary Jean Duckett, and Mary Clarkson of the Health Care Financing Administration, Joe Manes of the Bazelon Center for Mental Health Law, and staff of the National Information Center for Children and Youth with Disabilities (NICHCY).

Other individuals—both parents of children with special health care needs and professionals working with such children and families—gave their time to proofread drafts of chapters and offer corrections and suggestions. With this help, they added significantly to the final product: Joanne Mackey, Jo Shackelford, Mary Ann Allard, Karen Shannon, Joe Manes, Mary Cerreto, and Lynn Blanchard.

Joseph Lipscomb and Gordon Worley of Duke University, under a grant funded by the Kate Babcock Reynolds Health Care Trust, offered me the first structured opportunity to research a number of the topics covered in this book in a project between Duke and the Spina Bifida Association of North Carolina. Other mentors—Bob Smucker of the Independent Sector and Howell Baum of the University of Maryland School of Social Work and Community Planning—nurtured my desire for a more just and humane society and offered tools to work with and examples to follow in my efforts toward these ends.

Sarah Cheney, Kathy Boyd, and other staff of Paul H. Brookes Publishing Co. were a pleasure to work with. They offered helpful suggestions, support, and consideration throughout the process of writing and editing.

Finally, my husband and daughter allowed me the time I needed to pursue this project and see it to its end.

To all of these individuals I am most appreciative.

*Your Child
and Health Care*

1

Introduction

Help *is* available for families whose children need frequent or extensive medical and related care; that is the message of this book for both the families of children with chronic illnesses and disabilities and the people who help them. There *are* a variety of kinds of services to assess and improve children's functioning. There *are* educational and recreational programs to include children with special needs in society to the fullest extent possible. There *are* a variety of kinds of supports for families caring for such children at home. And, there *are* creative ways to keep to a minimum the amount a family must pay out of its own pocket for a child's medical and related care needs. For the portion a family may have to pay out of its own pocket, there *are* ways to pay for care over time so the child's access to other necessary services is not jeopardized. Furthermore, there *are* federal and state government provisions that allow reductions in income taxes for unusually large medical expenses paid by a family for children with special health conditions. The purpose of this book is to explore and outline the variety of resources available to families whose children require extensive and expensive medical care.

The number of families who could benefit from knowing about the help available to them and their children is growing. As many as 10%, or 7 million, of all U.S. children and youth from birth to 21 years of age are estimated to have chronic illnesses or disabilities that in some way alter their daily routines from others without these conditions (Newacheck & Taylor, 1992; Perrin, Shayne, & Bloom, 1993; *Statistical Abstracts of the United States, 1992*). With both the increase in premature infants born each year and the ability of advanced medical practices to care for very sick children, the number of children with chronic illnesses and disabilities is growing.

COMPLEX HEALTH CARE NEEDS, CHRONIC ILLNESSES, AND DISABILITIES

Many children with special needs begin life under difficult circumstances, spending months in intensive care nurseries hooked up to high-tech equipment. The complex health care needs of a number of these youngsters continue after they go home, many accompanied by ventilators, suction machines, and feeding tubes. Others, while requiring medical care for the rest of their lives, may not need such equipment (e.g., children with juvenile diabetes). These children, like others who appear more ill, must often limit their physical activity. Many develop at slower rates than other children their age. Compounding this problem, many children miss school frequently due to their illnesses or disabilities. This can interrupt their learning and efforts to keep up with other children their age. As they grow, for a child with a chronic illness or disability getting around may require the assistance of another person, a guide dog, braces, crutches, or a wheelchair. A number of children with disabilities require full-time home-based education due to the seriousness and instability of their illnesses or disabilities, or due to injuries resulting from accidents.

You may recognize your child in this description. Their conditions range from asthma, cerebral palsy, childhood diabetes, seizure disorders, sickle cell disease, and spina bifida to blindness, deafness, autism, Down syndrome, emotional, behavior, or mental disorders, and disabilities resulting from accidents (e.g., traumatic brain injury, extensive burns), to name some of the conditions that cause chronic illnesses or disabilities. With appropriate medical and related care, many of these children assume productive roles in society despite their continuing need for special assistance.

FAMILY INVOLVEMENT IN HEALTH CARE

All families are involved in multiple ways with caring for and obtaining services for their children who have chronic illnesses and disabilities. Parents and siblings help with daily care. Parents seek medical help and must be prepared to pay for necessary care that is not covered by health insurance or other public or private programs. Grandparents and other extended family may provide additional child care, transport sick children to medical care, or help pay for some of the costs of care. Family routines may be dictated by the medical requirements and schedule of the child who is sick or has a disability. Siblings may need to get by with less parental attention. All family members may need to limit themselves to only the minimum of necessary clothes, toys, and personal items to allow for expected and unexpected medical expenses. This is a family affair, affecting the lives of far more than the member with the chronic illness or disability.

THE COSTS OF HEALTH CARE

The costs of medical and related professional care for the children described above are expensive. Estimates for raising a child who has a chronic illness or disability to adulthood vary. One systematic study of U.S. children with spina bifida estimated that medical expenses would exceed one million dollars for a child in his or her lifetime (Rosenfeld, Worley, & Lipscomb, 1987). This estimate does not include any of the costs for related care (e.g., social services, counseling) or costs to society in public benefits given to the child (e.g., Supplemental Security Income, Medicaid). The estimate also does not include indirect costs (e.g., lost wages of the primary caregiver) or most of the routine expenses involved in raising a child without a chronic illness or disability.

Some of the costs of raising a child with a chronic illness or disability may be borne by private health insurance plans (which an estimated 37 million Americans lack) or public programs (e.g., Medicaid, Civilian Health and Medical Program of the Uniformed Services [CHAMPUS]). Still, a certain and increasing portion of the expenses of medical and related care comes directly out of the pockets of the families of children with chronic illnesses or disabilities. Examples of these costs include the following:

• Co-payments and deductibles in private insurance plans, which are generally increasing
• Services not covered in private or public health insurance plans (e.g., eyeglasses, experimental drugs, services not covered due to a pre-existing condition)
• Transportation to doctors' offices, clinics, and hospitals for children and youth

- Meal costs at hospitals (for all but the patients)
- Special diets required by premature infants or children with certain genetic or metabolic disorders
- Lost wages from work for a parent who has to cut back on work hours to take care of a sick child, or who loses pay to take a child to multiple medical appointments or for repeated hospital stays

THE JOBS THAT ACCOMPANY CARE OF YOUR CHILD'S HEALTH

Families with children who have chronic illnesses or disabilities live with a greater amount of fear and uncertainty than other parents. Will their child's condition get worse? Will the family be able to afford all of the recommended care? Can medical bills be paid to the satisfaction of the doctors and hospitals? If they cannot, will care for the child be withheld?

The suggestions in this book are meant to show you how to eliminate many of these worries by obtaining as much help as is possible from as many sources as you can. The single most important factor in helping to ensure the availability of services for your child and others will be your insistence that your child have the care he or she requires. To turn your insistence into effective action, you will have to undertake several jobs; these include the following:

1. ***Acknowledge and experience the grief you have for yourself and for your child.*** This grief is a perfectly normal and human reaction as you accept your child's condition and the possibility that he or she may fall behind other children over the years. It is also normal and compassionate to grieve over the physical and emotional pain you imagine your child may endure. If you can grieve, you will free up energy to problem-solve and advocate for your child and your fami-

ly. Grief that is buried can slow you down or surface inappropriately.

In recent years, *a variety of support and advocacy groups have developed* to help the families of children with chronic illnesses and disabilities. These groups, as well as community counseling services, can help you as you experience your grief. Many of these groups begin supporting a family when their child is in an intensive care nursery. The groups may offer emotional support and referral to information about the child's particular condition from the days immediately after birth. Other groups stay in periodic telephone contact with families, encouraging them to attend monthly meetings of disease-specific organizations (e.g., Head Injury Foundation, Easter Seal Society). These groups generally comprise parents of children in similar situations. Many such groups are also of value to families who are learning about services their children may need or who are trying to find their way through local service mazes and paperwork.

2. ***Realize that, as the child's parent(s) or caregiver(s), you will have the primary responsibility for obtaining the medical care and other services your child requires. Accept this role as fully as you can.*** When you accept this role, you empower yourself. In this case, you will look to professionals and other parents and caregivers as consultants or partners in information gathering and decision-making, rather than as primary problem-solvers.

3. ***Become as well informed as you can about the following:***

*   Your child's condition
*   High-quality services and supports in your community or state that could be of help to your child or other family members

• Your child's and family's rights to receive certain services, to be included in decision-making about care, and to be integrated fully into community living

There are a number of well-established regional, state, and national resources for information about diseases and disabilities, evaluation procedures, research findings, interventions and treatments, community health care and related services, funding of services and other family needs, counseling, family supports, and related advocacy. This book suggests a number of these.

    4. **Consult many sources of information, researching each question or problem you face systematically.** Inquire with many organizations, read articles or books, and talk with other parents and professionals you trust. Ultimately, however, make your own decisions and form a plan of action yourself.

    5. **Take advantage of all of the resources available to your child and family, including financial assistance.** Many of these resources are noted in this book. Included is information about public and private funding programs for medical care, other financial aid programs for your child and your family, and federal and state income tax savings to families with high medical bills and families with members with certain chronic illnesses or disabilities.

    6. **Assert yourself, as one family and with other families in a similar situation.** Speak up for the services your child and family need. If a certain service does not exist in your community, work with others to get such a service established and funded. Ask agency administrators and elected officials to help in your efforts.

    7. **Complain when your child's rights are ignored.** Consider legal action in cases of persistent discrimination. **Praise those who give exceptional service.**

8. ***Finally, take time off periodically from this job, as you would all others.*** Enjoy what you have and refresh yourself for more hard work and challenges ahead.

THE GOALS OF THIS BOOK

This book is designed to help with the business aspects of having a child with a chronic illness or disability. The suggestions and guidelines provided are intended to assist families in obtaining needed help for their children at costs they can afford. Specifically, this book will help each family have a better understanding of the following:

*   The variety of health and related care services available to children with chronic illnesses and disabilities in their homes and in the communities
*   The full range of ways to pay for medical and related care, and ways to make full use of these, including:
    —Private and public health insurance plans (e.g., Aetna, Blue Cross and Blue Shield, enrollment in Medicaid's program for kidney dialysis or kidney transplantation)
    —Other private and public programs that help pay medical expenses (e.g., Blue Cross and Blue Shield's "Caring" programs, County Departments of Human Resources Emergency Relief Program, County General Assistance medical [GA–Medical] programs)
    —Disease- and disability-related or civic organizations that offer some financial assistance for medical expenses
    —Negotiating with doctors, hospital business offices, and other professionals over fees, satisfactory reimbursement levels, and monthly payment plans for the portion of medical bills you will pay out of your own pocket

- Changes in the financing and reimbursement of health care services being discussed in every state legislature and in the U.S. Congress and White House, and how these changes might affect families with children with chronic illnesses or disabilities
- Other sources of financial aid to help families meet high medical bills and related expenses for their child, such as the following:
  —Supplemental Security Income (SSI) for the child, which in most states brings with it eligibility for Medicaid, and in some states brings a state supplemental payment
  —County Department of Human Resources Emergency Assistance for utilities, rent, rent deposits, moving, clothing, turkeys for Thanksgiving and Christmas, and Christmas gifts for children
  —Church ministries in your community for emergency assistance such as that described above
  —Free surplus food distribution
  —Aid to Families with Dependent Children (AFDC) for monthly cash assistance
  —Food Stamps to purchase some of the monthly groceries
  —WIC supplemental food program to qualified pregnant mothers, nursing mothers, and young children
- State and federal income tax deductions, exemptions, and credits available to families of children with chronic illnesses or disabilities
- Information about what bill collectors can and cannot legally tell you or do to you, and how to handle them when they call or show up at your home or place of work
- Contacts for help in monthly budgeting or for getting out of debt (e.g., Consumers Credit Counseling Services, U.S.D.A. Agricultural Extension Service, and other nonprofit organizations)

All of the information provided in this book is also designed to be helpful to the "natural helpers" of families in need of this kind of assistance. "Natural helpers" are defined here as those people to whom families turn to or with whom they come in contact during stressful times. They include professionals in medical environments— pediatricians, pediatric nurses, discharge planning nurses, social workers, and psychologists—as well as professionals and laypersons in other environments, including extended family, neighbors, clergy, teachers, special education coordinators, and family therapists. Such "natural helpers," if well informed and adequately respectful of family members' rights to make their own decisions, can be of great help to a family trying to get high-quality and appropriate services for their child at a cost the family can afford. It is hoped that "natural helpers" will find this information useful and that they will make use of it with families and individuals requesting or willing to be helped in this way. It is the hope of the author that families and their "natural helpers" will find the information in this book useful in getting needed services to children and in paying for their care.

2

Your Child's and Family's Legal Rights to Services and Protection

S ince the 1970s, the federal government and individual state governments have passed a number of laws to ensure that your child with special health care needs will have access to the services he or she needs and will be helped to assume his or her place in society. Courts have made a number of rulings in this area as well. This chapter outlines some of these laws and rulings for the following purposes:

- To illustrate the progress that has been made over the years in the area of "disability rights"

- To demonstrate the rights that children and families do have, under law, to services and inclusion in society
- To summarize benefits to children and families

Specific services that resulted from these and other laws to benefit children with chronic illnesses and disabilities and their families are reviewed in Chapters 3, 5, and 7.

Reviewing *federal laws* and the administrative agency regulations that evolve from laws and tell specifically how the laws will be put into practice is particularly useful. *Copies of many federal laws* can be obtained, free of charge, from the U.S. Capitol by calling (202) 224-3121; ask for the House or Senate Document Room to get copies of many laws. It is best to request a particular law by number. You should receive these within 2 weeks if they are available. If they are not available, you can go to any major library and ask a reference librarian to guide you to *U.S. Code Congressional and Administrative News.* This reference contains all Public Laws *and* the legislative history that led to their passage (e.g., subcommittee and committee reports, conference reports). It is also updated regularly.

Public Law numbers can be found by subject in *Shepard's Acts and Cases by Popular Names—Federal and State.*

Regulations to federal laws, issued by the executive agency with responsibility for overseeing implementation of particular laws passed by Congress, *state specifically how laws will be put into practice:* A reference librarian at a large public library, university library, or law school library can help you to locate the regulations that accompany a particular law. Parent Training and Information (PTI) Centers (see Chapter 3), as well as other national parent advocacy and disease- and disability-related organizations, should also be able to provide copies of major *laws* and *regulations.* Often such regulations, which are advertised for public comment in the

Federal Register, take 1–2 years after passage of the law to be issued.

It takes a while to get the hang of reading laws and regulations. If you prefer not to do this or you find it too difficult or time-consuming, *read summaries of laws and regulations.* These are often distributed by well established agencies or nonprofit organizations and can often be found in two publications in large libraries—*Congressional Almanac Quarterly* and *Congressional Quarterly Weekly Report.*

Judges' opinions or court rulings can be obtained from the clerk of the court in the district in which the specific opinion was rendered. In addition, noteworthy, precedent-setting opinions are sent to West Publishing Co. or Lexus Publishing Co. for entry into law books. Such rulings, as well as summaries and analyses of them, can be obtained with the help of a reference librarian at any law school library. Again, PTI Centers and national disease- and disability-related organizations discussed in Chapter 3 can provide copies of major court rulings. One caution: the court rulings themselves are in legal language and may be difficult to understand. Comprehensive summaries by reputable authorities will probably be more helpful to you.

State laws and court rulings can also be important in ensuring services and rights to your child and family. Check with your *state Protection and Advocacy Agency* (listed in Appendix B at the end of this book). The staff at these agencies can tell you which state laws, regulations, and court rulings are important for children with disabilities in your state and how to get copies and/or summaries of them.

Being aware of existing federal and state laws and court rulings as well as current issues being discussed regarding "disability rights" will help you better understand the issues you are facing. Such understanding will make you a more effective advocate for your child's and family's needs. For example, if you were interested in knowing which services your child with autism is entitled to receive in his or her third-grade class, you could find that information in the regulations to PL 101-476 (the Education of the Handicapped Act Amendments of 1990, now known as the Individuals with Disabilities Education Act [IDEA]), which was passed in 1990 and amended in 1991 by PL 102-119 (the Individuals with Disabilities Education Act Amendments). In reviewing the regulations for these laws, you would find that your child must receive, in addition to a "free, appropriate public education in the least restrictive environment possible," the following (as examples):

1. Assistive technology services and devices
2. Audiology
3. Counseling services
4. Early identification
5. Medical services for evaluation purposes
6. Occupational therapy
7. Parent counseling and training
8. Physical therapy
9. Psychological services
10. Recreation
11. Rehabilitation counseling services
12. Planning for transition from programs for infants and toddlers to those for preschoolers; programs for preschoolers to those in primary and secondary public schools; and secondary school programs to postsecondary education and job training, or adaptive and life skills training
13. School health services
14. Social work services
15. Communication development services
16. Transportation
17. Special education and related services

18. An individualized education program (IEP) and/or individualized family service plan (IFSP)

Because you had read the IDEA regulations, you would not be dependent on a school administrator to find out which services your child is entitled to receive. In some ways, it is in the financial interests of schools to provide only the services they must. You want to be sure that the school and other government agencies supply all services they should, including those that your child requires.

It is important to realize that some laws and rulings do not guarantee a particular child's access to services. The *Zebley* court decision (1990), for example, which opened the Supplemental Security Income (SSI) Program to more children with disabling conditions, requires that the child's condition meet the standards in the agency's regulations and that the child's family have limited income and resources. This ruling, although it may not give your child SSI benefits at this time, contributes to the general awareness of the needs of children with disabilities and to an environment that makes it easier to develop and fund programs that address these needs. **Some laws and court rulings, however such as IDEA, apply to all children with chronic illnesses and disabilities that meet a state's definition of "disability," regardless of family income or resources.**

The legislation and court rulings summarized below **do not by any means represent all of the legislation and court opinions of potential advantage to children with disabilities and/or their families.** These pieces of legislation and court rulings are described here because the author considers them particularly significant in ensuring the rights of individuals with disabilities and their families to full participation in society and in granting them specific access to needed health and related services. The examples that follow are also chosen because they represent the variety of

1. States are required to *identify children with disabilities as early as possible* (i.e., a Child Find Program must be established to find and refer children birth through 21, even though PL 94-142 only required states to serve eligible children and youth from 6 through 21 years of age).
2. *Children with disabilities must be educated at public expense* if they are 6 through 21 years old and in elementary or secondary school and meet the criteria described in #5 below.
3. *Preschool children* with disabilities must also be educated appropriately and at public expense *if* a state offers public education for other preschool children.
4. Schools must provide any necessary *related services* a child with a disability requires to be able to benefit from public education, and as much as is possible, in classes with children who do not have disabilities. Examples of such related services are transportation to and from school, physical therapy, occupational therapy, and selected health care services (e.g., assistance with intermittent catheterization, other assistive technology services and devices, social work services).
5. Every child who has a "developmental delay" according to the guidelines in the federal law and who meets a state's eligibility criteria must be provided an *individualized education program (IEP)*. This must be updated annually by a team of clinical and educational professionals with the child's parents and must be monitored periodically. An IEP is to include the following:
   - A description of the child's present level of educational performance
   - Instructional goals for the child for the school year
   - Educational services the child is to be provided by the school and the amount of time he or she will spend in a regular classroom

- The kind and duration of special services the child will receive and how the child will be evaluated (Palfrey et al., 1978)

6. The school system must *evaluate students' IEPs annually* and administer any testing that is part of the evaluation in a way that is nondiscriminatory and considers both a student's native language and his or her disability. (Current law requires an annual review of students' IEPs and full evaluations every 3 years.)

7. *Parents are to be included in team meetings and in any decision-making about their child's education.* Ideally, parents should be given copies of evaluation reports prior to a meeting to develop an IEP. Parents can bring anyone they want with them to meetings with school officials. A child and his or her family have a clearly defined way to challenge any decision made about a child's IEP or other education program or related services.

8. States must establish *inservice training for school personnel* in special education and services to other age groups, including information about related services students require to "benefit from" public school.

Later legislation, as you will see from the discussion below, increased the school's area of responsibility to include more related services, including general educational services to children from 3 through 5 years of age (or entry into kindergarten), and early intervention services for children birth through 2 years of age.

PL 98-199, the Education of the Handicapped Act Amendments of 1983

Important provisions of PL 98-199 included the following:

1. The creation of federally funded *Parent Training and Information (PTI) Centers* in each state to help parents

of children with chronic illnesses or disabilities understand their rights under PL 94-142 and participate more meaningfully in developing their child's IEP and in planning their child's education in general

2. The establishment of *Technical Assistance for Parents Program (TAPP)* agencies operated by PTI centers to help parents of children who have historically been underserved (e.g., minorities and those from disadvantaged environments) participate in planning the education of their children with disabilities (TAPPs have shifted their focus to offer peer-supported technical assistance to develop the leadership capabilities of PTIs, which serve all families in need.)

3. Expanded programs for the smooth *transition of children with disabilities from school for adult living*

4. Financial incentives to states to *expand their early intervention programs* for children from birth through 2 years old (Cutler, 1993) that were not mandated by federal law

PL 99-457, the Education of the Handicapped Act Amendments of 1986

PL 99-457 is known for the following:

- Its implication that young children with disabilities can best be understood, evaluated, and provided services in the context of their home environments
- Its commitment to more active involvement of parents of children with disabilities and chronic illnesses in treatment and other service plans
- Its emphasis on seeing children with disabilities as whole people who may require services from a variety of multidisciplinary providers

Part B of PL 99-457 required states to provide a "free, appropriate public education" for preschool children ages 3 through 5[1] with disabilities, by the 1990–1991 school year.

---

[1]IDEA actually states "children 3 to 5 inclusive." For readability, the author refers to "children from 3 through 5."

This extension of services to *preschool children* with disabilities and chronic illnesses was made possible by a federal expansion of aid to states for this purpose.

Part H of PL 99-457 gave additional incentives to states to develop *early intervention services* for infants and toddlers birth through 2 years old who have "developmental delays" or have diagnosed conditions with a "high probability of resulting in developmental delay" (National Early Childhood Technical Assistance System, 1992). At the state's discretion, a state may serve children "at risk" for developmental delay, as will be elaborated below. Currently these states do not receive additional federal funds for doing so.

The following guidelines are used by each state's Part H program:

1. States must develop *statewide, comprehensive, coordinated, multidisciplinary and interagency programs* (Trohanis, 1992) to serve infants and toddlers with disabilities, and their families.
2. Services must be available to *"children with developmental delays"* in one or more of the following areas: cognitive development, physical development, communication development, social or emotional development, or adaptive development.

    Children with *diagnosed conditions that have an established risk* (i.e., "high probability") *of resulting in developmental delay* must also be served. Examples of children with an "established risk" of delay might include those with Down syndrome, seizure disorders, chromosomal disorders, genetic or birth disorders, severe sensory impairments, inborn errors of metabolism, or fetal alcohol syndrome (Regulations 34 CFR, Part 303, Early Intervention Program for Infants and Toddlers with Disabilities, Final Rule, Federal Regulation, July 30, 1993, pp. 40958–40989, Vol. 58(145), *Federal Register*, § 303.16).

3. *A state establishes the definition of "developmental delay" it will use in implementing its early intervention program.*
4. A state has the *option to serve "children at risk of substantial delay* if early intervention services are provided." Examples of children "at risk" might include low birth weight babies, infants with respiratory distress syndrome or bleeding of the brain, and infants with prenatal exposure to cocaine or other substances of potential harm.

   Other examples of factors that could put infants and toddlers "at risk of delay" and make them potentially eligible for early intervention services include environmental factors, such as having a teenage mother, having a mother with a low educational level, living in poverty, or having a parent with a developmental disability.

   As of 1993, 13 states had elected to serve at least some categories of at-risk infants and toddlers under the Part H program (Shackelford, 1992; J. Shackelford, personal communication, May 12, 1993).
5. Service coordination must be provided to coordinate all evaluations, assessments, implementation of IFSP, and services given by other service providers.
6. Services must be in place by the beginning of a state's fourth year of participation in the federal program, and all eligible children must be served by the fifth year.
7. States have *"sliding scale fees" (based on a family's ability to pay) for a number of services.* Other services are provided at no cost to parents; these are Child Find, evaluation to determine eligibility, administration costs involved with IFSP development and procedural safeguards, and service coordination. With parental consent, Part H can bill a family's private health insurance policy for services.

Additionally, states offering Part H programs are required by PL 99-457 to do the following:

1. *Name a lead state agency to administer the state's early intervention program.* The U.S. Department of Education is the lead agency at the federal level.

2. Have the governor *name a 15-member Interagency Coordinating Council (ICC) with parent participation to serve in an advisory capacity to the state's lead agency.* The ICC must meet at least 3 times a year.

3. *Establish public awareness about the need for services* of young children with developmental delays, and how to get a child evaluated.

4. *Develop a "Central Directory"* of early intervention services, early intervention experts in the state, related research and demonstration projects in the state, and individuals and groups (including medical, psychological, legal, and parent support) who help children with developmental delays and their families.

5. *Develop and maintain a database* on infants and toddlers needing services, numbers being served, and kinds of services being provided (Early Intervention Advocacy Network, 1990).

All states have elected to offer Part H programs, although some requested an extension of time to meet all of the requirements for participation. *If a state elects to participate in Part H, it must provide all of the services identified through multidisciplinary evaluation and included in the IFSP.*

PL 99-457 emphasizes home- and community-based, family-centered care and notes that an assessment of a child with a developmental delay should be performed in context of the child's family and living situation. To this end, the law requires the following:

1. The development of an *individualized family service plan (IFSP)* within 45 days of the initial referral of a child (Early Intervention Advocacy Network, 1990). (Referral for service must be made 2 days following the identification of a child in need of service.)

2. An IFSP must include a statement of specific early intervention services needed to meet the child's and family's needs and other services that may be helpful to the family including those that are not covered under the state's early intervention program (e.g., respite care, child care).
3. *Procedural safeguards* must be followed, allowing parents or guardians full access to any records concerning the child, his or her evaluation(s), the family assessment, progress on the IFSP. Families must give their consent for service for their child or themselves, confidentiality must be maintained, and so forth.

PL 101-476, the Education of the Handicapped Act Amendments of 1990 and PL 102-119, the Individuals with Disabilities Education Act Amendments of 1991

The Individuals with Disabilities Education Act (IDEA) represents the reauthorization of PL 99-457 and a consolidation of previous laws regarding the education of children with chronic illnesses or disabilities. Therefore, IDEA provides the following:

1. Children who were previously described as "handicapped" are now referred to as "children with disabilities."
2. *Children with disabilities* are defined as children:

> with *mental retardation, hearing impairments* including *deafness, speech or language impairments, visual impairments* including *blindness, serious emotional disturbance, orthopedic impairments, autism, traumatic brain injury, other health impairments,* or *specific learning disabilities.* (Education of the Handicapped Act Amendments of 1990, Section 101, 602(A) (1)(B), emphasis added)
>
> For children from age *3 to 5 inclusive,* a State may include children experiencing developmental delays, as defined by the State and as measured by appropriate diagnostic instruments and procedures, in one or more of the following areas:

*physical development, cognitive development, communi-
cation development, social or emotional development,* or
adaptive development; and who by reason thereof *need
special education and related services* (Individuals with
Disabilities Education Act Amendments of 1991, Section
101, 602(A)(1)(B), emphasis added).

3. The entitlement of eligible children 3 through 21 years
   old to a "free, appropriate (public) education in the
   least restrictive environment possible," is reaffirmed.
4. The details of a particular child's entitlement to educational and related services will be spelled out in that
   child's IEP.
5. In Part H, the term "service coordination" replaced
   "case management." Vision services, assistive technology services and devices, and transportation and related costs were added to available services.
6. A child's IEP will be developed in collaboration with
   that child's parent or guardian and the latter shall have
   access to all records and have the right to challenge all
   decisions that are made concerning their child's education and needed support services. *IFSP assessments
   will be family-directed and will require the written
   consent of family members before services in an IFSP
   are delivered.*
7. *Every student, by age 16, must have a plan for transition to employment or postsecondary education ex-
   plicitly written in his or her IEP.* Funds for 3-year-olds
   can be flexibly provided by either Part H or Part B programs to ensure continuity of care.
8. Federal funding is expanded for the Early Education
   Programs for Children with Disabilities (EEPCD),
   which include outreach, demonstration, technical assistance, and research institutes.
9. Federal funding of *model programs for postsecondary
   education of individuals with disabilities* is increased.

10. Federal funding of *programs for children and youth with serious emotional disturbances* is increased.
11. *States may be sued in federal court for violating the provisions of IDEA.*

IDEA represents broad legislation covering the majority of children with chronic illnesses or disabilities and their families. By incorporating most of previous special education laws *and* expanding government responsibility in this area, **IDEA makes clear the federal government's and each state's responsibilities to educate and support children with disabilities.**

The process of educating and supporting children with disabilities begins at the birth of a child with special needs for Child Find's identification, referral, and services, and from 3 through 21 years old for service. Some children will not be identified for evaluation and services for a number of years. IDEA includes *identification, public education, support services required for children to benefit from public education,* and *transition to some kind of work or higher education. IDEA also provides a primary role in this process for the parent(s) or guardian(s) of a child with a disability or chronic illness and offers a child's family or guardians legal recourse if they believe their child is not offered their mandated benefits under IDEA.*

Many government agencies play a role in delivering services under this law, and in paying for them. A number of federally sponsored research, technical assistance, and family training and support programs were retained from past legislation or established to help states implement the provisions of this law.

The Guarantee of Full Access to All Public and Private Facilities

Advocates for children and youth with disabilities or chronic illnesses have worked hard to help ensure the full inclusion of such children and youth into society. This requires a guarantee, backed by federal law, of their full access to both public and private facilities, equal opportunities in the workplace, and the opportunity to communicate and travel.

PL 101-336, the Americans with Disabilities Act (ADA) of 1990

Under PL 101-336, the Americans with Disabilities Act (ADA) of 1990, *individuals with disabilities must be ensured access to the full range of services provided by both the public and private sectors, excluding religious entities and private clubs.* The provisions of the ADA cover an estimated 43 million Americans, including as many as 10% of all American children and youth from birth through 21 years old. As the American population ages, even more Americans will have access to services guaranteed as a result of the ADA.

The ADA was the **first federal law that required private businesses and organizations to help ensure individuals with disabilities access to all workplaces, retail stores, private schools, public transportation, restaurants, museums, hotels, and so forth, providing "auxiliary aids and services" where necessary.**

The ADA also provides for the *payment of attorneys' fees in any "action or administrative proceeding" in which the challenger is successful.* No monetary damages will be awarded in such hearings or suits (Williams, Simpson, & Bergman, 1991).

The same *functional definition of disability* offered in Section 504 of PL 93-112, the Rehabilitation Act of 1973, applies in the ADA (see pp. 35–36). According to Section 504, and the ADA, an individual is considered to have a disability if he or she meets one of the following criteria (Jones, 1991):

1. He or she must have "*a physical or mental impairment that substantially limits one or more of the major life activities of an individual*" (p. 33, emphasis added).

2. He or she must have *"a record of such an impairment"* (p. 33, emphasis added).

3. He or she must *"be regarded as having such an impairment"* (p. 33, emphasis added).

A **physical impairment** is defined as "any physiological disorder or condition, cosmetic disfigurements, or anatomical loss affecting one or more of the following body systems: neurological; musculoskeletal; special sense organs; respiratory, including speech organs; cardiovascular, reproductive; digestive; genito-urinary; hemic and lymphatic; skin; and endocrine" (Jones, 1991, p. 33). *Persons with communicable diseases* (e.g., acquired immunodeficiency syndrome [AIDS]) are covered by the ADA "unless they pose a direct threat to the health and safety of others . . . that cannot be eliminated by reasonable accommodations" (West, 1991a, p. xxviii).

A **mental impairment** is defined, as in Section 504 of PL 93-112, the Rehabilitation Act of 1973, as "any mental or psychological disorder, such as mental retardation, organic brain syndrome, emotional or mental illness, and specific learning disabilities" (Jones, 1991, p. 33). *Specific titles in the ADA relate to employment, public services, public accommodations and services offered by private entities, telecommunications, and miscellaneous provisions of the law.*

In the title related to **employment,** the ADA requires that by July, 1992 (July, 1994 for businesses with 15 or fewer employees) employers must consider hiring "qualified individuals with a disability who with reasonable accommodation can perform the essential functions of the employment" (West, 1991a, p. xxii). Provisions of this title apply even though an employer's health insurance may not cover a prospective employee with a disability or even if an employer would be charged more for the health insurance of such a prospective employee (Jones, 1991).

In a 1986 Louis Harris and Associates survey, it was estimated that 66% of individuals with disabilities between 16 and 64 years old were not working. Of those not working, 78% indicated that they would like to work (Harris & Associates, 1986).

Another indicator of the difficulty individuals with disabilities had in gaining access to public or private employment was noted in the late 1980s. Fifty percent of adults with disabilities had household incomes under $15,000 a year compared with 25% of adults without disabilities (U.S. Senate, 1989). This income level was just under the poverty level for a family of four.

In the ADA, the title relating to *public services* requires that as of January, 1992 (for most services) "no qualified individual with a disability shall be excluded from participation or derived benefit of the services, programs or activities of a public entity, or subject to discrimination by such an entity" (Americans with Disabilities Act, 1990, 42 U.S.C. 12131). This means that all state and local governments and departments or agencies of a state or local government (including publicly run railroads) must give individuals with disabilities access to their services. This augments the provision in Section 501 of PL 93-112, the Rehabilitation Act of 1973, that prohibits discrimination by the federal government or any agency of the federal government.

Under the ADA's title relating to *public accommodations and services offered by private entities,* as of January, 1992 (for most covered services), an individual with a disability cannot be excluded from hotels, restaurants, laundromats, museums, private offices of health care providers, retail stores, and so forth.

Additionally, under the same title of the law, as of July, 1992 (with some exceptions), private buses and rail carriers must provide "auxiliary aids and services" that would make these services accessible to individuals with disabilities. It

is estimated that in 1990 only 35% of transportation vehi-
cles were equipped with features to allow accessibility by
individuals with disabilities (West, 1991a), in particular
those with wheelchairs.

Aircraft carriers are not covered by the ADA, and businesses are not required to install elevators in buildings with
fewer than three stories of less than 3,000 square feet per
story (Americans with Disabilities Act, 1990).

Under the ADA title relating to *telecommunications,*
the Federal Communications Commission (FCC) must ensure that by July, 1993 interstate and intrastate telecommunications relay services are available to individuals with
hearing and speech impairments, so that such individuals
may use standard telephone equipment for communication.
Additionally, closed captioning television must be provided
for any public service announcement funded in part or full by
the federal government.

*All provisions of the ADA apply unless they would
cause "undue hardship" to an employer, service provider,
and so forth,* according to standards spelled out in the law
and the regulations that implement the law. *The consistent
emphasis in this law is on **enhancing the full inclusion and
participation in society of individuals with chronic illnesses and disabilities.***

Expansion of Services for Screening, Diagnosis, and Treatment Under Medicaid

An emphasis in all health care programs for children and
youth has been on the early detection of developmental delays, disabilities, or diseases and in providing needed intervention or treatment at the earliest possible time. In this
way, it is hoped that a child's delay or health problem can be
treated quickly and any associated problems minimized. Although the Early and Periodic Screening, Diagnosis, and Treat-

ment (EPSDT) Program under Medicaid was established to do just this for Medicaid-eligible children and youth, there were barriers in getting children evaluated and in getting them the needed treatment in all states.

PL 101-239, the Omnibus Budget Reconciliation Act (OBRA) of 1989, Including Medicaid Amendments

PL 101-239, the Omnibus Budget Reconciliation Act (OBRA) of 1989, *expands Medicaid's Early and Periodic Screening, Diagnosis, and Treatment Program* in a number of ways. Of most significance to the parents of a child with a chronic illness or disability, it *requires a state's Medicaid program to pay for any* **"medically necessary" services that a child who qualifies for the Medicaid program is shown to require whether or not that state's Medicaid plan includes coverage for that particular service.**

In addition, OBRA makes *the EPSDT Program more readily available to more children because a larger and more diverse group of professionals can evaluate a child, performing one or more of the required parts of the evaluation.* For example, the family of a child who is eligible for Medicaid can request an evaluation at least once a year at the local health department, outpatient pediatric department of a local hospital, or in most cases from the child's private pediatrician. (Frequency of encouraged evaluation follows the American Academy of Pediatrics guidelines offered in Figure 1 of Chapter 5.)

The OBRA of 1989 ruling regarding children in Medicaid's EPSDT Program has caused a stir in state governments because of the extra costs it means to states. Traditionally, states limit their expenses under Medicaid by limiting program beneficiaries and the number and extent of optional services offered in the program. This law does not allow states to do so for children in the Medicaid program evaluated under the EPSDT Program.

In addition to costing a state extra money (often money that cannot be easily anticipated and budgeted for), this ruling marks an important departure from the federal government's prior policy. Before 1989, the federal government made its share of Medicaid dollars contingent only on a state's provision of a uniform set of basic services, allowing a state to choose if it wanted to cover certain individuals and provide other optional services. This shift in federal policy positions the federal government to require that states provide more needed services to children with special health care needs most often if their families have low incomes.

It is important to remember that **it is the parent's or advocate's job to be sure that a child qualifies for Medicaid and is evaluated under the EPSDT Program. Additionally, after a child is evaluated, it is up to that child's parent or advocate to ensure that all services the child requires are provided.** This will often require a parent's or advocate's persistence with the state's Medicaid agency and other related groups (state's lead agency for administration of early intervention services) for the child to get the service he or she needs.

Reimbursement for Home- and Community-Based Services Under Medicaid (2176 Waivers)

It became clear over time that paying for home- and community-based services under Medicaid provided increased service choices for children and youth with disabilities or chronic illnesses and their families. Paying for home- and community-based care also has the potential of saving the state and federal governments money over the costs of institutional care.

PL 97-35, the Medicaid Amendments of 1981

PL 97-35, the Medicaid Amendments of 1988, *allows states to apply for waivers (i.e., exceptions to usual practice) for the use of Medicaid funds to provide home- and community-based services for children who are institutionalized or at risk of being institutionalized.* These are called 2176 waivers.

In most cases, your state must have successfully applied for such a waiver from the federal Medicaid agency for your child to receive home- and/or community-based services paid for by Medicaid. Although it is a lengthy process, you can request that your state Medicaid program apply for such a waiver if it does not already have one. A national parent-run organization can refer you to an advocacy group in your community or state to help you do this, or the national organization will help you. For a local referral or direct help, contact:

The Federation for Children with Special Needs
95 Berkeley Street
Boston, Massachusetts 02116
(617) 482-2915 (Voice and TT)

If your child qualifies medically for a 2176 waiver program, only his or her income and resources would be used in determining his or her financial eligibility for Medicaid services.

To find out what your state income and resource limits are and if they have such a Medicaid waiver covering children with chronic illnesses or disabilities, contact your local Medicaid agency, your State Medicaid Agency, or your State Department of Developmental Disabilities. You can find the address and telephone number of your local Medicaid Agency in the county government section of the white pages telephone book, or you can obtain it from your local information operator. Each state's Medicaid Agency and Department of Developmental Disabilities are listed in Appendix B at the end of this book.

Service Development and Coordination
for Children with Special Health Care Needs

Federal legislation in 1975 formally acknowledged the need to plan and coordinate services for individuals with disabilities, including children.

PL 94-103, the Developmental Disabilities Assistance and Bill of Rights Act of 1975

PL 94-103, the Developmental Disabilities Assistance and Bill of Rights Act of 1975, requires the **organization of Developmental Disabilities Planning Councils** in *each state* to fund and coordinate services for persons with severe long-term disabilities that developed before 22 years of age and are expected to last throughout that person's life. As a response to documented cases of neglect and abuse of individuals with mental retardation or mental illness in public hospitals, this law also *establishes* **a national system of independent Protection and Advocacy (P & A) organizations,** with a P & A agency in each state. P & A agencies are staffed principally by lawyers and social workers and provides information, referral, and advocacy services for individuals with disabilities in both institutional and community settings. Staff of P & A agencies will act as attorneys for their clients and do almost everything that any private attorney can do (e.g., provide representation at administrative hearings, sue in state or federal court). A list of each state's P & A agency is provided in Appendix B at the end of this book.

Access to Miscellaneous
Services, Rights, and Choices

A variety of laws help to guarantee broader inclusion of individuals with disabilities and chronic illnesses into everyday life; these include the following:

1. PL 98-435, the Voting Accessibility for Elderly and Handicapped Act of 1984,
2. PL 99-435, the Air Carrier's Access Act of 1986,
3. PL 100-430, the Fair Housing Act Amendments of 1988,
4. PL 100-407, the Technology-Related Assistance for Individuals with Disabilities Act of 1988,
5. Community Supported Living Arrangements (CSLA) (Section 4712 of PL 101-508, the Omnibus Budget Reconciliation Act of 1990).

Any of these Public Laws can be obtained free of charge from the House of Representatives or Senate Document Rooms, (202) 224-3121. A reference librarian at any large public library or university library can also assist you in locating copies and/or summaries of these laws as well as the federal agency regulations that specify procedures to implement the laws.

PROTECTION FROM DISCRIMINATION

A number of federal laws have been passed to protect individuals with disabilities or chronic illnesses—including children—from discrimination in a variety of settings and situations.

Antidiscrimination in Education and Hiring of Individuals with Disabilities

Advocates for children and youth with disabilities or chronic illnesses felt a pressing need for federal legislation prohibiting the discrimination of such individuals in educational and employment settings.

PL 93-112, the Rehabilitation Act of 1973, Sections 501, 503, and 504

One of the *earliest and most extensive laws that prohibited discrimination of individuals with disabilities* was PL

The intent of PL 99-372 was to *make it difficult for agencies to blatantly ignore various antidiscrimination laws* concerning persons with disabilities. If agencies ignore such laws, they could be sued and required to pay the legal fees for a family's challenge of agency practices, in addition to any damages awarded.

When considering legal assistance of any kind, individuals and families should discuss the expected cost of their legal actions and how they will be paid at a first meeting with an attorney (Cutler, 1993).

Provision of Supplemental Security Income Cash Benefits to Children and Youth with Chronic Illnesses or Disabilities

For many years, the families of children with chronic illnesses or disabilities—particularly those with mental illness or emotional and behavior disorders—were unsuccessful in qualifying their children for Supplemental Security Income (SSI) payments. This was due to restrictive eligibility procedures in the SSI Program, and represented a loss of significant monthly income to the children and their families.

Sullivan v. Zebley, a 1990 Decision of the U.S. Supreme Court

The 1990 *Sullivan v. Zebley* U.S. Supreme Court decision was the result of a 7-year lawsuit against the U.S. Department of Health and Human Services. The suit alleged that *children had been denied cash benefits under the Supplemental Security Income (SSI) Program because of unfair practices by the federal government restricting eligibility.*

According to the Judge David L. Bazelon Center for Mental Health Law (formerly called the Mental Health Law Project):

1. Children were not given as comprehensive an evaluation as adults to carefully determine if they had disabilities.
2. Children who were too young to evaluate were turned away from the SSI Program routinely if the impairments they had were not disabling to *all* children.
3. Children with more than one impairment were denied coverage if they did not meet all of the criteria for any one of their problems.
4. A child was declared "disabled" only if his or her "condition was the same or medically equivalent in severity to a condition on the Social Security Administration's List of Impairments" (Clark & Manes, 1991, p. 3). Not all disabling childhood diseases and conditions were included on that list (e.g., autism, AIDS).

As a result of the Zebley family's successful challenge of these eligibility practices, retrospectively as of 1980:

1. *The SSI Program was opened to thousands of children with chronic illnesses and disabilities* who could have been denied access to SSI before the *Zebley* decision.
2. *SSI was required to offer the more than 450,000 children denied benefits on or after January 1, 1980 the opportunity to have their cases re-evaluated.* If found eligible, these children would receive back payments from the time they were rejected by SSI to the time their eligibility was established.
3. *The Social Security Administration (SSA),* which administers the program, *was forced to change its policies for evaluating disabilities in children* in the following ways (Clark & Manes, 1991):
   • SSA must first see if a child's condition appears in the Social Security "Listing of Impairments." If so, and the child's family's income and resources are under the limit allowed, the child is eligible for SSI.

- If a child's condition or combination of conditions does *not* appear on SSI's List of Impairments, SSA must determine if the condition is either medically or functionally as serious as a condition that does appear on the list.
- If a child's impairment does not appear on the List of Impairments *or* is not considered as serious as a condition on the list, SSA must determine if the child's condition would prevent him or her from doing the same kind of things that most children their age can do. To determine this, SSA must conduct an "individualized functional assessment," at public expense, drawing on medical and nonmedical evidence. If this evaluation shows that a child is restricted in a number of activities of daily living, the child is considered "disabled" and eligible for SSI (Clark & Manes, 1991).

Children with one of 12 specified conditions can begin to receive payments immediately and for as long as 6 months while their applications go through the eligibility determination process. Historically children with these conditions are usually accepted into the SSI Program, so they are not made to wait to begin receiving benefits. These 12 categories include the following (Clark & Manes, 1991):

1. The loss of two limbs
2. The loss of a leg at the hip
3. A claim of total blindness
4. A claim of total deafness
5. Confinement or immobility due to a longstanding condition
6. Claim of a stroke or head injury more than 3 months in the past, with continued and obvious difficulty in walking or using a hand or arm

7. Claim of cerebral palsy, muscular dystrophy, or muscular atrophy, with obvious difficulty walking, talking, or coordinating hands or arms
8. Claim of diabetes, with the loss of at least one foot
9. Claim of Down syndrome
10. Claim of severe mental deficiency in a child 7 years or older
11. Claim of kidney disease requiring dialysis on a regularly scheduled basis
12. Human immunodeficiency virus (HIV) infection

It is important to remember that a child's disability is not enough to qualify him or her for benefits under the SSI Program. *A child's family income and resources (i.e., personal property, savings accounts) must not exceed program guidelines and the child and family must meet other program qualifications.* Information about a child's financial eligibility for SSI is provided in Chapter 7.

Permission for Individuals with Disabilities to Sue for Damages in Cases of Discrimination, Bias, or Harassment

If an individual with a disability experiences discrimination, bias, or harassment, he or she has legal recourse through PL 102-166, the Civil Rights Act of 1991.

PL 102-166, the Civil Rights Act of 1991

PL 102-166, the Civil Rights Act of 1991, permits individuals with disabilities (along with women and religious minorities) to *sue for damages where there is "intentional discrimination, unintentional bias, sex discrimination or harassment"* (Crosser, 1992, p. v, emphasis added). *This law is also important to individuals with disabilities because legal remedies available in the ADA are based on those available in the Civil Rights Act.*

Protection of Job Security When Caring for or Adopting a Child with a Disability or Chronic Illness

Until the late winter of 1993, working parents had no assurance that their jobs, health insurance, and other benefits would be secure if their child's disability or illness required the adults' frequent and occasionally extended absences from work.

PL 103-3, the Family and Medical Leave Act of 1993

PL 103-3, the Family and Medical Leave Act of 1993, protects *job security, seniority, and continued health insurance coverage for workers who need to take leave due to any of the following* (Children's Defense Fund, 1993a):

1. The birth or adoption of a child
2. A serious illness of the individual
3. The serious illness of a family member

Under this law, workers are entitled to as long as *12 weeks of **unpaid leave*** for any combination of the reasons listed above. This may allow the parents or relatives of a child with a chronic illness or disability to rotate responsibility for the child's care at home without any adult having to give up his or her job and income. This was often not possible before the passage of PL 103-3.

Benefits of PL 103-3, however, are *limited to workers employed at least 1 year with their current employers and to workers who work at least 25 hours a week.* Additionally, *employers with fewer than 50 employees are exempt* from the Family and Medical Leave Act, presumably because of the particular hardship this law could present for a small business or organization.

For more information on the Family and Medical Leave Act, contact:

The Women's Legal Defense Fund
1875 Connecticut Avenue, Northwest
Suite 710
Washington, D.C. 20009
(202) 986-2600

SUMMARY

As the above discussion indicates, *federal laws and court rulings have resulted in increased access to a variety of public and private services for individuals with chronic illnesses or disabilities and their families.* The discussion also demonstrates the evolution of government policies toward individuals with disabilities. The following list notes some of the significant changes that have occurred during this evolution:

1. Since 1973, the *language of laws has changed.* Later laws referred to children and youth with disabilities or chronic illnesses. Earlier laws called them "handicapped children."

2. As legislation evolved, *disabilities became defined more by empirical limitations in development or functioning than by a particular disease or disability.*

3. *Protection of rights and services to individuals with disabilities moved from primarily institutional settings to include institutional, home, and community settings with an emphasis on home- and community-based settings.*

4. Over time, *the rights of families of children with disabilities have been considered increasingly important,* and legislation has gradually *mandated active family*

involvement in the educational and other service planning for their children.

5. *Early identification* of children with disabilities and *early intervention* approaches have become increasingly popular. This was designed to reverse developmental delays, start appropriate education for children with disabilities and their families as soon as possible, and reduce the dependency of this population—in the long run—on public programs.

6. Finally, laws have been written to extend the access of individuals with disabilities and chronic illnesses to services and activities of living in both public and private settings.

A caution, however, is that laws and court rulings are not self-enacting. For a variety of reasons unrelated to malicious intent to thwart the rights of children or families, parents and guardians of children with disabilities must help employers and service providers to comply with the laws in this area.

Even with financial inducements, **organizations *do not* change readily and easily** unless their survival is threatened or they are helped and pressured to do so by others who stand to benefit from the change. In addition, many state governments, including local and state education agencies and state Medicaid agencies, are being asked to provide so much more service to children in recent years that a lot of additional expense is being incurred by the states. Therefore, many of these agencies will implement new legal mandates slowly.

Even so, parents and concerned professionals must keep their expectations of such agencies high. Additionally, disability advocates must be willing to do their share of work on boards, councils, and committees and in halls of local, state, and federal legislatures to see that the laws highlighted in this chapter and others of benefit are put into routine practice. Without participating in the process of change, you may not be able to help an organization resist its natural inertia. Parents of children with chronic illnesses or disabilities will be the most motivated to make the provisions of these laws a reality. Families have a special stake in whether or not an agency implements a service program or civil rights provision in the way intended.

With the support of each other and in numbers, well-informed parents have been and can continue to be effective advocates for their children and families. Such groups can call on professional assistance as needed—for example, to help them understand the latest research findings on intervention and treatment for one or more childhood disabilities or to help them learn about the state education agency's budgeting process and timetable.

A number of groups exist in each state and/or at the national level as a support or resource to any parent who wants to be an effective advocate for his or her child (*e.g., P & A agencies in each state, the Parent Training and Information [PTI] Centers in each state or region, Client Assistance Programs [for vocational rehabilitation in each state], staff of the national Judge David L. Bazelon Center for Mental Health Law, members of state and local disease- or disability-related organizations, local parent and family support groups*). The addresses and telephone numbers of the national, regional, and state organizations listed above are provided in Chapter 3, Appendices 6A and 6B, and Appendix B at the end of this book.

Your state's *P & A agency* or the *Judge David L. Bazelon Center for Mental Health Law* should be helpful in explaining in more detail the importance of any of the federal laws and court rulings discussed in this chapter. They can also *advise you of what to do if you believe any of these laws are not being followed* in the case of your child or family. The *PTI Centers will be particularly helpful with legislation relating to the education of your child with special health needs.*

3

Obtaining Services for Your Child and Family
Advocacy, Support, Medical, and Related Services

M any kinds of services are available in communities across the United States to help your child and your family. *The trend in the delivery of services to children with special health care needs and their families is to have as many services as possible in the community.* Furthermore, these services are to be flexible enough to fit differing needs. "Wrapping" as many services around a child and/or family as is needed is thought by many to be the most cost-effective way to serve children and families. *Knowing which services will best meet your needs and obtaining those services requires the following:*

1. Making a number of **telephone calls** or **writing a number of letters** to research service options in your community or state
2. **Describing your child's problems and needs** to many different people
3. **Persisting with your search** until you are satisfied that you know what your child's and/or family's choices are and you have applied for and received services that take care of these needs

There are a number of ways to proceed with these tasks. The following suggestions will help to ensure that you are aware of the largest number of appropriate resources, and that these resources are selected because they have a reputation for offering high-quality care or service. *Call or write to well-established national, regional, or state-level organizations for referrals to health care and related services in your community.*

For some people it will feel awkward to go to a national or regional organization before checking with local agencies. The author, however, believes that *locally provided information is most meaningful and useful when you have an overview of the many kinds of service programs and agencies that can meet your child or family's needs. A national, regional, or state-level organization can give you a "structure of possibilities" in which to "shop" for a local way to meet your child's or family's needs.*

National organizations maintain files of the most current information and research findings on a large variety of disabilities. They can also refer you to the best sources for information about high-quality services in your geographic area for your child and family. Even after you have chosen one or more local service programs, you can continue to consult with national, regional, and state-level organizations about the experiences you and your child are having with one or more local service providers.

However, *if you think that your child needs to be seen within a week,* call the Department of Pediatrics at the nearest children's hospital or call the nearest University Affiliated Program (UAP). Appendix B at the end of this book provides the address and telephone number for the American Association of University Affiliated Programs for Persons with Developmental Disabilities, which can refer you to the UAP nearest your home. After you reach the facility by telephone, ask to speak with a social worker for guidance about what to do. See if your child can be seen right away. *If you think that your child is having a life-threatening problem, take him or her directly to the emergency room of your nearest hospital or call 911 for an ambulance.*

*The information in the remainder of this chapter is for families who want to plan the most cost-effective ways to obtain care and to manage their children's conditions **over time.***

The purposes of this chapter are the following:

1. *To help you become aware of the large variety of services that exist to help children and families like yours*
2. *To make you aware of a number of national information and referral organizations for families with children who have disabilities or chronic illnesses that can refer you to high-quality services in your area*

This chapter is organized in the following way: *First, the variety of kinds of services potentially available to your child and family are listed by category.* Then, in the second part of this chapter, *a number of national, regional, and state-level referral organizations are provided to guide you to the most appropriate local sources of help.* You may also want to review the referral information you receive from these organizations with one or more professionals and parents experienced with your local medical and social service systems. This should help equip you to select services for your child and other family members.

SERVICES FOR YOUR CHILD AND FAMILY

A number of different kinds of services may be available to your child and your family in or near your community. These include services for diagnosis and evaluation, intervention and treatment, preventative and routine health care, service coordination, transportation, counseling, and respite care. When arranging services such as these for your child and your family, *it is important to remember that* you *are in charge of deciding which services your child receives, shaping the direction the services take, and evaluating any care or service.*

Try not to be intimidated by the knowledge and training of professionals. It is their job to share their expertise with you in a way you can understand and to be a resource to you and your child. Ask all of the questions you need to ask. All of your questions deserve courteous, informative answers.

You may find some resistance or impatience from professionals as you try to get the information you need to participate actively in your child's care. Some professionals are used to making these decisions for children and families. Parents may need intensive support from professionals at times, but decisions about your child are both your responsibility and your privilege to make.

Physical Diagnosis and Evaluation

Physical diagnosis and evaluation services should be able to give you a fairly precise idea of what is physically wrong with your child. This means telling you which areas of your child's body do not function well. Professionals should also be able to suggest medical and related therapies that could be helpful. They can be good sources of information about places in or near your community where your child can get the required help.

Medically related diagnostic and evaluation services are most commonly found in a number of places, including the following:

1. Government-funded speciality clinics in the community (e.g., University Affiliated Programs for the Developmentally Disabled, the Children's Special Health Care Needs Program, clinics that do Early and Periodic Screening, Diagnosis, and Treatment [EPSDT] under the Medicaid program, individual practitioners who screen under EPSDT)
2. Private speciality clinics associated with a hospital or medical center (e.g., Duke University Medical Center's Spina Bifida Clinic)
3. Private, free-standing speciality clinics in the community (e.g., the Charity League's Speech and Hearing Clinics at University of North Carolina Hospitals)
4. County and area public health departments
5. Rural health centers and migrant health clinics
6. The offices of a pediatrician or other physician

Not every facility will be able to conduct as comprehensive an evaluation as others. If it cannot, you can request that your child be referred to another site to conduct or complete the evaluation. You can also request that further evaluation be done of your child and his or her problem(s). In addition, in some cases, diagnostic and evaluation services for your child's physical condition will be available at a facility that offers other diagnostic and evaluation services (e.g., for your child's progress in mastering certain physical, intellectual, and social skills).

Diagnosis and Evaluation of
Emotional and Behavior Problems

If you suspect your child has an emotional or behavior problem, you can consult a diagnostic service designed especially to evaluate such problems. These services should be able to tell you more about the specific emotional and/or behavior problems your child has. They can also be good sources for both medical and nonmedical treatments that have helped others with similar problems, and may be able to direct your child to some of the sources of this help in your community.

Services for the diagnosis and evaluation of emotional and behavior problems are most commonly found in the following places:

1. Government-funded specialty clinics in the community (e.g., University Affiliated Programs for the Developmentally Disabled, Children's Special Health Care Needs Programs, clinics that do EPSDT screenings)
2. Private specialty clinics associated with a hospital or medical center (e.g., a university neuropsychiatry clinic or adolescent mental health clinic)
3. Private, free-standing specialty clinics in the community (e.g., a facility staffed by child psychiatrists and/or psychologists)
4. Developmental Evaluation Centers or Community Mental Health Centers
5. The offices of a solo practicing child psychiatrist, child psychologist, or other professional specifically trained to evaluate children

Diagnostic and evaluation services for your child's emotional and/or behavior problems will often be available at a location that offers other diagnostic and evaluation services (e.g., for progress in physical development).

Interdisciplinary Evaluation of Development

A number of professionals, including clinical child psychologists, developmental psychologists, general pediatricians, occupational therapists, physical therapists, speech-language therapists, and social workers, are trained to evaluate your child's developmental level. This is the level at which he or she can accomplish a number of physical, intellectual, and social tasks as compared with all other children his or her age. Your child's development will be measured based on an analysis of how he or she attempts a series of diagnostic tests and participates in meetings with one or more professionals. This is in addition to the information you provide about your child.

After your child's developmental evaluation is complete, the professionals conducting it should give you their opinions of your child's strengths and weaknesses. They should also be able to recommend services that can help your child's medical condition or functioning. This may include exercises or routines to follow at home as well as assistance you can receive from other professionals and parent groups in your community.

Developmental evaluation services are most commonly found in the following places:

1. Government-funded specialty clinics in the community
2. Private specialty clinics associated with a hospital or medical center, (e.g., a university child psychology or adolescent mental health clinic)
3. Private, free-standing, specialty clinics in the community (e.g., a facility staffed by developmental psychologists and/or child psychologists)
4. Psychologists employed at a local or area Department of Public Health
5. The offices of a solo-practicing child psychologist, developmental psychologist, or pediatrician

In some cases, developmental evaluations are available at a facility that offers other diagnostic and evaluation services (e.g., for evaluation of your child's physical condition).

Intervention and Treatment
for Your Child's Medical Condition

Treatment for your child's medical condition can occur in a number of places, including the following:

1. Your home
2. A specialized foster or family home
3. Your child's school
4. A doctor's office
5. An outpatient clinic
6. An acute or short-term inpatient facility like a hospital
7. A residential facility, such as a nursing home or group home

Intervention and treatment can include receiving physical or occupational therapy, taking prescribed medications, following a prescribed diet, and/or following a particular exercise regimen. It can also include having surgery or another medical procedure (e.g., having hip surgery to improve posture and walking). Finally, it may also entail such things as getting fitted for braces, a hearing aid, or eyeglasses to improve your child's ability to get around and interact more fully with his or her environment.

Services to Improve or Maintain
Your Child's Developmental Level

Intervention and treatment to improve or maintain your child's developmental level occurs in a number of settings, including the following:

1. Your family home (interventions and treatments such as speech-language therapy, occupational therapy, physical

therapy, taking medications, or behavior modification exercises, counseling, skills training, and family support and teaching)

2. Your child's school (interventions and treatments such as support for inclusion in public school classes, special education services, behavior modification exercises, counseling, and skills training)

3. A therapist's office (interventions and treatments such as physical therapy, occupational therapy, speech-language therapy, or the services of a pediatrician)

4. An outpatient clinic (interventions and treatments such as speech-language development therapy)

5. Other community settings, particularly social and recreational ones (e.g., YWCA, YMCA, Jewish Community Center, Boys and Girls Club, scouting)

6. An acute or short-term inpatient facility such as a general hospital

7. A rehabilitation hospital

8. Your child's residential home (e.g., nursing home, group home)

Intervention and treatment can include a variety of therapies. They can also include specific infant stimulation programs, specific programs to rehabilitate children with traumatic brain injuries, exercises in socialization, and special tutoring services.

Intervention and Treatment for Your Child's Emotional or Behavior Problem

Intervention and treatment for your child's emotional and/or behavior problem(s) can occur in a variety of settings, including the following:

1. Your family home (interventions and treatments such as individual counseling, behavior modification exercises, family support, and advocacy)

2. Your child's school (treatments such as individual or group support and counseling, a behavioral aide, taking medications, special education services, behavior modification exercises, vocational services or afterschool and summer programs)
3. A psychiatrist's, psychologist's, or social worker's office
4. An outpatient clinic (e.g., a Community Mental Health Center)
5. An acute or short-term inpatient facility (e.g., a general hospital or psychiatric hospital)
6. A specialized foster care home, group home, or supervised apartment

Based on a plan of care upon which you have agreed, intervention or treatment can include behavior management, individual psychotherapy, group counseling, family therapy and support, respite care, advocacy with the service system, taking prescribed medications and other supports and services identified by the family. It can also include supported inclusion in public school, extra tutoring after school hours, play or activity therapy, or family or group meetings.

Preventative and Routine Health Care Services

All children, including your child with special health care needs, require some routine and preventative care. If it is convenient for you and the pediatrician who manages your child's specialty care agrees to do it, you may want this pediatrician to oversee your child's routine and preventative care. Many community pediatricians are not well situated to coordinate interdisciplinary care or simply do not have the time. Pediatricians practicing in major academic medical settings focus on the special care needs of children with disabilities and chronic illnesses. They may not be the best practitioners to treat colds and coughs, broken legs, or immunizations.

Be careful. A local pediatrician treating a child with special health care needs should be aware of anything that might be different about the child's cough or cold, or its treatment, because of the disability. *It is always a good idea to have a local pediatrician stay in periodic contact with your child's specialty health care provider(s), so that the appropriate care can be given and coordinated.* You can talk with other parents of children with special health care needs to see how they handle the use of different pediatricians for different kinds of problems their children have.

Service Coordination

Service coordination (also known as care coordination or case management) is becoming more prevalent and its availability will probably continue to increase in the future. Children with special health care needs often require a number of services offered by different agencies. A service coordinator assists a family in obtaining appropriate, high-quality care for their child with special needs.

Another reason that service coordination is becoming increasingly popular is that it is mandated in the early intervention program for children from birth through 2 under the Individuals with Disabilities Education Act. Many corporate health insurance plans require employees to use service coordination in cases of complex or ensuing health problems. Many states offer service coordination as part of their state Medicaid plans. (They call it *case management.*) Finally, *there is a general consensus among health care planners and policy makers that planning and coordinating the care of frequent users of expensive services will save money.* Certainly, private insurance companies and budget-conscious staff of public health insurance programs such as Medicaid believe that some review of the use of extensive and expensive care is necessary. Service coordinators can help make this possible.

The **Child Find program,** which is used for identification and referral of children with suspected developmental problems, exists in every state. It can connect children from birth through 21 and their families to services, including service coordination.

A concern among families of children with special health care needs is that a service coordinator might limit a child's access to needed services or intrude on family privacy. Other parents in your situation can *share their experiences* dealing with service coordination. Other parents may be able to offer strategies that will help ensure that your child receives all needed and promising care without intruding on your family's privacy. Suggestions for how to get in touch with other parents in your situation are given in this chapter.

Transportation Services

Help getting to and from outpatient services is often available from local civic or church-related organizations on a volunteer basis (e.g., American Red Cross). *The specific groups that provide such services vary from community to community.*

Civic organizations (e.g., Kiwanis Clubs, Rotary Clubs, Civitans International) and church groups can be approached when they are planning their next year's projects to encourage them to establish funds to help children with special health care needs get to and from their required appointments. College sororities and fraternities can also be approached to provide driving services.

Additionally, families who receive Medicaid are required by law to be provided transportation to and from medical appointments or to be given the money to pay for

public transportation or cabs. Other clients with low incomes may receive this kind of help as well. County funds designated for this purpose, however, are often depleted before the end of the year.

Local and area health departments often have special funds to help families pay for transportation to and from the health department. Furthermore, *members of your church or synagogue or neighbors might be willing to help transport your child to appointments.* If you use this help, you may want to offer the driver a modest fee plus the cost of gasoline for his or her help.

Counseling and Support for Your Child and Other Family Members

There are a number of places you can get counseling and support for your child with special health care needs as well as for other members of your family. The extra stresses placed on individuals with chronic illnesses or disabilities and their families make it important to consider this extra help.

A number of questions and concerns of children with special health care needs and their families are not addressed adequately in conversations with pediatricians. Examples might be an adolescent's questions about sexuality and having children, discussions about the cause of a chronic illness or disability, fears about the child's future, and concerns about how the family will finance the expensive care required. Counseling and support services and programs have been established to fill this void. *Some of the places your child or other family members can receive such emotional support or counseling include the following:*

1. The offices of private practicing psychologists, social workers, marriage and family counselors, or other counselors

2. The offices of clergy trained in pastoral care
3. Nonprofit, community-based family counseling services
4. Parent support groups, where members receive training for this kind of counseling
5. Community Mental Health Centers, Community Health Centers, and Rural and Migrant Health Clinics
6. Other community programs (e.g., an Adolescent Sexuality Clinic for youth with disabilities, or a sibling support group sponsored by your county's chapter of The Arc [formerly the Association for Retarded Citizens of the United States])

Respite Care

Respite care programs are designed primarily to *give a break to the primary caregivers of individuals who require intensive and extensive care.* Children with disabilities also get a break from their regular routines and have a chance to get to know new people and to vary their activities.

Respite care is available for short-term needs (i.e., a few hours, a weekend, or in limited situations a week or longer). The cost for services varies from none to modest. If there are charges for these services, they are based on a family's income and ability to pay (i.e., a "sliding scale" fee system). These programs often serve families with children who have physical and/or behavior and emotional problems. *Common sources of respite care or referral to respite services include the following:*

1. Your state's Office for Developmental Disabilities, Mental Retardation, or Mental Health
2. A Community Mental Health Center or a county mental health agency
3. Specific respite care agencies
4. Disease- or disability-related organizations (e.g., the local Arc, the Easter Seal Society)
5. Selected civic organizations

Assistance Paying for Medical Care

The costs of providing care for a child with a chronic illness or disability can be enormous. Even generous health insurance policies have deductibles, and co-payments you must finance yourself, as well as limitations on the total amount a policy will pay. Some costs of caring for and raising a child with a chronic illness or disability are not covered by health insurance at all (e.g., transportation to and from medical care, the costs of special diets or clothing, some medical supplies and equipment, special tutoring). Chapters 5 and 6 give detailed information about ways to pay for children's medical and related care. Some organizations provide "flexible cash" to pay for medical and related care as well as other needed items (e.g., transportation, communication devices). A summary of the suggestions in Chapters 5 and 6 is provided here. Local parent support and advocacy groups can advise you of strategies for following through on these suggestions.

Private Sources of Help Paying for Medical Care

1. Obtain and use to the fullest one or more ***private health insurance policies*** through a family member's employer, a union or membership organization, or the private marketplace.
2. Explore insuring your child through a ***"risk pool"*** or "individual special health care plan" for medically uninsurable individuals.
3. Seek help from a Blue Cross and Blue Shield *"Caring"* ***Program*** if one exists in your community.
4. ***Negotiate fees*** with doctors, other therapists, clinics, and hospitals.
5. Set up ***payment plans*** with doctors, other therapists, clinics, and hospitals.
6. Seek help from ***disease- or disability-related organizations.***

7. Seek help from **civic or social welfare organizations,** including high school and college sororities and fraternities.
8. Seek help from **churches, community "ministries," and other religious organizations.**

Public Sources of Help Paying for Medical Care

1. Apply to the **Medicaid program,** which pays for a lot of medical care for eligible children and families. Medicaid includes the **Early and Periodic Screening Diagnosis, and Treatment (EPSDT) program** in all states, to screen for and treat developmental delays in children.
2. Use the **Children's Special Health Care Needs (CSHCN) Program** (sometimes known as the Crippled Children's Program) to help pay for medical care related to your child's chronic illness or disability.
3. Use the **Civilian Health and Medical Program of the Uniformed Services (CHAMPUS) health care insurance program** for dependents of the military. Within CHAMPUS, there is an additional "Program for the Handicapped" to pay for a lot of the needed care for such children.
4. If relevant, enroll your child in **Medicare's Program for Kidney Dialysis and Kidney Transplantation.** If your child qualifies, Medicare will pay a large portion of his or her medical bills.
5. If appropriate and it exists in your state or locality, apply for medical aid through a state or county **General Assistance—Medical (GA–Medical) program.**
6. Seek help from **Emergency Assistance programs** in your county's Department of Human Resources or Department of Social Services. These programs can pay for prescription medications, rent deposits, utility bills, and so forth.

7. Seek help paying for medical care or other household expenses you cannot manage from time to time from **Community Action Agencies (CAAs) or County Commissions for Economic Opportunity (CCEOs)** in your area.
8. Where available, use **county or city public hospitals** for the outpatient or inpatient care your child requires.
9. Use **Community Health Centers, Community Mental Health Centers, and Rural or Migrant Health Clinics** for the part of your child's health care they can provide.
10. Use provisions in the federal and state-funded **Vocational Rehabilitation (VR) Program** that allows payment for selected medical services for employable individuals enrolled in a VR Program.

Assistance Paying for Other Necessities of Life

A number of public and private programs are available to assist your family in paying for the basic services it needs—food, clothing, shelter, homemaker services, and medical care for other family members. Having assistance paying for some of your family's basic needs can free up money to pay for medical and related care for your child with a chronic illness or disability. Chapter 7 gives detailed information about these programs, including program benefits, eligibility requirements, and where to get more information. *Some specific service programs discussed in Chapter 7 are the following:*

1. **Supplemental Security Income (SSI)** for your child (a cash assistance program)
2. **Aid to Families with Dependent Children (AFDC)** (a cash assistance program for children in selected families with low incomes)
3. **Food Stamps**
4. **Surplus and other food distribution programs**

5. *The WIC program* (Supplemental Food Program for Women, Infants, and Children)
6. *Emergency Assistance programs* at county Departments of Human Resources for help paying for utility bills, rent deposits, medication, and so forth
7. *Ministries and other church-supported programs* to help individuals and families obtain food, clothing, and shelter
8. Cash assistance through state or county *General Assistance (GA) Programs*

Educational Services

As discussed Chapter 2, *federal law requires that State Departments of Education provide free or low-cost educational and related services to children with chronic illnesses or disabilities.* To receive these services, children from *birth through 2 years of age* must have developmental delays or have conditions with a high probability of resulting in developmental delay. Preschool children from 3 through 5 years old and school-age children through 21 must have one or more particular developmental disabilities or have developmental delays. *In both cases, each state defines "developmental delay" and conditions "with a high risk of resulting in developmental delay."* A number of educational programs are of potential benefit to your child with a chronic illness or disability. These are described on the following pages.

Early Intervention Programs

Early intervention programs (or *Part H programs*) are designed to assist children *from birth through 2 years old who have developmental delays or conditions with a high probability of resulting in a developmental delay* (e.g. spina bifida). *Each state defines these terms for their own programs.* Some states also elect to provide services to children from birth through 2 years old who are at risk of *developmental delay* (e.g., low birth weight babies, infants with respiratory distress syndrome, infants with have had prenatal exposure to alcohol or drugs) (J. Shackelford, personal communication, May 12, 1993). Most early intervention programs *are conducted in a child's home or in a community service setting.*

All 50 states participate in federally funded early intervention programs, although it is still optional that they do so. The *required services* a state must deliver to children from birth through 2 and their families include **assistive technology services, audiology, family training and counseling, health services, diagnostic or evaluative medical services, nursing services, nutrition services, occupational therapy, physical therapy, psychological services, service coordination, social work services, special instruction to families, speech-language pathology services, transportation, and vision services** (34 CFR 303.12(d)).

By the time a child in a Part H program reaches 30 months of age, an **individualized family service plan (IFSP)** must be developed for his or her family if they agree to this. States operating early intervention programs must also establish a **central directory** of services available in that state for this population. There is a **lead agency** designated to administer each state's early intervention program. In most states, this is either the state's Department of Education or the state's Office of Maternal and Child Health. The federal agency administering the early intervention program is the U.S. Department of Education.

Preschool Programs

Federally mandated Preschool Programs, or Part B programs, are designed for children **3 through 5 years old who have one of 12 developmental disabilities** listed in the regulations of the Individuals with Disabilities Education Act (IDEA). These conditions include, in alphabetical order, **au-**

tism, deaf-blindness, deafness, hearing impairment, mental retardation, multiple disabilities, orthopedic impairment, other health impairment, serious emotional disturbance, specific learning disability, speech or language impairment or traumatic brain injury, and visual impairment including blindness (34 CFR part 300, section 300.7).

Some states include an option to use the criteria of having a developmental delay in determining a child's eligibility for the Preschool Program. In these cases, all children having one of the 12 disabilities listed above would be served. Others, however, could be served as well, and no child would carry a particular disability label in being served. *Required services under Part B preschool programs include assistive technology services, audiology, counseling services, early identification and assessment of disabilities, evaluative medical services, occupational therapy, parent counseling and training, physical therapy, psychological services, recreation, rehabilitation counseling, school health services, social work services in school, speech-language pathology, transportation, and transition services* (34 CFR 300 sections 300.6, 300.7, 300.16, and 300.18).

According to each state's discretion, Preschool Programs must develop *individualized family service plans (IFSPs) or individualized education programs (IEPs).* IFSPs and IEPs outline the particular services a child and/or his or her family might need and the school's commitment to provide or help provide such services. The lead agency for preschool programs in all states is the State Department of Education, Division of Special Education.

School-Age Programs

School-age, or Part B, programs are federally mandated and designed for school-age children from *6 through 21 years of age who fall into one of the 12 categories for disability*

listed above for Preschool Programs. Required services are the same as those required for the Preschool Programs as well. In all 50 states, the lead agency for School-age Programs is the State Department of Education, Division of Special Education Services.

Head Start Programs

Head Start Programs are federally funded preschool education programs for children from 3 through 5 years old whose families have low incomes. Some siblings of current participants are admitted at 2 years of age, and expecting parents are encouraged to become involved before the delivery of their children.

The purpose of Head Start is to *improve the skills of children from disadvantaged backgrounds and to offer other services and support to the children and their families. Lunch, snacks, and transportation to and from the Head Start Program are provided to enrolled children at no charge.* **The federal government requires, as a condition of funding, that children with disabilities make up 10% of the enrollment of each Head Start Program.** This allows qualified families with a child who has special health care needs to get into a Head Start program sooner than many other children. *In addition, 10% of participants in Head Start may come from families whose incomes exceed program limits.*

Home-Based Teaching

Children who must stay at home for a significant part, if not all, of the time may receive schooling from public school teachers who come to the child's home. Local educational authorities vary on the minimum criteria necessary to warrant this method of teaching. They also differ on how frequently a teacher will come to the child's home to teach a child who cannot come to school.

You can receive more information about home-based teaching from your child's school, your local education agency, and/or your state's Department of Education. Local parent support groups can share their experiences with this service and offer tips about how to obtain such help for your child.

In-Hospital Teaching

Most children's hospitals have a staff of teachers to *help hospitalized children keep up with their school work.* The extent of these services, as well as the breadth of services covered, varies by hospital. Your child's medical team and/or local parent support groups can inform you about this service and their experience with it. They can also tell you how to obtain in-hospital teaching services for your child.

Higher Education

PL 101-336, the Americans with Disabilities Act (ADA) of 1990 requires that all colleges and universities be accessible and hospitable to individuals with disabilities. (A more detailed discussion of the ADA is provided in Chapter 2.) **Special sources of financial aid are available to students with disabilities as well.**

Two excellent sources of information about higher education for youth with chronic illnesses or disabilities include the following:

1. **HEATH (Higher Education and Adult Training for People with Disabilities) Resource Center** operates out of the National Center for Education in Washington, D.C. It is a clearinghouse of information about postsecondary education for youth with special health care needs. The staff at HEATH Resource Center can send your youth an information package about colleges, including support services available and sources of financial aid.

HEATH Resource Center
1 DuPont Circle
Washington, D.C. 20036-1193
1-800-544-3284 (Voice and TT)
(202) 939-9320 (Voice and TT, in Washington, D.C.
   area)

2. ***Vocational Rehabilitation (VR) Services*** is jointly funded
by the federal and state governments and is designed to help
individuals with disabilities become suitably employed. ***VR
services can be a source of training, help in financing a
technical or academic higher education, help in locating a job, and payment for medical care for young
adults.*** Youth can be referred to VR Services as early as
14 years old so that services will begin at age 16. This
should be part of the transition plans required by IDEA
for students with disabilities. ***Priority is given to individuals with more significant disabilities, and eligibility is not disease- or condition-specific.***

If college education or specific training is required for
an individual to be suitably employed (e.g., systems an-
alyst), ***VR services can assist in paying for tuition for
the training as well as any assistive services to help the
participant complete his or her educational program
and become employed.*** This could include but would
not be limited to providing reader services for the blind,
providing interpreter services for persons with hearing
impairments, funding Text Type (TT) and other sensory
aids, and financing transportation to and from the training site.

Both the federal and state parts of the VR Services
program are administered through State Agencies of Vocational Rehabilitation. You can call or write to them
for additional information about the program and/or application procedures. The addresses and telephone num-

bers of all State Agencies of Vocational Rehabilitation are provided in Appendix B at the end of this book. In addition, the national parent or advocacy groups listed on pages 83–85 and in Appendix B at the end of this book can help your youth apply to such a program. They can share the experiences of successful applicants.

Housing and Residential Services

A primary goal of maintaining children and youth with disabilities and chronic illnesses in the community is to have them *in family settings* to the greatest extent possible. These include birth families, foster homes, specialized home care, and group homes. An increasing number of services and subsidies are available to help families and communities care for children in such settings. Additionally, a number of programs exist to house youth with chronic illnesses and disabilities who are old enough to live independently. These include supervised apartments and other community residential placements.

Foster Homes and Specialized Home Care

Children with special health care needs who do not have parents able to care for them, or children who are having repeated problems living with their natural parents, can be placed in foster homes or homes set up specifically for the care of children with special health care needs (i.e., specialized home care).

Adults providing foster care or specialized home care to your child have received training about the physical or emotional and behavior problems of the children who live with them. These adults provide the routine health care the children require and take them to needed medical and related appointments. *Foster families and those providing specialized home care receive monthly stipends and payment for medical and other care they obtain for children in their care.* A child can remain in this kind of care for stays ranging from *short-term to indefinite*. Foster care can be a nurturing experience for a child and can provide a needed break in the routine for both a child and his or her parents.

Arrangements for foster care and specialized home care services can be made through your local Department of Social Services (or Human Resources), Department of Developmental Disabilities, Department of Mental Retardation, Department of Mental Health, or Department of Public Health. A list of state Directors of Developmental Disabilities and State Directors of Mental Health, Children and Youth Network, are included in Appendix B at the end of this book.

Group Homes

In many communities, children, teenagers, and young adults with special health care needs—whether physical and/or emotional and behavioral—have the opportunity to *live as a small group* in a home supervised by trained staff. In these settings, youth residents are encouraged to do as much of the housekeeping and personal care as they can. The have the opportunity to learn both individual responsibility and working with others. Individual and group counseling are generally available in group homes, or youth can be helped to receive counseling in the local community. For additional information about group home living for youth with developmental disabilities and/or behavior and emotional problems, contact your state's Office of Developmental Disabilities, Department of Mental Retardation, or Department of Mental Health, depending on the youth's condition and needs. The addresses and telephone numbers for these offices in each state are listed in Appendix B at the end of this book.

Supervised Apartments

Young adults with physical disabilities or a history of emotional and/or behavior problems are often able to *live alone or with others in supervised apartment settings.* In an instance like this, a trained professional does not live in the apartments with the young person but lives either on the grounds of the apartments much as a resident manager does in a large apartment complex or lives off the premises but stays in regular contact with the tenants. Individuals who are able to live in these apartments are able to care for themselves and conduct their daily routines with minimal help and supervision. A number of them attend school or work in the community.

Supervised apartments may be run by the local Community Mental Health Center or the local mental health authority. In some cases, a mental health authority actually purchases or leases apartments for this use. Some apartments are privately owned and leased by the young adults.

Currently, the federal Medicaid program is conducting demonstrations of Community Supported Living Arrangements (CSLA) as "optional services" in eight states— California, Colorado, Florida, Illinois, Maryland, Michigan, Rhode Island, and Wisconsin.

For more information about residential apartments and conditions for participation, contact your state's Department of Developmental Disabilities, Mental Retardation, or Mental Health, depending on your youth's condition. A contact for each of these is provided in Appendix B at the end of this book.

Other Residential Placements

In past years, some children and youth with chronic illnesses and disabilities used to live in nursing homes, residential schools, or other institutions, where they remained indefinitely. *The prevailing wisdom today is to have chil-*

dren and young adults with special health care needs remain and participate in their local communities and in family settings to the greatest degree possible. Thus, children who are still institutionalized usually have conditions that regularly threaten their lives. If you believe your child needs an institutional placement, talk this over with your child's doctor and/or contact a parent support group (see pp. 83–85 and Appendix B at the end of this book).

Life Skills/Job Training and Placement

Life skills/job training and placement services are available in a number of public and private agencies in the community. *The programs that offer such training and placement include public schools, Independent Living Centers, and Vocational Rehabilitation Services.*

Public Schools

In addition to the experiences and opportunities provided to all public school children, children with special health care needs receive additional training from local education agencies in life skills, job training, and job placement. IDEA, the public law guaranteeing a "free, appropriate public education" in "the least restrictive environment possible" for children with developmental delays, requires that public schools contribute to such a student's life skills and job training in the following ways:

1. Public schools must provide any support services a child with a disability requires to "benefit" from public education. These services may include occupational therapy and social work services, which can be directed at improving a child's social functioning and planning for his or her future.
2. IDEA requires that local education agencies include in a student's IEP a plan for that student's transition to work

or further education. The development of such a plan will likely include vocational counseling and may include life skills training and/or job training.

Independent Living Centers

Independent Living Centers are consumer founded and directed programs that **provide life skills training for both young and older adults with disabilities.** The goal of Independent Living Centers is to **help individuals with disabilities to function more effectively in local communities.** *Services are* not *residential,* although clients can be referred to residential programs along with other services and supports they might need. Advocacy and self-advocacy training is also emphasized.

Information about Independent Living Centers in your state is available at one of 10 regional Independent Living Center offices in the United States. A list of these offices can be found in Appendix B at the end of this book.

Vocational Rehabilitation (VR) Services

As discussed in connection with ways to finance higher education for employable young adults with disabilities, VR services are funded jointly by the federal and state governments and are specifically designed to help individuals with disabilities become suitably employed. Priority for service is given to individuals with disabilities that require more extensive support, and eligibility is not disease- of condition-specific.

Included in VR services are classroom and on-the-job training experiences, the provision of tuition costs for specialized training in the community, job development and placement, and post-placement assistance. Also included in VR services is **help with assistive technology devices** to allow a trainee to benefit from his or her training experience. This would include, but not be limited to, providing reader services for the blind, providing interpreter services for persons with hearing impairments, Text Type (TT) and other sensory aids, and financing transportation to and from training sites.

Individuals must be approaching the end of high school to apply for VR services. (They may apply at 14 years of age for services to begin as early as 16 years of age.) Additionally, applicants for VR services must meet the following requirements:

1. They must have physical or mental disabilities.
2. They must have disabilities that create or cause substantial difficulty in obtaining and maintaining employment.
3. They must have a reasonable chance of becoming employable after the provision of VR services (HEATH Resource Center, 1993).

The process of determining a young adult's eligibility for VR services is complex and often involves administering a number of tests, including physical examinations, aptitude and interest tests, vocational evaluations, employability examinations, and developmental and psychological testing. PL 102-569, the Rehabilitation Act Amendments of 1992, however, requires that eligibility determination be completed within *60 days* in most cases.

You can get additional information about services and eligibility requirements from your state's VR Agency listed in Appendix B at the end of this book. Parent organizations can share their experiences with this program and suggest ways to help ensure your youth's enrollment.

Other organizations in the community provide a variety of kinds of rehabilitation for job trainees. These include *disease- and disability-related organizations* (e.g., a local chapter of The Arc, which was formerly the Association for Retarded Citizens of the United States; the local United

Cerebral Palsy Association; Mental Health Association; Epilepsy Association), *civic organizations* (e.g., Goodwill Industries), which provide a variety of kinds of training opportunities for youth and adults with disabilities, and *Community Mental Health Centers* (CMHCs), which sponsor a variety of life skills training programs (e.g., general social skills, grooming and other adaptive skills, shopping, using public transportation, seeking a job, submitting a job application, interviewing).

Activities and Recreation

Activities and recreation for children with special health care needs are offered by a number of private agencies in most local communities. In many cases, these programs are open to other family members as well. Some of these agencies include disease- and disability-related organizations, the state and national park services, Special Olympics, the Boy Scouts and Girl Scouts of America, and YMCA organizations.

In the public sector, programs may be sponsored by your state's Department of Developmental Disabilities, Department of Mental Retardation, Department of Mental Health, and Department of Public Health. Activities include weekend and summer camping, year-round special activity programs, nature accessibility in wheelchairs, competitive sports, snow skiing, water skiing, bicycling, white water rafting, and horseback riding.

A local parent support group can inform you of the specific private and public agencies that provide recreational services for children with special health care needs and their families in your state.

Legal Services

Legal services are available in most communities. Families with relatively low incomes can use the more than 1,000 offices of the **Legal Services Corporation** (commonly known as "Legal Aid"). Funded by a variety of sources including federal, state, and local governments, this agency can offer free services to those who qualify.

Legal Aid attorneys can help you with routine legal work or **help you to obtain a service to which you believe your child is entitled.** They can also represent your child or family in a case in which you were discriminated against because of your child's disease or disability. *Some Legal Aid offices specialize in disability law.*

The Judge David L. Bazelon Mental Health Law Center can refer you to the Legal Aid office in your state most suited for your needs.

Judge David L. Bazelon Mental Health Law Center
1101 15th Street, Northwest
Washington, D.C. 20005
(202) 467-5730 (Voice)
(202) 467-4232 (TT)

Call ahead to the suggested Legal Aid office to see if your child or family qualifies financially for their services. If you do *not* quality, ask Legal Aid for a referral to a private attorney in your community or state suitable for your needs.

Protection and Advocacy agencies are independent and legally mandated agencies in each state. These agencies can also provide lawyers for children with disabilities in both community and institutional settings. A listing of each state's Protection and Advocacy agency is provided in Appendix B at the end of this book.

Advocacy Services

A number of public and private organizations represent the interests of children and other individuals with chronic illnesses or disabilities. These organizations help to ensure that needed services are made available in communities and obtained by individuals. They play a large role in seeing that laws and court rulings protecting individuals' rights are upheld. Finally, advocacy organizations teach self-advocacy skills to individuals with special health care needs so that they may be more assertive in obtaining the services and support they need and can challenge discriminatory practices they encounter.

The remainder of this chapter describes the major advocacy organizations that address all kinds of disabilities. Their addresses and telephone numbers are provided here as well as in Appendix B at the end of this book. *It is important to remember that the organizations described in this chapter are not the only ones you can contact. Many other organizations provide advocacy as a part of their other services.*

SOURCES OF REFERRAL TO HELP

There are many national, state, and regional sources of information about service programs and how to utilize them for families of children with chronic illnesses or disabilities. Some have information about diseases and disabilities or current interventions and treatments for different conditions, in addition to information about services available in particular states and communities. Others know more about laws and government policies affecting children with disabilities and their families.

Begin your search for any particular kind of information (e.g., counseling and family support services) with several of the organizations suggested below. You will obtain more information that way and can verify the accuracy and thoroughness of information you receive from any one source.

All of the organizations listed below maintain exten-
sive files of resources and are well suited to match your
need with resources available in your state or local commu-
nity. If one of these organizations cannot help you with a
particular request, it will refer you to other organizations
that can, including those at the local level. **Remember to**
persist until you get the information you need.

Information Clearinghouses

Information clearinghouses collect articles, reports, and other information from a variety of sources. They put this information together in brief fact sheets and other documents
that can be easily used by the public. Many also respond to
telephone inquiries by the public, answering questions,
sending written materials, and/or directing callers to other
information sources.

The National Information Center for
Children and Youth with Disabilities (NICHCY)

NICHCY has a large amount of information about chronic
illnesses and disabilities, service programs for such individuals, referrals to *advocacy and support groups*, information
about setting up a parent support group, the major pieces of
legislation concerning children with disabilities, and selected information about *programs to finance services* for
children with chronic illnesses and disabilities. The staff at
NICHCY are well acquainted with their resources and are
particularly helpful with callers who need help clarifying
the kind of information required. The staff can suggest other
resources that are related to the ones callers request.
NICHCY keeps an answering machine on during hours
when the office is not staffed, and calls are returned
promptly. For any information request you have about ser-

vices or any other aspect of chronic illness of disability and children, do not hesitate to contact NICHCY.

The National Information Center for Children and
    Youth with Disabilities (NICHCY)
Post Office Box 1492
Washington, D.C. 20013
(202) 884-8200 (Voice and TT) (If you call long
    distance, NICHCY will call you back.)

The National Center for
Education and Maternal and Child Health

The National Center for Education and Maternal and Child Health, affiliated with Georgetown University, can *provide information about diseases, disabilities, and service programs to benefit young children and their families.* Although it does not specialize in referral information for children with chronic illnesses or disabilities, it does have information regarding this group, including a large list of organizations working in the area of chronic illness.

The National Center for Education and Maternal and
    Child Health
2000 15th Street North
Arlington, Virginia 22201-2617
(703) 524-7802 (Voice)

The National Information
Clearinghouse (NIC) for Infants with
Disabilities and Life-Threatening Conditions

The NIC provides information for caregivers, health care providers and social service professionals involved with infants born with life-threatening conditions. Services they provide include information about parent support and training programs, community services and resources, early intervention programs, protection and advocacy agencies, child protective services, and special needs adoptions.

National Information Clearinghouse for Infants with
   Disabilities and Life-Threatening Conditions
Center for Developmental Disabilities
University of South Carolina
Benson Building, 1st Floor
Columbia, South Carolina 29208
1-800-922-9234 (Voice and TT) (toll-free)

The National Center for Youth with Disabilities (NCYD)

NCYD is a project of the Society for Adolescent Medicine
and the University of Minnesota's Adolescent Health program. It was established in 1985 as *an information and resource center focusing on adolescents with chronic illness
and disabilities and the issues that surround their transition to adult life.* NCYD's mission is to raise awareness of
the needs of adolescents with chronic illness and disabilities, expand the knowledge and involvement of those who
provide services to youth, and promote programs and strategies which enhance the ability of adolescents and young
adults to grow, develop, work, and participate in community life to their fullest capacity.

National Center for Youth with Disabilities
University of Minnesota
Box 721
420 Delaware Street, Southeast
Minneapolis, Minnesota 55455-0392
1-800-333-6293 (Voice) (toll-free)
(612) 624-3939 (TT)

HEATH Resource Center

HEATH (Higher Education and Adult Training for People
with Disabilities) Resource Center is a *national clearinghouse for information about postsecondary education for
individuals with disabilities.* Available help includes information about programs in American colleges and univer-

sities for individuals with disabilities, support services, and adaptations. It is also a *source of information about financial assistance for education programs after high school*, including special financial assistance programs for individuals with disabilities.

> HEATH Resource Center
> 1 Dupont Circle
> Washington, D.C. 20036-1193
> 1-800-544-3284 (Voice and TT; toll-free; outside
>   Washington, D.C.)
> (202) 939-9320 (Voice and TT; in Washington, D.C.
>   area)

National Parent Organizations for More than One Disease or Disability

These parent-founded and/or directed organizations can *provide referrals to established intervention, treatment, and service programs for children with special needs and their families.* They are also good sources of *information about laws and government policies affecting children with chronic illnesses, disabilities, or other special needs.* Finally, they can *refer families to support groups* in or near their home communities.

A Reader's Guide for Parents of Children with Mental, Physical, or Emotional Disabilities (Moore, 1990) is a readable and helpful book written by a parent and offers one of the best ways to get started learning about resources and how to use them.

The Federation for Children with Special Needs (FCSN)

FCSN provides a number of services to families of children with special health care needs. These include *information and referral to a variety of services in other states and local communities, parent training and the development of fami-*

ly education and support groups. FCSN conducts a number of national projects, including the Collaboration of Parents and Professionals (CAPP). It is also part of a network of parent centers that are all run by a coalition of parents.

> Federation of Children with Special Needs
> 95 Berkeley Street
> Boston, Massachusetts 02116
> (617) 482-2915 (Voice and TT)

Federation of Families for Children's Mental Health

This organization represents families of children who have mental illnesses or emotional and behavior problems. The Federation can *supply information to the public* about any of these conditions, *refer families* and others to local service providers and support groups, and *inform families* about how to get help for their children when faced with non-responsive service systems.

The Federation also represents the needs of such families with local, state, and national legislative bodies and administrative agencies (e.g., The National Governor's Association).

> Federation of Families for Children's Mental Health
> 1021 Prince Street
> Alexandria, Virginia 22314-2971
> (703) 684-7710 (Voice)

National Parent Network on Disability (NPND)

NPND is dedicated to improving the lives of children, youth, and adults with disabilities, and their families. Its goals include striving to *strengthen the family unit, improving the availability of service* to children and their families, and helping to *ensure that services are responsive to needs.*

National Parent Network on Disability
1600 Prince Street
Suite 115
Alexandria, Virginia 22314
(703) 684-6763 (Voice)

Family Voices

Family Voices is a *national parent network concerned primarily with representing the needs of children with chronic illnesses and disabilities, and their families, in state and national health care reform.*

Family Voices
c/o Polly Arango
Post Office Box 769
Algondones, New Mexico 87001

State Parent Training and Information (PTI) Centers

There is at least one PTI project in each state. Their primary purpose is to teach parents about the rights of their children with special health care needs, particularly under the Individuals with Disabilities Education Act (IDEA). Most of these centers also *teach advocacy skills to parents,* so that they can be more comfortable talking with their children's teachers, principals, and school board members about educational and other service needs. PTI Centers are excellent *sources of any kind of information concerning the rights of children with chronic illnesses or disabilities to a public education, strategies for parents to use in getting the local education authority to comply with federal legislation in this area, and any legal recourse open to a parent who believes that his or her child's school is violating the law.* A list of PTI Centers in each of the four regions of the United States is provided here:

Midwest Region (Pacer Center)
4826 Chicago Avenue, South
Minneapolis, Minnesota 55417
(612) 827-2966 (Voice and TT)

Northeast Region (Parent Information Center)
151A Manchester Street
Post Office Box 1422
Concord, New Hampshire 03302
(603) 224-6299 (Voice)
(603) 224-7005 (TT)

South Region (The Arc)
1851 Ram Runway
Suite 104
College Park, Georgia 30337
(404) 761-3150 (Voice and TT)

West Region (Washington State PAVE)
6316 South 12th Street
Tacoma, Washington 98465
(206) 565-2266 (Voice and TT)

National Disease- and Disability-Related Organizations

National disease- and disability-related organizations can be helpful to parents of children with chronic illnesses and disabilities. A discussion of these organizations appears in Chapter 6 and a list of the largest organizations, with addresses, telephone numbers, and descriptions of assistance offered, appears in Appendix 6A. In addition, *the National Information Center for Children and Youth with Disabilities (NICHCY) (see pp. 79–80) can provide any address and telephone number for the more than 100 disease- and disability-related organizations that exist.*

State Government Offices

State governments set up a variety of departments to handle the business of state government—meeting the public's need for services and information. These include, for example, matters ranging from housing, transportation, food services, and highway construction and maintenance to public education, police protection, and tax collection.

A number of state government offices deal particularly with the needs of children, including those with special health care needs. These are the government offices discussed below.

Children with Special Health Care Needs (CSHCN) Programs, State Office of Maternal and Child Health

Children with Special Health Care Needs (CSHCN) Programs, often called Title V Programs because of the section of the Social Security Act that authorizes them, can *direct you to evaluation or intervention and treatment services for your child* even if your child does not qualify for CSHCN services. **In general, CSHCN Programs pay for or provide disease- and disability-related health care for children with selected chronic illnesses or disabilities whose families have low to middle incomes.** *Requirements for eligibility and extent of services vary widely by state.* CSHCN Programs are listed in Appendix B at the end of this book.

Part H Coordinators
Administering States' Early Intervention Programs

Part H Programs are generally administered by the State Department of Education or the State Office of Maternal and Child Health. These programs provide early intervention services to children from birth through 2 years old who have developmental delays or conditions with a high probability of resulting in delays. In a number of states, however, other agencies have this responsibility. A list of states' Part H-Program Directors for early intervention programs is provided in Appendix B at the end of this book.

Part B Coordinators
State Departments of Education

Both Part B preschool (for children from 3 through 5 years old) and school-age programs for students 6 through 21 years old are administered by the Special Education Director in your state's Department of Education. This is the case in all 50 states. A list of Part B Program Directors (Special Education Directors) for each state appears in Appendix B at the end of this book.

State Departments of
Developmental Disabilities, Children and
Youth Division or Community Services Division

State Departments of Developmental Disabilities administer a number of institutional and community programs for individuals of all ages with developmental disabilities (e.g., mental retardation). They may be separate departments or may be combined with your state's Department of Mental Health and/or Department of Substance Abuse. Call the Community Services Division to find out about service programs for your child, including evaluation. To reach this office, contact your state's Department of Developmental Disabilities (see Appendix B at the end of this book).

State Department of Mental Health, Children
and Youth Division or Community Services Division

State Departments of Mental Health, which may be combined in your state with the Department of Developmental Disabilities, administer institutional and community programs for individuals of all ages with mental illness or severe emotional and behavior problems. Call the Children and Youth Division for information about services that are available for your child, including evaluation. To reach this office, contact your state's Department of Mental Health, Children and Youth Services (see Appendix B at the end of this book).

Other Organizations

A variety of other organizations are concerned with the needs of children with chronic illnesses and disabilities and their families. They are often nonprofit organizations (e.g., Association for the Care of Children's Health [ACCH]) or free-standing organizations established through federal legislation on behalf of children with special needs (e.g., University Affiliated Programs [UAPs], NEC★TAS [National Early Childhood Technical Assistance Systems]). These organizations play important and unique roles that *help to ensure that children with chronic illnesses or disabilities have access to the care and services they require.*

The Association for the Care of Children's Health (ACCH), National Center for Family-Centered Care

ACCH, composed of professionals, parents, and other advocates of children with chronic illnesses and disabilities, was started to help ensure appropriate and humane care for hospitalized children. Their work has reached out to homes and communities as more children with diseases and disabilities are receiving care at home or on an outpatient basis. The *organization's focus is family-centered care,* and it can supply information about family-centered care in hospitals and community programs, as well as referrals to family support and advocacy organizations. Call or write ACCH and/or the National Center for Family-Centered Care with your request for information about services for your child or family.

The Association for the Care of Children's Health,
  National Center for Family-Centered Care
7910 Woodmont Avenue
Suite 300
Bethesda, Maryland 20814-3015
(301) 654-6549

NEC★TAS

NEC★TAS (National Early Childhood Technical Assistance System) was formed as a result of PL 99-457, the Education of the Handicapped Act Amendments of 1986. *NEC★TAS's expertise is in clarifying the provisions of IDEA for state agencies and programs, particularly those serving infants, toddlers, and preschool children with disabilities.* **NEC★TAS also welcomes questions from parents of children with special health care needs and can provide information or referrals to a range of services available for children with diseases or disabilities and their families.** This includes information about state and federal education and health policies regarding these populations.

NEC★TAS
CB #8040
500 Nations Bank Plaza
Chapel Hill, North Carolina 27599
(919) 962-2001

University Affiliated Programs (UAPs)

University Affiliated Programs (UAPs) are located in major universities and teaching hospitals across the United States. They engage in different activities to *help support the independence, productivity, and inclusion in the community of individuals with developmental disabilities.* These activities include professional training, service delivery, research, and dissemination of information. The relative emphasis of each activity varies from location to location, depending on the strengths of the university with which a particular UAP is affiliated. There are currently 58 UAPs in 49 states, the District of Columbia, and Puerto Rico. For a referral to the UAP closest to your home, contact:

> American Association of University Affiliated
>   Programs for Persons with Developmental
>   Disabilities
> 8630 Fenton Street, Suite 410
> Silver Spring, Maryland 20910
> (301) 588-8252 (Voice)
> (301) 588-3319 (TT)

Developmental Disabilities (DD) Planning Councils

Developmental Disabilities (DD) Planning Councils have been established by federal and state laws for the following reasons:

- To help ensure that there are planned and coordinated services for individuals with significant long-lasting developmental disabilities
- To help change public policies and attitudes toward individuals with disabilities
- To foster the independence, productivity, and inclusion into society of individuals with disabilities
- To help establish additional personal care services for individuals with disabilities and programs of support for families with members with disabilities

There are currently 56 DD Planning Councils. Membership of each Council is required to be at least 50% persons with developmental disabilities. To obtain a referral to your state's DD Planning Council, contact:

> National Association of Developmental Disabilities
>   Planning Councils
> 1234 Massachusetts Avenue, Northwest
> Suite 103
> Washington, D.C. 20005
> (202) 347-1234

SUMMARY

As this chapter and the list of resources in Appendix 6A indicate, there is a *range of services of potential value to your child and your family*. In addition, the many national, state, and regional *referral sources can provide more detailed information about the services described* in this chapter. These organizations can also direct you to specific service programs and individual service providers in your area.

As you search for appropriate services for your child, you may find that some communities have fewer services than others. This occurs most often in the less populated areas of each state. If this applies to you, do not be discouraged. Although it is not always convenient, many families travel to nearby counties or states to get needed services for their child or other family members. If you find you must do the same, explore sources of reimbursement for your travel costs. Tips on how to do this are included in Chapters 5 and 6.

4

Dealing with Professionals, Hospitals, Insurance Companies, and School Systems

As the parents of a child with a chronic illness or disability, you will probably have frequent contact with doctors and other professionals, hospitals, and health insurance companies. In addition, you will develop a special relationship with the teachers and administrators at your child's school. These individuals play critical roles in your child's care and well-being.

You need not, however, feel intimidated by professionals, hospitals, insurance companies, and school systems. ***Try***

to get comfortable with your role as the primary individu-als responsible for your child's care. To do this, it is often helpful to gain whatever knowledge and support you can to help you advocate for your child's needs. Professionals can be viewed as partners in planning and managing your child's care, but decisions about the care your child receives are ultimately yours.

You will want to become acquainted with the full range of services that are available for your child, to be-come aware of your child's and family's legal rights to ser-vices, and to discover the most creative ways to finance the health care and related services your child requires. It will be important for you to become skilled and comfortable negotiating with doctors and other professionals, hospitals, health insurance companies, and school systems to help ensure that your child gets appropriate and high-quality care at a cost you can afford.

Although it is often difficult for laypersons to evaluate the quality of medical and related care, most people can evaluate the quality of the services they receive. Did your child have to wait too long to be seen? Were you treated courteously and informed about what would be done to your child that day? Were all of your questions addressed ade-quately? You will also have opinions about which treat-ments and/or programs helped your child and which did not. As parents, *you should feel free to give your opinions and preferences to professionals and to file complaints with clinic or hospital administrators when service is poor.* Sim-ilarly, you should give compliments when a doctor, hospital, insurance company, or school has been particularly helpful. This, in the long run, will help the professionals involved in your child's intervention and treatment to become more re-sponsive to the needs of your child and family, and others in similar situations.

It will take information, time, and practice to learn how to exercise this role effectively. There are many useful sources for information. A number of them are suggested throughout this book. **It is worth the time to read as much as you can about your child's conditions, services available for children with similar conditions, and the services offered in your community and state. Talk with other parents who have children with chronic illnesses and disabilities and those who have more experience with the available services than you do.** In terms of practicing your role as advocate for your child, the good news and the bad news is that you will get the opportunity for plenty of practice.

The referral sources in this book should help you in your job. Descriptions of major information and parent support and advocacy groups are included in Chapter 3 and Appendix B at the end of this book, along with information about how to reach them for assistance. *Other information services, books, and parent support and advocacy groups can also supply helpful information and emotional support as you educate yourself and/or advocate for your child.* If you write or call a number of the organizations suggested in this book they will send fact sheets, reading lists, and specialized referrals for more information on a variety of topics related to getting and paying for services for your child.

WHAT TO EXPECT FROM DOCTORS AND OTHER PROFESSIONALS IN OUTPATIENT CLINIC SETTINGS

The pediatrician or medical specialist who oversees the majority of your child's medical and related care will become an extremely important person in your child's and family's life. This professional's diagnostic and clinical skills, as well as the ability to get other professionals to cooperate with an overall intervention or treatment plan for your child, can have a major impact on your child's well-being and level of functioning.

Choose this professional carefully after reviewing possible choices with other parents and professionals you trust and who are familiar with the doctors you are considering. Before deciding on a service coordinator or a "primary care doctor," you may want to request a meeting with each of the candidates. You will want to ask the following kinds of questions that you have planned ahead of time:

- "How many other children with my child's condition have you treated?"
- "Can I call you at home for an emergency?"
- "Will you be willing to bill our family's health insurance company directly for payment?"
- "Will you accept whatever our insurance company pays as 'payment in full' for your services?"
- "Do you accept Medicaid?"
- "Can we set up a payment plan with you for services you give that are not covered by our health insurance plan?"

You should expect the person you select and his or her office or clinic staff to be *businesslike* and *courteous* to you and your child at all times. You should *not be expected to wait to see a professional for more than 30 minutes* on a regular basis in an office, a clinic waiting room, or a treatment room.

You should *feel listened to.* This means that you will feel that the professional is interested in your child and what you report about his or her condition or behavior and that the professional is absorbing and using what you report to form a diagnosis and plan of care for your child. Such a professional *should not appear to be threatened* by the active role you take in managing your child's care; rather, he or she should welcome your active participation, knowing that as parents you spend far more time with your child than any professional does and that it is your job to seek the best care for your child.

Professionals should be *willing to take the time and make the effort to explain to you, in easily understandable language, what they believe is wrong with your child and the rationale for recommending certain services to help.* Your questions should be welcomed, and professionals should be *able to refer you to sources for additional information about your child's condition* and state-of-the-art research concerning treatment and intervention.

Your child's primary care physician or other professional should be *willing and able to coordinate the services your child needs* in a way that is convenient and affordable for your family. He or she should also be willing to *communicate with your child's other providers*—with your permission—in other health care, educational, or social service environments.

Finally, the professionals you and your child see should be *willing to state or to approximate fees for services before performing them.* He or she should agree to supply your health insurance company with any written justifications it needs to pay your claims.

We all know there are few angels in the world and, in the case of rare disorders and in sparsely populated areas, you may not be able to choose the professional(s) who treat your child. However, if you do not expect an excellent standard of care and service for your child, he or she may not receive it.

WHAT TO EXPECT FROM HOSPITAL EMPLOYEES

You may be able to choose the hospital your child will use for diagnostic tests or medical procedures and surgeries. Some physicians have "admitting privileges" at more than one hospital, and psychologists and other mental health professionals may practice at more than one clinic in your area.

Hospital Staff

Both diagnostic and treatment staff in hospitals should be *professional, courteous,* and *caring* toward your child and your family. All staff should be *able and willing to tell your child what a test or treatment involves and whether it will hurt.* They should also be *able and willing to answer other questions you or your child may have.* Explanations should be given in a way that is sensitive and appropriate for your child's age. Again, the *amount of time you wait to see such personnel should be reasonable.* A limit of 30 minutes should be set, unless there is an acceptable reason given to you for a longer wait.

Business Office Personnel

Similarly, the personnel of the hospital's business office should be *professional* and *courteous.* They should be *able to tell you how much a service will cost in advance,* and they should be *willing to spend time explaining charges on bills, filing for payments from your health insurance company, and providing justifications your insurance company needs* to pay your claims. They should also help you to *set up a payment plan* with the office, clinic, hospital, or a local bank for charges not covered by insurance.

Some hospital business offices will try to get you to pay a large portion of your child's total hospital bill for an inpatient stay or for a costly outpatient procedure or treatment *before* your child is discharged from the hospital or clinic. You are not legally required to do this. You may pay a modest amount of the bill and set up a monthly payment plan for the estimated portion of the bill you will owe after your health insurance company pays its part.

As with professionals in outpatient clinics, it is important to *file complaints with hospital administrators when you believe a clinical or business staff member behaved inappropriately. Similarly, it is important to let hospital administrators know when their staff have performed their job(s) competently.* Your child and your family are the hospital's customers. As many hospitals compete for your business, what you think and feel matters to the hospital's administrators.

Hospitals can be quite aggressive in collecting fees owed to them. A number of hospitals contract with collection agencies to recover money from unpaid bills. Bill collectors may call you repeatedly and come to your workplace trying to collect money, particularly if you have not responded to their written requests for payment. To minimize the chances of this annoyance, *arrange a monthly payment plan with the hospital(s) or clinic(s) to whom you owe money and try to make the payments.* Contact the hospital or clinic if you cannot make your agreed-upon payment for a particular month.

Collection agency practices are regulated by the Federal Trade Commission (FTC) in regional offices across the United States. A summary of acceptable practices is found in Chapter 9. If you believe that a representative of a collection agency has threatened you, report it to the FTC office closest to your home and call the local police. A list of FTC regional offices, including addresses and telephone numbers, appears in Appendix B at the end of this book.

WHAT TO EXPECT FROM YOUR HEALTH INSURANCE COMPANY OR PLAN

If you are fortunate enough to have your child's care covered by a health insurance policy or plan, **be sure to read the policy or plan information carefully.** Verify coverage, exclusions from coverage, and any special conditions that must be met for part or all of your child's care to be paid by the health insurance company. ***To minimize the costs you will pay out of your own pocket,*** follow the policy or plan guidelines as you obtain services for your child.

Filing Claims

A representative of your health insurance company or self-administered plan should be able to tell you *what information you need to supply to file a claim and in what time frame the claim must be filed to receive the maximum reimbursement* possible for your child's care. If you have any trouble obtaining this information, ask to speak with the representative's supervisor.

If you have more than one health insurance policy, the one that is "primary" will pay its part of a claim first. The "secondary" policy will then pay its share of the remaining balance. Your insurance company is required to send you a "claims form" within 15 days of your written notice of a claim and to pay benefits for that claim within 60 days after receipt of proof of a claim. This assumes that you have complied with your responsibility to report all claims within 20 days of their occurrence. *Remember, self-insured health insurance plans are not required to comply with this timetable.*

Rejected Claims

Most state laws require your health insurance company to tell you in writing the reason(s) for rejecting any claim. Generally, you have as long as 60 days from the date of the rejection notice to appeal a claim. A representative of your health insurance company should tell you how to do this. Again, self-insured health care plans are exempt from this state regulation and therefore do not need to comply with this law. Many comply, however, on a voluntary basis.

Obtaining Reimbursement

If you are having trouble obtaining reimbursement under your health insurance policy or plan, contact your state's Department of Insurance for assistance. These departments regulate all insurance companies doing business in their state, except those that are self-insured. Ask to speak with a staff member in the Consumer Affairs Division for Personal Health Insurance. A list of every state Department of Insurance, including addresses and telephone numbers, is provided in Appendix B at the end of this book.

WHAT TO EXPECT FROM YOUR CHILD'S TEACHERS, PRINCIPAL, AND SCHOOL DISTRICT

Under federal law (i.e., the Individuals with Disabilities Education Act [IDEA]), your state education agency and your local school district—often in conjunction with your state's Department of Maternal and Child Health, Department of Health, and/or Department of Mental Health—*have a number of major responsibilities to your child with special health care needs and to your family.* These responsibilities include Child Find services; a free, appropriate, public education in the least restrictive environment; services to allow a child to benefit from public education; an annual individualized education program (IEP); and in some cases, an individualized family service plan (IFSP). Each of these responsibilities is discussed here.

First, children with special health care needs must be *identified at the earliest age possible* by one of the state departments listed above and referred to care that is designed to enhance his or her functioning and well-being. Each state must develop and publicize *procedures for the referral of children to services* and for information about services, and each state must develop a directory of services.

This program is known nationally as Child Find. Many states have developed statewide toll-free telephone numbers for information and referral.

Second, *states must provide a "free, appropriate, public education" to children 3 through 21 years of age if they meet the state's definition of "disabled."* Although not yet mandated for children birth through 2 years of age, there are strong financial incentives for states to provide early intervention services to infants and toddlers. Children must be provided early intervention (i.e., early treatments and other services to minimize the effects of delays) services if they meet their state's definition of "developmentally delayed" or have a condition that has a "high probability of resulting in developmental delay." Some states also choose to serve children "at risk" of developmental delay.

Third, children with chronic illnesses or disabilities, who must be educated at public expense in the "least restrictive environment possible," also must be provided with *auxiliary aides and services* that allow them *to benefit from such an educational setting.* Examples of such services include physical, occupational, and speech-language therapies; transportation to and from school; and social work services. A number of other services could qualify as "auxiliary aides and services."

Fourth, each child must be provided an *annual, written individualized education program (IEP).* The child's family *must be encouraged to participate in the development of the IEP.* Additionally, families of children receiving early intervention services must be provided annual *individualized family service plans (IFSPs).* This federal requirement acknowledges that a child's family may need some support services to provide for the child adequately. Families must also be encouraged to participate fully in the development of their IFSPs. The details of what must be included in IEPs and IFSPs are provided in Chapter 5.

As your child's parent or legal guardian, **you should expect your child's teachers and school principal to be fully informed about their responsibilities under federal law to help ensure your child's optimal development and functioning.** If they are not fully informed, you should expect them to seek out this information so they can provide your child with the education and services to which he or she is entitled by law.

Complying with IDEA is costly to school districts, area education agencies, and the other human service organizations that may be involved. Not all of the expenses are reimbursed by the federal government. For this reason, *you may find waiting lists for services for children* birth through 2 years old (i.e., for early intervention services) or for children 3 through 5 years old (i.e., for preschool services). You also may encounter some resistance in getting your child's teachers, principal, and school district to provide both the education and support services that are mandated by law. **If you are having problems getting compliance with the law at your child's school, you can do several of the following things:**

1. **Contact the Part B lead agency (Office of the Special Education Director) for your child's school district or area education agency.** He or she may be able to help you to find a remedy for the problem(s). A list of Part B lead agencies for each state appears in Appendix B at the end of this book.

   If another agency is responsible for the program your child needs (e.g., early intervention services provided by your state's Office of Maternal and Child Health), contact that office. A list of addresses and telephone numbers for each state's Office of Maternal and Child Health also is provided in Appendix B at the end of this book.

2. **Contact a parent advocacy group that specializes in education for children with special health care needs.** These groups can help you resolve problems with an early intervention program, preschool program, or school, based on the ways in which similar complaints were favorably resolved elsewhere. They can also refer you to advocacy resources in your community or state. Parent Training and Information Centers for each region of the country are provided in Chapter 3 and Appendix B at the end of this book. These organizations specialize in teaching parents how to get school systems and other government agencies to provide federally mandated services for children with special health care needs.

3. **If you do not get any relief using the suggestions above, contact your local Legal Aid Office or a private attorney** for advice about how to handle your situation. A number of lawsuits (including class action lawsuits on behalf of large numbers of people) have been brought against school districts that restricted full compliance with federal law regarding the public education of children with special health care needs. Call your local information operator for the telephone number of a Legal Aid or Legal Services Corporation office near your home. If you cannot locate help this way, call the national office of the Legal Services Corporation for a referral:

> Legal Services Corporation
> 750 First Street, Northeast
> 11th Floor
> Washington, D.C. 20002-4250
> (202) 336-8800

As with other program of benefit to your child, it will be up to you to be certain your child obtains the educational benefits and support services he or she is entitled to receive through the public education system.

SUMMARY

Your child depends on you to advocate for his or her best interests with professionals, hospitals, insurance companies, and school systems. You may be required to obtain additional information (e.g., about your child's condition, available interventions and treatments, arrangements you can make to pay medical bills, services to which your child is entitled) and *to develop skills you can use with confidence* (e.g., filing and appealing health insurance claims effectively). Others (e.g., physicians, teachers) can provide help and support to you in this role, but specific decisions about your child's health care and education are up to you. Furthermore, you should expect to be listened to, assisted, and treated with respect by all of the professionals you consult as you seek services for your child.

5

Paying for Medical Care—Public Sources of Help

The high cost of medical care is becoming a problem for many Americans. Parents worry about whether they will be able to afford the medical care their children require—from preventative checkups and immunizations to diagnostic tests, medical procedures, and surgeries. This is of particular, and often critical, concern for the parents of a child with a chronic illness or disability. Almost certainly, such children will require more medical and related care than their peers who do not have chronic illnesses or disabilities. This means more medical bills and higher out-of-pocket expenses for parents.

Fortunately, *a number of public and private programs provide care directly or help American families to pay for medical and related care.* Some programs require that a child's family has limited income and "resources." Other programs require a child to fit a certain category of need. However, some programs can provide emergency or periodic help for any child or family in need. This chapter reviews the major public programs that can offer help to your child with a chronic illness or disability, and in some cases to your family. Private sources of help are described in Chapter 6. The public programs described here include the following:

1. The Medicaid program, including the following:
   - Required eligibility groups
   - Optional eligibility groups, including TEFRA 134
   - Categorically Needy Program
   - Medically Needy Program
   - Federally mandated Basic Services
   - Optional Services
   - Home-Based and Community-Based Care 2176 Waivers
   - Early and Periodic Screening, Diagnosis, and Treatment (EPSDT) Program
2. The Children's Special Health Care Needs (CSHCN) Program
3. State Departments of Education and Local Education Agencies
   - Part H (early intervention) programs under the Individuals with Disabilities Education Act (IDEA) (for infants and toddlers from birth through 2 years of age)
   - Part B programs under IDEA (for preschoolers from 3 through 5 years of age and school-age children and youth from 6 through 21)
4. Civilian Health and Medical Program of the Uniformed Services (CHAMPUS) (health care for dependents of the military)
5. Medicare's coverage of kidney disease in children and youth

6. State and local General Assistance–Medical programs (GA–Medical)
7. Emergency assistance programs, county Departments of Human Resources (or Departments of Social Services)
8. County or area Public Health Departments
9. Public hospitals
10. Community Health Centers and Community Mental Health Centers
11. Rural and Migrant Health Clinics
12. Community Action Agencies (CAAs) or County Commissions for Economic Opportunity (CCEOs)
13. Vocational Rehabilitation (VR) Programs
14. The Hill-Burton Free Care Program, U.S. Department of Health and Human Services

It is important to keep in mind that if a health care reform bill passes in the U.S. Congress, a number of these programs may be changed. You will have to check with the agencies administering the programs presented here to see whether their roles have been affected. No matter how benefit programs are organized, one of the goals of health care reform is to bring at least a minimum package of health benefits to *all* Americans. ***The minimum package for children with chronic illnesses or disabilities should reflect that their "minimum" needs are greater than those of children who do not have chronic illnesses or disabilities.***

THE MEDICAID PROGRAM

Medicaid is designed to provide medical and related health care to certain individuals and families with low incomes. It is financed jointly by the federal and state governments. ***All states have some kind of Medicaid program,*** although both available benefits and number of eligible children are much greater in some states than in others. As you will see below, each state determines the benefits package it offers (beyond the required "basic services") as well as, in most cases, the state's eligibility requirements that are not mandated by the federal government.

Individuals enrolled in Medicaid services do not pay for the care. In a few cases, however, to discourage overuse of a service, a small co-payment (50¢ or $1.00) is charged. This co-payment must be paid by the individual receiving the Medicaid service. With the exception of recipients who are enrolled in a health maintenance program under Medicaid, recipients may choose to go to any qualified provider who agrees to accept Medicaid patients. It is important to note that *not all health care providers accept Medicaid as payment* for their services. This is something all families must ask when considering the use of a particular doctor or other health care provider.

Which Children Are Eligible for Medicaid Services?

There are "required" and "optional" eligibility groups under Medicaid. "Required" eligibility groups are those a state must serve under its Medicaid program. "Optional" eligibility groups are those a state *may* serve.

Required Eligibility Groups

Each state's Medicaid program must provide for at least "basic" medical services for any child who fits one of the following descriptions:

1. The child is eligible for Aid to Families with Dependent Children (AFDC), a cash assistance program that is offered by most states and is jointly funded by the federal and state governments; income levels for AFDC eligibility vary by state.
2. The child is eligible for Supplemental Security Income (SSI), a federal cash assistance program for older adults and people with disabilities. In 38 states and the District

of Columbia, qualification for SSI is accompanied by automatic enrollment in Medicaid. In the other states, you must apply for Medicaid.

3. The child is younger than 6 years old and a member of a family whose income does not exceed 133% of the federal poverty level is eligible. The federal poverty level for a family of three in 1993 was $11,890. For example, if 100% of the poverty level for a family of three was an annual income of $11,890 in 1993, a family could earn 33% more than this—or one-third more—and still qualify financially for Medicaid. This means they could earn $11,890 plus one-third of $11,890 (i.e., $3,924), or a total of $15,814 a year.

4. The child comes from a two-parent family with low income and limited resources.

5. The child is born after September 30, 1983 into a family whose incomes does not exceed 100% of the federal poverty level. (By the year 2002, all such children younger than 19 years of age will be covered.)

6. The child receives adoption assistance and foster care in programs under the Title IV-E of the Social Security Act.

7. The child is part of a "protected group." Protected groups are generally composed of children who lose their cash assistance for a period of time due to their family's increased income. Protected groups may include children of two-parent unemployed families where cash assistance is limited by a state to such families. Children in such "protected groups" can receive Medicaid coverage for 12 continuous months.

Optional Eligibility Groups

There are several groups of children that states have the option of including in their Medicaid program. The primary ones relevant here are *Categorically Needy, Medically Needy,* and those eligible under *TEFRA 134.* A number of children fall into each grouping.

Criteria for the Categorically Needy Program

Categorically Needy groups include any of the following:

1. Infants up to 1 year of age and pregnant women not covered under "required eligibility groups," if family income is less than 185% of the federal poverty level (Each state sets the income percentage below the federal poverty level at which individuals are eligible.)
2. Children younger than 21 years of age who meet income and resource limits for participation in AFDC, but are not otherwise eligible for that program
3. Children receiving care under home-based and community-based waivers
4. Children receiving State Supplemental Payments to SSI
5. Children qualified under Medicaid's Medically Needy Program described below

Criteria for the Medically Needy Program

Another group of children is eligible for Medicaid services in certain states. These are children whose families earn more than their state's maximum amount to receive AFDC or more than the federal limit for SSI, but who otherwise meet the eligibility requirements of the Categorically Needy listed above. ***Children can become eligible for Medicaid under the Medically Needy Program if they qualify as "categorically needy" and their families meet the following criteria:***

1. The family must have an income above 133⅓% of the maximum income level allowed in the state to receive AFDC, *and*
2. The family must have *incurred* enough medical expenses that, if paid, would lower their incomes to a level that would qualify them under the Categorically Needy Program.

3. In some states, families can become eligible for Medicaid by making monthly cash payments to the state for the difference between their family income without medical expenses and the income level allowed for Medicaid eligibility.

It should be emphasized that the federal government does not require states to serve "medically needy" children and their families under the Medicaid program. States may or may not choose to offer services to them. *As of January, 1992, 41 states had some form of Medically Needy Program.*

In addition, states are not required to offer the same services to recipients in the Medically Needy Program as recipients in the Categorically Needy Program. *In some states, Medically Needy programs are extensive; in other states, they are quite limited.* Check with your state's Medicaid agency to see whether your state offers a Medically Needy Program under Medicaid. If so, ask for the details of the program. You can find a list of each state's Medicaid Agency in Appendix B at the end of this book.

TEFRA 134

TEFRA 134 (i.e., Section 134 of the Tax Equity and Fiscal Responsibility Act of 1982) gave states the option of providing home- and community-based Medicaid services for children under 18 years of age who could be cared for cost effectively at home and who would otherwise require institutionalization. As in the 2176 waiver program (see pp. 116–118), *only the income of the child or youth is counted in determining Medicaid eligibility under TEFRA 134.* A child's inclusion in Medicaid through TEFRA 134 allows him or her to receive services under the *Early and Periodic Screening, Diagnosis, and Treatment (EPSDT) Program* (see pp. 118–119), giving him or her access to a range of medical and family support services (except habilitation for MR/DD, home modification, and respite care offered without other services). This program was formerly known as the Katie Beckett Waiver Program in Medicaid. It is not currently a waiver program, but is an optional eligibility group.

What Services Are Available
Under the Medicaid Program?

There are both *"required Basic Services"* and *"Optional Services"* in the Medicaid program. States must offer the required services if they are to receive federal Medicaid funds. Although the federal government encourages states to offer Optional Services, these are not mandatory. Both kinds of services are described below.

There are also *Waiver programs,* which generally waive existing eligibility requirements for services. Waiver programs can also provide services not usually covered by Medicaid.

Finally, there is the *Early and Periodic Screening, Diagnosis, and Treatment (EPSDT) Program* within Medicaid, which offers regular screenings of children. *Under EPSDT, services are also available to reduce the impact of developmental delays detected in a screening, **regardless of whether such services are in a state's Medicaid plan.***

Federally Mandated *"Basic Services"*

The federal government requires each state to offer "Basic Services" to all citizens who are eligible for Medicaid according to the state's guidelines. These Basic Services include the following:

1. Inpatient hospital services
2. Outpatient hospital services
3. Physician services—the services provided by a physician in or out of the hospital
4. Services in rural health clinics

5. Laboratory and x-ray services not provided by a hospital or rural health clinic
6. Care in skilled nursing facilities (commonly known as *nursing homes*) for individuals *21 years and older,*
7. Home-based health care
8. Family planning care and supplies
9. Services of a nurse or midwife
10. Services under the EPSDT Program to screen and treat children for developmental delays

It is important to note that, with the exception of the EPSDT Program, your state and others may set limits on the benefits offered, even under the required Basic Services program. These limits pertain to the "amount, duration, and scope" of services. For the EPSDT Program, the only limit is that the service be "medically necessary." A number of states, for example, place limits on the number of days a Medicaid recipient is covered for hospital care. Other states limit the number of outpatient hospital visits a Medicaid recipient may make per year or per month. These limits, however, must be consistent for all diseases and disabilities (Laudicina & Lipson, 1988).

Optional Services
In addition to the services described above, your state may cover a large number of other health care and related services. If your state has chosen to provide any of these optional services, it receives money from the federal government to help pay for such care. Optional Services your state may provide include the following:

1. Prescription medications
2. Medications that can be bought without a prescription (e.g., Tylenol, cough syrup, Milk of Magnesia)
3. Services in clinics, including Community Health Centers, Community Mental Health Centers, and school-based clinics

4. Services in hospital emergency rooms
5. Transportation to and from medical care facilities
6. Dental care for those not in the EPSDT Program
7. Services in skilled nursing facilities for persons *under 21 years of age*
8. Services in inpatient psychiatric hospitals for persons *under 21 years of age*
9. Personal care services to individuals who need help with the basic activities of daily living (e.g., dressing, eating, bathing)
10. Outpatient rehabilitative services to improve functioning

A list of Medicaid's "optional services" that may be offered by your state appears in Table 1. The availability of these services changes often. If your child or family qualifies for Medicaid, contact your state's Medicaid agency for a list of current Optional Services.

Also, *even if a state includes an "optional service" in its Medicaid plan, a physician or other licensed professional must recommend the care for it to be covered by Medicaid. In some cases, prior authorization is required from a state's Medicaid agency as well.* A list of addresses for each state's Medicaid agency is provided in Appendix B at the end of this book.

Waiver Programs

There are a number of kinds of Waiver programs for which a state can apply from the federal Medicaid program. If the state's application is approved, it can then offer services not usually offered by Medicaid to those who qualify for them. Only the Home- and Community-based Care Waiver program, or 2176 Waiver program, applies particularly to children with disabilities or chronic illnesses.

Table 1. "Optional Services" that may be offered by your state's Medicaid program

Chiropractors' services	Nursing facility services for persons younger than 21 years old
Christian Science nursing	
Christian Science sanitariums	Occupational therapy
Clinic services	Optometrists' services
Dental services	Personal care services
Dentures	Podiatrists' services
Diagnostic services	Physical therapy
Emergency hospital services	Prescribed drugs
Eyeglasses	Preventative services
Inpatient hospital services[a]	Private-duty nursing
Inpatient psychiatric services for persons younger than 21 years old	Prosthetic devices
	Rehabilitative services
	Respiratory care services
Intermediate Care Facilities for Persons with Mental Retardation	Screening services
	Service coordination
Medical social workers' services	Speech, hearing, and language services
Nurse anesthetists' services	Transportation services
Nursing facility services[a]	

Source: U. S. Department of Health and Human Services, Health Care Financing Administration, Intergovernmental Affairs Office, Medicaid Bureau (1992).

[a]For persons 65 years or older in Institutions for Mental Diseases.

Since the early 1980s, the federal government has issued Waivers to states to allow them to offer *home- and community-based care* to qualified recipients. **These 2176 Waivers are designed for individuals who require intensive home- or community-based care to avoid being institutionalized.**

All states currently have 2176 Waiver programs; however, not all of them cover children. If your child qualifies for such a waiver, he or she may remain at home or in the community and Medicaid will pay for a large portion of his or her medical and related care, including special tutoring, selected transportation costs, and so forth. **Under a 2176 Waiver program, only your child's income and "resources" are counted in determining your child's eligibility for the program.**

Your state's Medicaid agency can tell you if your state has a 2176 Waiver program covering children. If so, ask to have information about available benefits and eligibility requirements sent to you. Often these programs have a limited number of approved "slots" and thus a waiting list for waivered services.

The Early and Periodic Screening, Diagnosis, and Treatment (EPSDT) Program

The EPSDT Program is available to all children younger than 21 years old who are eligible for Medicaid. *The goal of the EPSDT Program is to ensure that all children in the Medicaid program are screened on a regular basis and are provided any necessary treatment to correct detected delays or problems. This is particularly important for children who have or are at risk of developmental delays.*

Under the EPSDT Program, periodic developmental screenings must occur at least once a year and include, at a minimum, the following (Hill & Breyel, 1991):

1. A comprehensive health and developmental history, including health, education, nutrition, immunizations, and development
2. An unclothed physical examination
3. Laboratory tests
4. Vision testing
5. Hearing testing
6. Dental screening

In addition, federal law requires states to screen all children between 1 and 5 years old for lead poisoning.

The American Academy of Pediatrics recommends having children screened on a regular basis. The contents of such a screening are included in Figure 1 on pages 120–121. PL 101-329, the Omnibus Budget Reconciliation Act of 1989, attempted to strengthen the EPSDT Program and improve the health status of children from families with low incomes by doing the following:

1. **Requiring states to encourage the participation of all eligible children in the EPSDT Program** (A goal of 80% participation of all eligible children was established in the legislation.)

2. **Requiring states to provide and fund services that any Medicaid-eligible child was found to need as a result of an EPSDT screening—whether or not this service was normally covered by the state's Medicaid plan** (Exceptions to these required services are habilitation for MR/DD, home modification, and respite care offered as a discrete service. Prior to passage of the 1989 federal legislation, the Optional Services most often not covered in a state's Medicaid plan were services for children with mental illnesses and developmental disabilities.)

3. **Increasing the pool of professionals who could administer developmental screens by:**
   - Allowing providers to participate in the EPSDT Program even if they could only administer a part of the required developmental testing while having others perform the other parts, *and*
   - Requiring states to show each year that the reimbursement they provide pediatricians is adequate to retain enough participation in the program to make covered benefits available to eligible children (Hill & Breyel, 1991)

Another advantage of Medicaid's EPSDT Program is that **children in the program are eligible for preventative services that may not normally be provided under the rest of that state's Medicaid program.** These include *vision care including eyeglasses, dental care, and developmental testing.* **By enrolling in Medicaid, a child is automatically enrolled in the EPSDT Program. No separate enrollment in the EPSDT Program is needed.**

Each child and family is unique; therefore, these **Recommendations for Preventive Pediatric Health Care** are designed for the care of children who are receiving competent parenting, have no manifestations of any important health problems, and are growing and developing in satisfactory fashion. **Additional visits may become necessary** if circumstances suggest variations from normal. These guidelines represent a consensus by the Committee on Practice and Ambulatory Medicine in consultation with the membership of the American Academy of Pediatrics through the Chapter Presidents. The Committee emphasizes the great importance of **continuity of care** in comprehensive health supervision and the need to avoid **fragmentation of care.**

A **prenatal visit** by first-time parents and/or those who are at high risk is recommended and should include anticipatory guidance and pertinent medical history.

	INFANCY							EARLY CHILDHOOD					LATE CHILDHOOD					ADOLESCENCE[7]			
AGE[3]	2–3 d[1]	By 1 mo	2 mo	4 mo	6 mo	9 mo	12 mo	15 mo	18 mo	24 mo	3 y	4 y	5 y	6 y	8 y	10 y	12 y	14 y	16 y	18 y	20 y+
HISTORY Initial/Interval	•	•	•	•	•	•	•	•	•	•	•	•	•	•	•	•	•	•	•	•	•
MEASUREMENTS Height and Weight	•	•	•	•	•	•	•	•	•	•	•	•	•	•	•	•	•	•	•	•	•
Head Circumference	•	•	•	•	•	•	•	•	•	•											
Blood Pressure											•	•	•	•	•	•	•	•	•	•	•
SENSORY SCREENING Vision	S	S	S	S	S	S	S	S	S	S	S	O	O	O	S[4]	S[4]	O	O	O	O	S
Hearing	S	S	S	S	S	S	S	S	S	S	S	S	O	O	S[4]	S[4]	O	S	S	S	S
DEVELOPMENTAL/ BEHAVIORAL ASSESSMENT[5]	•	•	•	•	•	•	•	•	•	•	•	•	•	•	•	•	•	•	•	•	•
PHYSICAL EXAMINATION[6]	•	•	•	•	•	•	•	•	•	•	•	•	•	•	•	•	•	•	•	•	•
PROCEDURES[7] Hereditary/Metabolic Screening[8]	•↓																				
Immunization[9]		•	•		•			•	•			•					↓	•↓	•↓		
Tuberculin Test[10]							↑	•↓				↑ •	•↑		•↑			•↑	•↑		
Hematocrit or Hemoglobin[11]						•			↑ •				•↑		•↑			•↑	•↑		
Urinalysis[12]						↓		↑					•↑		•↑			↑	↑		
ANTICIPATORY GUIDANCE[13]	•	•	•	•	•	•	•	•	•	•	•	•	•	•	•	•	•	•	•	•	•
INITIAL DENTAL REFERRAL[14]											•										

1 For newborns discharged in 24 hours or less after delivery.

2 Adolescent-related issues (e.g., psychosocial, emotional, substance usage, reproductive health) may necessitate more frequent health supervision.

3 If a child comes under care for the first time at any point on the schedule, or if any items are not accomplished at the suggested age, the schedule should be brought up to date at the earliest possible time.

4 At these points, history may suffice: if problem suggested, a standard testing method should be employed.

5 By history and appropriate physical examination: If suspicious, by specific objective developmental testing.

6 At each visit, a complete physical examination is essential, with infant totally unclothed, older child undressed and suitably draped.

7 These may be modified, depending upon entry point into schedule and individual need.

8 Metabolic screening (e.g., thyroid, PKU, galactosemia) should be done according to state law.

9 Schedule(s) per *Report of the Committee on Infectious Diseases*, 1991 Red Book, and current AAP Committee statements.

10 For high-risk groups, the Committee on Infectious Diseases recommends annual TB skin testing.

11 Present medical evidence suggests the need for reevaluation of the frequency and timing of hemoglobin or hematocrit tests. One determination is therefore suggested during each time period. Performance of additional tests is left to the individual practice experience.

12 Present medical evidence suggests the need for reevaluation of the frequency and timing of urinalyses. One determination is therefore suggested during each time period. Performance of additional tests is left to the individual practice experience.

13 Appropriate discussion and counseling should be an integral part of each visit for care.

14 Subsequent examinations as prescribed by dentist.

NB: **Special chemical, immunologic, and endocrine testing** is usually carried out upon specific indications. Testing other than newborn (e.g., inborn errors of metabolism, sickle disease, lead) is discretionary with the physician.

Key: ● = to be performed S = subjective, by history ○ = objective, by a standard testing method

The recommendations in this publication do not indicate an exclusive course of treatment or serve as a standard of medical care. Variations, taking into account individual circumstances, may be appropriate.

Figure 1. American Academy of Pediatrics' suggested schedule for the screening of children. (From American Academy of Pediatrics. [1991, July]. *Recommendations for preventive pediatric health care.* Elk Grove Village, IL: Author; used with permission of the American Academy of Pediatrics).

Where and How Can You Apply for Medicaid?

You can apply for Medicaid at the following places:

1. Any local Medicaid office
2. The "Special Programs" office of most large, academic teaching hospitals
3. Many local Health Departments and Community Health Centers

Begin by calling your county's Department of Social Services (DSS) or Department of Human Services (DHS) to find out where you can apply in your area. These departments should be listed in the blue pages of the local telephone book. If you provide the name of the county where you live, your local information operator can also supply the number of your county's DSS or DHS.

If you decide to call a location at which you can apply for Medicaid, rather than to stop by the office for information, ask to speak with a person handling Medicaid eligibility. Ask that person to send you written information about Medicaid eligibility in your state, including income and "resource" limits and descriptions of all Medicaid programs offered by your state (e.g., Categorically Needy Program, Medically Needy Program).

Whether you call or write, *be sure to note the name of the person with whom you speak, particularly if he or she is helpful to you.* If you have to follow up on your request or if you have any questions after you review the material, it is often more useful to talk with the same person you talked to the first time. *You should receive information you requested by telephone within 10 days.* If there is anything in this information you don't understand, contact the person from whom you requested the information to answer your questions.

If you choose to visit your local Medicaid office or one of the offices listed above, ask to meet with someone to discuss your child's eligibility for the Medicaid program. Ask the following questions:

* What are family income and "resource" limitations for your family size?
* Does your child or family fit into one of the required categories for coverage?
* Does your state currently have a Medicaid program for families who are medically needy?

If your child or family meets the requirements of an eligibility category and your family income is anywhere near the limits the Medicaid worker describes, apply for Medicaid for your child. Before formally filing an application, however, it is recommended that you contact one of the referral groups listed below to review your strategy in applying for Medicaid. Members and staff of these organizations have a great deal of experience working with families who have applied for Medicaid and other public programs. They can refer you to families for tips to increase your child's chances of being accepted into the program. Organizations that can advise you on successful strategies for applying for Medicaid include the following:

Federation for Children with Special Needs
95 Berkeley Street
Boston, Massachusetts 02116
(617) 482-2915 (Voice/TT)

Federation of Families for Children's Mental Health
1021 Prince Street
Alexandria, Virginia 22314
(703) 684-7710

National Parent Network on Disabilities
1600 Prince Street
Alexandria, Virginia 22314
(703) 683-NPND

Parent Training and Information (PTI) Centers may also be helpful. Contact the PTI in your region or state:

Midwest Region—Pacer
  Center
4826 Chicago Avenue,
  South
Minneapolis, Minnesota 55417
(612) 827-2966
  (Voice and TT)

South Region—The Arc
1851 Ram Runway
Suite 104
College Park, Georgia
  30337
(404) 761-3150
  (Voice and TT)

Northeast Region—Parent
  Information Center
151A Manchester Street
Post Office Box 1422
Concord, New Hampshire
  03302
(603) 224-6299 (Voice)
(603) 224-7005 (TT)

West Region (Washington
  State PAVE)
6316 South 12th Street
Tacoma, Washington
  98465
(206) 565-2266
  (Voice and TT)

When you do go to one of the Medicaid offices to fill out your child's application for Medicaid, you are permitted to bring someone with you to help you complete the application or for support. Try to get a specific appointment time. Plan to spend about 45 minutes filling out the application and some time in line waiting to be seen. You may want to bring something with you to do. If you bring children with you, be sure to bring toys for them, a diaper change, and a snack.

What Information Do You Need to Complete Your Medicaid Application?

When you go to a Medicaid office to complete your child's application, you want to *be sure you have everything you need.* Generally, if you have your "Family Information File" with you, you will have most of the information you need. The full contents of such a file are described in Chapter 10. You may need to update some items before you begin the application (e.g., wage stubs or statements, bank account statements). You will also need to take proof of your family income, other resources, and expenses when you apply. ***The kind of information that will be requested on your application for Medicaid includes the following:***

1. Your name, address, and telephone number
2. Your child's name, address, and telephone number
3. The first name, maiden name, and Social Security number of each person in your household
4. The citizenship status of each person in your household
5. The date of birth of each person in your household
6. The gross amount (i.e., before taxes) of income earned by you, your spouse, and others in your family in the last year, including self-employment income
7. The amount of income you, your spouse, and/or others in your family received in the last year from Social Security, Supplemental Security Income (SSI), unemployment benefits, veterans benefits, military allotment, worker's compensation, or any similar source
8. The amount of cash gifts from family, church, or friends that you, your spouse, and others in your family received in the last year
9. The amount of interest, dividends, or other income from banks, stocks, or bonds that you, your spouse, or others in your family received in the last year
10. A record of your monthly expenses (rent receipts, current utility bills, etc.)

Also, for proof of identification, you will want to have available, birth certificates and Social Security cards for you and your child.

How Long Will It Take to
Find Out If Your Application Is Accepted?

The federal government requires that your state's Medicaid agency let you know whether your application is accepted within 45 days of when your application is signed and completed. **Your state Medicaid agency is required to notify individuals with disabilities within 30 days of their application.**

Some individuals are "presumed to be eligible" and benefits for them can begin as soon as an application is made. Check with your local or state Medicaid agency to see which individuals or families can begin using the Medicaid program before the application is fully processed.

What Can You Do If You or
Your Child Is Denied Medicaid Coverage?

If you or your child is not considered eligible for Medicaid, *the reason(s) for the denial must accompany formal rejection from the program.* **Applications are frequently denied simply because they were not completed or were completed improperly. You may appeal the decision to deny benefits by sending a written request for a hearing to your state Medicaid agency within 60 days of your rejection notice.**

THE CHILDREN'S SPECIAL
HEALTH CARE NEEDS (CSHCN) PROGRAM

The Children's Special Health Care Needs (CSHCN) Program is a federally funded program in each state *to provide or pay for disability-related services to children with chronic illnesses or disabilities.* In many cases, the child must be from a family with a low income. It is administered by the state Office of Maternal and Child Health Programs. Until

1985, the CSHCN Program was called the Crippled Children's Service in most states, and it is still known by that and other names in a few states.

Funds for this program will probably increase in the coming years as a result of a 1989 federal requirement that states spend 30% of the funds from their Maternal and Child Health Services block grants on the CSHCN Program. This should bring CSHCN services to more children in need.

The federal government has also asked all states to "improve the service system for these children and their families by promoting family-centered, community-based, coordinated care" (Ireys & Nelson, 1991). This represents a broader mandate for the CSHCN Program and one that could signal more comprehensive and coordinated care with greater family involvement.

States vary in the range of services offered, the way care is made available, and the numbers of disease- and disability-related groups served. Many state programs focus on a relatively narrow range of orthopedic and surgical conditions. Others have expanded their eligibility criteria to include more medical illnesses. A few programs also cover children with chronic behavior or developmental disorders (Ireys & Nelson, 1991).

What Services Are Offered in the CSHCN Program?

As mentioned previously, state CSHCN Programs vary a great deal, both in the disease- and disability-related categories covered and the range of services offered. *All programs cover health and related care* **for the child's disease or disability only.** Services needed for injuries or illnesses not related to the disease or disability (e.g., service for repair of a broken bone resulting from a fall on the sidewalk) are not covered. A comprehensive program might offer the following services or reimbursement for the following services for income-eligible children with most diseases or disabilities:

1. Physician services in an outpatient specialty clinic
2. X-ray and other diagnostic services in a hospital or outpatient clinic
3. Required inpatient hospitalization
4. Medical and surgical fees in connection with an inpatient or outpatient hospital visit
5. Home health care
6. Prescribed medications and nutritional supplements
7. Prescribed medical equipment
8. Medical supplies, including catheters, rubber gloves, diapers for any child older than 3 year of age, and so forth
9. Inpatient and outpatient prescribed physical therapy, occupational therapy, speech-language therapy, and so forth
10. Services of a psychologist for educational testing or counseling

A more limited CSHCN Program might consist only of an outpatient orthopedic clinic for children with spina bifida or a neurology clinic for children with seizure disorders. It is hoped that, with the 1989 federal requirements, all states will provide more services with greater uniformity across the country to more children with chronic illnesses or disabilities under the CSHCN Program.

Which Children Are Eligible to Participate in the CSHCN Program?

The federal government, specifically the Maternal and Child Health Bureau, defines *children with special health care needs* as children "with disabilities and handicapping conditions, with chronic illness and conditions, with health-related educational or behavioral problems, and [children who are] at risk for disabilities, chronic conditions, and health-related educational and behavioral problems" (Ireys & Nelson, 1991). This is a broader definition than has been used in the past at the federal level, in that it includes more children with special health care needs.

To be eligible for a CSHCN Program, a child must meet the following three criteria:

1. Have a disease or disability that his or her state's CSHCN Program serves (It is important to note, however, that the 1989 federal legislation mentioned previously *requires that the service system for children with special health care needs be increasingly "generic" and for all children with special needs rather than children with specific diseases or disabilities* [Ireys & Nelson, 1991].)
2. Come from a family whose income is no greater than the maximum allowed by a particular state
3. Be ineligible for Medicaid or a private health insurance coverage

How Can You Learn More About Your State's CSHCN Program or Apply for Services?

To obtain information specific to your state's CSHCN Program, use the addresses and telephone numbers listed in Appendix B at the end of this book. Ask to have a description of the program, including eligibility information and covered services and an application form, sent to you.

STATE DEPARTMENTS OF EDUCATION AND LOCAL EDUCATION AGENCIES

The Individuals with Disabilities Education Act (IDEA) and the preceding legislation that culminated in this law in 1990 require that **all children from birth through 21 years old** *who have developmental delays, conditions with a high probability of resulting in delays, or disabilities receive a "free and appropriate public education" in the "least restrictive environment" possible.* Using federal guidelines, each state has written its own definition of "developmental delay." Some states also serve children from birth through 2 years old who are at risk of developmental delay.

The IDEA legislation also requires that State Departments of Education and Local Education Agencies *arrange to provide and have paid for all support services required for a child with a developmental delay or disability to "benefit from public education."* Examples might include speech-language therapy, physical therapy, social work services, and transportation to and from school. Other state agencies actually provide many of these support services and fund them from their own budgets. A list of required services for infants and toddlers (i.e., birth through 2 years old), preschoolers (i.e., 3 through 5 years old), and school-age children (i.e., 6 through 21 years old) is provided in Chapter 3.

IDEA and the services it will generate have the potential to provide your child with a number of the health-related services he or she may require. For example, one of the required services for school-age children who qualify for services under IDEA is the annual development of an individualized education program (IEP). Some states may require the development of an IEP for preschoolers as well. An IEP describes in detail the educational and support services to be provided to your child as part of his or her total education program, and how often each support service is to be offered each week. According to IDEA, a parent must be actively involved in the development of his or her child's IEP, and a parent can challenge any provisions of the final program.

To obtain more information about the health care and related services your child is entitled to under IDEA, including health-related care, contact your state's Part H or Part B program and any PTI, as they were established by parents specifically for this purpose. (National parent advocacy groups, including PTI Centers, are listed in Chapter 3.) You can reach the regional PTI nearest your home by consulting the list of such programs on page 124. (Each state's Part H and Part B programs are listed in Appendix B at the end of this book.)

Part H Programs Under IDEA

Part H programs were created to provide early intervention services to infants and toddlers from **birth through 2 years old** *who have developmental delays, conditions with "high probability of resulting in a delay," or "high risk" of delay (states are not required to serve the latter group, but many do). Children who are 3 years old and are not eligible for a preschool program until the next school year may be served by Part H programs. Provision of early intervention programs is still optional by states, although the federal government has included strong financial incentives for all states to offer programs. Currently all states participate in Part H.* States are required to develop a variety of kinds of services including assistive technology and services, service coordination, transportation to and from services, and, if the family agrees, the development of an individualized family service plan (IFSP), for children and their families (see Chapter 3). **Services are free to families or provided at low cost, based on the family's ability to pay.**

States participating in Part H must also develop a statewide *Interagency Coordinating Council* and local coordinating councils to field referrals for services, catalog relevant resources, and divide responsibilities among the numerous state agencies involved (e.g., the State Medicaid agency, the State Department of Health, the State Department of Education).

You can get information about your state's Part H program, including eligibility criteria, from the program office. This office may be administered by your state's Department of Education or another agency (e.g., Office of Maternal and Child Health). The addresses and telephone numbers of each state's Part H program are provided in Appendix B at the end of this book. In addition, it may be a good idea to *talk with other parents* who have firsthand experience with the Part H program. You can reach such parents through your regional PTI office listed on page 124. Additional information about Part H programs, including required services, can be found in Chapters 2 and 3.

Part B Programs Under IDEA

Part B programs under IDEA serve **preschool children 3 through 5 years of age and school-age children from 6 through 21 years of age** *who fall into one of the categories that would qualify him or her as "disabled." Preschoolers, in some states, may also be enrolled in a Part B program if they are found to have "developmental delays" even if they do not meet the categorical criteria* (e.g., mental retardation, orthopedic impairment). You can get information about your state's Part B programs from that program's office. In all cases, this will be administered by your state's Department of Education. The addresses and telephone numbers for each state's Part B program are provided in Appendix B at the end of this book. Additional information about Part B programs, including categories qualifying a child as "disabled," is found in Chapters 2 and 3.

CIVILIAN HEALTH AND MEDICAL PROGRAM
OF THE UNIFORMED SERVICES (CHAMPUS)

*The Civilian Health and Medical Program of the Uni-
formed Services (CHAMPUS) is a program to help pay for
the cost of health care from civilian doctors and hospitals
for families in the U.S. military service. The CHAMPUS
program offers* **a great deal of coverage for general medical
care and some coverage for disability-related care for eligible individuals.** *Families who use these benefits fully and
persist in seeking the care their children need will receive a
great deal of financial help in paying for medical bills.*

Families of all seven uniformed services—the Army,
Navy, Marine Corps, Air Force, Coast Guard, Public Health
Service, and Oceanic and Atmospheric Administration—*are
eligible.* **CHAMPUS does** not **cover active-duty military
persons,** only dependents of active-duty military personnel,
retired military personnel and their dependents, widows and
divorcees of military personnel, and so forth.

**CHAMPUS is designed to supplement care that depen-
dents and families can receive at little or no cost in military
hospitals and clinics.** Families who live in areas close to
military hospitals or clinics often must seek the desired service at the military facility. In a number of cases, CHAM-
PUS will only help families share the cost of their private
medical care if that service is not available at the nearby
military hospital or clinic.

Which Children Are Eligible for CHAMPUS?

Children who are dependents of active-duty, retired, or de-
ceased members of the uniformed services are covered by
the general CHAMPUS medical program (CHAMPUS,
1990). Children of reservists who are ordered for active duty
for more than 30 days are covered during the reservist's
active-duty tour.

Only children of active-duty members of the uniformed service are eligible for the CHAMPUS Supplemental Program for the Handicapped (PFH). These eligible children are accepted into the program by application, and service for them is covered on a case-by-case basis. This program is discussed in more detail below.

All CHAMPUS-eligible persons must be enrolled in the DEERS eligibility-checking system before any non-emergency care in military hospitals can be received or any CHAMPUS claims can be paid. CHAMPUS eligibility for a dependent child ends at midnight of the day the active-duty sponsor is discharged or leaves the service for reasons other retirement (CHAMPUS, 1990).

What Services Are Covered Under the General CHAMPUS Medical Program?

As of January, 1993, CHAMPUS shared the cost of most medically or psychologically necessary health care with covered individuals (CHAMPUS, 1990). *In general, CHAMPUS will help to pay for allowed outpatient services provided by the service provider you choose.* **All inpatient services must be preauthorized by obtaining a "non-availability of services" statement, which certifies that the services needed are not available in the nearest military hospital.** Allowed services include the following:

1. Physician bills in connection with inpatient and outpatient care
2. Hospital bills for semi-private rooms
3. Meals served while in a hospital, including any special diets that are required
4. Diagnostic testing, including computed tomography (CT) and magnetic resonance imaging (MRI) scans if less expensive tests have been tried first

5. Outpatient medical and surgical treatment
6. Ambulances in emergency situations
7. Skilled nursing care at home
8. Genetic testing when indicated
9. Maternity care during the pregnancy, the delivery of the baby, and the first 6 weeks after the baby is born
10. Newborn and pediatric care, including well-baby visits
11. Prescription medications
12. Durable medical equipment and medical supplies accompanied by a doctor's prescription (unless you live near a military hospital where durable equipment is available on loan) (CHAMPUS, 1990)
13. Physical and occupational therapy
14. Family planning services
15. Eye examinations (one per year, available to active-duty families only)
16. Selected organ transplants
17. Plastic and cosmetic surgery needed to restore functioning (e.g., from a cleft palate, accident, disease, breast removal)
18. Detoxification for alcoholism (as long as 7 days; these days count toward an individual's 60-day limit for mental health inpatient care)
19. Inpatient or outpatient mental health or drug abuse treatment (as long as 60 days for inpatient mental health care)
20. Alcohol and other rehabilitation services (as long as 21 days per year as part of the 60-day inpatient mental health care limit; also limited to three inpatient lifetime admissions)
21. Outpatient therapy for alcohol rehabilitation (as many as 60 visits per year)
22. Inpatient treatment for children and adolescents who need mental health care (with approval)

23. Family therapy (as many as 15 visits per year)
24. Acquired immunodeficiency syndrome (AIDS) medication, including azidothymidine (AZT)
25. Miscellaneous other care (e.g., intraocular surgery, wigs for persons undergoing cancer treatment)

CHAMPUS does not cover the following:

1. Routine dental care (CHAMPUS does cover dental care that is a part of another medical treatment and some of the inpatient costs for a person with hemophilia who must be hospitalized for routine dental care.)
2. Eyeglasses and contact lenses
3. Food, food substitutes, or food supplements for home intravenous feeding, except under authorization from the Program for the Handicapped
4. Most foot care
5. Hearing aids, except when purchased under the Program for the Handicapped
6. Routine mammograms
7. Most pap smears
8. Routine annual physicals
9. Orthopedic shoes and arch supports
10. Speech-language therapy, unless related to a specific illness or injury

CHAMPUS also will not pay for services of providers employed by the military. Military families must seek providers who are not federal medical personnel. A list of acceptable private providers is available in the *CHAMPUS Handbook* (1990).

It is also important to note that ***any long-term care may require certain reviews and paperwork that must be processed during the course of treatment.*** Similarly, ***some care requires special authorization regardless of how long it will last.*** Be sure to read the most recent *CHAMPUS Handbook* carefully to see when such authorization is needed.

CHAMPUS Handbooks are available from your Health Benefits Advisor (HBA) at the military hospital or clinic nearest your home. Get to know this person. He or she can answer any questions you have about benefits and will be the one to negotiate coverage for your child with military authorities.

Also, *if your base or post has an Exceptional Family Members Program, become familiar with it.* (It may be called something else at different locations.) It is a group of military families with members who have special health care needs. The group gets together to share information and support.

What Costs Will a Family Pay to Participate in CHAMPUS?

Depending on the status of the CHAMPUS sponsor (i.e., the person whose status makes a dependent eligible for benefits) employed by the military, *the portion of the costs you will share with CHAMPUS will vary.* The following discussion describes the way CHAMPUS handles most outpatient services. Inpatient services are discussed on pages 138–139.

Outpatient Services

Families of active-duty members of the military pay the first $150 or $50 per person (i.e., deductible) plus 20% of the remaining bill (i.e., co-payment) each year for covered services given by a provider who participates in the CHAMPUS program. (A year begins October 1 and ends September 30.) These rates for deductibles and co-payments are for 1993 and will probably vary in the future. *Before agreeing to care, ask your provider if he or she will participate in CHAMPUS.* If a family chooses a provider who does *not* participate in CHAMPUS, that provider can charge you whatever he or she wants. In these cases, CHAMPUS will only pay its 80%

share of the amount it considers an "allowable charge." This means that *the family is responsible for 20% and the balance of the "allowable charge," or 20% plus 100% of any cost you were charged in excess of the "allowable charge."* To avoid this extra fee, ask your provider if he or she will absorb any charge in excess of what CHAMPUS "allows." Families are responsible for 100% of the charges for all services that are not covered by CHAMPUS.

The military puts a limit on the amount of out-of-pocket expenses a family must pay for health care under the CHAMPUS program. *Families of active-duty service members share no more than $1,000 of the allowable cost of the family's care per year, including all deductibles and co-payments.* All other CHAMPUS-eligible families pay no more than $10,000 a year for the allowable cost of medical care. **However, it is important to note that costs paid by families under the CHAMPUS Program for the Handicapped are not counted in figuring this out-of-pocket limit.**

Inpatient Services

CHAMPUS-covered families pay no deductibles for most inpatient care. Families of active-duty service members pay either a $25 co-payment for each admission or a small daily fee—whichever is *greater.* As discussed previously, **if you live near a military hospital, you must try to use that hospital for nonemergency inpatient care.** Otherwise CHAMPUS will not share the cost of that stay with you. Check with your HBA to see if your home address falls into a zip code where this regulation applies. **If the military hospital near you cannot provide the inpatient care you need, ask them for a "non-availability of services" statement** (i.e., DD Form 1251). If the hospital is filing your claim, you will need this statement the day of admission. Otherwise, you will need to turn this statement in with your claim for

CHAMPUS payment for a hospital stay at a nonmilitary hospital.

Filing Claims Under **CHAMPUS**

Claim forms are provided by your HBA, the CHAMPUS claims processor in the state where you live, or by writing to the following address:

CHAMPUS
Aurora, Colorado 80045-6900

The **CHAMPUS** Handbook *explains in detail how to determine which forms must be completed for different claims and how to complete them.* If you have any additional questions after consulting the *CHAMPUS Handbook*, contact your HBA.

Every time you file a claim, be sure to send originals of all necessary forms with any additional paperwork required (e.g., doctor's letter prescribing a certain piece of durable medical equipment, military hospital's "non-availability of services" statement). *Be sure to keep a photocopy of everything you send to CHAMPUS and a record of the dates you send them. CHAMPUS states that it will respond to properly completed claims within 1 month of receipt.*

CHAMPUS's Program for the Handicapped

CHAMPUS offers *supplemental coverage to provide health-related care for individuals with serious disabilities who are dependents of active-duty service members.* This coverage is provided through the Program for the Handicapped, which *operates in addition to CHAMPUS's general medical program.* Any eligible child's health care that is *not* related to his or her disability would be covered by the General Medical Program. According to the Program for the Handicapped, *handicapped individuals include the following:*

1. Individuals with "moderate" or "severe" mental retardation
2. Individuals with a major physical "handicap"
3. Individuals with "moderate" or "severe" mental retardation and a major physical "handicap"

Decisions regarding which individuals are included in the program are made on a case-by-case basis; however, general guidelines describing mental retardation and physical handicaps are available. In determining whether an individual has "moderate" or "severe" mental retardation, CHAMPUS considers the following (CHAMPUS, 1990):

1. Whether the medical and life history indicates this
2. Whether the individual is unable to perform tasks typical for his or her age group
3. Whether IQ tests or developmental tests show "moderate" or "severe" mental retardation

General guidelines used by CHAMPUS to determine whether an individual has a major physical handicap include the following (CHAMPUS, 1990):

1. Whether the individual is expected to have the "handicap" for at least 1 year and whether he or she is expected to die from the "handicap"
2. Whether the individual needs help in his or her activities of daily living (e.g., eating, getting dressed)

Applying for the Program for the Handicapped

To apply for the Program for the Handicapped, active-duty members must submit an application on Form 2532, "Request for Health Benefits under the Program for the Handicapped." You can get an original copy of Form 2532 from your HBA or your state's CHAMPUS claims processor. *With the completed Form 2532, have your child's doctor send a management plan, including the following:*

- A report of your child's physical examination
- Your child's diagnosis
- A family history
- A history of the handicapping condition and summary of earlier treatment
- Results of any diagnostic tests
- Reports from any consultants
- The method of planned care, including how long care will be needed
- The professional status of those who will provide the care
- Your child's prognosis
- An estimate of the monthly cost of care
- Medical reports from your child's current facility, if a change will be recommended

Periodically, your child's doctor must send a progress report along with an updated management plan, which includes a letter indicating that public funds and facilities are either not available or not appropriate for your child's care.

In addition, an updated Form 2532 and another letter like this must be sent each year and whenever your family moves to a different CHAMPUS claims processing area. A completed Form 2532 and letter must also be submitted by each service provider (e.g., speech-language therapist, wheelchair vendor) when appropriate. This application must also be resubmitted if you change providers or vendors.

After the application is filed, approval for services is back-dated to your date of application as long as the services began no more than 90 days before approval. Service providers can bill for back-dated services on Form 2532.

Filing Claims Under the Program for the Handicapped

To file a claim for care your child receives under the General Medical Program of CHAMPUS, use Forms DD 2520, DD 500, or other forms used by individuals without a disability.

Program for the Handicapped claims are also filed on DD 500. (Form 2532 authorizes the billing of the claim.)

Again, members of your base or post's *Exceptional Family Members Program* can advise you about how to file claims to help ensure that you limit your out-of-pocket costs. **As a general rule, do not pay any medical bills from doctors, clinics, and so forth until you hear from CHAMPUS.** CHAMPUS will let you know which charges are allowed, what your share of the costs are, and if there are any non-allowed charges you must pay in full.

Costs to Enroll in the Program for the Handicapped

CHAMPUS charges a monthly cost to individuals who use the Program for the Handicapped. This cost is based on the pay grade of the active-duty military sponsor. In 1990, this cost ranged from $25 to $250 per month. The *CHAMPUS Handbook* gives the exact contributions required for each pay grade.

After a sponsor has paid the monthly charge, CHAMPUS will pay as much as $1,000 per month more for care your child requires. If your child's costs exceed this amount, your family must pay 100% of the additional amount. The cost for particularly expensive items (e.g., a wheelchair) can be spread out over a maximum of 6 months, thus allowing the purchase of a $6,000 piece of equipment if needed.

If there are two or more individuals with disabilities in your family enrolled in the Program for the Handicapped, you are only required to pay the monthly charge for one. CHAMPUS will pay for as much as $1,000 of care per month for each individual with a disability in your family.

Appealing a CHAMPUS Decision

If you are not satisfied with a decision made by CHAMPUS—either through the General Medical Program or the Program for the Handicapped—you can appeal the

decision in a number of ways. The *CHAMPUS Handbook* gives details on how to do this and describes possible remedies. You can also consult with your HBA for information about how to proceed.

It is important to appeal denied claims. *Some claims are denied simply because claim forms were not completed properly or because needed documents were not included with the claim. If such a claim was submitted by your service provider, ask him or her to resubmit the claim.* Service providers are interested in being paid and are usually happy to resubmit a claim if you show them the copy of the statement of denial or partial payment.

MEDICARE'S COVERAGE OF
KIDNEY DISEASE IN CHILDREN AND YOUTH

The Medicare program, generally considered the public insurance program for older Americans, is available to individuals of all ages to help pay for care for kidney disease. Most of such care is for kidney dialysis or kidney transplantation and related services. In 1991, more than 150,000 American received treatment under this program (*Medicare Q & A*, 1991, updated for 1993).

Some of the services related to kidney disease are provided under Part A of the Medicare program; others are covered in Part B. Part A of Medicare mainly addresses inpatient care, and Part B focuses on physician services; all outpatient services; and related prescription medications, medical equipment, and medical supplies. A summary of the coverage available to your child in the two parts of this program follows. Tables 2 and 3 outline the services provided by each part.

Part A Coverage for Children
and Youth with Kidney Disease

Part A of Medicare is financed primarily from the Social Security payroll tax deduction. There is no monthly premi-

Table 2. **Medicare (Part A):** Hospital insurance-covered services per benefit period

Services	Benefit	Medicare Pays[b]	You Pay[b]
Hospitalization: Semi-private room and board, general nursing, and miscellaneous hospital services and supplies	First 60 days 61st to 90th day 91st to 150th day[a] Beyond 150 days	All but $676 All but $169 a day All but $338 a day Nothing	$676 $169 a day $338 a day All costs
Post-hospital skilled nursing facility care: You must have been in the hospital for at least 3 days and enter a Medicare-approved facility generally within 30 days after hospital discharge	First 20 days Additional 80 days Beyond 100 days	100% of approved amount All but $84.50 a day Nothing	Nothing $84.50 a day All costs
Home health care	Visits limited to medically necessary skilled care	Full cost of services; 80% of approved amount for durable medical equipment	Nothing for services; 20% of approved amount for durable medical equipment
Hospice care: Available to persons with terminal illnesses	As long as 210 days if doctor certifies need	All but limited costs for outpatient drugs and inpatient respite care	Limited cost sharing for outpatient drugs and inpatient respite care
Blood	Blood	All but first 3 pints per calendar year	For first 3 pints[c]

Source: Medicare Q&A (1991).

[a]60 reserve days may be used only once; days used are not renewable.

[b]These figures are for 1993 and are subject to change each year.

[c]To the extent the blood deductible is met under one part of Medicare during the calendar year, it does not have to be met under the other part.

A benefit period begins on the first day you receive service as an inpatient in a hospital and ends after you have been out of the hospital or skilled nursing facility for 60 consecutive days.

These figures may change annually. Call The Social Security Administration at 1-800-772-1213 each year for the latest information.

Table 3. **Medicare (Part B):** Medical insurance-covered services per calendar year

Services	Benefit	Medicare pays[a]	You pay[b]
Medical expense: Physician's services, inpatient and outpatient medical services and supplies, physical and speech-language therapy	Medical services in or out of the hospital	80% of approved amount (after $100 deductible)	$100 deductible[a] plus 20% of approved amount (plus any charge above approved amount)[b]
Home health care	Visits limited to medically necessary care	Full cost of services; 80% of approved amount for durable medical equipment	Nothing for services; 20% of approved amount for durable medical equipment
Outpatient hospital treatment	Unlimited if medically necessary	80% of approved charges (after $100 deductible)	Subject to deductible plus 20% of approved amount
Blood	Blood	80% of approved amount (after $100 deductible and starting with fourth pint)	First 3 pints plus 20% of approved amount (after $100 deductible)[c]

Source: *Medicare Q&A* (1991).

[a]Once you have had $100 of expense for covered services in that year, the Part B deductible does not apply to any further covered services you receive for the rest of the year.

[b]You pay for charges higher than the amount approved by Medicare unless the doctor or supplier agrees to accept Medicare's approved amount as full payment for services rendered.

[c]To the extent the blood deductible is met under one part of Medicare during the calendar year, it does not have to be met under the other part.

um cost to recipients for services received. Payments are made directly to the providers of care. Coverage includes the following:

1. Needed *inpatient hospital care* up to a limited number of days and after a specified deductible is paid (In 1992, Medicare paid in full for the first 60 days of inpatient care in a "benefit period," after a deductible of $676. From days 61–90, patients had to pay a co-payment of $169 per day. From days 91–150, patients must pay $388 per day.) Medicare-eligible individuals have a one-time reserve of 60 inpatient days they can use after 150 days of hospitalization in a "benefit period." A "benefit period" starts the day you enter a hospital (or skilled nursing facility) and ends when you have been out of the hospital (or skilled nursing facility) for 60 consecutive days.

2. Medically necessary care in a *skilled nursing facility* following at least a 3-day hospital stay, with no deductible or co-payment for 20 days; and a subsequent daily co-payment (in 1993 was $84.50), limited to 100 days of care per benefit period.

3. *Hospice care,* for as long as 210 days if a physician certifies the care is needed; no deductible but small co-payments for outpatient drugs and inpatient respite care.

Part A would cover a child's inpatient hospital services when he or she was in preparation for kidney transplantation and when he or she was admitted for kidney transplant surgery.

Part B Coverage for Children and Youth with Kidney Disease

Part B of the Medicare program is optional and is financed by the premiums paid by recipients, which fund 25% of the program's cost, and federal general revenues, which fund

the remaining 75% of the program's cost. In 1993, the monthly premium cost to recipients for Part B coverage was $36.60. In general, services covered under Part B are reimbursed at 80% of the "allowable charge" after an annual deductible has been met. In 1993, the Part B annual deductible was $100.

Part B covers most of the services and supplies needed by children with permanent kidney failure. These include physician services, outpatient hospital services, outpatient physical and speech-language therapy, medical supplies, and some self-administered drugs. Part B also covers most services in connection with kidney dialysis, including the following:

1. Outpatient maintenance dialysis
2. Staff-assisted dialysis
3. Self-dialysis training
4. Home dialysis including hemodialysis, home intermittent peritoneal dialysis (IPD), continuous cycling peritoneal dialysis (CCPD), and home continuous ambulatory peritoneal dialysis (CAPD)

Part B also covers many services related to kidney transplantation; these include the following:

1. The kidney registry fee
2. Laboratory and other evaluative tests for the recipient and potential donors
3. Costs of obtaining a suitable kidney donor
4. Costs of care for a kidney donor, including physician fees (No deductible or daily co-payment is required for this.)
5. Surgeon's fees to perform the transplantation operation, including pre- and postoperative care
6. Immunosuppressant drugs for 1 year after discharge from a transplantation operation

Services Not Covered by Medicare
for Children with Permanent Kidney Failure

Neither Part A nor Part B of Medicare covers the following costs associated with permanent kidney failure:

1. Transportation costs to and from routine outpatient dialysis, including ambulance trips
2. Fees for dialysis aides to help with home dialysis
3. Charges for inpatient hospitalization or care in a skilled nursing facility solely for maintenance dialysis
4. Costs for lodging (e.g., when inpatient dialysis is conducted some distance from your home)
5. Lost wages you or your partner might have in connection with your child's treatment or self-dialysis training

Private health insurance, CHAMPUS (for families of U.S. military employees), and other programs may help pay for the services not covered by Medicare.

If your family income is below the national poverty level, *the Medicaid program can pay a number of your costs for your child's participation in the Medicare program.* It can pay the monthly premium for participation in Part B as well as some of the deductibles and co-payments required under Parts A and B. Contact your state or local Medicaid agency if you think you may qualify for this type of assistance.

In addition, some states have Kidney Commissions to pay for some of the costs of dialysis or transplantation that Medicare does not cover. Contact your local Kidney Association to inquire about this help. You can find it listed in the business section of your white pages telephone directory.

For more information about Medicare's coverage of children and youth with permanent kidney failure, call the Social Security Administration:

(800) 772-1213 (Voice)
(800) 325-0778 (TT)

You can request a copy of the latest edition of *Medicare Coverage of Kidney Dialysis and Kidney Transplant Services: A Supplement to the Medicare Handbook.* (The 1992 edition's publication number was HCFA 10128.) This publication, together with a general explanation of the Medicare program, will give you all of the information you need to understand your child's entitlement for services and the benefits he or she can receive under the Medicare program.

STATE AND LOCAL GENERAL ASSISTANCE—MEDICAL PROGRAM (GA–MEDICAL)

General Assistance (GA) is the term used to describe state and local financial assistance programs for persons with low incomes (Lewin/ICF, Bell, & Associates, 1990). These programs can be known by other names, such as General Relief or Poor Relief.

Many General Assistance programs have a Medical Assistance component or a companion Medical Assistance program. **State and locally funded Medical Assistance programs pay for health care services of individuals and families with low incomes who are not covered by any other health insurance program** (e.g., Medicaid, private insurance). The GA–Medical Assistance program is described here. The General Assistance program that provides cash supplements to individuals and families with low incomes is described in Chapter 7.

According to the most recent comprehensive survey, which was conducted in 1989, *39 states had GA–Medical Assistance programs of some kind, with benefit availability ranging from "emergency" to "short-term" to "ongoing"* (Lewin/ICF et al., 1990). If your state has a program like this, your child may be able to make some use of GA–Medical

Assistance programs. ***This would most likely be possible if your family lacks health insurance or during times when your child or family is between private health insurance programs or waiting to be accepted into the Medicaid program.***

Who Is Eligible for State and Local GA–Medical Assistance?

As mentioned previously, GA–Medical Assistance programs are *designed primarily for individuals and families who have no other way to pay for health care.* Family income limits to qualify for GA are generally *lower* than the income limits to qualify for Medicaid. Applicants may also be required to show that they have a permanent residence and that they are American citizens. Individuals who qualify for the GA monthly cash supplements are automatically eligible for GA–Medical Assistance.

What Medical Services Are Covered Under GA–Medical Assistance Programs?

States and localities offering GA–Medical Assistance programs vary considerably in the services they cover and in the length of time they will provide help. Of the 39 states with a GA–Medical Assistance program, 15 have extensive benefits similar to the Medicaid program. Both inpatient and outpatient benefits, as well as payment for physician services, laboratory and x-ray services, and care in skilled nursing homes, are available in these cases (Lewin/ICF et al., 1990). The other 24 states have benefits that are less comprehensive than those offered in the Medicaid program. A number of the GA–Medical Assistance programs that are less comprehensive limit medical coverage to outpatient care. A few programs only cover medical emergencies. ***States with more generous Medicaid programs are more***

likely to have GA–Medical Assistance programs, and those tend to be more comprehensive in coverage (Lewin/ICF et al., 1990).

How Can Your Child Apply for GA–Medical Assistance Coverage?

To apply for GA–Medical Assistance coverage, call your county's Department of Social Services (DSS) or Department of Human Resources (DHR). You can find their number in the county government section of your local telephone book. Ask whether your county or state has a GA–Medical Assistance program. This information changes from year to year.

If your state or county has a GA–Medical Assistance program, ask which services it covers and on what basis— emergencies only, short-term help, or help for as long as needed. If you think this program would benefit your child and your family, ask about income eligibility and other requirements to enroll in the program. If you think your child has some chance of qualifying, request that an application form be sent to your home and ask where you would go to submit the completed form.

When you receive the application, fill it out as completely as possible. Take all necessary personal papers with you when you submit the application. Be certain agency staff make photocopies of important documents and letters you submit and return the original copies to you.

Ask how long it will take before you will hear about your child's application for the GA–Medical Assistance program. Note the name of the staff person with whom you talked. If you have not heard from the agency by the time that was indicated, call that person and inquire about the status of your child's application.

EMERGENCY ASSISTANCE PROGRAMS, COUNTY DEPARTMENT OF HUMAN RESOURCES (OR DEPARTMENT OF SOCIAL SERVICES)

Each county's Department of Human Resources (DHR) or Department of Social Services (DSS) has an office or an individual to handle requests for emergency assistance. Included in the emergency assistance offered is help paying for medical emergencies.

What Kind of Help Is Available to Pay for Medical Care?

Your county's DHR/DSS can help you do the following:

1. Pay for needed *medication, medical supplies,* and *special foods* for your child on an emergency basis
2. Pay for or provide *transportation to and from medical care* if your child receives Medicaid
3. Find *longer-term sources of help* to pay for your child's medical care and/or supplement your family's income

Counties have varying policies on how help will be offered. DHR/DSS may arrange to buy a needed medical item for your child or may give you the cash to purchase it yourself. For transportation costs, DHR/DSS may provide bus tickets, transport you and your child in a county vehicle, or give you a voucher for a cab company with which it contracts for service. *It is important to note that direct, immediate help is usually only offered on an emergency basis and only from time to time for one individual or family.* This is to help ensure that limited county funds for this purpose are available to all who need them.

How Can You Request Emergency Help for Medical Care and Related Services Through DHR (or DSS)?

To request emergency help for medical care from your county's DHR (or DSS), call and ask to be connected with the

Office of Emergency Assistance. You can find the telephone number in the county government section of your local telephone directory. You can also call your local information operator for the number.

After you reach DHR/DSS and the office or individual that handles emergency assistance, explain your child's condition and the medical help he or she needs and request assistance. ***Do not be shy about asking for this help.*** DHR/DSS emergency assistance programs are arranged to give this kind of help to children like yours and other members of the local community.

COUNTY OR AREA
PUBLIC HEALTH DEPARTMENTS

Public Health Departments provide a variety of medical services and sponsor health promotion programs for fees that are based on an individual's or family's ability to pay.

What Services Do
Public Health Departments Provide?

Some of the services provided by Public Health Departments include ***immunizations*** and ***checkups*** for babies and children younger than 19 years old, ***prenatal care,*** and ***family planning.*** Public Health Departments also have ***laboratories and pharmacies,*** where tests and medications are available to residents of the county or area the department serves. Some health departments also have funds to pay for ***transportation*** to and from the Public Health Departments or will help pay for gas expenses if you drive. ***Your child may be able to get routine medical care (e.g., immunizations, care for a bad sore throat, care for a cut finger) at the Public Health Department nearest your home. The author recommends that care for your child's chronic illness or disability be given by a specialist trained to treat children*** *with conditions similar to your child's.* This kind of speciality care is often not available at the Public Health Department, but it can give you a referral to specialty care.

Where Is the Public
Health Department Nearest Your Home?

For additional information or to receive services for your child, look in the county government section of your local telephone book or call your local information operator and request the number of your county's Public Health Department, or call your state's Office of Maternal and Child Health. A list of states' Offices of Maternal and Child Health, including their toll-free telephone numbers, is provided in Appendix B at the end of this book.

PUBLIC HOSPITALS

A number of public hospitals in the United States provide health care at little or no cost to families and individuals who are not covered by any private or public insurance plan (e.g., Blue Cross and Blue Shield or Medicaid). The health care provided at public hospitals is paid for by a combination of government sources. *Each state has at least one public hospital, which is most often located in a large city but is available to all state residents.*

What Services Are Available at Public Hospitals?

Public hospitals usually offer a *full range of health care services,* including inpatient and outpatient care for routine illnesses and surgeries, maternity clinics and the delivery of babies, well-child clinics, vision and hearing clinics, dental clinics, and so forth. *Speciality care for children with chronic illnesses or disabilities is usually referred to other medical centers* better equipped and more experienced in treating children with special needs.

How Can You Use a Public
Hospital for Your Child's Care?

If you do not have private health insurance, CHAMPUS (for dependents of members of the military), or Medicaid coverage for your child, *you can use a public hospital for the routine care your child requires.* This might include care for a broken wrist, a high fever, or a persistent cough, if you are reasonably certain these problems do not require the attention of physician well acquainted with your child's condition.

COMMUNITY HEALTH
AND MENTAL HEALTH CENTERS

Community Health and Mental Health Centers exist in every state to provide health and mental health care to families and individuals living in the specific geographic areas these centers serve. Using a Community Health Center (CHC) or a Community Mental Health Center (CMHC) is another way to fund some of the medical and related care your child requires.

Community Health Centers

There are 600 federally funded CHCs in the United States. They offer a variety of outpatient medical services. Each state has at least one of these centers; they may be located in urban or rural areas.

CHCs may be a good source of low-cost care for your child's *routine outpatient health care* needs (e.g., immunizations, ear infections, a sprained ankle). *You will be charged for the care your child receives at a CHC based on your family's income and expenses.* For more information about CHCs or to find the CHC closest to your community, contact the National Association of Community Health

Centers. Ask for a local referral to a certified CHC in your area:

> National Association of Community Health Centers
> 1330 New Hampshire Ave., N.W.
> Suite #122
> Washington, D.C. 20036
> (202) 659-8008

Community Mental Health Centers

There are more than 2,000 CMHCs and other community mental health programs in the United States, with a number located in each state. *CMHCs offer a variety of services for children with mental, emotional, or behavior problems. Some CMHCs are larger than others and offer a broader range of services.* The kinds of services that may be offered at a CMHC in your area include the following:

1. Inpatient care
2. Outpatient therapy
3. Day support and programs
4. Supervised living in group homes or apartments
5. Drug abuse and alcohol services
6. Mental retardation services
7. Developmental disability services
8. Emergency assistance
9. Consultation and education (e.g., prevention work in the community)

Fees for services are based on your family's ability to pay. For more information about a CMHC in your community or to make an appointment, call your community's Information and Referral Service or your community's 24-Hour Crisis Line. You can get these telephone numbers from your local information operator. Ask for referral to a federally funded CMHC near your home. Federally funded CMHCs are required to meet higher standards of care than other CMHCs.

RURAL AND MIGRANT HEALTH CLINICS

There were more than 600 certified Rural and Migrant Health Clinics in 1990, with 44 of the 50 states having at least one. Generally, they are *located in sparsely settled areas.* Many Rural and Migrant Health Clinics are also Community Health Centers. *These clinics generally provide only routine health care* (e.g., physical examinations, immunizations, routine blood work, diagnostic testing). They can also refer you to professionals or clinics that could diagnose and/or treat your child with special health care needs.

If you live in a rural area of your state and would like to know if there is a Rural or Migrant Health Clinic serving your area, contact your state's Office of Maternal and Child Health. Each state's MCH office, including a toll-free telephone number, is listed in Appendix B at the end of this book.

COMMUNITY ACTION AGENCIES OR COUNTY COMMISSIONS FOR ECONOMIC OPPORTUNITY

Each state has a number of Community Action Agencies (CAAs), or County Commissions for Economic Opportunity (CCEOs), as they are often known. These agencies are funded largely by the federal government to *help families and individuals with low incomes in a number of ways.*

Among the services provided by CAAs and CCEOs are the following:

1. Administration of the Head Start Program, which offers preschool programs for children from disadvantaged environments

2. Distribution for some of the U.S. Department of Agriculture's food programs
3. Job training and development
4. Teaching of parenting skills
5. Alcohol and drug prevention services
6. ***Provision of emergency financial assistance for food, housing, utility bills, and prescription medications***

As with county Department of Human Resources emergency assistance programs, CAAs and CCEOs are usually only able to provide these kinds of assistance on an emergency or intermittent basis. To contact the CAA or CCEO nearest your home, call your statewide CAA or CCEO office for a local referral. The addresses and telephone numbers of all state offices of CAAs/CCEOs are listed in Appendix B at the end of this book.

VOCATIONAL REHABILITATION (VR) PROGRAMS

Federal and state governments jointly fund vocational rehabilitation (VR) programs in each state. These programs are ***designed to help eligible individuals with disabilities "define a suitable employment goal and become employed"*** (HEATH Resource Center, 1993, p. 4).

Eligibility for Vocational Rehabilitation Services

Children must be at least 14 years of age to become involved with a vocational rehabilitation program. Between 14 and 16 years old, their health status and skills are evaluated to determine if they meet the requirements for enrollment in a VR Program. This evaluation is now mandated under "transition" services in IDEA. *Individuals with disabilities are eligible for VR assistance if the following three circumstances apply:*

1. They have a physical or mental disability,
2. Their disability creates or causes a substantial handicap to employment, *and*

3. There is a reasonable expectation that the provision of vocational rehabilitation services can make them employable. (HEATH Resource Center, 1989, p. 2)

In the VR Program, **individuals with more severe disabilities are given priority, eligibility is not disease- or condition-specific, and individuals must have the potential to be "employable" to be considered eligible for VR services.** In this case, "*employable*" means able to "*obtain and retain employment consistent with an individual's capacities and abilities in the competitive labor market, self-employment, homemaking, farm, or family work, sheltered employment, homebound employment, supported employment, or other gainful work*" (HEATH Resource Center, 1989, p. 2).

The process of determining a young adult's eligibility for VR services is complex, and often involves the administration of a number of tests, including physical examinations, aptitude and interest testing, vocational evaluations, employability examinations, and developmental and psychological tests. **Eligibility determination, however, must be made within 60 days in most cases.** *If your child is found ineligible for VR services for any reason, he or she must be notified in writing of this decision and given the reasons for this decision. Additionally, your child must be notified of his or her right to appeal this decision, and the procedure to do so must be described.*

What Services Are Offered by Most VR Programs?

In addition to evaluation, VR programs offer the following services (State Department of Education, Division of Rehabilitation Services, 1992):

1. Counseling and guidance
2. Physical restoration, including medical and psychological treatment, surgery and hospital care, and the purchase of needed assistive devices

3. Training, including specific skills training in school and on-the-job training, tuition expenses, reader services for the blind, interpreter services for persons with hearing impairments, other prescribed aids and devices to assist study and training, TT and other sensory aids, and other goods and services that help make an individual with a disability employable
4. Transportation and equipment, as needed to get to training and/or employment
5. Job development and placement
6. Post-placement assistance

These services are offered primarily for eligible individuals in vocational training or for those seeking undergraduate degrees.

After eligibility has been determined, the rehabilitation counselor assigned to a young adult or adult entering the VR Program develops a *individualized written rehabilitation plan* (IWRP) with the new enrollee. Services are provided by the VR Program to be consistent with the goals and objectives of the IWRP.

When Do VR Services End?

After your child is considered successfully rehabilitated or it is found that he or she cannot achieve vocational goals as planned, VR services will no longer be available. VR defines an individual as "satisfactorily rehabilitated" when he or she has been employed for at least 60 days.

How Are VR Services Funded?

VR agencies pay for all of the services required to establish an individual's eligibility for VR services with the state and federal assistance they receive. However, after an individual is eligible for VR, services are paid for by a combination of government funds and contributions from individuals receiving services. *Individuals are charged for services based on their ability to pay. In many cases, with young adults, their family's income is counted in determining the contribution the young adult must make.*

For more information about VR services or to apply for services, contact your state's Department of Vocational Rehabilitation. In many cases, VR services are offered through a Division of Rehabilitation Services under the State Department of Education. The addresses and telephone numbers for each state's Department of Vocational Rehabilitation are provided in Appendix B at the end of this book.

THE HILL-BURTON FREE CARE PROGRAM, U.S. DEPARTMENT OF HEALTH AND HUMAN SERVICES

Free or low-cost health care is available in hospitals, nursing homes, and other health facilities as a "payback" from the U.S. government for federal construction or modernization funds. Facilities that have received such funds and are "paying them back" are participants in the Hill-Burton Free Care program. *These participating facilities have agreed to do the following:*

1. Provide a reasonable amount of service to individuals who cannot pay for care
2. Make services available to all individuals living in the particular facility's geographic area

Many facilities have already paid back their Hill-Burton funds, and are no longer required to offer free or low-cost care under this program. To find out which facilities in your state are still offering free or low-cost care under this program and if your child or family would qualify for services, call the Hill-Burton Hot Line:

1-800-638-9742
1-800-492-0359 (in Maryland only)

SUMMARY

A number of government programs exist to help make the medical and related care your child requires more affordable. Try to take advantage of any public assistance programs you can. Although these programs are not designed specifically to pay for medical care, they can or can free up your personal funds to do so. *All families can receive some help from one or more of these programs on an emergency or temporary basis.*

6

Paying for Medical Care—Private Sources of Help

A number of private sources of support are available for medical and related care. The largest, and currently the best source for funding ongoing medical needs, is *private health insurance.* In addition, many *disease- and disability-related organizations and civic, social welfare, and religious organizations* as well as a number of *charitable foundations* help families pay for care for children with chronic illnesses or disabilities. All of these potential resources for paying for your child's health and related care are presented in more detail in this chapter.

One caution must be mentioned here. *Health insurance or health care reform will possibly change the way health insurance is purchased and the way health care is delivered.* Thus, some of the information provided here may change in the next few years. Try to keep up with newspaper and magazine articles discussing health insurance reform proposals. If substantial changes in health care financing or delivery occur, you will be better informed about what to do on your child's behalf (see Chapter 12). The national offices of the larger disease- and disability-related organizations should also be able to inform you of any major changes that are made and how these changes are likely to affect your child's access to health care and the costs you will have to pay.

PRIVATE HEALTH INSURANCE

Having private health insurance with generous coverage of many health care and related services continues to be the most reliable way to get your child's medical, surgical, and related therapy, medication, and equipment expenses paid. Having such a policy that covers your child with a chronic illness or disability will provide some assurance that you can obtain the care your child needs at a cost your family can afford.

However, it is important to note that, ***even with private health insurance, you will be responsible for some of the expenses involved.*** These expenses include deductibles, ongoing co-payments, items not covered in the policy, and often 100% of any charges that exceed the "usual and customary rate" (UCR) or "maximum allowable charge" of which the insurance company will pay its share.

Whether a more traditional fee-for-service plan or a managed care plan, private health insurance is most often obtained as a benefit of your or another family member's employment. However, private health insurance is available through sources other than employment (e.g., nonprofit and fraternal organizations, union groups); these sources of insurance are discussed on pages 192–195. When your employer offers health insurance, most commonly you pay a set amount (i.e., a premium) each month or quarter, and your employer provides you with access to a group health insurance plan. Your employer is the actual "policyholder," and as an employee you are eligible for health insurance coverage for yourself and often for other members of your immediate family. In many cases, your employer will pay part of your premium as an employee benefit. Usually, you must pay the portion of the "premium" that covers other family members.

Plans vary widely in extent of coverage and cost to the insured. There are hundreds of Blue Cross and Blue Shield contracts with employers and dozens of contracts with any given health maintenance organization (HMO) or preferred provider organization (PPO). Plans are usually negotiated yearly between employer and insurance company, and benefits and rates may change.

In seeking health insurance coverage through your employer, you can select any plan the employer offers. *Services covered, as well as premiums, deductibles, and copayments, vary in plans.* Information to help you evaluate different plans is provided on pages 167–180.

In a growing number of cases, large companies are "self-insuring," meaning they arrange and fund their own health insurance plans. There are several incentives for businesses to do this, most notably that their insurance plans cannot be regulated by state agencies that oversee private health insurance companies doing business in their state. The lack of state regulation on companies that "self-insure" may not work to the benefit of insured employees.

There are several rules of thumb in the health insurance industry regarding cost, coverage, and the size of the insured group. Knowing these may help you to obtain the most adequate health insurance coverage for your child's needs. *These rules include the following:*

- The more employees insured, the more generous the benefit package available

- The more employees insured by a given plan, the lower the cost to any individual employee
- The more employees insured, the more able the plan is to carry a few frequent and/or high-cost service users without increasing rates for anyone

For these reasons, **parents whose children have chronic illnesses or disabilities are advised to look for employment with large companies or government organizations.** This is addressed in more detail on page 182.

Making Full Use of a Comprehensive Health Insurance Policy

Having an adequate health insurance policy or plan is in some ways beyond your control. As mentioned previously, an employee can only choose from one of the health insurance plans his or her employer offers. *After you have chosen a plan, however, knowing how to use your health insurance to obtain a maximum amount of care with a minimum of out-of-pocket cost is an art worth learning.* The following discussion reviews:

1. How a family with a child who has a chronic illness or disability would decide among available health insurance plans
2. Provisions of health insurance policies of most concern to families with children who have chronic illnesses or disabilities
3. How to use your health insurance policy to get the most service for your child at the least cost to you
4. What to do if you are having a problem getting your insurance company to pay for medical or related care or equipment you believe is covered in your policy
5. How to try to get private health insurance if your employer does not offer it

Deciding Between Available Health Insurance Plans

If you have a choice between types of private health insurance, **you need to consider the advantages and disadvantages of all options carefully:**

1. You may need to decide between a less and more comprehensive, traditional fee-for-service plan.
2. You may need to choose between a plan using a traditional fee-for-service approach and one with a prepaid managed care approach (e.g., an HMO or a PPO).

These options and others are discussed in Table 1 and below. Highlighted are the general characteristics of each kind of insurance plan, including their strengths and weaknesses, particularly for a child with a chronic illness or disability.

Regardless of the option you eventually choose, there are several general guidelines for evaluating health care plans; these include the following:

- Your main concern will be to have adequate coverage of services your child with special needs requires or may require in the future.
- A second concern will be that you can afford to pay your share of the cost of premiums and the covered health care services you expect your child and other family members to use.

Remember, different plans cover different health care services to greater or lesser extents. Different plans also require different premiums, co-payments, and deductibles each year.

Be sure to get a copy of your health insurance policy, which is actually called the "certificate." Become very familiar with all of the services covered by your health insurance plan. Learn which services are not covered, and find out what portion of the cost of care you will be asked to pay out of your own pocket.

Table 1.   A comparison of fee-for-service and managed care health insurance approaches

FEE-FOR-SERVICE APPROACHES

- Fees charged for each service as insured receives it
- Often emphasize treatment for illness; little coverage for preventative care (e.g., routine physical examinations, immunizations, well-baby care)
- Insured are free to choose any qualified physician or other provider to provide services; insured can contact a generalist or a specialist to provide any covered service at any time; therefore, care may not be coordinated
- Increasingly have requirements for prior approval for a hospital admission and greater reimbursement for using outpatient rather than inpatient care for certain tests, procedures, and surgeries (In this way, fee-for-service plans have acquired some aspects of managed care plans.)
- Often require evidence of insurability and may limit coverage for "pre-existing conditions" entirely or for a period of time
- Premiums are often higher than for managed care plans, as are co-payments and deductibles
- Often easier to get reimbursement for an out-of-state consultation than with a managed care plan that uses a specific network of providers
- There are two kinds of plans using a fee-for-service approach; the insured may have access to either one or both combined in one package.

1. Basic coverage plans	• Cover a limited number of services, which are reimbursed according to a scheduled rate that is lower than actual charges • Each service may be subject to a deductible and/or co-payment • Little or no coverage of preventative care • May be an inexpensive way to cover a limited number of services if fee-for-service approach is preferred
2. Major medical plans	• Generally offer reimbursement for a large variety of medical and related services • Reimbursement based on the usual and customary rate (UCR) for such services in a particular geographic area; generally reimbursed at 80% of UCR after an individual has met an annual deductible, up to a lifetime limitation • Some services subject to further limitations (e.g., services for psychiatric and substance abuse treatment, substance abuse care)

(continued)

Table 1.   (*continued*)

> - May include a "stop loss" provision to limit an insured's out-of-pocket loss (commonly to $1,000 or $2,500 per year)

MANAGED CARE APPROACHES

- Tries to control costs by limiting services used to the minimum necessary and by using a network of providers who agree to accept lower fees in exchange for a guaranteed flow of patients
- Insurance and service provider organization may be the same, as in some health maintenance organizations (HMOs)
- Primary care provider coordinates all care received and access to specialists
- Approval for many services, including use of the emergency room, required
- Limits choice of doctors
- Often do *not* refuse participation or limit coverage due to "pre-existing conditions"
- Preventative services covered in addition to services for illness
- Can often offer lower premiums than fee-for-service approaches due to strict utilization review
- Managed care approach can be combined with a fee-for-service approach, as in preferred provider organizations (PPO) plans or point-of-service (POS) plans (see below)

1. Health maintenance organizations (HMOs)

- May both insure and deliver services (e.g., Kaiser–Permanente, Group Health) or insure through a network of participating providers across a geographic area (e.g., Complete Health of Alabama)
- Insured pays one fee for health care services each year; no fee charged with each service except for small co-payments in some cases to discourage overutilization of services (e.g., prescription medications)
- Have limits on some services (e.g., psychiatric care)
- Usually insured must pick a primary care provider from the HMO's list of participating physicians; insured must go through this provider to receive all other care under the HMO plan except in situations that are life-threatening
- May offer financial incentives to participating service providers to limit amount of care offered to plan members
- Emphasize preventative care; cover routine examinations, immunizations, and well-baby care

(*continued*)

Table 1.   (*continued*)

2. **Preferred provider organizations (PPOs)**	• Use a network of generalists and specialists to provide care at discounted rates (In addition, certain hospitals belong to PPO networks so they can offer inpatient care at discounted rates.)
	• Insured persons get maximum reimbursement if they use a provider or hospital in the PPO network—often 100% reimbursement less a small co-payment; or insured persons may choose to go outside of the network for care and be reimbursed at a lower rate than if they had chosen a provider in the network
	• Approval by a generalist is *not* required to use specialty care within the PPO or other covered care outside of the PPO
	• May impose limits on services used by insured (e.g., for psychiatric care)
3. **Point-of-service (POS) plans**	• Use a network of providers and hospitals who agree to charge lower rates in exchange for a guaranteed flow of clients (This is also a characteristic of PPOs.)
	• Insured must use a primary care provider in the POS network to coordinate care and obtain referral to any specialist (This is also a characteristic of HMOs.)
	• Insured is reimbursed at a higher rate for using a provider or facility in the POS network

It is also important to **make your child's health care providers aware of your plan's benefits and limitations. Encourage them to plan and coordinate your child's care around these provisions whenever possible** (Rosenfeld, 1993).

Fee-for-Service Health Insurance Approach

Health insurance plans using a fee-for-service approach separate payment for care from delivery of services. You, the insured, are free to consult any health-related professional whose services are covered by your plan at any time for any reason. You do not need to call or visit a primary care physician or an internist before making an appointment with a specialist, and you do not need to get an internist's approval to go to a specialist. You may pick up the telephone and request such an appointment whenever you feel it is needed. You and your dependents may go for care to any hospital that meets standards set by the American Hospital Association.

If health insurance and health care reform is implemented, this procedure is likely to change for many individuals. *More individuals will have to obtain referrals from general pediatricians, internists, or other generalists to consult specialists.* This type of reform is designed to contain health care costs, but it may also make it more time consuming and difficult to consult specialists. However, *generalists will have to coordinate most of the care their patients receive.* This may result in more efficient and effective treatment and intervention.

Plans using a fee-for-service approach vary in the types of services they cover and the amount of deductibles and co-payments the insured is required to pay out of his or her own pocket.

Basic Coverage Plans

Basic coverage plans commonly provide more limited coverage according to a scheduled rate of reimbursement, often well below the actual fee you are charged by a doctor or a hospital. Each hospital admission may be subject to a deductible, commonly $250, and you may be required to provide a modest co-payment toward the cost of the hospital room each day. Furthermore, preventative care (e.g., immunizations, routine checkups) is often not covered at all. These exclusions limit costs to the insurance company while providing you and your dependents reimbursement for some of the costs of more expensive outpatient medical and surgical procedures, inpatient medical and surgical procedures, and hospital room and board. Generally, the more costly the plan (i.e., the higher the monthly premium the insured pays), the more adequate the reimbursement available for covered medical services.

Major Medical Plans

Major medical plans make less use of limited reimbursement for specific types of services. Instead, these plans contain an overall lifetime limitation on total reimbursements and, as with basic coverage plans, use deductibles and copayments to limit overutilization of services. Only selected services are subject to additional limitations (e.g., reimbursement for inpatient and outpatient psychiatric care).

An example of how major medical plans limit their expenses is the common practice of requiring you and one or more of your family members to pay an annual deductible of at least $100 before receiving any reimbursement and requiring at least a 20% co-payment on most outpatient services. That means you must pay out of your own pocket at least 20% of the cost of care for you and your family members. This percentage could be higher if the insurance company declares that the fee the professional charged you is more than the "usual and customary rate" (UCR) for your geographic area. In that case, the insurance company will pay only its 80% share of costs on the "usual and customary rate." You, the insured, will be responsible for 100% of the difference between what the insurance company pays and what the health care provider or facility charges.

It is also important to note that in major medical plans, an employee's or dependent's lifetime limitation or "overall maximum benefit" can be partially or totally restored. This can happen if the insurance company is presented with evidence of insurability that meets its satisfaction. This often means that your policy has not had major claims charged against it during the previous year. Reinstatement of "maximum benefits" is easier for the insurance company to do when the insurance pool involved is large.

Historically, both basic coverage plans and major medical plans have most adequately paid for inpatient and outpatient physician and medically related care, including some of the cost of prescription drugs. This was largely because lobby or advocacy groups for physicians and hospitals were the principal authors of the first health insurance plans.

Basic coverage and major medical plans have not been as good at reimbursing insured individuals for medical equipment and supplies, home health care (although this has changed since the cost of inpatient medical care has increased so dramatically), and other medical and related costs your child with a chronic illness or a disability might incur (e.g., the cost of special formulas and foods, the cost of tutoring and special private education, family counseling, homemaker services, the cost of refitting a house or a car to accommodate a child in a wheelchair).

In their efforts to provide services efficiently and at reasonable costs, health care plans using a fee-for-service approach are taking on aspects of those based on managed care. *The emerging emphasis is on service coordination— trying to provide and coordinate the services necessary to return your child to his or her routine as soon as possible.* This new emphasis has also opened the door for a number of nonmedical and home- and community-based services to be delivered and paid for through traditional health insurance mechanisms. This is addressed further on pages 175–176.

"Evidence of Insurability" and "Pre-existing Condition" Exclusion Clauses

In a health insurance plan based on a fee-for-service approach, *the insurance company may require (if state law permits) "evidence of insurability" for you and your family members.* This means that **an insurance company can exclude from coverage or limit benefits for "pre-existing conditions."** These are generally defined as "injuries or sicknesses that have existed for a specified period—such as 3 or 6 months—prior to a person's becoming insured" (Health Insurance Association of America, 1992a, p. 195). The company can require you and the dependents you want to insure to answer questions about your health and health history. It can even require you and your dependents to undergo a physical examination (at the company's expense).

However, **if you elect to participate in your company's health insurance plan within 30 days of becoming employed or during an "open enrollment" period, you do not have to demonstrate insurability** for yourself and your dependents, and are thus not subject to coverage limitations for "pre-existing conditions."

Managed Care Health Insurance Approaches

Health insurance plans based on managed care, which include HMOs, PPOs, and POS plans, try to provide health care services while controlling costs. The primary ways cost control is achieved may include one or more of the following:

1. Financial and other incentives offered to health care providers—all of whom work directly for or contract with the HMO, PPO, or POS plan—to provide only basic, essential services
2. The requirement in some cases that you select a primary physician (usually any pediatrician, family practice physician, or internist) to direct and coordinate all of the care you receive
3. Financial incentives to you (i.e., lower premiums, small deductibles) if you use doctors who have agreed to charge the plan less in exchange for a guaranteed amount of business

4. The agreement in some cases that if you make un-authorized use of health care services either within or outside of the plan, you must pay for this care yourself
5. The plan administrators' aggressive review of utiliza-tion of health care services by all insured individuals in the plan

Recently, health insurance plans based on a fee-for-service approach have introduced requirements and finan-cial incentives for those insured with them to try to save money; these include the following:

1. Offering reimbursements for surgery or medical proce-dures done on a less costly outpatient basis
2. Requiring prior approval for an inpatient hospital stay
3. Requiring use of particular hospital, with which the in-surance plan has negotiated lower rates
4. Requiring that testing needed before an inpatient stay be done on an outpatient basis
5. Disallowing weekend admissions to hospitals

Service Coordination

HMOs helped popularize the notion of service coordination, which was once known as "case management" or "care coordination." This began in the mid 1980s to help con-trol costs associated with the care used by individuals with chronic illnesses and long-term disabilities. These costs account for a large share of health care expenses because of the large amount of care—often highly specialized and expensive—that must be given over a long period of time.

Service coordinators, usually registered nurses or social workers with at least several years of experience, are being used by most health insurance plans. Service coordinators work for employers either directly or by contract. *Their job is to research a patient's health insurance coverage, includ-ing policy limitations. Together with the patient's "primary care physician" or internist, they arrive at a plan of inter-vention or treatment. The goal of such an intervention or treatment plan is to offer needed services as efficiently as possible and at the least cost possible, thereby restoring the patient to maximum functioning as soon as possible.*

In the future, **all health insurance plans will make in-creasing use of service coordinators in the interest of sav-ing money. However, a good service coordinator can also coordinate services for your child with a chronic illness or disability in a way that benefits your child and your fami-ly's finances, too.**

Preferred Provider Organizations (PPOs)

Use of a preferred provider organization (PPO) is one way to control costs, through discounted arrangements with pro-viders, while still preserving freedom of choice for the in-sured. Preferred provider organizations give financial incen-tives to insured individuals to use one hospital and a given network of health care providers. Within that network, you may choose any doctor and go to specialists when you be-lieve it is necessary. If you choose to use health care pro-viders who are not part of the prescribed network, you will be reimbursed at a lower rate. PPOs can offer better reim-bursements to you for health care services within the PPO network because health care providers have agreed to accept lower fees in exchange for a greater volume of customers.

"Point-of-Service" (POS) Programs

A "point-of-service" (POS) program combines the concepts of an HMO and a PPO. The insured is given financial incen-tives (i.e., higher reimbursement and lower co-payments) to use physicians and services in a PPO network. When seek-ing care within this network, you must use a "primary care physician" to coordinate care and direct referrals to special-ists. If seeking care outside the network, you can choose any health care provider and any service, and can self-refer to specialists. It will cost you more to do the latter.

A Comparison of Options for Families with Children Who Have Chronic Illnesses or Disabilities

Brief descriptions of fee-for-service versus managed care approaches in health insurance plans, including advantages and disadvantages of each, are reiterated in Table 1.

The major advantage of a traditional fee-for-service health insurance plan is that that you have total freedom to choose any health care professional in your plan for any covered health service. Professionals, including specialists, can be consulted as often as you feel is needed, and services may be used as frequently as desired. *This privilege may be limited in cases of chronic illness or when extremely high expenses are incurred for care. If the employer has elected a service coordination option in the company's insurance plan, you may be obliged to work with a service coordinator to plan your child's future care as efficiently and cost-effectively as possible.*

Where state law permits, health insurance plans using fee-for-service approaches can refuse to reimburse you or your dependents for care for pre-existing conditions. Thus, while you are paying the full premium amount for your insurance, you or your dependents may be refused coverage or have to wait as long as 2 years to be covered for services related to any prior or existing medical problem. In larger group plans, pre-existing condition provisions are generally waived if you enroll in the insurance plan within 30 days of beginning work for the given company.

Premiums for a plan using a fee-for-service approach tend to be higher than for those based on managed care because of your right to choose more costly providers and more care. Furthermore, fee-for-service premiums, co-payments, and deductibles are likely to increase more rapidly than in plans using managed care because there are few controls for overutilization of services.

Another disadvantage of plans using a fee-for-service approach is that care may not be coordinated. Although the requirement for service coordination in a managed care approach is primarily designed to save money, service coordination can be quite helpful to you or your child. In this case, a physician or nurse evaluates all of the reports from specialists and puts this information together to assess and treat your child. This does not happen automatically in fee-for-service plans, particularly if your child uses a variety of health care providers associated with different group practices and hospitals.

An HMO may not be the best alternative for a family with a child who has special health care needs. Generally, costs are limited through strict control of service use. Although an HMO legally cannot deny a plan member needed care, it may be difficult for you to know what care is needed and to ask for it. This might be particularly true regarding durable medical equipment and assistive technology services and devices. You want to be able to get the most up-to-date and appropriate items to help with your child's development and general mobility. Historically, many pediatricians and other practitioners who contract with HMOs have not been experienced in treating children with chronic illnesses and disabilities. As indicated previously, your child's pediatrician or primary care physician must be willing to learn about your child's condition and any special requirements for his or her care.

Under the following conditions, an HMO can be a workable option for some families with children who have disabilities or chronic illnesses:

1. You meet with your child's prospective primary care provider and feel confident that he or she will make

every effort to become familiar with your child's condition, current research on the condition, and state-of-the-art interventions and treatments

2. You meet with your child's prospective primary care provider and feel confident that he or she will make all necessary referrals to specialists and order any durable medical equipment or other assistive technology services and devices that could be of help to your child

HMOs generally charge lower premiums for insurance coverage and have fewer deductibles and co-payments. In addition, federally qualified HMOs cannot withhold coverage or charge more for insured persons with pre-existing conditions. They must also have an appeals process for service that is denied under the plan. From the first day of enrollment in the plan, your child with special needs will be covered for all of the care that other plan participants will be.

Another benefit of HMOs is their emphasis on preventative services. More routine kinds of care are covered that are not connected to any illness or sickness (e.g., routine physical examinations, immunizations, diet and exercise programs).

PPO and POS plans may offer a good compromise between the freedom of choice currently available in a fee-for-service plan and cost saving to you and the greater preventative care for your family offered in an HMO.

One additional suggestion: *concerning health insurance plans based on both fee-for-service and managed care approaches, you should find out how the plans reimburse or provide for the following:*

1. Treatments that are still considered experimental
2. Out-of-state services that are the most appropriate

You may have to formally request that your health insurance plan cover these services.

The advantages and disadvantages of each health insurance option must be weighed against your child's needs, what you can afford, and your comfort with one insurance arrangement or the other. *No matter which type of plan you choose, you will be called on to be your child's advocate and, from time to time, you will need to push the insurance or health care system to do more for your child. You will be the one to make the plan work* (Rosenfeld, 1993).

Health Insurance Concerns for a Family with a Child Who Has a Chronic Illness or Disability

To be certain that your child with special needs is insured and that his or her insurance remains active, **there are a number of areas in which you need to be alert. To get the most service for your child for the the least out-of-pocket cost to your family, try to observe the following:**

1. *If you have a choice of insurance plans, be sure to study all plans your company offers and select the one that looks like it will give you and your dependents the most coverage for the least out-of-pocket cost.*
2. *It is very important for you to enroll in an employer's group health insurance at the first opportunity possible, but no later than 30 days after employment begins.* In the case of larger employers, this will help to ensure that coverage begins promptly and that there will be no pre-existing condition clause that limits coverage for you and your dependents.
3. *Be sure you have a "family coverage" plan in effect at least 2 months before your baby is due.* If an infant is born to you and you have *not* requested the change in status from "single" or "couple" to "family," the insurance company may refuse to cover your baby for a certain period of time. Currently, this can be as short as 10 days after birth to as long as 90 days. Parents of a

child born with a severe health problem or a disability know that such a baby requires a large amount of expensive medical care in the first weeks of life. ***Without "family" coverage in place, you could be responsible for 100% of your child's medical bills until such coverage is in place and the insurance company assumes its share of the bills.***

There should be a staff person at your place of employment who handles all dealings with the health insurance company. This is the person to speak with to request "family" coverage. Each time you expect another child, it is a good idea to notify your insurance company 2 months before the child is expected.

You will pay an increased premium for "family" coverage, but it will give you coverage for your first and future dependents from their first day of life. If you get "family" coverage well in advance of your first child's due date, he or she will be insured even if born early.

4. *Be sure that your portion of the health insurance premium and your employer's part is paid to the insurance company as agreed, whether monthly, quarterly, or annually.* This will ensure that there is no gap in health insurance coverage. The easiest way for you to pay your part is to request an automatic payroll deduction for it. It is possible that this may be done before your pay is taxed, which means that you will be paying taxes on a smaller salary because your health insurance premiums will be deducted from your gross pay *before* figuring the income tax you owe each week or month.

5. ***If you are considering a job change, ask to review your prospective employer's health insurance plans.*** *Be sure the coverage will be adequate for your family's needs. If you are still interested in the job, be certain that your child with a chronic illness or disability will*

be covered under all of the insurance plans you would consider.

In your family's situation, a good job with poor health insurance coverage will probably not be appealing to you. The quality of the health insurance options will in many cases be as important as the job description itself and the salary to be paid.

Some state laws, while requiring an employer to cover a newborn if "family" coverage is in effect, do not require the employer to offer coverage to a child who comes with his or her family to the new insurance plan. If this were so in your case, again the new job might not be as appealing.

Larger employers—both public and private—offer comprehensive health care benefits at a modest cost to the employee. In addition, they will most often cover a child with special needs together with an employee and his or her other dependents. This is because large organizations insure so many people that they can absorb the higher medical costs of some insured members without increasing their overall premium costs. **It is therefore a general rule of thumb for families with children who have chronic illnesses or disabilities to seek and maintain employment with as large an employer as possible.**

Insurance coverage for your dependent with special needs, however, must be negotiated along with other work issues. You cannot assume your dependents will be automatically covered by the company's health insurance plan.

6. *Most health insurance policies no longer cover a child after he or she is out of school (18–24 years old), unless the child has a disability and is incapable of supporting him- or herself.* **In many states, it is up to you to notify your insurance company that your child has a**

disability and to request that he or she be kept on your family policy as a "dependent" indefinitely. You must make this request of your insurance company before your dependent child would be dropped from the policy because of his or her age. Your insurance company will probably request a letter from your doctor indicating your child's medical condition and extent of disability.

7. *Your child with a chronic illness or disability, as with any other dependent on your policy, will have the option to convert his or her coverage to an individual policy of his own.* For a child dependent, this conversion privilege is a one-time option that can be exercised when the child is no longer able to be covered on his or her parents' policy because of age. As with the request to retain a child as a dependent beyond the usual allowable age, it may be the family's responsibility to contact the insurance company to exercise this conversion privilege. The insurance company should be contacted before the dependent would be dropped from the parents' policy because of age.

    Conversion policies, however, tend to provide less comprehensive coverage and cost more than coverage available under large group plans. Therefore, having a child with special needs convert to an individual policy is only advised if you believe your child will be capable of supporting him- or herself on a fairly sustained basis. In this case, the conversion policy can provide coverage until he or she obtains personal coverage as a benefit of employment.

8. **Be aware of the lifetime limitation on your "major medical policy."** *As soon as your family exceeds this level of health care expenses, your insurance company may not cover future medical costs.* Many families with a child with costly medical needs live in fear of

exceeding this lifetime limitation. Although it a valid concern and may be a factor in a family's decision about an elective surgery, families should try not get so scared off by this that they avoid seeking recommended care for their children.

Some insurance companies will restore part or all of the lifetime limitation over time. This is most likely to occur in plans that insure large groups of individuals and when there has not been excessive use of the insurance policy.

9. *If you are considering an HMO or other managed care insurance plan, be comfortable that your primary care physician is capable of treating your child with special needs and that he or she will make all necessary referrals to specialists.*

10. *If it is not given to you when you enroll in a health insurance plan,* **request a copy of the papers or booklet (often called a "certificate") describing in detail the health insurance coverage you have selected for your family. Study this booklet inside and out!**

Becoming familiar with the benefits offered and limitations on them, will help you plan any needed medical care for your child. Benefits will be listed with required co-payments and deductibles. Situations in which deductibles can be waived (e.g., using a particular hospital for an inpatient admission) will be described in your health insurance certificate or plan outline.

Limitations on health care use will be noted as well. An example of a limitation that could be costly to you if you overlooked it would be the insurance company's request that all inpatient hospital stays be pre-approved by the insurance company. If you do not get such an approval, your hospital stay would be reimbursed at a lower rate than if you had gotten the stay pre-approved.

11. ***Make your doctors and other health care providers aware of what your policy will cover and what it will not. Ask for their help in scheduling medical and surgical procedures in a way that will yield the maximum insurance reimbursement.***

Doctors, like health care consumers, are quite aware of the high costs of medical care. However, they often do not think about it in terms of a particular patient's insurance coverage or financial situation. In most cases, it will be up to you to inform you doctor about your needs in this area.

12. *Your family should* ***negotiate with doctors, hospitals, and other health care providers by requesting that they accept as "payment in full" whatever your insurance company will pay.*** Physicians and other health care providers in private practice can agree to accept a reduced fee for their services (Rosenfeld, 1993). Some states have laws that require this. Many health care professionals associated with academic medical centers and teaching hospitals have some authority to do so as well (Rosenfeld, 1993). Try to explain the extra financial burden you have due to the large amount of medical and related care required by your child with special needs. If you are truly undergoing financial hardship, explain this to your health care providers. They may be able to relieve you of some of your medical bills.

You may feel awkward or embarrassed asking doctors or other professionals for a discounted fee. Many families fear that professionals will withhold care from families who cannot pay full fees. Try to overcome these concerns. Professionals treating your child will try to help you in any way they can. It will be up to you, however, to make them aware of your family's concerns and needs.

13. *If you do not have health insurance and/or have ac-cumulated a large amount of out-of-pocket expenses you cannot pay, ask your physicians and hospital bus-iness office personnel if you* **can set up a "payment plan"** *to pay on these bills monthly.* This will be easier to do with physicians and other health care providers and more difficult to do with hospitals and other in-stitutions. It is costly for hospitals to bill you and collect small payments each month over a long period of time. In some cases, hospitals receive greater finan-cial benefit from writing off your outstanding medical bills. Some hospitals have established relationships with area banks to refer clients for financing their med-ical debts.

In any case, do not withdraw your child from needed intervention or treatment because you do not have the money to pay for it or you are shy about negotiating with your doctors, other professionals, and hospitals. Try to work something out.

14. **If you use a health care plan based on a fee-for-service insurance approach, establish relationships with both the staff person at your company who works most closely with the insurance company and a responsive claims representative at the insurance company. If you are a member of an HMO or other managed care plan, establish a good working relationship with your primary care physician.**

The claims representative or primary care physician can be helpful in clarifying coverage in your policy and how to best use it to your advantage. In the case of the claims representative, you can send all of your claims to him or her to be sure items get properly coded for reimbursement. This should shorten the time it takes for you to be reimbursed. Furthermore, if you have any problems, you have one person to whom to talk. He or she knows your personal situation, and in many cases can act as an advocate for your family with the insurance company.

Your primary care physician in an HMO is the gatekeeper to all other care you might need or want for your child. He or she is also the person who receives reports from all other caregivers and puts their information into a coherent whole picture. This is important for your child both diagnostically and in selecting preferred treatments and interventions.

Try to remember to acknowledge the help these individuals provide your family, with a periodic "thank you" note, a small gift around the winter holidays, or homemade cookies. For a family with numerous frequent medical bills and claims, this is an extremely important relationship to nurture.

15. **If a health insurance claim is denied, the insurance company must tell you why. With this information in hand, submit the denied claim again, including any additional information requested.**

Insurance companies can be quite particular about the language used in describing a medical problem, a medical need, or a treatment procedure. *Many claims are denied for small, technical reasons.* If needed, enlist the help of your claims representative to clarify what will be needed to get your claim paid.

Write a letter to your doctor or other health care provider telling them of the problem. **Give them guidelines for the language your insurance company prefers in supporting a claim.** A sample of such a letter appears in Appendix A at the end of this book.

16. *If your insurance company refuses to pay a claim you have submitted at least twice, you can contact your State Department of Insurance, Office of Consumer Affairs. This remedy is discussed on pages 188–189.*

17. *When your child is hospitalized, try to stock up on medical supplies your child will use after discharge.* These supplies are often covered at 100% as part of an inpatient stay but are not reimbursed as fully or at all on an outpatient basis.

What to Do If Your Insurance Company Will Not Pay

If you believe that you were denied payment for care that your employer's health insurance policy clearly covers for you or your dependents, you *can* do something about it. The author recommends taking the following steps in the following order:

1. *Appeal your denied claim to your health insurance company at least twice.*

2. *If you are not reimbursed after these appeals and do not believe you were given an adequate explanation,* **contact your State Department of Insurance.** Each state has such an agency whose primary job is regulating insurance companies who do business in their state. They will respond to your complaint and problem in some way. Some State Departments of Insurance, however, are more consumer oriented than others. A list of State Departments of Insurance for each state, including their addresses and telephone numbers is provided in Appendix B at the end of this book.

    Call this state agency to report your problem with getting reimbursement. Ask to speak with someone in the Office of Consumer Affairs regarding a health insurance problem. Request the name of the staff person to whom you should write to submit a formal complaint, and determine the kind of information he or she will need to investigate your complaint. *Note the name of the person you talked with on the telephone as well.*

    Send the person to whom you are told to write a description of your problem and a copy of the section in your insurance certificate, booklet, or plan summary that states that you are covered for the service for which you are having trouble getting covered. Include any other information you feel would be important in establishing your case as well as any information the State Department of Insurance requests when you call.

Make a copy of your letter before sending it and begin a file for letters like it (e.g., "Health Care Reimbursement Problems, 1993"). Keep all correspondence on this problem in this file, including notes you make of related telephone conversations. This gives you a central place to store all information about this topic and allows you to return to this problem easily at a later date.

Give your State Department of Insurance 2 weeks to reply to your letter. At the end of 2 weeks, call and ask to speak with the person to whom you sent your letter. When you reach this person, ask for the status of your complaint.

Wait another 2 weeks. If you still have no satisfactory response from your State Department of Insurance and the amount of money is sizeable, consider the next step.

3. *Contact a lawyer.*

   a. *Call the nearest* **Legal Services Corporation office** (e.g., "legal aid program") **to see if you are eligible for its services.** Ask to speak to an information specialist to discuss your situation. If you are eligible, an attorney on the program's staff may be able to help you recover your reimbursement. The charge for this service will be based on your income, but is generally less expensive than hiring a private attorney.

   Call the local information operator for the number of the legal aid office in your area. If you have trouble reaching such an organization locally, call the national office of the Legal Services Corporation in Washington, D.C. This number is listed in Appendix B at the end of this book. They can refer you to the legal aid office nearest your home.

b. **If you do not qualify for legal aid, contact the law school nearest to your home.** It may have law students in clinic programs available to help you. If there is a charge for this service, it would be based on your family's ability to pay and should be less than the cost of hiring a private attorney.

c. **If you are not able to get help from legal aid or a law school in your state or if you can afford to use a private lawyer, contact your county or state Bar Association's lawyer referral service and your state's Protection and Advocacy agency.** Ask for the name of two to three private attorneys experienced in recovering health insurance payments. Screen the recommended lawyers by telephone. Ask each if he or she will meet with you to review your case. At such a meeting, you can also decide if you want him or her to handle your case.

When you speak with any attorney by telephone, be sure to ask what his or her fee will be and when you have to pay it. Fees can be high—as much as one-third of the money recovered—but usually you do not need to pay until you receive your reimbursement from the insurance company. **Many private lawyers will meet with you once at no charge.**

Any lawyer, after hearing the facts of your case, may tell you that he or she will not take your case. This is because he or she believes you do not have a good chance of getting reimbursed for the money you claim is owed you.

If you do end up owing money you did not anticipate to a doctor, hospital, or other health care provider, you can pay for this expense over time. Set up a monthly payment plan with them.

What to Do If Your Job Is Terminated or If You Resign
Under federal law (COBRA, 1985), **any public or private employer with 20 or more employees** (except the federal

government and some religious organizations) **must offer continued health insurance coverage for all employees who are terminated, unless they are terminated for "gross misconduct."** Some company health insurance policies will cover employees who resign as well. *This extended group coverage can be for as long as 18 months for an employee, and as long as 36 months for the employee's spouse and other dependents.*

The departing employee must pay the full premium cost for the extended coverage. That means he or she would pay the part of the premium he or she paid before *plus* the part paid in the past by the employer.

For more information about this, you may contact your employer's Department of Human Resources or the individual who handles personnel issues. *For private employee plans,* you can also get detailed information about this program from:

U.S. Department of Labor
Pension and Welfare Benefits Administration
Division of Technical Assistance and Inquiries
200 Constitution Avenue, N.W.
Room N-5658
Washington, D.C. 20210

For public employee plans, you can also get detailed information about this program from:

U.S. Public Health Service
Office of the Assistant Secretary for Health
Grants Policy Branch (COBRA)
5600 Fishers Lane
Room 17A-45
Rockville, Maryland 20857

At the end of this temporary extension of health care benefits, employees can elect to "convert" their group poli-

cy to an individual policy. Generally, the cost of an individual policy will be higher and the coverage will not be as comprehensive. They would, however, have health insurance coverage available to them and their families.

Employees may also extend health care benefits after they leave employment with the federal government. For more information, they should contact the personnel office serving their agency. Employees of state and local governments who are seeking extended health care benefits after termination of their jobs should contact their state and local Departments of Health and Human Services.

Other Sources of Private Health Insurance

If you cannot obtain private health insurance through an employer, there are several other places to look for it. This might be the case if your employer does not offer health insurance or his or her plan will not cover your child, or if you are self-employed or unemployed and not eligible for a public insurance program such as Medicaid.

Unions, Professional Associations, and Fraternal and Civic Organizations

If you belong to a union, professional association, or civic association, you may be able to get health insurance for yourself and your dependents through one of these groups. Many such groups offer health insurance plans as a benefit of membership. If you do not belong to such a group, you might be able to find one with appealing health benefits and join it.

Plans among the different groups vary, and many require "evidence of insurability." This means they can deny you insurance or limit your coverage (i.e., a pre-existing condition clause) based on your responses to questions about your current health and medical history or on the results of a medical examination they arrange for you.

Small Group Insurance Plans

If you work for a small employer, health insurance coverage may not be offered at all, or it may not cover your dependents. You can investigate, with your co-workers and supervisor, the possibility of a number of small employer groups joining together to get health insurance coverage as one group.

Many states have recently developed legislation to make it easier for small employers to obtain group health insurance coverage and offer it to their employees. In the past, it has been too expensive. *Premiums in small group plans will still be higher than in a much larger plan insuring many individuals, where the insurance company's "risk" is spread among a much larger number of people.*

Contact your State Department of Insurance or Communicating for Agriculture to find out it there are small employer health insurance programs your company can join. A list of State Departments of Health Insurance can be found in Appendix B at the end of this book. The address and telephone number of Communicating for Agriculture, a large advocacy group working for more and better health insurance options for self-employed people and small employers, is:

> Communicating for Agriculture
> 2626 East 82nd Street
> Suite 325
> Bloomington, Minnesota 55425
> 1-800-445-1525 (toll-free)
> (612) 854-9005

Health Insurance "Risk Pools"

As of January, 1994, individuals who have been refused health insurance because of their current health problems or health history can get health insurance in 27 states. These states have developed health insurance "risk pools." In "risk pools," *individuals are offered fee-for-service health coverage at rates that usually cannot exceed 125% of the private market rate for similar insurance.* Deductibles and copayments tend to be higher than those not in "risk pools," coverage tends to be less comprehensive, and there are often "pre-existing condition clauses" that limit or exclude coverage of certain conditions for as long as 2 years.

States with "risk pools" as of January, 1994 include the following:

Alaska	Missouri
California	Montana
Colorado	Nebraska
Connecticut	New Mexico
Florida	North Dakota
Georgia	Oregon
Illinois	South Carolina
Indiana	Tennessee
Iowa	Texas
Kansas	Utah
Louisiana	Washington
Maine	Wisconsin
Minnesota	Wyoming
Mississippi	

For more information about "risk pools," contact your State Department of Insurance (listed in Appendix B at the end of this book) or Communicating for Agriculture.

Special Individual Health Insurance Plans

Some states that do not have "risk pools" have individual special health insurance plans designed for individuals considered "medically uninsurable." This designation may be due to current health problems or a health history (e.g., congenital heart defect) that insurance companies believe puts the individual at risk of health problems.

Special individual health insurance plans operate in a way similar to "risk pools" and tend to be more costly and provide less coverage than private fee-for-service group insurance plans. If you can afford one, however, it can offer you health insurance for some major medical expenses you anticipate that would not be covered without such a program. *If your state is not included in the list of states with "risk pools" and you want to find out if your state has a special individual health insurance plan, contact your State Department of Insurance listed in Appendix B at the end of this book.*

The federal government and local and state governments are debating a number of health insurance proposals that would try to provide health insurance coverage to more Americans at more affordable costs.

PRIVATE NONPROFIT FOUNDATIONS

A number of private, nonprofit foundations provide help in paying for medical and related care, mostly on an outpatient basis. The referral sources provided in Chapter 3 suggest the names of such foundations you can approach in your area.

Among them are 25 "Caring" Programs across the United States established primarily to help pay for needed medical care for children. One of the program's priorities is helping families with children who have chronic illnesses and disabilities to afford the medical and related care their children need.

Each "Caring" Program varies in the organization of its programs, sponsorship, and range of services covered; however, the Blue Cross and Blue Shield organization pays a major role in most programs. To help ensure that there are enough funds to go around for all children in need, *all "Caring" Programs emphasize payment for preventative care* (e.g., well-child visits, immunizations) *and outpatient services* of all kinds including physician office visits for illness, diagnostic services, emergency care, outpatient medical and surgical procedures, outpatient therapies (i.e., physical therapy, occupational therapy), medical equipment, medical supplies, and prescribed medications. As an example, the "Caring Program for Children" based in Pittsburgh, Pennsylvania, has provided $8 million worth of health care and related services for children in western Pennsylvania since the program began in 1985.

Most of these programs try to help children from birth through 19 years of age (as long as they are still in school) when their families are considered "working poor." This means their families have incomes that are low but generally not low enough to make them eligible for Medicaid.

In addition to Blue Cross and Blue Shield's role in sponsoring "Caring" programs, contributions from businesses, religious organizations, civic groups including schools, and private individuals make these programs possible. The addresses and telephone numbers of the 25 "Caring" programs in existence as of January, 1993 are listed in Appendix B at the end of this book.

If your state does not yet have a "Caring" Program, and your family meets the general description above—lacking private health insurance, not eligible for Medicaid, seeking medical care for a child 19 years old or younger—you might want to call the Caring Program for Children in Pittsburgh, Pennsylvania, at (412) 645-6202. It is one of the oldest "Caring" Programs and may have some leads for you on private sources of help in your state.

Disease- and Disability-Related Organizations

For nearly every chronic illness and disability, there is a related organization that has developed to increase public awareness about the disease or disability, to disseminate information about the illness or condition to interested parties, and to serve as an advocacy group. Many such organizations fund basic research on the illness or condition of their interest. *In most cases, organizations can direct you to sources of different kinds of financial assistance even if they do not provide financial aid for medical care themselves.*

Consistent with the approach taken throughout this book, this author recommends calling a national parent support or advocacy organization before contacting any organization listed below. Such parent organizations have years of experience seeking resources. Let them know what you or your child's particular needs are. At a minimum, get their response to your plan of action in seeking private assistance to pay for medical and related care.

Ask which organizations have been particularly responsive in their experience, and what approaches to getting help from such groups have been successful. After you have done this, you can more comfortably and confidently approach a number of private sources of help. *At that time, approach as many organizations as seems reasonable,* including the disease- or disability-related organization that represents children with conditions similar to your child's.

In the spring of 1992, the executive offices of 45 national organizations representing a range of chronic illnesses and disabilities affecting children were sent a 2-page survey asking several questions, including the following:

• Does your national organization or its local chapters provide any financial assistance to families of children with the illness or disability represented by your organization, to help them pay for medical and related care?
• If yes, is assistance provided on an emergency or other basis for any of the following:
    Prescription medicines
    Medical equipment (e.g., braces)
    Medical supplies (e.g., catheter tubes, syringes)

Medical transportation

Other needs (please specify)

Organizations that did not respond to the initial questionnaire were sent a duplicate survey 2 months later with a follow-up letter urging them to respond. Appendix 6A highlights the kinds of help available from the disease- and disability-related organizations that responded to the survey. From the list in Appendix 6A (pp. 207–222), you will see that *most disease- and disability-related organizations that offer financial help for medical care often offer help for medical equipment, medical supplies, and prescribed medications. Many, however, only offer such help on an emergency or short-term basis.*

A number of disease- and disability-related organizations also offer financial assistance for other necessities of life and a number of kinds of loans and scholarships, and can refer individuals and families to other sources of financial help.

Help is most often offered at the local level through chapters of these national organizations. The national offices (listed in Appendix 6A and Appendix B at the end of this book) can refer you to the chapter nearest your home. If you need financial help for any medical or related care for your child, or for any other need, *be sure to try one or more of the organizations related to your child's condition.* Try this along with other ideas for assistance outlined in this book.

Civic, Social Welfare, and Religious Organizations

In addition to disease- and disability-related organizations, *a number of civic, social welfare, and religious organizations help children with special health care needs.* They do this largely by raising money to give to a group of children or by purchasing needed medication, equipment, or supplies directly.

Civic Organizations

Many *civic organizations* have a specific charity they sponsor on a national basis (e.g., Grottoes of North America provides dental care for children younger than 18 years of age with mental retardation, cerebral palsy, muscular dystrophy, or myasthenia gravis). In other cases, local chapters of national organizations sponsor specific illness or disability groups in their area. Still other local chapters of national civic organizations decide annually on a charity or "cause" to sponsor for a given year.

Again, **before approaching any particular organization, talk with members of one or more national parent advocacy organizations** (listed in Chapter 3 and Appendix B at the end of this book). **These groups can supply leads for you and help you plan a strategy to approach a number of groups.** These parent groups have knowledge of which groups fund which kinds of needs, particularly at the local level.

After you have consulted with a national parent advocacy organization, contact civic, social welfare, and religious organizations locally. **A civic group may help you or your group by sponsoring an ongoing activity or specific fund-raising event for this purpose.** This has a better chance of happening if one of the members of the civic group has a child or a grandchild with a chronic illness or disability. *It also helps if a member of the civic group introduces the idea to his or her fellow members.* If you do not know a member of the civic group to approach, a friend, relative, or co-worker may be able to introduce you to that person.

Be sure to find out about the planning cycle of the groups you want to approach. In most cases, each group has a specific time in the year when proposals are put forward for discussion of possible fund-raising events.

If a civic organization cannot raise funds for you, it may help you or a local group to set up a fund-raising event

to collect money for medical care for children with chronic illnesses and disabilities in your local community. Civic groups are experienced with organizing these kinds of projects in local communities.

Community high schools and area college sororities and fraternities are not formally surveyed in this book, but in the author's experience, they have demonstrated a great deal of enthusiasm and skill in fund-raising for charitable causes. As with other local groups, you might approach them to hold benefits or to set up ongoing funds for medical equipment, supplies, prescription medications, and transportation for children with chronic illness and disabilities in your community.

University Benevolent Funds can also be a source of financial aid for medical emergencies. Many universities collect funds in addition to what they might collect for an organization such as United Way. These additional funds are usually available on an emergency basis to employees of the university and their dependents. Requests for help generally must be submitted to a committee in the university for approval. Contact any university in your community where one of your family members works to see if they have such a benevolent fund.

Social Welfare Organizations

Many social welfare organizations provide families with needed medical equipment, supplies, pharmacy items, or transportation to medical care, or they offer to pay for these needs. Again, as with disease- and disability-related organizations, this seems most possible **on an emergency or temporary basis.** This is largely due to funding limitations and a belief that public organizations should provide for these needs on a permanent basis. **Social welfare organizations can and do help many families enroll in programs to provide this kind of help on a more permanent basis** (e.g.,

Medicaid) or other programs that could provide additional income to pay for medical care (e.g., SSI).

More than 60 national civic, social welfare, and religious organizations were sent a questionnaire in the spring of 1992 and, if they had not responded, a duplicate survey and letter 2 months later. More than two dozen organizations were interviewed by telephone between January and April of 1993 to follow up on the survey responses. Questions asked were similar to those asked in the questionnaire sent to disease- and disability-related organizations (see pp. 197–198).

Most organizations responding indicated the kind of financial aid they could give, even if it was not for medical and related care. ***Most civic, social welfare, or religious organizations noted that they could help families get such aid if they could not supply it directly.*** The civic and social welfare organizations that responded that they can assist families are listed in Appendix 6B, along with brief descriptions of the help they can offer and addresses and telephone numbers.

Religious Organizations

Religious organizations can also provide help to a family trying to manage any difficulty involved with raising a child with a chronic illness or disability, including the stress on the family because of the high costs of care. In times of stress, it is natural for a family to turn to a member of the clergy for help. Clergy can often provide both emotional support and specific leads to help resolve problems causing stress.

In addition, ***most churches have emergency assistance funds and emergency loan funds. Clergy can also refer you to sources of both temporary and longer-term financial help, including multidenominational sponsored "ministries."*** Certainly, you can approach your own clergy if possible. If this is not possible, or you do not want to speak to someone you know, you may follow the guidelines given below by the pastoral offices of the major religious denominations.

Baptist

To request help from the Baptist Church, you have one of two choices:

1. *Contact the minister of any Baptist church in your community.* You can find these churches listed in the yellow pages telephone directory under "Churches" or "Churches and Synagogues."
2. *Call the "Baptist Association" closest to your home.* You may be able to find their telephone number in the business section of the white pages telephone directory or in the yellow pages directory under "Churches" or "Religious Organizations." If you have trouble getting their telephone number, call your local "Information Operator" or one of the Baptist churches in your community.

Catholic

For help through an organization affiliated with the Catholic Church, you can try one of two things:

1. *Contact the nearest "Catholic Charities" office.* This agency can be reached directly, through the business section of the white pages telephone directory, or through a local priest, parish office, or diocese office. Telephone numbers for Catholic churches in your community can be found in the yellow pages telephone book under "Churches" or "Churches and Synagogues." Telephone numbers for parish or diocese offices of the Catholic church can usually be found in the business section of the white pages telephone book.

2. If you are not able to reach a "Catholic Charities" office, *contact the social services department of Catholic Charities U.S.A.* This organization can refer you to an agency in your community that can help.

    Catholic Charities USA
    1731 King Street
    Suite 200
    Alexandria, Virginia 22314
    (703) 549-1390

Episcopal

You can receive help through the Episcopal Church in one of two ways:

1. *Contact the minister of any Episcopal church in your community.* The listings for all Episcopal churches in your area are usually given in the yellow pages telephone book under "Churches" or "Churches and Synagogues."
2. *Contact your local Episcopal diocese.* You should be able to find it listed in the business section of the white pages telephone directory under "Episcopal Diocese."

Jewish

To receive financial assistance from a Jewish synagogue, temple, or Jewish organization:

1. *Contact the rabbi of any synagogue or temple in your area.* Synagogues and temples are listed in the yellow pages telephone directory under "Churches and Synagogues" or "Religious Organizations."
2. *Contact the Jewish Family Services Agency or the Jewish Federation Office in your area.* These organizations will either help you directly or refer you to someone who can. You can find these Jewish organizations listed in alphabetical order in the business section of the local

white pages telephone book, or you can ask your local information operator for the number.

Lutheran

For help through the Lutheran Church, you have two options:

1. *Contact the minister of any Lutheran church in your area.* You can find a listing of Lutheran churches in the yellow pages telephone directory under "Churches" and "Churches and Synagogues."
2. *Contact the Lutheran Social Services Agency nearest to your home.* If this agency is not listed in the business section of the white pages telephone book, you can get their number from an information operator or from any Lutheran church in your community.

Presbyterian

The Presbyterian Church can help in one of two ways:

1. *Contact the minister of any Presbyterian church in your community.* Presbyterian churches are listed in the yellow pages telephone book under "Churches" or "Churches and Synagogues."
2. *Call the "Presbytery" (regional office) in the major city closest to your home.* They will give you a referral for help in your local community. Check the business section of the local white pages directory for the telephone number or call your local information operator.

Methodist

To receive help from a church or organization affiliated with the Methodist Church:

1. *Contact the minister of any Methodist church in your area.* The telephone number of all Methodist churches in your community can be found under

"Churches" or "Churches and Synagogues" in the yellow pages telephone directory.

2. *Contact your area Methodist Bishop's Office.* You can get the telephone number from the local information operator or from any Methodist church in your community.

Other Denominations

Contact the minister of any church in or near your community. He or she can help direct you to the most promising sources for assistance with your child's or family's particular need. **Church-sponsored "ministries"** are often inter-denominational and exist in many large communities to help families. **They offer emergency help for food, clothing, shelter, prescription medications, furniture, rent, and so forth. They can refer a family to a variety of longer-term assistance** (e.g., Supplemental Security Income for Children, Medicaid, Aid to Families with Dependent Children, Food Stamps, Surplus Food Distribution). You can locate such a "ministry" by calling your community Information and Referral Service (often sponsored by United Way) or any church or synagogue in your community.

SUMMARY

Private health insurance, even with its current limitations, remains one of the best ways to pay for medical and related care for your child. A comprehensive private health insurance policy of any kind that covers your child will limit your out-of-pocket medical costs and give you peace of mind that you can obtain the care your child needs.

If you do not have private health insurance or have a modest policy that leaves you with many medical bills, there are other private sources of help for medical and related care for your child. Many disease- and disability-

related, civic, social welfare, and religious organizations have funds available for at least emergency or short-term medical needs. Local charitable foundations can help as well.

This chapter is only intended to be a starting point as you think about possible resources in your community or region. Ask the professionals you consult with and local advocacy groups for leads on private sources of help for financing your child's care. Also ask your Chamber of Commerce about local businesses who have donated money at Christmas or other times during the year to causes that help children. Pursue these leads yourself or with other parents whose children have chronic illnesses or disabilities.

Think creatively and be as resourceful as possible. Try not to become frustrated when a source or two cannot or will not help you. Realize that it will take time and effort to get the help you need. Your efforts and persistence should be well worth the time your search will require. In the process, you will be educating a large number of business and community leaders about the needs of children like yours and the ways community leaders can get involved and help.

*Selected
Disease- and
Disability-
Related
Organizations*

This appendix lists disease- and disability-related organizations that responded to the survey the author conducted to develop this book (see Preface). For each organization, a brief overview of the help it provides is listed, as well as the organization's address and telephone number(s). Other organizations of potential help are listed in Appendix B at the end of this book.

American Council of the Blind

This organization provides scholarships to postsecondary students who are blind, for academic, professional, and technical training programs. For more information, contact:

American Council of the Blind
1155 15th Street, N.W., Suite 720
Washington, D.C. 20005
1-800-426-8666 (toll-free)
(202) 424-8666

American Foundation for the Blind

Although this group does not provide direct financial assistance for medical care or supplies, it does provide personal loans for Kurzweil automated readers that scan book pages and read them. This organization also provides a variety of kinds of scholarships and can direct you to sources of financial assistance. For more information, contact:

American Foundation for the Blind
15 West 16th Street
New York, New York 10011
1-800-232-5463 (toll-free)

American Heart Association

No direct financial assistance for medical care is offered by the national office of this organization. Many state and local chapters offer such support. If not, they can refer you to other sources of financial assistance for children with heart conditions and their families. For more information, or referral to a chapter near you, contact:

American Heart Association
7272 Greenville Avenue
Dallas, Texas 75231-4596
1-800-242-8721 (toll-free)
(214) 373-6300

American Juvenile Arthritis Organization

This group is primarily an information and advocacy organization for parents of children with arthritis or rheumatic diseases. Although the national office does not provide financial assistance to families themselves, some local and state chapters do. The national office can direct families to state and local chapters and other sources of help. For more information, contact:

American Juvenile Arthritis Organization
1314 Spring Street, N.W.
Atlanta, Georgia 30309
(404) 872-7100

American Lung Association

The national office of this organization was not aware of any chapter programs to provide financial help to families for their children's medical needs. Many chapters, however, are trained to refer families to other sources for financial assistance. For more information, contact:

American Lung Association
1740 Broadway
New York, New York 10019
(212) 315-8700

American Lupus Society

No direct financial aid for medical care is available through this national organization. Its staff can, however, refer you to a number of sources for financial assistance. For more information, contact:

American Lupus Society
3914 Del Amo Boulevard
Suite 922
Torrance, California 90503
1-800-331-1802 (toll-free)
(310) 542-8891

American Society for Deaf Children (ASDC)

No financial aid for medical care is directly available from this organization, but it can refer you to a number of resources for financial aid for children with hearing problems.

American Society for Deaf Children
814 Thayer Avenue
Silver Spring, Maryland 20910
1-800-942-ASDC (Voice or TT) (toll-free)

The Arc (formerly The Association for Retarded Citizens of the United States)

No financial aid for medical care is available at the national level. Some local chapters provide assistance directly, and all can provide referral to sources of financial aid for children with mental retardation and related disorders. Look for your local Arc chapter in the business section of your telephone directory, or call the national office of The Arc for a referral:

The Arc
500 East Border Street
Suite 300
Arlington, Texas 76006
1-800-433-5255 (toll-free)

Asthma and Allergy Foundation of America

This organization offers pilot programs to provide prescription medications to children with severe asthma and low family incomes. They can also refer you to other resources for financial assistance. For more information, contact:

Asthma and Allergy Foundation of America
1125 15th Street, N.W.
Suite 502
Washington, D.C. 20005
1-800-7-ASTHMA (toll-free)
(202) 466-7643

Autism Society of America

No direct financial assistance for medical care is available from this national organization. The staff can, however, refer you to state and local chapters that may offer financial help and other sources for aid for children with autism and their families. For more information, contact:

Autism Society of America
8601 Georgia Avenue
Suite 503
Silver Spring, Maryland 20910
(301) 565-0433

Candlelighters Childhood Cancer Foundation

Local chapters provide financial help to families to pay for medical equipment, medical supplies, prescribed medications, transportation to medical care, and medical procedures not covered by private or public insurance. For more information, contact the Candlelighters Childhood Cancer Foundation for referral to the chapter nearest your home:

Candlelighters Childhood Cancer Foundation
1312 18th Street, N.W.
Suite 200
Washington, D.C. 20036
1-800-366-2223
(202) 659-5136

Children and Adults with Attention Deficit Disorders (CH.A.D.D.)

No financial aid for medical care is offered by this national organization. It can, however, offer help seeking aid elsewhere for children with attention deficit disorders and their families. For more information, contact:

Children and Adults with Attention Deficit Disorders
499 Northwest 70th Avenue
Suite 308
Plantation, Florida 33317
(305) 587-3700

Cleft Palate Foundation

This group does not provide financial assistance itself, but suggests March of Dimes, Grottoes of North America, and National Association for the Craniofacially Handicapped for aid for medical and related care for children with cleft palates. For more information, contact:

Cleft Palate Foundation
1218 Grandview Avenue
Pittsburgh, Pennsylvania 15211
1-800-24-CLEFT (toll-free)
(412) 481-1376

Crohn's and Colitis Foundation of America, Inc.

This national organization has a program to help families purchase prescribed medications and vitamins at reduced costs for children affected by these conditions. State and local chapters may offer additional financial help. The national organization and chapters can refer families to a number of resources for financial assistance. For more information, contact:

Crohn's and Colitis Foundation of America, Inc.
386 Park Avenue South
New York, New York 10016-7374
1-800-343-3637 (toll-free)
(212) 685-3440

Cystic Fibrosis Foundation (CFF)

This group provides some medical services in the community (this varies by chapter), sponsors a cystic fibrosis pharmacy that provides 150 medications at discount prices, has a national network of home health care services specifically designed for individuals with cystic fibrosis that costs less than other home health care, provides general medical care and treatment for individuals with cystic fibrosis in 120 CFF centers across the United States, offers vocational rehabilitation, gives financial assistance to students, and can connect you with other resources for help paying for medical care. For more information, contact:

Cystic Fibrosis Foundation
6931 Arlington Road
Bethesda, Maryland 29814-5200
1-800-FIGHT CF (toll-free)
(301) 951-4442

Epilepsy Foundation of America

Members of this organization can purchase prescription medications at a discount through a mail-order program of the American Association of Retired Persons (AARP). Some local and state chapters offer additional financial aid.

The Epilepsy Foundation of America can direct families to local and state chapters and to other resources for assistance paying for medical care. For more information, contact:

Epilepsy Foundation of America
4351 Garden City Drive, Suite 406
Landover, Maryland 20785
1-800-EFA-1000 (toll-free)
(301) 459-3700

Federation of Families for Children's Mental Health

No financial aid for medical care is offered by this group, but it can help direct families to sources of aid for medical care and other necessities of living. For more information, contact:

Federation of Families for Children's Mental Health
1021 Prince Street
Alexandria, Virginia 22314-2971
(703) 684-7710

Juvenile Diabetes Foundation International

This organization funds research on diabetes and provides information to families, teachers, and other professionals who live or work with children with diabetes.

Some chapters provide limited financial assistance for medication, and most chapters can refer a family to sources for financial help in their community. For more information, contact:

Juvenile Diabetes Foundation International
432 Park Avenue South
New York, New York 10016
1-800-JDF-CURE (toll-free)

Learning Disability Association of America

This organization does not provide financial assistance to families, but chapters can refer them to other sources for this help. For more information, contact:

Learning Disability Association of America
4156 Library Road
Pittsburgh, Pennsylvania 15234
(412) 341-1515 or (412) 341-8077

Leukemia Society of America

Patient Aid Program of Leukemia Society gives as much as $750 a year to individuals in outpatient care for costs not covered by health insurance or other programs, prescription medications, x-rays, blood services, and transportation to medical care. Some local chapters provide additional financial aid to families. The national organization and its chapters can also help individuals and families locate other sources of financial aid for medical care and other needs. For more information, contact:

Leukemia Society of America
600 Third Avenue
New York, New York 10016
1-800-955-4LSA (toll-free)
(212) 573-8484

Lupus Foundation of America

No financial assistance for medical care is available from this national organization, but this group can steer you to local chapters and other sources of aid. For more information, contact:

Lupus Foundation of America
4 Research Place
Suite 180
Rockville, Maryland 20850-3226
1-800-670-9292 (toll-free)
(301) 670-9292

March of Dimes Birth Defects Foundation

No direct financial assistance to families is provided by this national organization, but its staff can refer families to local chapters and other places for this kind of help. For more information, contact:

March of Dimes Birth Defects Foundation
1275 Mamaroneck Avenue
White Plains, New York 10605
(914) 428-7100

Muscular Dystrophy Association, Inc. (MDA)

MDA sponsors a network of services from approximately 235 clinics across the United States for diagnostic services, therapy, and rehabilitative services for individuals with any muscular dystrophy, amyotropic lateral sclerosis, Charcot-Marie-Tooth disease, myasthenia gravis, and other spinal muscular atrophies. Genetic and social service counseling is also offered to individuals and families.

Individuals with muscular dystrophy can also purchase selected orthopedic appliances and daily living aids and have them repaired through the MDA.

Also provided are physical and occupational therapy evaluations; help in paying for physical, occupational, and respiratory therapy treatments; orthopedic equipment (e.g., braces, wheelchairs, walkers, hospital beds, hydraulic lifts) rental and repair; and other medical equipment (e.g., aspirators, nebulizers); influenza shots, educational and recreational activity, and assistance with transportation.

For more information about any of these services or for a referral to other sources of financial aid, contact:

Muscular Dystrophy Association, Inc.
3300 East Sunrise Drive
Tucson, Arizona 85718
(602) 529-2000

National Alliance for the Mentally Ill (NAMI), Children and Adolescent Network (CAN)

CAN does not provide direct financial assistance, but can refer families to such help. For more information, contact:

National Alliance for the Mentally Ill, Children and
  Adolescent Network
2101 Wilson Boulevard, Suite 302
Arlington, Virginia 22201
(703) 524-7600
1-800-950-NAMI (toll-free)

National Association of the Deaf (NAD)

No financial assistance for medical care is available, however NAD can refer you to other sources for aid. It also has a legal defense fund. For more information, contact:

National Association of the Deaf
814 Thayer Avenue
Silver Spring, Maryland 20910
(301) 587-1788 (Voice and TT)

National Association for Sickle Cell Disease, Inc.

Local chapters of this organization provide some financial assistance for medical care for children with sickle cell disease. They can also refer you for additional help paying for medical care and other needs.

Consult the business section of your local telephone directory for the number of the local chapter nearest your home, or call the national organization for a referral:

National Association for Sickle Cell Disease, Inc.
3345 Wilshire Boulevard
Suite 1106
Los Angeles, California 90010-1880
1-800-421-8453 (toll-free)
(213) 736-5455

National Association for the Visually Handicapped

No financial assistance for medical care is offered. This organization, however, can make some suggestions for resources for financial help. Contact:

National Association for the Visually Handicapped
22 West 21st Street, 6th Floor
New York, New York 10010
(212) 889-3141

National Down Syndrome Congress (NDSC)

No financial aid for medical care is available from this group directly, but they can refer you to sources of aid elsewhere. For more information, contact:

National Down Syndrome Congress
1800 Dempster Street
Park Ridge, Illinois 60068-1146
1-800-232-6372 (toll-free outside Illinois)
1-800-823-7550 (toll-free in Illinois)

National Down Syndrome Society

As a general rule, this organization does not provide financial assistance for a child's medical care. It can, however, refer families to community resources for this assistance. For more information, contact:

National Down Syndrome Society
666 Broadway, Suite 810
New York, New York 10012
1-800-221-4602 (toll-free)

National Easter Seal Society

The National Easter Seal Society maintains a "Technology-Related Loan Fund" to help families buy assistive technology (e.g., wheelchairs, braces, communication devices) on an installation plan.

Additionally, 100 Canon Communicators are available to help individuals with hearing and speech problems, motor disabilities, and those who are both deaf and blind.

The National Easter Seal Society also offers computer-assisted technology services (CATS) to provide affordable technology to facilitate employment and quality of life for individuals with disabilities.

This organization also provides services for the following:

- Speech-language therapy
- Medical and nursing treatment
- Physical therapy and prosthetic care
- Home health services
- Vocational education, occupational therapy, and job training and placement
- Individual and family counseling
- Camping, recreation, and social services

Finally, the National Easter Seal Society can refer individuals and families to other resources for financial assistance for medical care or other needs. For more information on any of these programs, contact:

National Easter Seal Society
70 East Lake Street
Chicago, Illinois 60601
1-800-221-6827 (toll-free)
(312) 726-6200
(312) 726-4258 (TT)

National Fragile X Foundation

No financial assistance for medical care is offered directly, but this group can help direct you to assistance. For more information, contact:

National Fragile X Foundation
1441 York Street, Suite 215
Denver, Colorado 80206
1-800-688-8765 (toll-free)

National Head Injury Foundation

No financial aid for medical care is offered directly by the National Head Injury Foundation; however, it can refer individuals to financial help through the "Family Helpline." For more information, contact:

National Head Injury Foundation
1140 Connecticut Avenue, N.W.
Suite 812
Washington, D.C. 10026
1-800-444-NHIF (toll-free "Family Helpline")
(202) 296-6443

National Hemophilia Foundation (NHF)

The national office of the National Hemophilia Foundation does not provide financial assistance to individuals and families to pay for medical and related care. The 46 local chapters of the Foundation, however, have emergency assistance funds that can pay for emergency medical expenses (e.g., prescribed medication, wheelchair repair). They can also refer you to other sources of financial aid. If you cannot find a chapter of the National Hemophilia Foundation in the business section of your telephone book, contact the national office for a referral:

National Hemophilia Foundation
The Soho Building
110 Greene Street, Suite 406
New York, New York 10012
(212) 219-8180

National Kidney Foundation, Inc.

Some local chapters of the National Kidney Foundation offer financial assistance to children with kidney disease. Typically, they might help pay for prescription medications or transportation to medical care. This organization can also refer you to other sources for financial aid.

Contact the local chapter nearest your home. You can find its telephone number in the business section of your white pages telephone directory, from your local information operator, or by contacting the national office:

National Kidney Foundation, Inc.
30 East 33rd Street, 11th Floor
New York, New York 10016
1-800-622-9010 (toll-free)

National Organization for Rare Disorders, Inc. (NORD)

NORD does not generally provide financial assistance for medical care for children with rare disorders, but it can refer families for this help. Through NORD, the Sandoz Pharmaceutical Company provides all of the drugs it manufactures and a drug called Carnitor at no charge to children whose families have low incomes. For more information, contact:

National Organization for Rare Disorders, Inc.
Post Office Box 8923
New Fairfield, Connecticut 06182-1783
1-800-937-NORD (toll-free)

National Spinal Cord Injury Association

No financial aid for medical care itself is available from this national organization; however, Malmberg travel group offers members travel discounts, including hotel costs. For more information, contact:

National Spinal Cord Injury Association
600 West Cummings Park, Suite 2000
Woburn, Massachusetts 01801-6379
1-800-962-9629 (toll-free)
(617) 962-9629

Spina Bifida Association of America

No financial assistance is available for medical care directly from this national organization. Some state and local chapter offer help paying for some medical care. The national organization can refer you to the chapter nearest your home and to other resources for help. For more information, contact:

Spina Bifida Association of America
4590 MacArthur Boulevard, Suite 250
Washington, D.C. 20007
1-800-621-3141 (toll-free)
(202) 944-3285

United Cerebral Palsy Association (UCP)

The national office of UCP does not provide financial aid for medical care for children with cerebral palsy. Many local chapters of UCP provide some help.

Contact the local chapter of UCP nearest your home. You should be able to find them listed in the business section of your white pages telephone book. If you cannot, call the national office of UCP for referral to that chapter:

United Cerebral Palsy Association
1522 K Street, N.W.
Washington, D.C. 20005
1-800-872-5827 (toll-free)
(202) 842-1266 (Voice or TT)

Appendix 6B

Selected Civic and Social Welfare Organizations

This appendix lists civic and social welfare organizations that responded to the author's survey of private sources of help for families with children who have chronic illness and disabilities (see Preface). For each organization, a brief description of available help is given, in addition to the organization's address and telephone number(s).

Aid Association for Lutherans

Local offices of this national association help families pay for medical equipment, medical supplies, and transportation to medical care. They do not, however, help pay for prescription medications. As examples, local offices have supplied wheelchairs to children, and have helped equip vans to carry wheelchairs or to be driven by individuals with disabilities who require special modifications of vans to drive themselves.

Contact your local Aid Association for Lutherans for more information. You can find local telephone numbers in the business section of the white pages telephone directory, or you can call your local information operator for the number. If you have any trouble reaching your local chapter, contact the national office for a referral to the chapter:

Aid Association for Lutherans
4321 North Ballard
Appleton, Wisconsin 54919-0001
(414) 734-5721

American Friends Service Committee

No financial aid is available from this organization for medical care; however, it can assist individuals and families in reaching other sources of financial assistance. For more information, contact:

American Friends Service Committee
1501 Cherry Street
Philadelphia, Pennsylvania 19102
(215) 241-7000

American Red Cross

The national office of the American Red Cross does not provide financial aid for medical or related care for individuals. Wealthier chapters may give emergency help for this on a case-by-case basis.

In addition, some local chapters have volunteers who provide transportation for individuals with disabilities to and from doctors' offices and other medical care facilities.

To find out if these services are available in your local community, call your local chapter of the American Red Cross. You can find their telephone number in the business section of the white pages telephone book. For more information, contact:

American Red Cross
17th and D Streets, N.W.
Washington, D.C. 20006
(202) 737-8300

Association of Jewish
Family and Children's Agencies, Inc.

The national office of this organization does not provide aid for medical care. Some of the 145 member agencies *do* provide help for medical equipment, medical supplies, prescribed medications, transportation to medical care, and so forth. Those that do not can connect families to other resources for assistance. You can find out about the availability of these services in your local community by contacting the national office:

Association of Jewish Family and Children's
   Agencies, Inc.
Post Office Box 248
Kendall Park, New Jersey 08824
1-800-821-0909 (toll-free)

Association of Junior Leagues International, Inc.

The international office of this organization does not provide financial aid for medical care of any kind. Some local Junior Leagues do, but usually on a special project basis.

Contact your local Junior League to see if it can help you. You can find their telephone number in the business section of the white pages telephone directory, or you may contact the international office:

Association of Junior Leagues International, Inc.
660 First Avenue
New York, New York 10016-3241
(212) 683-1515

Catholic Charities, U.S.A.

Local Catholic Charities offices fund some medical care. Contact the Catholic Charities nearest your home to see what kind of assistance they can provide. You should be able to find their number in the business section of the white pages telephone directory, or you may ask your local information operator for the telephone number. If you have trouble locating your local Catholic Charities agency, contact:

Catholic Charities, U.S.A.
1732 King Street
Suite 200
Alexandria, Virginia 22314
(703) 549-1390

Civitan World Headquarters

Local chapters of this organization can help families purchase prescription medications, medical equipment, and supplies for children with mental retardation or developmental disabilities. Of the money collected in Civitan candy boxes, 100% goes exclusively to helping families and children in these ways. Civitan chapters are also experienced in directing families to other sources for financial help. For more information, contact:

Civitan World Headquarters
1401 52nd Street South
Birmingham, Alabama 35213
1-800-CIVITAN (toll-free)
(205) 591-8910

Council for Health and Human Service Ministries

This organization does not provide financial help to individual families for medical and related care. It can, however, make referrals to other sources for financial assistance with medical care and other needs. For more information, contact:

Council for Health and Human Service Ministries
700 Prospect Avenue
Cleveland, Ohio 44115
(216) 736-2250

Elks National Foundation

The national office of the Elks does not provide payments for medical care. Local Elks lodges may provide some of this help to children with chronic illnesses or disabilities.

Contact your local Elks lodge to see if it funds any medical help for children or could be encouraged by you to do so. You can find their telephone number in the business section of the white pages telephone book. If you have any trouble reaching a local lodge, contact the national office for a referral:

Elks National Foundation
2750 Lake View Avenue
Chicago, Illinois 60614
(312) 929-2100

General Grand Chapter, Order of the Eastern Star

This national organization does not provide assistance for medical care; however, state chapters may be approached to do so.

Each state chapter selects its own fund-raising project each year. A state or local chapter could be approached to set up a fund to provide for medical equipment, medical supplies, prescription medications, and/or medical transportation for children with chronic illnesses or disabilities who do not have a way to pay for these needed items. Contact the national chapter to get a referral to your state chapter:

General Grand Chapter
Order of the Eastern Star
1618 New Hampshire Avenue, N.W.
Washington, D.C. 20009
(202) 667-4737

Grottoes of North America

Grottoes of North America pays for dental care on a pre-authorized basis for children younger than 18 years old who have mental retardation, cerebral palsy, muscular dystrophy, or myasthenia gravis. Both inpatient and outpatient dental care is covered, except for orthodontics and reconstructive jaw surgery. For additional information or a referral to a dentist, contact:

Supreme Council, M.O.V.P.E.R.
1696 Brice Road
Reynoldsburg, Ohio 43068
(614) 860-9193

International Association of Lions Clubs

The international organization does not assist in paying for children's medical care; however, local chapters do. Local chapters can help provide eye care, with a priority given to children with visual impairments. Some chapters provide *at no cost to qualified applicants* eye examinations, eyeglasses, prescription eye medications, artificial eyes, emergency hospital care, and surgery and hospital fees as funds permit.

For help, contact your local Lions Club chapter. You should be able to find their telephone number for it in the business section of the local white pages telephone directory. If you cannot, contact the international office for a referral to the chapter nearest your home:

Association of Lions Clubs
300 22nd Street
Oak Brook, Illinois 60521-3137
(708) 571-5466

International Sunshine Society

As funds allow, they are available from this organization for medical equipment, medical supplies, prescription medications, and transportation to medical care. For more information, contact:

International Sunshine Society
105 Marsh Boulevard
Wilmington, Delaware 19809-3137
(302) 764-1405

Kiwanis International

The international organization does not fund medical care for children; however, local clubs may have such funds available. Local clubs could also be encouraged to establish a fund for emergency needs for medical equipment, supplies, prescription medications, and transportation for local children with chronic illnesses or disabilities. For more information or a referral to a local chapter, contact:

Kiwanis International
3636 Woodview Trace
Indianapolis, Indiana 46268-3196
1-800-879-4769 (toll-free)
(312) 875-8755

Knights of Columbus

Most Knights of Columbus chapters can provide financial assistance for children who need prescription medications, medical equipment, medical supplies, and transportation to medical care.

Although the Knights of Columbus is a civic organization affiliated with the Catholic Church, *families seeking financial assistance for medical care for their children do not have to be Catholic.*

Look for their telephone number for your local Knights of Columbus chapter in the business section of the white pages telephone directory. If you have any trouble reaching the local chapter, contact the national organization:

Knights of Columbus
1 Columbus Plaza
New Haven, Connecticut 06510-3326
(203) 772-2130

National Coalition of Hispanic Health and Human Services Organizations

This national organization does not provide payments for medical care directly, but it can refer families to local resources in their community. For more information, contact:

National Coalition of Hispanic Health and Human
  Services Organizations
1501 16th Street, N.W.
Washington, D.C. 20036
(202) 387-5000

National Flotation Health Care Foundation

This organization does not provide financial assistance directly for medical equipment and supplies, prescription medications, or medical transportation.

The organization does, however, provide flotation bedrest devices to individuals with medical and financial needs with the recommendation of a professional. These devices are often used for arthritis, back ailments, or burn injuries and to prevent decubitus ulcers. *Flotation bedrest devices*

are donated to those in need. For an application or more
information, contact:

> National Flotation Health Care Foundation
> Attention: Review Committee
> 5757 West Century Boulevard, Suite 512
> Los Angeles, California 90045
> 1-800-221-2928 (toll-free)
> (213) 417-8075

New Eyes for the Needy

This project of the Junior League of Short Hills, New Jersey
pays for eyeglasses for individuals with low incomes who
need eyeglasses but have no other way to obtain them.

New Eyes for the Needy suggest using Lions Club
chapters or low-vision clinics of public city hospitals for
free or low-cost eye examinations. For more information,
contact:

> New Eyes for the Needy
> Post Office Box 332
> 549 Millburn Avenue
> Short Hills, New Jersey 07078
> (201) 376-4903

Ruritan National

Local Ruritan clubs, of which there are 1,428 across the United
States, help families pay for medical equipment and supplies, prescription medications, and medical transportation.

Check the business section of your local white pages
telephone directory for a listing of the Ruritan chapter in
your community. If you cannot find a local chapter or would
like more information, contact:

Ruritan National
Post Office Box 487
Dublin, Virginia 24984
(703) 674-5431

Salvation Army

Local units of the Salvation Army can offer emergency financial assistance to families. You can find a local office in the business section of the local white pages telephone book, or you can get the telephone number from your local information operator. If you have a problem or need more information, contact:

Salvation Army
National Headquarters
615 Slaters Lane
Post Office Box 269
Alexandria, Virginia 22313
(703) 684-5500

Shrine of North America
and Shriners Hospitals for Crippled Children

Shriners Hospitals provide free care to children with orthopedic problems or burns. They do not, however, offer direct financial help for outpatient medications or medical transportation. For more information or to get an application for service, contact:

Shriners Hospitals for Crippled Children
Post Office Box 31356
2900 Rocky Point Drive
Tampa, Florida 33631-3356
1-800-237-0555 (toll-free outside Florida)
1-800-282-9161 (toll-free in Florida)

St. Jude Children's Research Hospital

St. Jude Children's Research Hospital does not offer direct financial aid, but offers free medical care to children with cancer of any kind, including AIDS-related cancers. For more information, contact:

> St. Jude Children's Research Hospital
> One St. Jude Place Building
> 501 St. Jude Place
> Post Office Box 3704
> Memphis, Tennessee 38103
> 1-800-USS-JUDE (toll-free)
> (901) 522-9733

Support Dogs for the Handicapped, Inc.

This organization provides training and placement of service dogs to increase the independence of individuals 17 years old and older who have one or more disabilities.

Younger children with disabilities are visited at home weekly or bi-weekly by TOUCH dogs for companionship.

A small charge is requested for these services. For more information, contact:

> Support Dogs for the Handicapped, Inc.
> 301 Sovereign Court, Suite 113
> St. Louis, Missouri 60311
> (314) 394-6163

Traveler's Aid International

Local Traveler's Aid agencies help individuals and families in crisis; however, *only short-term crisis intervention is available.* This could include a situation in which a child had a medical emergency.

Traveler's Aid is listed in the business section of the local white pages telephone book or under "Social Service

Agencies" in the yellow pages directory. If you have a problem reaching this agency, you can get a referral to an office near your home from the international office:

Traveler's Aid International
918 16th Street, N.W.
Suite 201
Washington, D.C. 20006
(202) 659-9468

United Methodist Association of Health and Welfare Ministries

The national office of this organization does not provide direct financial aid. Member organizations are direct service organizations that provide services, including medical and related care at reduced or negotiated rates. For information about agencies in your area that belong to this network, contact:

United Methodist Association of Health and Welfare
    Ministries
601 West Riverview Avenue
Dayton, Ohio 45406-5543
(513) 227-9494

Uniformed Service Organization (USO) World Headquarters

This international organization does not offer direct financial aid of any kind. For active-duty service personnel, however, local USO organizations sponsor family and community centers to help families on a crisis intervention basis.

You can find your local USO organization in the business section of the white pages telephone directory or through your local information operator. If you are having trouble contacting a local USO organization, contact:

Uniformed Service Organization World Headquarters
601 Indiana Avenue, N.W.
Washington, D.C. 20004
(202) 783-8121

Venture Clubs of the Americas

This national organization does not offer financial assistance for medical care, but it does award two scholarships to individuals with physical disabilities who are 15–35 years old and are seeking further education. For further information or referral to a local chapter, contact:

VCA Coordinator
Venture Clubs of the Americas
1616 Walnut Street, Suite 700
Philadelphia, Pennsylvania 19103
(215) 732-0512

Volunteers of America, National Headquarters

No direct financial assistance for medical care is available from this organization. Among the programs it does sponsor to help individuals and families with low incomes across the United States is Minnesota's Bar-None Residential Program for children with severe autism.

Requests for assistance must be written on the letterhead stationery of a physician or other health care professional, and should include a statement of the physical condition of the patient as well as his or her financial hardship. For more information, contact:

Volunteers of America, National Headquarters
3813 North Causeway Boulevard
Metairie, Louisiana 70002
(504) 837-2652

7

Other Sources of Financial Help for Your Child or Your Family

A number of other financial assistance programs are available to help you. *These programs help provide for your family's basic living needs—food, clothing, shelter, and so forth. Some of them can pay for medical expenses as well.* If you receive extra income from any of these programs, or if one or more of them pay for items you would generally fund out of your monthly budget, you might be able to afford extra medical care for your child that month. *The following public and private programs are reviewed in this chapter.*

1. The Supplemental Security Income (SSI) Program
2. Emergency and temporary cash assistance programs

3. Aid to Families with Dependent Children (AFDC)
4. The Food Stamp Program
5. The Special Supplemental Food Program for Women, Infants, and Children (WIC)
6. Surplus and other food distribution programs of the U.S. Department of Agriculture other than WIC

THE SUPPLEMENTAL
SECURITY INCOME (SSI) PROGRAM

SSI is a cash assistance program for older adults and other children and adults who are blind or have other disabilities. It is funded and administered by the federal government through its Social Security Administration (SSA) offices located throughout the United States. *Every individual enrolled in the SSI Program receives a monthly check to help with support.* In 1992, a child or adult received as much as $422 per month in assistance, regardless of the county or state where he or she lived. *Many states provide supplements to federal SSI payments.* In 1992, 23 states supplemented the federal SSI payment each month. You can call the Social Security Administration (SSA) at 1-800-772-1213 (VOICE) or 1-800-325-0778 (TT) to find out if this is the case in your state, and, if so, the amount of the supplement.

Enrollment in SSI also brings with it another major benefit—automatic eligibility for the Medicaid program, which in most states provides payments for a large list of health care services. For more information about Medicaid, see Chapter 5.

Which Children Are Eligible for SSI Cash Payments?

If your child is younger than 18 years old (or younger than 22 if he or she is a full-time student) *and has a chronic illness or disability, he or she may be eligible to receive SSI payments.* Children whose chronic illness or disabilities cause them to lag behind their peers without disabilities in development and the tasks of daily living (e.g., communicating, walking, dressing, learning, playing with other children) are eligible for SSI payments, *if their family income and resources meets program standards.*

Eligibility for SSI Based on Disability

Until recently, it was difficult to get children with chronic illnesses or disabilities into the SSI Program. This was particularly so for children with mental illnesses or a serious emotional or behavior problem. This was so because of the following:

1. The evaluations given to children were not as comprehensive as those given to adults to determine whether they had disabilities.
2. Children who were too young to evaluate were turned away from the program routinely if the impairments they had were not disabling to all children.
3. Children with more than one impairment were denied coverage if they did not meet all of the criteria for any one of their problems.
4. Children were only declared as having disabilities if "their condition was the same or medically equivalent in severity to a condition on the Social Security Administration's 'List of Impairments.'" Not all disabilities and conditions were included on that list (e.g., spina bifida, Down syndrome, autism, AIDS) (Clark & Manes, 1992).

As a result of these restrictions, it is estimated that prior to 1980 less than one-third of potentially eligible children with low incomes and disabilities and chronic illnesses received SSI cash assistance each month.

In 1983, Community Legal Services of Philadelphia filed a lawsuit against the SSI Program for all of the children who had been denied cash benefits because of the restrictive eligibility policies described above. As a result of the success of this lawsuit, known as the *Zebley* case (for the last name of one of the children involved), the SSI Program as of 1980: 1) *was opened to thousands of children with chronic illnesses and disabilities who would not have been accepted into the program before,* and 2) *was required to offer the more than 450,000 children denied benefits on or after January 1, 1980 the opportunity to have their cases re-evaluated. If found eligible, these children would receive back payments for the time between their rejection by the SSI Program and the time their eligibility was established.* **If you applied for SSI benefits for your child before January 1, 1980 and your child was turned down, you are urged to apply again. If your child is found eligible, SSI cash payments would begin immediately and you would receive a check for back payments from the date of your child's original application to the date the current SSI payments begin.**

SSI was also forced by the lawsuit to change its policies for evaluating disabilities in children. New policies to evaluate children require that the SSI Program (through its Disability Determination Service [DDS]) evaluate children in the following steps:

1. Determine if a child's condition appears on the Social Security Administration's "List of Impairments," which include physical and mental conditions thought to be severe enough to "disable" a child.
2. If a child's condition does not appear on the "List of Impairments," determine if his or her condition is either medically or functionally as serious as a condition on the list.
3. If a child's impairment is not on the "List of Impairments" *or* is not considered as serious as a condition on the list, determine if his or her condition would prevent

him or her from doing the same kind of things most children that age can do, and is of comparable severity to "disable" an adult.

To make this last determination, the SSI Program's DDS has to conduct an *individualized functional assessment (IFA)* at government expense for each applicant meeting other program requirements. This assessment includes obtaining information from both medical and nonmedical sources (e.g., parents, neighbors, teachers, child care workers, medical sources). If the answer to any of the above questions is "yes," the SSI Program would consider your child as having a disability and being eligible to receive SSI payments *if he or she is financially eligible.* A child's or family's income and resources must fall within limits for participation in this program.

Income Eligibility for SSI

It is important to remember that a child's disability is not enough to qualify him or her for the SSI Program. As mentioned previously, a child's family also must not exceed the SSI Program's limits on the amount of annual income and resources (e.g., bank accounts, jewelry) they have. Income includes both "earned income" (e.g., wages from a job) as well as "unearned income" such as gifts of money, child support payments, and payments from most public assistance programs. Not all earned and unearned income is counted in determining a child's financial eligibility for SSI. In 1991, for example, $400 a month of income earned by an unmarried student with a disability who was younger than 18 years old was not counted. Excluded also were a child's payments from public assistance programs. Because a certain amount of income does not count in determining a child's eligibility for SSI, and because family size is also taken into account, a family of two parents and one child with a disability could earn more than $21,000 a year and still financially qualify their child for SSI (Clark & Manes, 1992).

Limits on "Resources" for SSI Participation

"Resources" are *things a child or family owns* (e.g., furniture, a bank account, property). Although there is a limit on the amount of "resources" a child or family can possess for the child to be eligible for SSI, a number of resources are *not* counted in determining a child's eligibility. These include, but are not limited to the following:

1. The family home and the land on which it sits
2. As much as $2,000 worth of personal property, including jewelry, furniture, and cars not needed to go to work or for medical care
3. Any family member's life insurance policy with a cash value of up to $1,500
4. Any retirement funds

The Social Security Administration (1-800-772-1213 [Voice]; 1-800-325-0778 [TT]) or your state's SSI Disability Determination Office can provide you with the exact, up-to-date guidelines used in determining your child's financial eligibility for SSI. These requirements change from time to time.

How Can You Apply for SSI for Your Child?

The following three ways may be used to begin the application process:

1. *You can go to any field office of the Social Security Administration (SSA) to get a copy of an application form* and instructions for completing it, including any papers or items that must be included with the application. While there, you can make an appointment to return your completed application and have it reviewed by

a staff person. According to the SSA, applicants are supposed to have the opportunity to meet with a staff person the same day they walk in if they choose. ***The author recommends that you study the application and instructions, or have a friend or neighbor review the application with you, before talking to a SSA worker. It is also suggested that you locate another parent who has been through an SSI application process and talk with him or her before filing your child's SSI application.*** Another parent may be helpful in suggesting ways to increase your child's chances of being accepted into the program. The national- and regional-level parent advocacy groups listed in Chapter 3 and Appendix B at the end of this book can provide this help or refer you to local groups for assistance. Keep in mind that ***the date of your first visit to the SSA field office is considered your child's "filing date" for SSI,*** if you in fact file his or her completed application within 60 days of your visit to the office.

2. You can call the Social Security Administration's toll-free number (1-800-772-1213 [Voice] or 1-800-325-0778 [TT]) between 7 A.M. and 7 P.M. Eastern Standard Time Monday through Friday to *make an appointment for a telephone application interview.* For the best chance of getting through to this busy office, try to call before 9 A.M. or after 5 P.M. Avoid Mondays and the first week of each month, which are particularly busy times for SSA. ***The day you place a call to SSA to request a telephone application interview is considered your child's "filing date" for SSI,*** providing you file his or her completed application for SSI within 60 days of the initial call.

3. *In rare cases, SSA can send a representative to your home to assist you in filing an application for SSI.* SSA would consider this if the parent or child could not trav-

el to a SSA field office because he or she is hospitalized or unable to leave their home for medical reasons. In this case, *your child's "filing date" for the SSI application is the date you request a home visit* to make an application for your child to be enrolled in the program.

Information Needed to Complete an Application

Be sure to call ahead to SSA to ask what information and supporting documents you will need to file a completed application for your child for SSI. Allow yourself enough time to gather the papers if you do not keep most of them in one place. *Do not delay, however, applying for SSI for your child if you are lacking a few pieces of information.* Submit the items you are lacking as soon after you submit your other paperwork as possible. *Examples of the kinds of information you will need to show or give to the SSA include the following:*

1. Your child's Social Security number
2. Proof of your child's age and citizenship
3. Wage stubs, bank book, cash value of life insurance policies, car registrations, other information about the family's income (both earned and unearned) and "resources"
4. Names, addresses, and telephone numbers of any doctors, hospitals, clinics, and other therapists that have treated your child
5. Names, addresses, and telephone numbers of relatives, neighbors, teachers, social workers, and so forth who can provide information about your child's functional ability

It is important to keep photocopies of everything you give SSA, including your child's completed application. If possible, do not send important documents through the mail or leave them with a worker at SSA. Send or give photocopies whenever they are acceptable.

If you bring your personal documents and records to a SSA field office for review, request that they be given back to you that day. If SSA insists that you leave important documents (e.g., your child's birth certificate) **make a list of what you are leaving and ask the worker to sign and date the list.** If something is not returned to you in a reasonable amount of time, it will be SSA's responsibility to replace it.

It is also important to **note the names of any workers you talk with at SSA, by telephone or in person. Try to talk with the same worker each time you call or go to SSA's field office.** This can save you time and energy, as you will have some continuity in the process and will not have to repeat your story over and over again to different workers.

Your child's "filing date" begins when you make your first telephone call to request an application for SSI, stop by the SSA field office to get an application, or request a home visit to complete an application. As explained previously, this applies as long as you submit a completed application for SSI within 60 days of your first inquiry with SSA.

When Will You Know If Your Child Is Accepted into the SSI Program?

The local SSA office will **determine,** based on its review of the information you provide, **if your child is financially eligible for SSI** and, if so, the level of the monthly payment he or she will receive if determined to have a disability according to SSI standards.

Your state's Disability Determination Service (DDS), which is a branch of SSA, reviews the medical and related information you provide to **determine if your child has a disability.** DDS staff may write or call you to obtain more information. They may also want *to have a doctor who works for SSA examine your child. Try to answer all of their requests as soon as possible* and keep any scheduled appointments with doctors. This will speed up your child's disability determination process.

Feel free to submit additional information to the DDS that you feel will strengthen your child's case for enrollment in SSI. You might want to write up a summary of your child's past and current medical and/or developmental problems. If you do this, indicate the areas in which you believe your child's functioning is limited and behind other children his or her age. Mention similar comments you have received from professionals. Discuss both physical and emotional problems. In addition, *be sure to send a note to all of the individuals whose names you submitted to SSA and DDS.* Let them know that you are applying for SSI for your child and that a worker from SSA or DDS might be contacting them to comment about the extent of your child's condition. Give them an idea of what the DDS will be looking for (e.g., ways your child's condition prevents him or her from doing things that peers without his or her condition can do).

It can take 4–6 months for SSA to decide whether your child is eligible for SSI payments. (Priority in determining SSI eligibility based on disability is given to children with terminal illnesses.) *However, as soon as SSI payments start, your child will be paid from the original "filing date" of the application.*

In select cases, the SSI Program can make payments before it fully reviews an applicant's eligibility. These cases include the following:

1. *"Presumptive eligibility"* can occur if a child has one of the following 12 severe impairments and meets all other eligibility requirements:
    a.   Amputation of two limbs
    b.   Amputation of one leg at the hip
    c.   Allegation of total blindness
    d.   Allegation of total deafness

e. Confinement to bed or inability to move around because of a long-standing condition
f. Allegation of a stroke more than 3 months prior, with significant difficulty in walking or using a hand or arm
g. Allegation of cerebral palsy, muscular dystrophy, muscular atrophy, and marked difficulty walking, speaking, or coordinating hands or arms
h. Allegation of disabilities with amputation of a foot
i. Allegation of Down syndrome
j. Allegation of severe mental deficiency in a child at least 7 years old
k. Allegation of renal disease requiring dialysis on a regularly scheduled basis
l. Human immunodeficiency virus (HIV)

If a child qualifies for presumptive eligibility, payments can begin immediately and continue for as long as 6 months. If, after a full review of eligibility, a child given payments under presumptive eligibility is found to be ineligible for SSI, the child is *not* required to return any payments.

2. If a child needs an ***emergency advance*** while awaiting eligibility determination, SSA can do this once and for as much as the monthly maximum SSI can pay (plus any state supplement). The advance will be deducted out of the child's first check. An emergency is defined as a "threat to health or safety" (Clark & Manes, 1992).
3. An immediate, ***one-time payment of $200*** can be made to a child whose application has been delayed.

Only SSA field office workers can make the decisions described above, and there is no way to formally appeal if your child is denied early or emergency payments under one of these provisions.
While waiting to hear about your child's eligibility, you can make followup calls to your state's DDS office to check

on the status of your child's SSI application. Ask if you can help by collecting any additional information to help with the decision.

Several months after the SSA has collected all of the information it needs to determine if your child is eligible to receive SSI payments, you will receive a notice in the mail. This notice will tell you if your child is eligible for SSI or not. If he or she is eligible, the monthly benefit amount to be paid by SSI will be specified. If SSA informs you that your child is *not* eligible for the SSI Program, *the reason(s) for this "denial of benefits" will be given.* For example, the notice may say that the family's annual income exceeds program limits or that the child has not been determined to have a disability according to SSA guidelines.

Appealing SSI's Denial of Benefits

A parent or youth has 60 days after receiving a denial notice from SSI to appeal the decision to deny the child benefits. It is recommended that you *request an appeal immediately* after being denied, as the appeals process can take a long time. *It is important to note that a number of "denials" result simply because applications were incomplete or improperly completed.* There are several steps in the appeal process; these include the following (Clark & Manes, 1992):

1. *To ask the SSA to reconsider its denial, ask for the form to "request reconsideration."* You can write or call for this form, remembering that it must be filed within 60 days of your child's denial. Include on this form any new or additional information you believe reflects more favorably on your child's case or shows any changes in your child's condition.

   If your child is again denied enrollment in SSI after reconsideration of his or her case, ***appeal again!*** *Many children who are not found to have a disability after* *two reviews of their cases are accepted into the program following the next appeal.*

2. *Request a hearing before an administrative law judge (ALJ) to review SSA's two denials.* This request must be made within 60 days of the last denial. **More than 50% of SSA's denials are reversed as a result of these hearings** (Clark & Manes, 1992).

The Judge David L. Bazelon Center for Mental Health Law (formerly known as the Mental Health Law Project), a consumer-oriented disability law firm in Washington, D.C., suggests that you hire a lawyer to prepare for such a hearing. If you can afford a private attorney, contact:

National Organization of Social Security Claimants
   Representatives (NOSSCR)
1-800-431-2804

Call them for a referral to private attorneys who handle SSI-related cases. If you cannot afford an attorney, your local Legal Aid office can help you. You can get the telephone number from your local information operator by asking for "Legal Aid" or "the Legal Services Corporation." When you call the Legal Services Corporation, ask to speak to an information specialist.

3. If the decision is not reversed in a hearing by an ALJ, the family can *appeal further to an Appeals Council within 60 days of the last denial.*
4. Finally, if still unsuccessful, the family can *appeal to a federal court.*

To obtain more details about how to request any of these appeals, contact:

Judge David L. Bazelon Mental Health Law Center
1101 15th Street, Northwest
Washington, D.C. 20005
(202) 467-5730 (Voice)
(202) 467-4232 (TT)

Appeals are most likely to be successful at some stage in the appeals process if your child's denial is because SSA determined that your child did not have a disability according to its guidelines.

Your child's enrollment in the SSI Program can bring a significant amount of regular monthly income to your family to help pay for medical bills and other extras your child's condition requires. Although you may feel a bit fearful about challenging the Social Security Administration, the potential loss of family income that a denial represents may motivate you to do so.

Remember also that if your child *is* eligible for SSI, he or she may also be eligible for a state supplement to SSI. Contact the Social Security Administration at 1-800-772-1213 (Voice) or 1-800-325-0778 (TT) to find out if your state offers such a supplement to SSI payments.

There is one aspect of SSI that requires caution. If your child is found eligible to receive SSI payments, SSI may overpay your child and later ask you to pay back any excess amount. This can happen if, for example, your family income increases. It can take SSA several months to react to this fact and reduce your child's monthly payments. In the meantime, SSA will be overpaying your child. If overpayment occurs, you can usually work out an arrangement with the SSI Program to take a part of what you owe in your child's overpayment out of future monthly checks until your child's debt is cleared.

EMERGENCY AND TEMPORARY CASH ASSISTANCE PROGRAMS

Emergency and temporary cash assistance programs are public and private programs designed to provide prompt help to individuals or families in need. *Their assistance can include cash, paying for prescription drugs and/or utility bills, and*

providing rent deposits, food, clothing, and shelter. A discussion of organizations that provide emergency or temporary cash assistance and the services they offer follows.

Ministries and Churches

There are two kinds of church and related religious groups that offer emergency cash assistance: 1) local churches and synagogues, and 2) church-sponsored "ministries."

Local churches and synagogues usually have an emergency fund to help their members in times of need. Most often, the minister, priest, or rabbi controls this fund, and any cash gifts or loans to families are kept confidential. There are no guidelines in common regarding what churches and synagogues can fund. The individual or family in need has to approach the clergy member about the need. *Providing financial assistance and the amount of such help is most often at the discretion of the clergy.* As suggested above, *both gifts and loans may be available.* Details about financial aid available from churches is provided in Chapter 6.

Church-sponsored ministries, many of which are nondenominational, can offer cash assistance as well. They can offer payment, similar to your county's DHR, for some items (e.g., **rent deposits, utility deposits or payments, moving expenses**) in addition to prescription medications and medical supplies.

"Ministries" also offer other types of help (e.g., **clothing, bedding, home furnishings**) that might free up money in your monthly budget. Most of this help is offered **on an emergency or short-term basis only**, and a family usually needs to go to a ministry's office to apply for assistance. Many ministries will pay a bill or purchase an item your child or family needs instead of giving you cash to buy it. *Requirements for receiving help are generally not as strict* *as for enrolling in a public assistance program such as General Assistance or AFDC.*

The clergy of any large church or the rabbi of any synagogue can tell you if there is a ministry in or near your community. You can also get this information from an area office of United Way, an area crisis service, or a women's center. Your local information operator can provide these telephone numbers.

Local Departments of Human Resources/Social Services

As discussed in Chapter 5, each county's Department of Human Resources (DHR)/Social Services (DSS) has an office or an individual to handle requests for ***emergency assistance.*** *In addition to providing help buying needed prescriptions or medical supplies, a DHR or DSS can provide the following:*

1. Rent deposits or monthly payments
2. Moving expenses
3. Payment of utility bills

At the discretion of a particular DHR/DSS, the agency may pay a client's bill directly instead of giving the client cash for this purpose (e.g., send a check to the utility department or landlord).

*It is important to remember that this help offered by a county's DHR is **usually available on an emergency basis only.*** If your child or your family needs help, feel free to contact your DHR for the kinds of assistance listed above. If it cannot be of help, it may be able to direct you to an agency that can. You can find the telephone number of your county's DHR/DSS in the county government section of your local telephone directory. Your local information operator will have their telephone number.

State and Local General Assistance Programs

The term *General Assistance* (GA) is used to describe *state and/or local programs of financial assistance for persons with low incomes* (Lewin/CF, Bell, & Associates, 1990). These programs can also be called by other names (e.g., General Relief, Poor Relief).

General Assistance programs are designed to **provide small amounts of cash assistance to individuals who are not eligible for AFDC or SSI, or who are awaiting enrollment in another income subsidy program.** According to a 1990 survey, 45 states and the District of Columbia have General Assistance programs. Some of these programs are statewide; others exist only in certain counties or cities (Lewin, 1990). As of 1990, the states *without* GA programs were the following:

Arkansas	Tennessee
Louisiana	Texas
Oklahoma	West Virginia

What Cash Assistance Is Available?

GA programs provide emergency, short-term, or ongoing cash payments. Ongoing payments are generally made monthly. Monthly payments in 1989 (for one person) ranged from $27 in Charleston, South Carolina, to $385 in Portland, Maine. The average in all programs providing ongoing assistance was $210 a month (Lewin, 1990).

State and local GA programs that served all individuals with low incomes who could not receive SSI, AFDC, and so forth paid more than programs that served only some individuals with low incomes (e.g., those unable to work). Ongoing programs paid more per month than programs that gave only cash payments on an emergency basis.

Additional Benefits in GA Programs

In addition to cash payments for daily needs, GA programs may offer other forms of assistance that can be used as cash, such as *vouchers to pay for rent or shelter*. Most GA programs also have a medical component that pays for selected medical care and supplies. A full description of the GA–Medical programs is offered in Chapter 5.

Who Is Eligible to Receive GA?

Some GA programs are available to those in need who cannot qualify for other income assistance. Other programs are only available to some of these individuals (e.g., individuals with disabilities, "unemployable" individuals). *Applicants must demonstrate the following:*

- That they have applied to the SSI Program and AFDC and have been denied or are waiting for word about their eligibility
- That they have low incomes and meet the income guidelines for a particular GA program
- That the value of their "assets" or personal possessions (e.g., furniture, clothing) does not exceed a particular GA program's limit.

Of 34 GA programs available to employable individuals, 29 require recipients to seek paying jobs actively.

Where Can You Apply for a GA Program?

Your county's Department of Human Resources/Social Services can tell you if your state or county has a General Assistance program. If so, they can tell you where to call or go to apply. You can find their telephone number in the county government section of your white pages telephone directory. Your local information operator will also have their number.

Disease- and Disability-Related Organizations

State and local chapters of disease-related organizations, such as the Easter Seal Society, Spina Bifida Association, or Alliance for the Mentally Ill, may have *emergency cash assistance to help children whose families are members of their organization, or who have other special health care needs. Each organization has different policies on the kind of problems with which they can help.* Chapter 6 discusses some of the kinds of assistance available, according to a 1992 survey of the national offices of 45 disease- and disability-related organizations.

It is also a good idea to check directly with the local and state affiliates of national organizations that could help your child or family. State and local chapters add and delete services from time to time. You should be able to find the telephone numbers of any disease- or disability-related organization in the business section of your local telephone directory, or you can get their number from your local information operator. The national disease- and disability-related organizations listed in Appendix B at the end of this book can also provide the telephone numbers of their local affiliates.

"Crisis Services"

Many communities are served by "crisis services" that can be reached by telephone as much as 24 hours a day. The organizations that run these services do not have cash to distribute for emergencies, but trained volunteers can give you telephone numbers for one or more agencies that do. You can find out if there is such a crisis service in your community by calling the nearest chapter of United Way, a local women's center, or your local information operator. Any of these sources should be able to provide the number of one or more crisis services in your area.

AID TO FAMILIES WITH
DEPENDENT CHILDREN (AFDC)

Aid to Families with Dependent Children (AFDC) is a joint federal and state funded program that offers **monthly checks for the care of dependent children who are in financial need because their parent(s) cannot provide them with needed financial support.** Recipients are most often single parents.

As of October, 1992, all states operating AFDC programs are also required by the federal government to provide AFDC to children in *two-parent families* who are in need because of the *unemployment of the household's principal wage-earner. There is a requirement, however, that most AFDC recipients participate in a JOBS program or attend educational activities, unless they meet one of the following requirements.*

1. If they are ill, have disabilities, or are taking care of someone in their homes who is ill or has a disability
2. If they are the primary caregivers of children younger than 1–3 years of age (Each state has different rules about this.)
3. If they are 16 years old and full-time students in an elementary, secondary, or technical school
4. If they are working at least 30 hours a week

Monthly reporting of income and resources is required by a number of states.

What Benefits Are Available Under AFDC?

Each AFDC recipient receives a **monthly payment** based on his or her family size, ranging from $120 in Mississippi to $924 in Alaska as of January, 1992 (Committee on Ways and Means, U.S. House of Representatives, 1992). **Child care payments** *are also available to AFDC recipients who meet one of the following requirements:*

1. If they are under 16 years of age and attend full-time secondary or technical school
2. If they are required to participate in a JOBS program for educational, training, or employment purposes
3. If they are younger than 20 years old, have no high school degree or equivalent, are the primary caregiver of a dependent child, and are required to participate in full-time educational activities

Transportation costs *are provided for most recipients who receive child care payments to attend school, a JOBS program, or educational activities.*

In most states, enrollment in AFDC brings with it automatic eligibility in the Medicaid program (see Chapter 5). It also usually allows recipients to receive Food Stamps (Committee on Ways and Means, U.S. House of Representatives, 1992) and vouchers for the Women, Infants, and Children (WIC) Food Supplement program if AFDC recipients meet other eligibility requirements.

Who Is Eligible for AFDC?

In the AFDC program, each state defines which children are eligible in their state, by setting a standard of need. States also set benefit levels and allowable income and resources limits for eligibility within federal guidelines. *To receive AFDC, families must be eligible in a number of ways, including the following:*

1. A dependent child who otherwise qualifies for AFDC must be younger than 18 years of age or, at a state's discretion, younger than 19 years of age and a full-time student in secondary or vocational school.
2. A child who otherwise qualifies for AFDC must be without parental support because his or her mother or father is absent from the home on a continuous basis *or* is unemployed (i.e., generally working less than 100

hours per month) but has recently been employed more than this.

3. The family unit of a dependent child cannot have a *gross* income that exceeds 185% of their state's "need standard." (Certain items are excluded in figuring gross income.)

4. The family unit of a dependent child cannot have a *net* income that exceeds 100% of their state's "need standard."

5. The family "resources" of recipient children must not exceed $1,000, excluding the home they live in, one car worth not more than $1,500, furniture, and clothing.

It is important to note that a number of states allow "special needs items" (e.g., special diets, the extra cost of medical care, the extra cost of shelter) to be added to their state's basic "need standard" in determining eligibility for a dependent child.

Where Can You Apply for AFDC?

To apply for AFDC, call your county's Department of Human Resources (DHR)/Department of Social Services (DSS). You can find this agency listed in the county government section of your local telephone book. You can also get their number from your local information operator.

The author strongly suggests that you **talk with another family who has applied for AFDC successfully before you give any information to the DHR/DSS or make a formal application for AFDC.** One or more families already in the AFDC program can best advise you how to help ensure that your application is accepted. You can get the names and telephone numbers of AFDC recipients in your area from one or more of the parent advocacy organizations listed in Chapter 3.

FOOD STAMP PROGRAM

The Food Stamp Program is one of the major assistance programs operated by the U.S. Department of Agriculture. **Coupons, or "food stamps," are issued monthly to qualified individuals and families to help them purchase food.** *The value of food stamps given depends on a family's size and income, among other standards.* In 1992, the Food Stamp Program served more than 25 million people each month, with average monthly benefits of $68 per person (U.S. Department of Agriculture, 1992). If you want more information about the program or want to apply for food stamps, contact your county's Department of Human Resources/ Department of Social Services for a referral to the Food Stamp Program office nearest your home. You can find the telephone number for your county's DHR/DSS in the government section of your local telephone directory. You can also call your local operator for their number.

SPECIAL SUPPLEMENTAL FOOD PROGRAM FOR WOMEN, INFANTS, AND CHILDREN (WIC)

The federally sponsored Special Supplemental Food Program for Women, Infants, and Children (WIC) **provides vouchers for the purchase of selected food items** for the following:

1. Pregnant women
2. Women who have recently delivered babies
3. Breastfeeding women
4. Infants and children up to age 5

Potential recipients must also be found to be at "nutritional risk," which means they are lacking proper nutrition that endangers their health or the health of an unborn child. "Nutritional risk" includes a number of conditions, such as anemia, low weight for height, and in children "failure to thrive."

If you or your child is accepted into the program, you can receive monthly vouchers for certain food items. These vouchers are usually available at more than one location in a community. Be sure to ask to receive your vouchers at the location nearest your home or the location most convenient to you. Call your local Department of Health or your county's DHR/DSS for information about the WIC program and instructions for how to apply. You can find either agency in the county government section of your local telephone book, or you can ask for their telephone number from your local information operator.

SURPLUS AND OTHER FOOD DISTRIBUTION PROGRAMS OF THE U.S. DEPARTMENT OF AGRICULTURE (OTHER THAN WIC)

Food is purchased by the U.S. Department of Agriculture and donated to a number of programs to help children and adults in need. Examples of these programs include the following:

1. The National School Breakfast and School Lunch Program
2. Food distribution to people who are unemployed or have low incomes (through the Temporary Emergency Food Assistance Programs [TEFAP])
3. Food distribution to charitable institutions for individuals in need (e.g., food pantries, soup kitchens—Soup Kitchen/Food Bank [SKFB])

Information about the distribution of food and eligibility for it can be found in the newspaper or by contacting your local Community Action Agency (CAA) or County Com-

mission for Economic Opportunities (CCEO). State contacts for all CAAs and CCEOs can be found in Appendix B at the end of this book. You can also contact a regional office of the U.S. Department of Agriculture's Food and Nutrition Service that administers these programs. Call the regional office that covers your state; these addresses are listed in Appendix B at the end of this book.

SUMMARY

As you can see, **many programs are available to help your family meet its basic needs.** They include the SSI Program, emergency and temporary cash assistance programs, AFDC, the Food Stamp Program, and WIC and other food distribution programs. Both public and private agencies participate in this kind of relief. Taking advantage of some of the help they offer may free up some of your resources for your child's medical care. Try to take advantage of as many of these programs as you can.

8

Saving Money on Your Income Taxes

Deductions, Exemptions, and Credits

It is quite common for families of children with chronic illnesses and disabilities to have extremely high medical expenses. Health insurance, if available, only pays a part of these costs (see Chapter 6). These families might have higher child care costs as well, because they have to hire more child care assistance and pay for more skilled people to care for their children.

There is one time, however, when the families of children with special health care needs can recover some of their out-of-pocket expenses for medical and related care. When individuals or couples file federal and state income taxes, it is possible to pay less tax because of some of the exceptional expenses they incurred during the year. You can take as many income tax deductions, exemptions, and credits as you are eligible for. In most cases, there will be more than one.

Be sure to order a free copy of the ***Internal Revenue Service (IRS) Publication 907: Tax Information for Persons with Handicaps or Disabilities*** (Department of the Treasury, Internal Revenue Service, 1991i). It details the numerous income tax savings you may be eligible to receive. If you have any questions about the information in this or any other publication mentioned in this chapter, call the IRS district office's toll-free telephone number: 1-800-829-1040 (Voice) or 1-800-829-4059 (TT). ***If you want to speak to a person and not a recording, wait until the end of the "menu" choices you are given when you call.*** You will be connected with an IRS information specialist. A lot of federal tax information (e.g., regarding proper forms to use, Child and Dependent Care Credit, Charitable Deductions, amending tax returns) is available on pre-recorded tapes you can listen to free of charge, by calling TELETAX (1-800-829-4477). Specific federal tax reporting forms can be ordered by calling 1-800-TAX-FORM (1-800-829-3676).

Call your state's Department of Revenue as well to find out about the tax savings that are available to you in your state. Each state's Department of Revenue is listed in Appendix B at the end of this book.

Remember to check with both the IRS and your state's Department of Revenue each year before filing taxes on the status of these deductions, exemptions, and credits. Tax laws change from year to year.

FEDERAL INCOME TAX SAVINGS

The federal government provides a number of ways for taxpayers to reduce their income tax bills and recover some of their expenses during the year. Reductions in income tax can be in the form of tax deductions, tax exemptions, and tax credits.

A tax deduction is an expense that reduces your income tax bill because all or part of the expense may be deducted from your tax bill.
A tax exemption is a status or condition (e.g., dependent, "disabled") *that reduces a taxpayer's tax bill because of presumed expense associated with that status or condition.*
A tax credit is allowed for certain expenses. Such a credit is applied against your final income tax bill, reducing it one dollar for each dollar of expense allowed to be credited in this manner.

Income tax deductions and exemptions, unlike credits, allow you to recover only a portion of your out-of-pocket costs for allowable items. Examples of income tax deductions or exemptions, respectively, include the possible medical deduction for out-of-pocket medical expenses for any member of the family or the personal exemption allowed all individuals in the family unit reported on a federal income tax return.

In addition to the deductions allowed all taxpayers with medical expenses above a certain level, there are additional deductions, exemptions, and credits given to individuals with disabilities. Families of individuals with disabilities are also eligible for additional reductions in their income taxes for certain expenses made on behalf of their children with special needs (e.g., the installation of ramps at home, adding a wheelchair lift to a family van).

It is important to note that for federal income taxes and most state income taxes, an individual or couple must claim itemized deductions instead of the standard deduction in order to take advantage of medical deductions. Itemizing deductions or filling out the "long form" (Form

1040 for federal taxes) is *not* required to take advantage of other deductions, exemptions, or credits (e.g., the credit for child care expenses for parents who are both working or looking for work, the Earned Income Credit for working families with low incomes).

Federal Income Tax
Deductions for Medical and Related Care

A *deduction* can be taken for all out-of-pocket expenses for medical and related care for any member of the family who is listed on the tax return. To claim this deduction, however, *out-of-pocket costs must exceed 7.5% of your family's adjusted gross income (AGI).* Additionally, a family must usually itemize deductions, counting up the cost of all of the allowable deductions they had during the year (e.g., medical expenses, home interest charges, other taxes, charitable giving).

When families do *not* take the "standard deduction" given by the IRS, but itemize their deductions, they file a Form 1040 to report their federal income taxes and report their itemized deductions on Schedule A. *If you choose to itemize your income tax deductions, you must hold onto receipts and cancelled checks showing you paid for deductible items.* Medical expenses that can be deducted include the following:

1. *Health insurance premiums* (Remember that an employee's portion of this premium is often deducted directly from his or her paycheck. This can still be counted as an out-of-pocket expense to you unless your employer deducted your share of the premium "before taxes.")
2. *Payments to hospitals, clinics, doctors, dentists, physical therapists, psychologists, and other providers of medical and related care*

3. *Payments for x-rays, laboratory work, and other diagnostic tests*

4. *Payments for prescribed medications, medical equipment, or medical supplies (***Prescriptions can also be written for items that do not normally require a prescription** [e.g., special foods, aspirin, adhesive tape] **if you regularly purchased them for your child because of his or her condition.** *Ask your doctor to write a prescription for items such as these to make them tax deductible.)* **Diapers are tax deductible for all children who are required to wear them after they are 3 years old.**

5. *Purchase and installation of ramps, bathtub transfer bars, or other items to make your home accessible and usable* (These items are tax deductible to the extent that they do *not* increase the value of your home.)

6. *Maintenance, repair, and operating costs* associated with purchase and installation of the above-mentioned items and any other medical equipment your child needs (e.g., ventilator)

7. *Mileage or transportation costs* to get to and from medical appointments, a hospital, the pharmacy, a medical supply store, or an equipment store, or to discuss your child's medical problem (e.g., school)

8. Payment for *parking* at hospitals or clinics and offices of doctors, dentists, physical therapists, psychologists, and other service providers

9. Payments for *room and meals* provided at any hospital away from home

10. Payment for *lodging* (as much as $50 a night per person) when out of town in connection with a child's medical care

11. Payment for *meals* for a parent who accompanies his or her child to the hospital, as long as the meals are provided by the hospital or a similar institution

12. Payments for *long-distance telephone calls* related to scheduling medical appointments for your child, order-

ing medical equipment or supplies, or discussing your child's medical condition with a service provider
13. Any other *out-of-pocket expense you have in connection with your child who has a chronic illness or disability* that you would not have with one of your other children without such a medical condition

Keeping track of mileage (see #7 above) can be a nuisance. The author recommends that you make a one-time record of the round trip mileages to each doctor, clinic, and hospital your child visits and keep those mileage figures in a safe place until the end of the year when you are working on your income taxes. During the year, you only need to record the initials of the particular doctor or clinic you visited and the date of the visit. This is often conveniently done on a 12-month calendar in the kitchen. As an example, "Doctor. S." marked on a particular day on your kitchen calendar could stand for a trip to Dr. Stone's office (Figure 1). At the end of the year, you can add up the total number of trips to Dr. Stone's office that year. From your initial record of the mileage to and from Dr. Stone's, you can multiply the number of trips made by the round trip mileage for one trip to Dr. Stone's to arrive at the total number of deductible miles for appointments with that doctor. You can do this for each doctor, pharmacy, medical supply store, and so forth visited in any one tax year. Be sure to add the miles to the places you visited less frequently for your child's medical problem. Add the miles you traveled for medical appointments for other members of your family as well. This will give you a figure for medical mileage you can include in your total out-of-pocket expenses for medical items. *For the 1991 tax year, the reimbursement rate for medically related mileage was 9¢ per mile.*

For additional information on medical deductions, the Internal Revenue Service issues a special publication called IRS Publication 502: Medical and Dental Expenses (Depart-

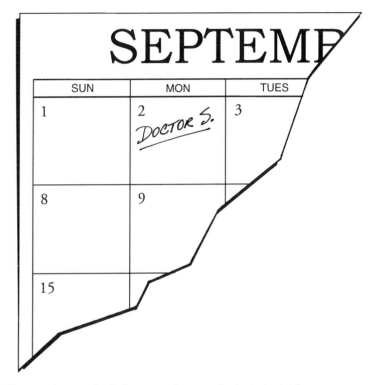

Figure 1. An example of mileage records on a wall calendar kept at home.

ment of the Treasury, Internal Revenue Service, 1991d) at no charge. It includes details about allowable medical and related deductions. You can get a copy by calling the IRS at 1-800-TAX-FORM. If, after reviewing this publication, you still have questions, call the IRS District Services office at 1-800-829-1040 (Voice) or 1-800-829-4059 (TT).

Self-Employed Health Insurance Deduction

An additional deduction is available to individuals who are self-employed and had a net profit for the tax year. This deduction is also available to individuals who received wages from an S corporation in which they own more than 2% of the shares. *Individuals who meet this description may take a federal income tax deduction for part of the health insurance premiums they paid to insure themselves, their spouses, and their dependents during the tax year in question.* This deduction is not limited to families with children with chronic illnesses or disabilities. It is a deduction, however, that was recently added to the federal income tax laws. Under several proposals for health insurance reform, including President Clinton's, a self-employed individual would be allowed to deduct 100% of the premium paid to insure him- or herself, a spouse, and dependents.

The IRS provides a worksheet to calculate the portion of health insurance premium expenses you can deduct in these cases. You can find the worksheet in the "Forms and Instructions" booklet that is sent to all taxpayers at the end of each year. You can also get instructions for figuring out your deduction, as well as other information about this deduction in **IRS Publication 535: Business Expenses** (Department of the Treasury, Internal Revenue Service, 1991g).

Charitable Contributions

If you itemize your deductions, you can take an income tax deduction for the amount of money or goods you donated to one or more charitable organizations. This means that, in addition to money, you can deduct the following kinds of items you donate to private nonprofit organizations that have 501(c)3 (i.e., tax-exempt) status:

1. *Clothing* (*You* decide on the value of the items you are donating, and the recipient organization will give you a receipt and form on which to record their value.)
2. *Food*
3. *Furniture and other household items*
4. *Books and records*

5. *Professional services* (e.g., as a mechanic, you might repair your church's bus at no charge)

If you buy tickets to a church supper or a school play and fundraiser, the part of the ticket that is profit to the charitable organization may be taken as a deduction. **Be sure to obtain a receipt from the organization(s) to which you made contributions.** This is particularly important when you give cash or goods. When you contribute by check, your cancelled check will serve as your receipt.

When you claim total contributions (cash and goods) of more than $500, you must attach Form 8283 with your federal income tax return. This form gives more detail about the contributions you made. There are limits on the amounts you can deduct as a percentage of your adjusted gross income, but you can carry over contributions in excess of your limit for 1 year into the next.

Examples of qualifying charitable organization are churches, synagogues, schools, libraries, the United Way, the Salvation Army, the Red Cross and the Boy Scouts. For more information about federal income tax deductions for gifts to charity, *consult* **IRS Publication 526: Charitable Contributions** (Department of the Treasury, Internal Revenue Service, 1991f), which is available at no charge.

Federal Income Tax Exemptions

For the 1992 tax year, all tax filers whose adjusted gross income was $78,950 or less could take an exemption of $2,300 for each taxpayer and any dependents they claimed. **There are no additional exemptions allowed families with children who have chronic illnesses or disabilities.**

Federal Income Tax Credits

There are two income tax credits that may be of value to families who have children with a chronic illness or disability.

Credit for Child and Dependent Care Expenses

One income tax *credit* is available for the cost of paying someone to provide care for either of the following:

1. A child who is younger than 13 years of age
2. A dependent or spouse who is unable to care for him- or herself.

A couple may file for a credit only if both of them are working or looking for work. The IRS's definition of "looking for work" is that the person was successful in his or her job search and earned some income in the tax year for which he or she is claiming the credit.

Child and/or dependent care costs qualifying for a tax credit cannot exceed the annual earnings of an individual taxpayer, or the lower of the two annual earnings for married taxpayers filing jointly. If you were eligible for a Child and Dependent Care Credit in 1993, you were able to reduce your total federal income tax bill by 20%–30% of your qualifying expenses up to $2,400 per child or dependent or $4,800 for two or more children or dependents.

*As the discussion above indicates, a family with a child who has a chronic illness or a disability is eligible to take a credit for child and dependent care **regardless of the age of their sick child.*** If both parents live in the household, are working or looking for work, and have to hire someone to care for this child, a percentage of those costs can be taken as a federal income tax credit. *The family's caregiver can even be a family member, as long as he or she is 19 years of age or older and does not live in the home of the child or dependent for whom he or she is giving care.*

For more information on this type of credit, contact the IRS (1-800-TAX-FORM) to request *Publication 503: Child and Dependent Care Expenses* (Department of the Treasury, Internal Revenue Service, 1991e).

Earned Income Credit (EIC)

The **Earned Income Credit (EIC)** *is a federal income tax credit for individuals or families who work, have adjusted gross incomes of less than $21,250 per year (1991 tax year), and have at least one child living with them.* **There are two types of EICs;** these are described below. *For a family to qualify for any of the EICs, the dependent child must also meet the following criteria:*

1. He or she must be the son, daughter, adopted child, or a direct descendent (e.g., grandchild, stepchild, foster child) of a taxpayer who meets the qualifications above.
2. He or she must live with the qualifying family for at least 6 months (12 months for a foster child) in a residence in the United States.
3. He or she must be less than 19 years old at the end of the tax year in question, be 24 years of age or younger and a full-time student, *or have a permanent or total disability.*

Taxpayers who want to take one or more of the two types of EIC credits described below must also do the following:

1. File a federal income tax return even if no tax is owed or an individual or family did not earn enough income to file a return
2. File a joint federal income tax return if married
3. File a federal income tax return covering a 12-month period
4. Provide a Social Security number for a qualifying child more than 1 year of age (Taxpayers can request a Social Security number for any child by filing Form SS-5 at their local Social Security Administration office. At the time of the request, ask for Form SSA 5028, which documents your application for a Social Security number for your child.)

The following are the two types of EICs:

1. ***The basic credit*** is based on the number of children living with you. In the 1991 tax year, a credit of as much as $1,192 was available for qualifying individuals or families with one child. A credit of as much as $1,235 was available for qualifying individuals or families with two or more children.

2. ***An extra credit for a child born during the tax year*** is available, but limited to one qualifying child who is younger than 1 year old. This credit was as much as $357 in the 1991 tax year and was not used to determine eligibility for most welfare programs. ***A taxpayer must elect to take this credit or the credit for Child and Dependent Care.*** Both credits may not be taken for the same child in 1 tax year.

If you find you are eligible to take either EIC, you can subtract them from the federal income taxes you owe at the end of the year. You will do this as you or your tax preparer completes your federal income tax return and calculates your federal income tax. ***If you do not owe any federal income taxes for the year in question, you can file a federal income tax return and receive your EIC as a tax refund.*** In both cases, be sure to attach IRS Schedule EIC with your federal income tax return 1040 or 1040A. It is included in the federal income tax packet you may have received from the IRS in January. If not, request one by calling 1-800-TAX-FORM or pick one up at your nearest library, post office, or federal government offices.

Another option is to *let the IRS figure your EIC for you.* In this case, simply complete the top portion of Schedule EIC and attach the incomplete form with your federal income tax return. ***Individuals and families who are owed EICs can get an advance EIC credit during the next year.*** This can be done by filing a Form W-5 (Earned Income Credit Advance Payment Certificate) with their employers. For more information on the Earned Income Credit, request *IRS Publication 596: Earned Income Credit* (Department of the Treasury, Internal Revenue Service, 1991h) by calling 1-800-TAX-FORM. If you have questions you want to ask an IRS staff member, you can call the IRS district office at 1-800-829-1040.

Credit for the Elderly or the Disabled

In spite of its name, the Credit for the Elderly or the Disabled is *not* a federal income tax credit available to families because they have or must pay for the care of children with chronic illnesses or disabilities. This federal income tax credit is for individuals who are:

1. 65 years or older, *or*
2. Younger than 65 years old and retired on permanent and total disability

This credit does not cover most children and youth with a chronic illness or disability, as they do not meet these criteria.

Reductions in State Income Taxes

A review of the 1992 income tax laws of all 50 states indicated that *states offer reductions in state income taxes primarily to individuals who are classified as "permanently and totally disabled."* Although this appears discouraging at first glance, it is important to consider the criteria for "permanent and total" disability. In most states, *an individual who has been or is expected to be ill or have a disability for at least 12 months is considered "permanently and totally disabled."* Therefore, reductions in state income taxes are indeed a potential source of savings for families with children who have chronic illnesses or disabilities.

The following are general comments about state income taxes and tax reductions that are offered before details about each state's deductions, exemptions, and credits:

1. Some states are similar to the federal government in that they have both a more simple ("short form") and a more detailed ("long form") form for filing personal income taxes. Readers are advised to determine which way yields the most tax savings to them.
2. As with the federal government, some states will not let you take certain income tax deductions unless you itemize your deductions.
3. A number of states do not have a special income tax deduction for medical expenses. In some cases, this is because a state does not allow itemized deductions of any kind on personal income tax returns.
4. More states are offering a reduction in the taxpayer's adjusted gross income for at least part of the premium self-employed individuals pay to obtain health insurance for themselves, their spouses, and their dependents.
5. Many states give taxpayers and/or their spouses an extra income tax exemption if either the taxpayer or spouse is blind. A number of states do so as well if the taxpayer or spouse is deaf.
6. Several states have eliminated or reduced special income tax savings offered to individuals with chronic illnesses or disabilities. (North Carolina, for example, recently limited special exemptions for such children to those in families with low incomes. Prior to this, there were special exemptions offered to any taxpayer or dependent who fell into one or more of at least a dozen categories of disease of disability [e.g., spina bifida, head injury, wheelchair use].)

7. If you did not file for a tax deduction, exemption, or credit you were entitled to, you can file an "amended return" to claim the savings. Most states require filing of "amended returns" within 3 years of the filing of the original return.

Potential reductions in state income taxes are detailed by state in the appendix to this chapter. *For more information about specific state tax reductions and how to claim them, contact your state's Department of Revenue.* As with the IRS, remember to check with your state's Department of Revenue on tax reductions at least once a year, as state tax laws also change from time to time. The addresses and telephone numbers of each state's Department of Revenue (often carrying a different name) are provided in Appendix B at the end of this book.

GENERAL SUGGESTIONS FOR FILING INCOME TAX RETURNS

For both federal and state income tax returns, **Exceptional Parent** *magazine ("Annual income," 1993) recommends that you include the following with both your federal and state income tax returns:*

1. Your own statement about your child's illness or disability, the extent of medical care he or she requires, and any special tax deductions
2. A statement from your child's primary doctor certifying his or her medical condition and the prescribed treatments he or she requires

Including these statements should help you to avoid being audited by the IRS if you are claiming a large reduction in the taxes you owe ("Annual income," 1993).

Read your federal and state income tax preparation instructions carefully when you receive them each year in your income tax packet. Note the particular tax deductions, exemptions, and credits available to you as well as the procedures for taking advantage of them. Remember, you *may* be entitled to a refund even if you do not owe any income taxes that year and would otherwise not file an income tax return.

If a tax preparer is figuring your taxes, make sure he or she is aware of your child's condition and the special reductions in taxes your family is entitled to receive.

If you forget to take any deduction, exemption, or credit when you file your income tax returns, file an amended return. Usually, you have 3 years from the date the original return was filed or 2 years after a tax was paid (whichever was later) to do so.

SUMMARY

Reductions in federal and state income taxes are available to all taxpayers with exceptional expenses relating to the care of a child with a chronic illness or disability. To take advantage of some tax savings, individuals or couples must itemize their income tax deductions (e.g., medical deductions) in most cases. For others, this is not necessary (e.g., Child and Dependent Care Credit). *Some states require that a physician or other professional certify a child's condition the first time a special exemption or deduction is claimed. Other states require that such a certification be sent in each year with your income tax return.*

Remember, to receive additional information about *federal* income tax savings, contact the IRS district offices at 1-800-829-1040 (Voice) or 1-800-829-4059 (TT). Their staff can suggest particular publications offered free of charge to give you details about income tax reductions and how to claim them.

For *state* income tax savings, contact your State Department of Revenue. In some states, this department carries a different name. A list of each state's Department of Revenue (or its equivalent) is given in Appendix B at the end of this book.

Health insurance and/or health care reform measures at the state or federal level will change the nature and extent of income tax deductions, exemptions, and credits allowed. Contact your state's Department of Revenue (and the federal IRS) before preparing your income tax returns each year to be sure you are taking all income tax benefits to which you are entitled.

Appendix **8A**

*State Income
Tax Deductions,
Exemptions,
and Credits
Related to
Having a Child
with a Chronic
Illness or Disability*

The following state-specific information regarding income tax deductions, exemptions, and credits related to having a child with a chronic illness or disability is based on the author's review of the 1991 state income tax packets.

Alabama

- Alabama allows a deduction for out-of-pocket medical expenses greater than 4% of a taxpayer's state adjusted gross income.

Alaska

- Alaska does not collect a state personal income tax.

Arizona

- An additional personal exemption of $1,500 is available in Arizona for taxpayers who are blind.
- Out-of-pocket medical and dental expenses may be deducted if they exceed 7.5% of the federal adjusted gross income.
- A property tax credit is available, even for renters, if taxpayers earn less than $3,751 (living alone, 1991) or $5,500 (living with other, 1991). Some income is not counted in arriving at a taxpayer's income figure (e.g., payments from the Aid to Families with Dependent Children program).

Arkansas

- In Arkansas, taxpayers who are blind or deaf and/or their spouses receive an additional personal tax credit. Blindness is defined as any person who cannot tell light from darkness or whose eyesight in the better eye does not exceed 20/200 with corrective lens, or whose field of vision is limited to an angle of 20 degrees. Deafness is defined as an average loss of speech frequencies in the better ear of 86 decibels or more.
- Since 1983, there has been an additional $500 personal credit each for a taxpayer with one or more children with mental retardation.
- Since 1991, if a taxpayer has a child with a permanent and total disability in his or her home, he or she can take an adjustment to gross income of $500. Both physical and mental impairments are included in the definition of disability. Certification of the child's condition is required the first year this tax reduction is claimed.

- All medical and dental expenses that are not reimbursed in some way and that exceed 7.5% of state adjusted gross income may be taken as a state income tax deduction.
- The premium paid for health insurance coverage for a self-employed taxpayer and his or her spouse and dependents is deductible in full as an adjustment to state gross income.
- A credit is given for 10% of the child and dependent care expenses a taxpayer claimed on his or her federal return.

California

- In California, part of the federal reduction for health insurance paid by a self-employed taxpayer is allowed as an "adjustment to state gross income."
- An additional personal exemption for a taxpayer and/or spouse who is "visually impaired" is permitted. "Visually impaired" is defined as someone who cannot see better than 20/200 while wearing glasses or contact lenses and whose field of vision is not greater than 20 degrees. The first year this benefit is claimed, a doctor's statement certifying this condition must be attached to the income tax return.
- Medical and dental expenses that are not otherwise reimbursed can be deducted from California income taxes as soon as they exceed 7.5% of federal adjusted gross income.
- Taxpayers can take a portion of the federally claimed Child and Dependent Care Credit as a credit on their state income tax returns. The amount of the credit varies with taxpayer income.
- A percentage of the health insurance premium paid by a self-employed taxpayer for him- or herself, a spouse, and dependents can be taken as an "adjustment to state income."

- A low-income tax credit is offered for individuals who earn less than $11,430 (in 1991) and couples who earn less than $22,840 (in 1991).
- A renter's credit on personal income tax is available (up to $120 in 1991) for individuals renting property in California and earning less than $20,500 (in 1991). This credit is also available to couples earning less than $41,000 (in 1991).

Colorado

- Out-of-pocket expenses that are not otherwise reimbursed and that exceed 7.5% of federal adjusted gross income can be taken as deductions to your state adjusted gross income.
- Property tax, rent, and heat rebates are offered for individuals who had disabilities for an entire tax year and had incomes under $7,500 (single individual in 1991) or $11,200 (married couple in 1991). A maximum credit of $500 for property tax or rent and $160 for heating expense is given.
- The state government collects a small tax from taxpayers with federal adjusted gross incomes above $15,000 to help finance its health insurance risk pool for those who are medically uninsurable by the private health insurance market.

Connecticut

- As of early 1992, Connecticut had no deductions, exemptions, or credits for medical expenses, dependent care expenses, or disability.

Delaware

- In Delaware, there is an additional standard deduction of $1,000 for taxpayers and/or their spouses who have disabilities and do not itemize their state income taxes.

- Medical and dental expenses that have not been reimbursed can be deducted from adjusted gross income to the extent that they exceed 7.5% of federal adjusted gross income.
- You can deduct one-half of the premium paid for the health insurance of a self-employed person and his or her family after this amount is reduced by the allowable medical and dental expenses claimed as medical deductions. (Delaware defines a self-employed person as "one who derives more than one-half of his or her gross income from self-employment.")
- Delaware offers a state income tax credit for child and dependent care at the rate of 50% of the federally claimed credit.

District of Columbia

- The District of Columbia offers a personal exemption of $1,370 each for a taxpayer who is blind and/or a spouse.
- Medical and dental expenses that have not been reimbursed can be deducted from adjusted gross income to the extent that they exceed 7.5% of federal adjusted gross income.
- A credit for Child and Dependent Care expenses is given at the rate of 32% of the federally claimed credit.
- A low-income (nonrefundable) tax credit is offered. The average credit is $250 for an individual taxpayer and $350 for married taxpayers filing jointly.

Florida

- Florida does not collect a personal state income tax.

Georgia

- Georgia offers a taxpayer who is blind and/or a spouse an extra state income tax deduction of $700 each if the standard deduction is used in filing.

- Medical and dental expenses that have not been reimbursed can be deducted from your adjusted gross income to the extent that they exceed 7.5% of federal adjusted gross income.

Hawaii

- If a taxpayer or spouse in Hawaii is blind, deaf, or "permanently and totally disabled," he or she can claim an income tax exemption of as much as $7,000 per individual or $14,000 per couple instead of taking the standard exemption of $1,040 per individual. In Hawaii, the definition of blind is "central visual acuity [that] does not exceed 20/200 in the better eye with correcting lenses, or . . . visual acuity [that] is greater than 20/200 but is accompanied by a limitation in the field of vision such that the widest diameter of the visual field subtrends an angle no greater than 20 degrees." Hawaii's definition of deaf is "average loss in the speech frequencies (500–2,000 Hertz) in the better ear . . . [of] 82 decibels, A.S.A., or worse." Hawaii's definition of "totally and permanently disabled" is "a physical or mental disability, which results in the . . . inability to engage in any substantial gainful business or occupation."
- Medical and dental expenses that have not been reimbursed can be deducted from adjusted gross income to the extent that they exceed 7.5% of federal adjusted gross income.
- Taxpayers in Hawaii can deduct 25% of the cost of premiums for health insurance for themselves and their families as an adjustment to gross income.

Idaho

- Medical and dental expenses that have not been reimbursed can be deducted from adjusted gross income to the extent that they exceed 7.5% of federal adjusted gross income.

- Idaho allows a state income tax credit for Child and Dependent Care expenses; 100% of the federally allowed expenses can be credited.
- A grocery credit of $15 per person in the household is allowed for taxpayers and/or spouses who are blind. This is a refundable credit, which means that Idaho taxpayers who do not need to file state income taxes can request a cash refund for this refund.

Illinois

- Since 1990, Illinois has allowed an additional state income tax exemption for any taxpayer or taxpayer's spouse who is legally blind.
- No itemized deductions are allowed in filing state income taxes in Illinois, including for medical expenses and Child and Dependent Care expenses.

Indiana

- Indiana allows an additional state income tax exemption for any taxpayer or taxpayer's spouse who is legally blind.
- Indiana does not allow any itemized deductions in filing state income taxes, including for medical costs and Child and Dependent Care expenses.
- In Indiana, under "Other Deductions to Adjusted Gross Income," there is a Human Services Tax Deduction for individuals who: 1) receive Medicaid; 2) do not live at home; *and* 3) receive care in a hospital, skilled nursing facility, or an intermediate care facility.
- Indiana offers a renters' income tax deduction of as much as $1,500 or actual rent for the year (whichever is less) in any property subject to Indiana property tax.

Iowa

• In Iowa, medical and dental expenses that have not been reimbursed can be deducted from adjusted gross income to the extent that they exceed 7.5% of federal adjusted gross income.

• An additional exemption of $20 is allowed on the Iowa state income tax return for a taxpayer and/or spouse who is blind.

• Iowa allows a deduction, not to exceed $5,000, on its state income taxes for care of a child, grandchild, parent, or grandparent with a disability in your home. This person must be unable to care for him- or herself due to physical or mental disability and must be receiving or be eligible to receive Medicaid.

• A self-employed taxpayer is allowed a deduction from state adjusted gross income of 25% of the premium cost of health insurance for him- or herself and his or her family. This deduction is *not* available if the taxpayer's spouse could receive health insurance for the family at his or her place of employment.

• A refundable Child and Dependent Care Credit is available through Iowa's state income taxes. Its value is 10% – 75% of the taxpayer's federally declared credit, depending on the taxpayer's income.

• Iowa also offers a nonrefundable Earned Income Credit of 6.5% of the federally declared EIC for Iowa taxpayers whose federal adjusted gross incomes are less than $21,250 and who have dependent children.

Kansas

• In Kansas, medical and dental expenses that have not been reimbursed can be deducted from adjusted gross income to the extent that they exceed 7.5% of federal adjusted gross income. Couples filing jointly who earned more than $100,000 together can only deduct a portion of these expenses.

• Kansas offers a credit on individual income tax for taxpayers who made their principal dwelling, an existing building, or an income-producing facility accessible to persons with disabilities.

• The full premium cost for health insurance for a self-employed taxpayer and his or her family is allowed as a deduction to gross income in Kansas. This deduction is not allowed if the taxpayer or his or her spouse's place of employment offers a health insurance plan they could join.

• Child and Dependent Care expenses can be taken on state income taxes as a credit at the rate of 25% of the federally claimed credit the same year.

Kentucky

• Medical and dental expenses that have not been reimbursed can be deducted from adjusted gross income in Kentucky, to the extent that they do *not* exceed 7.5% of federal adjusted gross income.

• Kentucky allows an additional income tax credit for taxpayers and/or spouses who are legally blind.

• Kentucky allows a credit against income tax to employers and employees for a percentage of premiums they pay for health insurance to a health care trust.

• Child and Dependent Care expenses are allowed as an income tax credit equal to 20% of the federally declared credit.

• A low-income credit is allowed for "single persons and married couples whose combined Kentucky adjusted gross income does not exceed $25,000. Credits range from 5% to 100%, depending on adjusted gross income. However, if taxpayers claim a federal supplemental young child credit as part of the federal Earned Income Credit, they cannot claim a Child and Dependent Care Credit on their federal income taxes.

Louisiana

- Louisiana gives an additional state income tax exemption to taxpayers and/or spouses who are blind.
- Taxpayers are allowed a credit of $100 for themselves, their spouse, or any dependent for any one of the following conditions:
  - Deafness, which is defined as the inability to understand speech through auditory measures alone (even with the use of amplified sound) and the need either to use visual measures or to rely on other forms of communication
  - Loss of limb, which is defined as the loss of one or both hands at or above the wrist, or one or both feet at or above the ankle; *the credit also applies if the use of the limb or limbs has been permanently lost*
  - "Mentally incapacitated," which is defined as the inability to care for oneself or to perform routine daily health requirements due to one's mental condition
  - Blindness, which is defined as "total blindness" and a central field of acuity that does not exceed 20/200 with corrective lenses in the better eye and a field of vision not greater than 20 degrees

  Only one credit may be claimed for each individual in any 1 year. The first year the credit is claimed, a doctor's statement of the condition must accompany the Louisiana income tax return.
- Louisiana allows a state income tax credit for Child and Dependent Care expenses equal to 10% of the declared federal credit for this expense.
- A tax credit equal to 10% of that declared on the taxpayer's federal return is allowed for taxpayers with "permanent and total" disabilities.

Maine

• Medical and dental expenses that have not been reimbursed can be deducted from adjusted gross income in Maine to the extent that they exceed 7.5% of federal adjusted gross income.

• Maine allows 20% of the credit for persons with "permanent or total disabilities declared on the federal income tax return as a credit on state income taxes.

• There is a deduction for long-term–care insurance.

• Maine allows a credit on its state income taxes for Child and Dependent Care expenses equal to 25% of the declared federal credit.

Maryland

• Medical and dental expenses that have not been reimbursed can be deducted from adjusted gross income in Maryland, to the extent that they exceed 7.5% of federal adjusted gross income.

• Maryland gives an additional income tax exemption of $1,000 to taxpayers and/or spouses who are blind.

• Maryland also permits the full federally allowable deduction for Child and Dependent Care expenses from any state income taxes due.

• Maryland also allows an income tax deduction for taxpayers whose earned income and federal adjusted gross income are less than the poverty level for a household of that size. Eligibility for this and amount of deduction depends on the results of a "Poverty Level Income Worksheet" included in the Maryland state income tax packet.

Massachusetts

• Medical and dental expenses that have not been reimbursed can be deducted from adjusted gross income in Massachusetts to the extent that they exceed 7.5% of federal adjusted gross income. All taxpayers may claim this deduction, as Massachusetts does not allow itemized deductions on its state income tax return.

• Massachusetts allows an additional state income tax exemption of $2,200 each for taxpayers and/or spouses who are blind.

• A deduction of $600 per child is allowed on state income taxes *or* employment-related expenses for the care of a dependent child. Allowable child care expenses differ from those of the federal government in the following ways:

1. Massachusetts allows you to deduct child care expenses for children younger than 15 years old, while the federal government only allows the credit for children younger than 13 years old.

2. The federal government requires taxpayers to include any employer-provided dependent care benefits in calculating a taxpayer's allowable expenses. A Massachusetts taxpayer does not have to include these in figuring his or her state credit.

3. In Massachusetts, a taxpayer may claim both a Child and Dependent Care Credit on state income taxes *and* the "federal supplemental young child credit" (part of the Earned Income Credit) if eligible for both. The federal government requires the federal taxpayer to choose one or the other.

• A "Limited Income Credit" on Massachusetts state income taxes is available to single individuals with income between $8,000 and $14,000 or married couples filing joint returns with incomes between $12,000 and $21,000.

Michigan

• Michigan offers additional personal exemptions on its state income taxes for taxpayers and/or spouses who are deaf or blind, or have disabilities. In Michigan, "disabilities" refer to hemiplegia, paraplegia, quadriplegia or "total and permanent" disabilities.

- There are no deductions for medical expenses, as no itemized deductions are allowed in figuring your Michigan personal income tax.
- Michigan taxpayers can include under "Miscellaneous Subtractions" the benefits from a discriminatory self-insured medical expense reimbursement plan, if the taxpayer includes the reimbursement in their Michigan adjusted gross income. A discriminatory self-insured medical expense reimbursement is simply any medical plan that reimburses a taxpayer for medical expenses.
- There is a homestead property tax credit available for Michigan taxpayers who are blind or have disabilities and whose incomes are $82,650 or less. This credit is reduced by 10% for every $1,000 the taxpayer household income exceeds $73,650. These taxpayers can be reimbursed for part or all of property taxes paid (up to a maximum of $1,200), even if they rent.
- A home-heating credit is available for Michigan taxpayer families with low incomes. This credit is based on the number of individuals living in the household.

Minnesota

- Medical and dental expenses that have not been reimbursed can be deducted from adjusted gross income in Minnesota to the extent that they exceed 7.5% of federal adjusted gross income.
- A credit for Child and Dependent Care expenses is allowed on Minnesota state income taxes if you meet the following criteria:

    1. Your federal adjusted gross income is less than $27,640.

2. You incur expense to provide care for a child younger than 13 years old, a spouse with a disability, or a person with a disability who receives at least half of his or her support from you, the taxpayer.
3. You paid for child care while you were looking for work.
4. The person on whose behalf you paid for dependent care lived with you.
5. You are single or married and filing a joint income tax return.
6. You paid someone other than your dependent child or stepchild under the age of 19 for the child care service.
7. You provided more than half the cost of running the household for the year.

This credit is refundable, meaning that even if you are *not* required to file a state income tax return, you can get a check from the state of Minnesota for the amount of the credit for Child and Dependent Care to which you are entitled.

Mississippi

• Medical and dental expenses that have not been reimbursed can be deducted from adjusted gross income in Mississippi to the extent that they exceed 7.5% of federal adjusted gross income.
• Mississippi allows an additional state income tax exemption of $1,500 for each taxpayer and/or spouse who is blind.

Missouri

• Medical and dental expenses that have not been reimbursed can be deducted from adjusted gross income in Missouri to the extent that they exceed 7.5% of federal adjusted gross income.

- Missouri has a "Special Needs Adoption Tax Credit" to help defray the costs of adopting a child with special medical needs. Information about this can be obtained from the Missouri Division of Family Services, Post Office Box 88, Jefferson City, Missouri 65103-0088; 1-800-877-6881.

Montana

- Medical and dental expenses that have not been reimbursed can be deducted from adjusted gross income in Montana to the extent that they exceed 7.5% of federal adjusted gross income.
- In Montana, a taxpayer with a child who has a disability is entitled to an additional exemption of $1,320 provided that child meets the following criteria:

    1. He or she must be claimed as a regular exemption.
    2. He or she must be at least "50% permanently disabled" as certified by a physician. (A copy of a physician's certification must be submitted with the Montana income tax return each year.)

- Montana allows an additional state income tax exemption of $1,320 for each taxpayer and/or spouse who is blind.
- The full cost of long-term–care insurance is deductible from your gross income in Montana if your policy meets the minimum standards established by the Montana State Auditor's Office, Insurance Commission Division.
- A taxpayer may deduct from his or her Montana state income taxes any payments made for "Child or Disabled Dependent Care" if the taxpayer and spouse both worked or looked for work and met the following criteria:

    1. The taxpayer maintains a home that includes one or more children younger than 15 years old, other dependents, or a spouse who was unable to care for him- or herself.

2. The taxpayer's income is not more than $22,800 with one child, $25,200 with two children, and $27,600 with three or more children.

Nebraska

- Medical and dental expenses that have not been reimbursed can be deducted from adjusted gross income in Nebraska to the extent that they exceed 7.5% of federal adjusted gross income.
- Nebraska allows an additional exemption in state income taxes of $1,290 each if the taxpayer and/or spouse is blind.

New Hampshire

- New Hampshire allows an extra exemption of $1,200 each (1991 rate) in its personal income taxes if a taxpayer and/or spouse is blind.
- An extra exemption of $1,200 each is allowed in New Hampshire if a taxpayer and/or spouse has a disability.
- New Hampshire does not allow itemized deductions in filing state income taxes.

New Jersey

- Medical and dental expenses that have not been reimbursed can be deducted from adjusted gross income in New Jersey to the extent that they exceed 2% of New Jersey's adjusted gross income. *All taxpayers may take this deduction, whether they itemize their state income taxes or not.*
- New Jersey allows an additional exemption of $1,000 each in its state income taxes for taxpayers and/or spouses who are blind or "disabled." "Disabled" in this case is defined as "total and permanent inability to engage in any substantial gainful activity by reason of any medically determinable physical or mental impairment."

Certification of a physician must be attached to the New Jersey income tax return the first time this exemption is claimed.

Nevada

• Nevada does not collect a state personal income tax.

New Mexico

• Taxpayers who are blind and live in New Mexico may be eligible for a state income tax deduction of as much as $8,000 based on federal adjusted gross income.
• Taxpayers who adopt a child with special needs on or after January 1, 1988 can claim a deduction of as much as $2,500 for each child who is younger than 18 years old. To claim this deduction, taxpayers need to attach a copy of the certification issued by the Human Services Department in New Mexico or the licensed child placement agency for each child for which this deduction is claimed.
• In New Mexico, a "Child Day Care Credit" is available to individuals who work and have incomes of $17,680 or less. This is a refundable credit, which means that even individuals who are not required to file state income tax returns can be rebated money by the state of New Mexico for child care expenses.

New York

• Medical and dental expenses that have not been reimbursed can be deducted from adjusted gross income in New York to the extent that they exceed 7.5% of federal adjusted gross income.
• A state income tax credit for Child and Dependent Care expenses is available in New York. The credit on New York state income taxes is 20% of the credit claimed on the federal income tax return.

North Carolina

- Medical and dental expenses that have not been reimbursed can be deducted from adjusted gross income in North Carolina to the extent that they exceed 7.5% of federal adjusted gross income.
- North Carolina offers its taxpayers an income tax credit if they have "permanent and total" disabilities. This credit equals one-third of the credit claimed for this item on the taxpayer's federal income tax return.
- North Carolina also offers a credit on state income taxes for "permanently and totally disabled" spouses and dependents. This credit, however, is limited to taxpayers with low incomes. Credits range from $40 to $80, depending on the household income and filing status of the taxpayer. To qualify for a spouse or dependent disability credit, a taxpayer must attach a statement to his or her income tax return each year the benefit is claimed. The taxpayer, spouse, or dependent must be "unable to engage in any substantial gainful activity by reason of a physical or mental impairment that can be expected to result in death or that has lasted or can be expected to last for a continuous period of not less than 12 months."
- Taxpayers in North Carolina may also be able to take a state income tax credit for Child and Dependent Care expenses. This credit is as follows:

    1. Seven percent of qualified federal expenses if care is for a dependent 7 years or older who is physically and mentally capable of caring for him- or herself
    2. Ten percent of qualified federal expenses if care is for a dependent younger than 7 years old or a dependent *not* physically or mentally capable of caring for him- or herself

North Dakota

- In North Dakota, all medical and dental expenses that have not been reimbursed can be deducted from state adjusted gross income, as long as the taxpayer has also itemized medical and dental deductions on his or her federal income tax return.

Ohio

- Medical and dental expenses that have not been reimbursed can be deducted from adjusted gross income in Ohio to the extent that they exceed 7.5% of federal adjusted gross income.
- Ohio allows a Child and Dependent Care Credit for taxpayers whose Ohio adjusted gross income is under $30,000. The credit is $360 or 25% of the federal Child and Dependent Care Credit claimed, whichever is *less.*

Oklahoma

- Medical and dental expenses that have not been reimbursed can be deducted from adjusted gross income in Oklahoma to the extent that they exceed 7.5% of federal adjusted gross income.
- Oklahoma allows a "Disability Deduction" for physical disabilities that constitute "substantial handicaps" to employment. When this applies, taxpayers may deduct some expenses from Oklahoma state income taxes, including those to modify a motor vehicle, home, or workplace to compensate for the handicap.
- Oklahoma allows a child care credit on its state income tax return equal to 20% of the credit the taxpayer claimed on his or her federal income tax return.

Oregon

- Medical and dental expenses that have not been reimbursed can be deducted from adjusted gross income in Oregon to the extent that they exceed 7.5% of federal adjusted gross income.
- Oregon offers an additional state income tax deduction of $1,000–$1,200 for taxpayers and/or spouses who are blind.
- Oregon offers a credit on state income tax for taxpayers who are "permanently disabled. This credit is equal to 40% of the federal credit declared on the taxpayer's federal income tax return.
- An extra income tax exemption is available in Oregon for taxpayers with a "severely disabled child." To qualify, the child must meet the following criteria:

1. He or she must be 17 years old or younger.
2. He or she must be eligible for early intervention services or diagnosed as "disabled" for special education purposes. (Learning disabilities alone do not generally count for this exemption.)
3. He or she must have a health-related disability requiring special education as defined by the Oregon Department of Education (i.e., autism, visual impairment, "trainable mental retardation," hearing impairment, orthopedic impairment, or multiple disabilities).

To claim this exemption, taxpayers must attach a statement of eligibility confirming one of the disabilities listed above and the cover sheet from one of the following:

1. The child's individualized education program (IEP)
2. The child's individualized program plan (IPP)
3. The child's individualized family service plan (IFSP)

- Oregon also offers a child care credit on state income taxes of 4%–30% of qualified expenses for taxpayers with incomes between $5,000 and $45,000.

Pennsylvania

- Pennsylvania does not allow itemized deductions in filing state income taxes, including for medical expenses and Child and Dependent Care costs.

Rhode Island

- Medical and dental expenses that have not been reimbursed can be deducted from adjusted gross income in Rhode Island to the extent that they exceed 7.5% of federal adjusted gross income.
- There is a credit on state income taxes in Rhode Island for Child and Dependent Care expenses, equal to the amount declared on the taxpayers' federal income tax return.
- Rhode Island offers a property tax credit to persons with disabilities who have collected Social Security Disability during the tax year in question and who meet certain household income limitations.

South Carolina

- Medical and dental expenses that have not been reimbursed can be deducted from adjusted gross income in South Carolina to the extent that they exceed 7.5% of federal adjusted gross income.
- South Carolina offers a credit on its state income taxes for 20% of expenses paid to a skilled or intermediate care nursing home.
- South Carolina offers a tax credit for Child and Dependent Care expenses equal to 7% of federally qualified expenses.

South Dakota

• South Dakota does not collect state personal income tax.

Tennessee

• Taxpayers who are blind qualify for "total exemption" from state income tax in Tennessee. A written statement from a medical doctor must be sent to tax authorities to substantiate the condition.
• When taxable interest or dividend income is received jointly by a blind person and a sighted spouse, only half of the jointly received income is exempt from state income tax.
• Tennessee does not allow itemized deductions in filing state income taxes, including for medical expenses.

Texas

• Texas does not collect state personal income tax.

Utah

• Medical and dental expenses that have not been reimbursed can be deducted from adjusted gross income in Utah to the extent that they exceed 7.5% of federal adjusted gross income.
• Utah offers an additional exemption of $1,613 on its state income tax for individuals with disabilities (not necessarily the taxpayer or spouse) who fall into certain categories:

   1. "Disabled infants and toddlers birth through 2 years" who are enrolled in an early intervention program monitored by the Utah Department of Health
   2. "Disabled school-age persons 3 through 21" who must be diagnosed by a local school district as "pre-

school handicapped," "intellectually handicapped," "severely intellectually handicapped," "deaf," "orthopedically handicapped," "visually handicapped," "severely multiply handicapped," "deaf and blind," or "autistic." The child must also be enrolled in a school district special education program or in the school for the deaf and blind, and not currently receiving residential services from the Division of Services to People with Disabilities (Department of Human Services) or from the school for the deaf and blind. *Children with learning disabilities and behavior disorders are not eligible.*

3. *"Adults with disabilities"* (18 years of age and older unless they are enrolled in a school district special education program) (Adults eligible for this exemption must have a severe chronic disability that is attributable to mental and/or physical impairment that is likely to continue indefinitely. The disability must result in substantial functional limitation in *three* or more of the following: adaptive skills [i.e., self-care], receptive and expressive language, learning, mobility, self-direction, capacity for independent living, or economic self-sufficiency. In addition, the individual must require a combination or sequence of special interdisciplinary or generic care, treatment, or other services that may continue throughout life and must be individually planned. "Disability" means, but is not limited to, "persons with autism, central nervous system damage [other than mental illness] due to birth defects, genetic disorders, trauma or disease," and includes encephalitis and meningitis, cerebral palsy, mental retardation, severe dyslexia, or severe sensory, orthopedic, or neurological impairments.)

Vermont

- Medical and dental expenses that have not been reimbursed can be deducted from adjusted gross income in Vermont to the extent that they exceed 7.5% of federal adjusted gross income.
- Vermont offers a "V-Script" program for individuals receiving disability payments. This is a pharmaceutical assistance program for those *not* eligible for Medicaid but still in need of financial help. The maximum qualifying income in 1991 was $11,600 for individuals and $15,500 for married couples.
- Vermont offers a children's comprehensive dental health program called "Tooth Fairy," a reduced cost dental care program for children under 18 years old whose families have low incomes. For families with incomes under $16,000 (1991 level), dental care costs are reduced as much as 50%. If a family's income is less than $8,500, the costs of dental care are reduced as much as 75% of the retail cost. This program is *not* for Medicaid recipients.
- Vermont offers a homeowner's or renter's credit on its state income taxes for taxpayers whose income is less than $45,000. The maximum credit possible is $1,350. Twenty percent of rent can be claimed as property tax.
- Vermont offers an Earned Income Credit for families who qualify for the federal EIC. The credit on Vermont state income taxes is 28% of the federal EIC.

Virginia

- Medical and dental expenses that have not been reimbursed can be deducted from adjusted gross income in Virginia to the extent that they exceed 7.5% of federal adjusted gross income.

- Virginia offers an extra state income tax exemption of $800 each for taxpayers and/or spouses who are blind according to federal income tax guidelines.
- In Virginia, a taxpayer can reduce his or her gross income by deducting disability income used to compute federal credit for "totally and permanently disabled under 65."
- Child and Dependent Care expenses are available as a credit to state income taxes, equal to all federally qualified expenses up to $2,400 for one child and $4,800 for two or more children.
- Beginning in the 1991 tax year, landlords in Virginia can qualify for an income tax credit of 50% of the total rent reductions he or she makes for tenants with mental or physical disabilities. Landlords must reduce the rent of these individuals by 15% or more. The maximum credit a landlord can take per year is $10,000, with any amount in excess of this carried for the next 5 taxable years.

Washington

- Washington does not collect a state personal income tax.

West Virginia

- West Virginia does not allow itemized deductions in its state income taxes, including for medical, dental, and related expenses.
- In West Virginia, a taxpayer can take a reduction in his or her gross income for tax purposes if he or she has a "total and permanent" disability. Such individuals must be "unable to engage in any substantial gainful activity by reason of any medically determinable physical or mental impairment that can be expected to result in death *or* that has lasted or can be expected to last for a continuous period of not less than 12 months." A West Virginia taxpayer trying to claim this credit must include a doc-

tor's certification of his or her condition. A reduction in West Virginia adjusted gross income as much as $8,000 (1991 level) is available for each qualified individual.

• West Virginia allows an adjustment to a taxpayer's gross income for premiums for health insurance they paid if self-employed. Premiums can cover insurance for both the taxpayer and his or her family members. The allowable reduction in adjusted gross income is equal to that allowed on the federal income tax return.

Wisconsin

• Wisconsin allows a 5% credit (1991) for excess expenses over the standard deduction available in figuring state income taxes. Items that can be itemized on a taxpayer's federal income tax return can be included in arriving at the Wisconsin credit.

• A deduction of 25% of the cost of health insurance a self-employed taxpayer pays for him- or herself, his or her spouse, and any dependents is allowed on the Wisconsin state income tax.

• Taxpayers with household incomes below $19,154 (1991) are allowed a homestead credit in figuring their state income taxes. Both home owners and renters can qualify for this credit.

• Wisconsin also offers a renter's or home owner's credit on state income tax for school property taxes. The maximum credit is $200 (1991).

• Wisconsin has an Earned Income Credit (EIC) available on state income taxes if the taxpayer claimed one on his or her federal income tax return. The children who qualify the taxpayer can be claimed as dependents on the taxpayer's Wisconsin state income tax return.

Wyoming

• Wyoming does not collect a state personal income tax.

9

Managing Your Debts

When Is It Time to Seek Outside Help?

F requent medical and related care often results in high medical bills, only a portion of which may be covered by public or private health insurance. This can put a tremendous strain on any family's budget. There are a number of things you can do to relieve some of this pressure. This chapter presents strategies to help. Information about resources to help you manage your medical bills and other debts is presented. Bill collectors and credit repair services are discussed as well. *Try to use as many of the following suggestions as you can.*

BUDGETING AND SPENDING CAREFULLY

Budget your family income and spend money as carefully as possible. This is helpful for every household, but is particularly important for families with frequent and often large medical bills. Figures 1 and 2 provide an example of a sample monthly budget and an expense record to give you an idea of how to plan and track your family's expenses. *It is not that difficult or time-consuming to budget and track your expenses; however, these activities put you face to face with your family's financial well-being.* For many of us, this is a painful "meeting," as our expenses exceed our income and we are not sure what to do about it. Planning for and keeping track of your expenses by category can suggest areas where expenses can be trimmed.

Planned expense	Amount
Mortgage payment	675.00
Utilities (gas, electric, water and sewer)	100.00
Telephone (including long-distance calls)	70.00
Gasoline and oil	65.00
Food	350.00
Child care	400.00
Clothing	50.00
Doctors and dentists	100.00
Other therapies	100.00
Prescription drugs	30.00
Allowances and school lunches	90.00
Car insurance (two cars)	75.00
Car repairs (two cars)	50.00
License plates (two cars)	15.00
Life insurance	30.00
Homeowner's insurance	30.00
Real estate taxes	70.00
Union dues/professional dues	30.00
Entertainment (including magazines, evening babysitting)	70.00
Miscellaneous	50.00
Total	$2,450.00

Figure 1.   Sample of a monthly budget.

Expense	Actual expense
Housing and housing maintenance	
Rent or mortgage payment	
Taxes	
Insurance	
Electricity	
Gas	
Water and sewer	
Trash/garbage collection	
Telephone	
Repairs or maintenance	
Home furnishings	
Cleaning service	
Lawn service	
Food	
Grocery items	
Nonedible items	
Pet food	
Snacks	
Meals prepared outside of the home	
Transportation	
Car insurance(s)	
Car payment(s)	
Title and tag(s)	
Repairs	
Personal property tax	
Gasoline/oil	
Automobile maintenance items	
Public transportation	
Education	
Tuition	
Books	
Supplies	
Work	
Union and/or professional dues	
Journal subscriptions	
Special equipment	
Uniforms, special clothing	

(continued)

Figure 2.   Sample monthly expense record.

Figure 2. (*continued*)

Expense	Actual expense
Medical/dental	
Health insurance	
Physicians	
Dentists	
Other professionals	
Hospitals	
Clinics	
Therapies	
Prescription medications	
Medical equipment and supplies	
Over-the-counter drugs and supplies	
Prescribed diet	
Vitamins	
Exercise club	
Child care	
Preschool	
Daytime babysitter	
Child support	
Recreation/entertainment	
Movies/plays	
Sports events	
Hobbies/special interests	
Vacations	
Toys	
Home entertaining	
Clothing	
New purchases	
Repairs/alterations	
Dry cleaning	
Laundry service	
Gifts/charity	
Birthdays	
Holidays	
Synagogue/church donations	
Nonprofit organization donations	
Personal	
Cosmetics	
Gifts for self	
Hairdresser	

You can also get free or low-cost help budgeting your family's income from a number of organizations and groups in or near your community. Some of these groups include the following:

- A *Consumer Credit Counseling Service (CCCS)* is a non-profit community organization that will help you budget your expenses and manage your debts. These services have trained professional or volunteer staffs who are also skilled at teaching individuals and families how to use credit wisely. A CCCS may charge you a small fee for these services, and there may be a short waiting list for help in some communities. To locate the Consumer Credit Counseling Service nearest your home, call the *National Foundation for Consumer Credit* (1-800-388-CCCS) for a referral.

- Your county's *Agricultural Extension Service or Cooperative Extension Service* may be helpful. In some states (e.g., North Carolina), this agency has arranged *Money Management Centers* that help individuals and families budget their expenses and use credit. To reach the Agricultural Extension or Cooperative Extension Service nearest your home, call your local information operator. Tell the operator your county of residence.

- A number of *local churches* have established and trained groups of volunteers to help individuals and families learn to manage their money. Contact your local church to inquire about such a program, or call your local United Way for information about church-based money management programs. You can find the United Way listed in the business section of the white pages telephone directory or you can ask your local information operator for the telephone number.

- *Women's centers* across the United States offer free or low-cost counseling on balancing your checkbook, managing your money, applying for and using credit, and so forth. To reach a women's center in or near your community, contact a United Way Information and Referral Service or a 24-hour crisis service. Call your local information operator to obtain any of these telephone numbers.

If you find yourself unable to pay all of your bills and developing a poor credit record, ***avoid individuals or services that claim they can "repair" your bad credit or "fix" your credit report.*** These services will charge you as much as $1,000 to do this. In reality, they cannot repair or erase poor credit records. Credit reports are maintained by private companies, who cannot erase accurately reported bad debts that appear on your credit report for a 7- to 10-year period.

SEEKING APPROPRIATE
SERVICES AT THE LOWEST COSTS

Seek appropriate services for your child with a chronic illness or a disability at the lowest cost possible. Chapter 3 details the many kinds of services available, as well as strategies to obtain and pay for them. *Advocacy and parent support groups* can help you sort through the many available services. Chapter 3 discusses ways these and other groups can help; Appendix B at the end of this book lists a variety of such national and regional groups that can recommend a local service or put you in contact with an agency or parent group that can. As discussed previously, ***it is recommended that you use this routing to get help. This way local referrals will be screened for you regarding the quality and appropriateness of services available.*** Professionals in your area can also offer suggestions and recommendations for appropriate services. *Gather information from several sources before making a decision about which services to use.*

NEGOTIATING WITH HEALTH CARE PROVIDERS

Ask health care providers to accept what your health insurance will pay as "payment in full."

Physicians and other health care providers in private practice are at total liberty to accept a reduced fee for their services. Most health care providers associated with teaching hospitals and academic medical centers have some authority to do so as well. (Rosenfeld, 1993, p. 19)

Try to overcome any discomfort you may feel discussing fees with your child's doctors and other professionals. It can save you a great deal of money.

ARRANGING PAYMENT PLANS

Set up payment plans with health care providers for the portion of service costs you will have to pay out of your own pocket. Agree to pay your creditors only what you can comfortably afford each month. If you are not able to make your agreed-upon payment one month, contact the doctor, hospital, or other health care provider. Also let the provider know when you can resume your payments. This will keep you out of credit trouble and may keep the bill collectors away.

ENROLLING IN PUBLIC ASSISTANCE PROGRAMS

Enroll your child and family in any public assistance programs possible. Examples of these include the federal government's Supplemental Security Income (SSI) Program for older people and people who are blind or have disabilities, Medicaid, Aid to Families with Dependent Children (AFDC) for children from families with low incomes, the Food Stamp Program, and so forth. Chapters 5 and 7 suggest many public programs of potential help. Strategies to obtain help successfully are offered in these chapters as well.

SEEKING HELP FROM PRIVATE ORGANIZATIONS

Seek medical care or cash assistance from private organizations in your community or state. Examples of these organizations include your *church, area ministries, civic and disease- or disability-related organizations.* Chapter 6 offers detailed information about private sources of help in paying for medical and related care for your child. This section of the book also suggests strategies for obtaining such help.

The important thing to remember is not to withdraw your child from useful medical or related care simply because you find you cannot pay your child's medical bills. Discuss your situation with your child's doctors. Find a social worker in the hospital or clinic where your child receives a lot of his or her care. Ask the social worker to direct you to help, so you can ease your financial situation, avoid embarrassment, and continue to get your child any required care.

DEALING WITH BILL COLLECTORS

It is important to know that, regardless of the state you live in, all bill collectors are regulated by federal law, and *there are fairly strict limits on what bill collectors can and cannot do to collect funds.* For example, according to PL 95-109, the Consumer Credit Protection Act Amendments of 1977, and PL 99-361, the Fair Debt Collection Practices Act Amendments of 1986; *bill collectors must obey the following rules:*

1. Debt collectors may not contact you at unreasonable times or places, such as before 8 A.M. or after 9 P.M., unless you agree that this is acceptable.
2. Debt collectors may not contact you at work if you inform the collector that your employer disapproves of this practice (Federal Trade Commission, 1991).
3. A debt collector may not contact you again if you send the collection agency a letter stating that you do not owe money to their creditor. You must send this letter within 30 days of your first contact by the collector.

4. Debt collectors are prohibited by law from using threats of violence or harm against a person, property, or reputation (Federal Trade Commission, 1991); from calling you endlessly to annoy you; or from advertising your debt.

You should also know that, under federal law, **you have the right to sue a bill collector in a state or federal court within 1 year of the date you believe the creditor violated the law.** If you are successful in your suit, you are entitled to recover your attorney's fees and any court costs from the debt collector in addition to the money damages you are awarded by the court (Federal Trade Commission, 1991).

The Federal Trade Commission (FTC) is responsible for monitoring the behavior of bill collectors to see that they comply with federal law. The regional office of the FTC closest to your home can send you more complete information on federal regulations regarding debt collection practices and steps to take if you feel a debt collector has violated the law. Addresses and telephone numbers for FTC Regional Offices are listed in Appendix B at the end of this book.

If you feel personally threatened by a bill collector, hang up the telephone and report the incident to your local police. Be sure to get the name of the bill collector or the collection agency he or she represents, so you can pass this information on to the FTC or your local police.

SUMMARY

Probably one of the most challenging jobs associated with having a child who has a chronic illness or disability is trying to fit all of the medical and related bills for that child into your family's budget. Most families in this situation have some problem affording the care their children require. Family budgeting and other community services can help you manage these expenses, avoid irritating bill collectors, and keep your credit in good standing. Some of the ways to obtain these services have been suggested in this chapter.

10

Keeping It All Together
Organizing the Paperwork

W hen you have a child who requires frequent health-related care, including a variety of specialized services, it is useful to keep certain kinds of information at your fingertips. If you do so, you can obtain additional services for your child, save money, and have a greater sense of control over your child's care. This chapter explains why this is important and suggests the kinds of information you will want to have readily available. Some ways to organize and store this information are presented as well.

REASONS TO BE ORGANIZED

The major reason to keep information about your child and your family close at hand is that most of the programs to which you will apply for services for your child will request it. The staff usually ask for a lot of information about your child, his or her condition, and the prior intervention services and treatments he or she has received. These agencies and others to which you may apply for financial assistance will also want to know about your family, including the amount of family income and other "resources" and assets your family has.

In addition to **applying for services or financial assistance for your child or family,** keeping a variety of kinds of information about your child and your family in a central location can help you in other ways. In keeping summaries of your child's inpatient and outpatient visits to professionals, you can **track the tests, medications, procedures, and surgeries your child has had over time.** You will often be asked to provide this information to a service program or a new professional your child is consulting. With such records easily available to you, you can also **evaluate the interventions and treatments your child has received over time and chart his or her progress in development and functioning.** Storing receipts, bills, and records will also **help you to stay on top of medical bills for clinics, hospitals, doctors, and other professionals, and to take advantage of special federal and state income tax deductions, exemptions, and credits** available to many families with a child who has a chronic illness or a disability or with large medical expenses. Finally, having certain paperwork about your child and his or her treatment at hand can help you more easily **appeal a denied health insurance claim or present your case if you challenge any part of your child's individualized education program (IEP), your family's individualized family service plan (IFSP), another entitlement to service** (e.g., Supplemental Security Income [SSI]), or any other matter relating to your child's care.

To serve many of the purposes described above, it is recommended that you *keep the following kinds of informa-*

tion organized and in a place that is always accessible to you. In many cases, quite a bit of information about your child will need to be organized and stored. ***Where and how you keep this information is up to you.*** It does not matter if you keep it in a series of shopping bags, shoe boxes, looseleaf notebooks, or file drawers. The most important thing is to keep the information in a way that is comfortable for you to use and easy to update from time to time, and that organizes the information in a way you will get the most use out of it.

INFORMATION TO KEEP
READILY AVAILABLE ABOUT YOUR CHILD
WITH A CHRONIC ILLNESS OR DISABILITY

You will want to keep the following information about your child with a chronic illness or disability:

1. Birth certificate or a copy of it
2. Social Security number
3. The full name, address, and telephone number of your child's doctor(s) and the other professionals he or she sees
4. Your child's primary diagnosis, any secondary diagnoses, and a description of developmental delays and/ or functional limitations in daily living
5. A list of all of the medications your child takes, including the dose of each
6. The name, address, and telephone number of the pharmacy (or pharmacies) where you fill your child's prescriptions
7. The name, address, and telephone number on the medical equipment and supply company (or companies) you have used to purchase equipment or supplies for your child
8. Yearly summaries of your child's diagnosis, including updates, delays, and functional limitations, along with

major illnesses and medical procedures that have occurred throughout the year (K. Shannon, written communication, 1993) (This can be useful for tracing your child's progress).

9. A copy of all of your child's bills for medical and medically related treatment for the last calendar year (e.g., doctor bills, dental bills, clinic visits, hospital stays, prescription medications, medical equipment and supplies, eyeglasses, medically prescribed diet, psychotherapy, diagnostic testing, modifications to your home to improve access)

10. A record of payments you made for all of your child's medical and medically related care

11. A copy of your child's IEP for each year, as required by Part B of IDEA for preschoolers and school-age children with disabilities

12. A copy of your family's IFSP for each year, as required by Part H of IDEA for infants and toddlers from birth through 2 years old

13. A copy of a physician's certificate stating that your child has a particular chronic illness or disability (specified in the statement) and/or certain functional limitations in daily living (also specified in the statement) (This is often required to claim extra income tax exemptions available in many states.)

Another way to stay organized and "keep it all together" is to develop a list of "key contacts" in your child's care. These contacts may include your child's doctors and therapists, as well as hospitals, insurance companies, and school staff. Figure 1 contains a sample form for compiling this information. You may want to use a form like this or design one that more clearly matches your child's and family's needs.

Key Contacts

Child's name: _____

Child's date of birth: _____

Child's Social Security number: _____

Health insurance policy covering this child:
    Company name: _____
    Company address: _____
    _____

    Company telephone number: _____
    Policy number: _____
    Contact person: _____

Community pediatrician: _____
    Address: _____
    _____

    Telephone number: _____
    Nurse's name: _____

Medical specialists: _____
(For each, include _____
telephone number _____
and nurse's or _____
assistant's name) _____
_____

Other therapists: _____
(For each, _____
include _____
telephone _____
number and _____
nurse's or _____
assistant's _____
name) _____

Hospital your child usually uses: _____
(Include name and telephone _____
number) _____

(*continued*)

Figure 1.   A sample form for listing key contacts in managing your child's health and related care.

Figure 1. (*continued*)

Pharmacy: _____
(Include name _____
and telephone _____
number)

Medications _____
child is taking: _____
(Include names _____
and dosages) _____
_____
_____

Medical supplies and/or equipment: _____
(Include name and telephone _____
number) _____
_____

Your child's teacher: _____
(Include name and _____
telephone number)

Your child's principal: _____
(Include name and _____
telephone number)

Contact at Part H Program: _____
(Include name and _____
telephone number) _____
_____

Special Education Director: _____
(Include name and _____
telephone number) _____
_____

Other: _____
_____
_____
_____
_____

INFORMATION TO KEEP READILY AVAILABLE ABOUT YOUR FAMILY

It is important to keep the following information about your family in an easily accessible place (e.g., a "Family Information File"):

1. The birth certificates (or copies) for the parents of the child with a chronic illness or disability, and those for other children or dependents claimed on your income tax return
2. Social Security numbers of the parents of a child with a chronic illness or a disability and those for all individuals living in the household
3. All wage stubs or payroll receipts for the past 18 months for anyone in your family who earns income
4. A list of the resources or assets members of your family own with an estimated value of each (e.g., for home, car[s], bank accounts, savings bonds, home furnishings)
5. The names, addresses, and telephone numbers of all employers for individuals in your household who work
6. A copy of your past year's federal and state income tax returns
7. If both parents work or your household is headed by a single parent who works, a record of your expenses for "child and dependent care" for the last 18 months
8. A summary of the health insurance benefits covering your child with a chronic illness or disability and other members of your household (e.g., a summary of benefits under a private health insurance policy, CHAMPUS, the Medicaid Program including the Early and Periodic Screening, Diagnosis, and Treatment [EPSDT] Program, your state's Department of Maternal and Child Health's "Children's Special Health Services Program")

9. A note about the kind of written justification each of the public and/or private insurers of your child or other family members requires to be reimbursed for a claim
10. A dozen extra forms to file health insurance claims for your child or other family members, including the address to which to send completed claims
11. Copies of all medical bills for all family members other than your child with special health care needs for the last 3 years (Keep bills for your child with special health care needs separately.)
12. A record of payments you made for all of your family's medical bills
13. A copy of any life insurance policies a parent or parents have, with the policy number and any cash value highlighted
14. A copy of the parent or parents' will(s)

Some families keep track of medical and medically related expenses by maintaining a separate checking account solely for this purpose. *For temporary storage of bills*, payment receipts, and clinic reports, it is recommended that you carry a large manilla envelope or folder with you and a smaller envelope (Figure 2) in your purse or car's glove compartment. This way you will always have a place to put any important papers. You can transfer papers from this portable file into your more *permanent storage system* when you return from trips to the clinic, pharmacy, and so forth.

SUMMARY

Setting up information files may take some time, as will updating the files from time to time. Doing so, however, should bring many extra benefits to your child and family. First, having such files will save you many anxious hours of

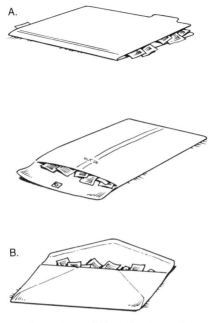

Figure 2. A large manilla envelope or folder (A) and a smaller envelope (B) that can easily be carried with you or kept in your car as a temporary storage system for bills and payment receipts.

searching through your house for a particular medical bill, birth certificate, or payment receipt. Second, with all of the information you will store and update periodically, you will be superbly positioned to apply for services and financial assistance for your child and family. Third, you will also be able to know fairly easily which programs you and your child can qualify for, and whether or not your family can realize any additional income tax savings at the end of the tax year. Finally, you will be better informed about your child's health status, treatments, and progress he or she has made, and you will be able to participate more meaningfully with your child's doctors and teachers in decisions about your child's care and education.

11

Tips for Getting What You Need

This chapter discusses the most effective ways to solve problems and get help, whether you are seeking information about your child's disease or disability, interventions and treatments that could help, the best school program for him or her, or ways to finance medical care. Specific groups and organizations come and go. Effective strategies, such as the following, that use whatever group or organization is in place will serve you well into the future:

1. ***Remind yourself regularly that the information or help you are seeking is needed by your child or your family.*** Know in your heart that you are fulfilling your responsibility as that child's parent(s) to do everything and anything you can—within the law—to get your child the medical and related care that he or she needs. This effort will help your child to function and participate in life as fully as possible. Remembering this will keep you on track and will help

immunize you to others' lack of appreciation for, or even criticism of, your dogged determination and assertiveness.

2. **When your child or family has a need, call as many individuals and organizations as necessary to get that need met.** Stay on the telephone until you get the information you need. This can be frustrating as you may have to call a number of organizations and speak to several individuals there. Keep in mind that your child's welfare depends on your persistence. Do not give up until at least one of the individuals you contact says "yes," that he or she can help.

3. **Commitment to your job and persistence are the names of the game. Your determination to solve a problem your child or other family member has will generally pay off.** In researching solutions, do not look only at what was or is the case or policy. Also look at what could be.

Who would have thought that Julie Beckett could get the U.S. Congress and the federal Medicaid agency to reverse a major policy of not covering children with severe disabilities under Medicaid if the children were not in institutions? With a few good research skills and a lot of determination to change a policy that she believed was not reasonable, Julie did exactly that.

Every state in the United States now has some kind of *home- and community-based waiver program* for at least a limited number of individuals. Most of them cover children and only count the child's income in determining their eligibility for Medicaid. That's progress.

4. Similarly, **consider it unreasonable for your child with a disability or chronic illness to go without needed medical care. Develop an informed opinion about who you would like your child's care providers to be, and try your best to have your child treated by such individuals or at such facilities.**

Do not discontinue your child's medical and other needed care just because you are having trouble paying the bills. You will be able to work something out with your child's provider. But, until you do, keep getting your child the care he or she needs. Doctors and hospitals will work with you to reduce fees and finance medical bills.

5. *Also decide that it is not reasonable for a family paying for expensive care of a child with special health care needs to go without adequate food, heat, or medical care in order to afford the child's medical bills.* Your strong beliefs about what is not reasonable and your determination and persistence to do what you can about it are the most important ingredients in solving your child's and family's problems.

6. *Learn all you can about the disease, disability or condition your child has. Learn about recommended interventions, treatments, and available services in your community or state.*

Remember, organizations and programs change focus and location over time. *Update your resource list at least once a year.* If you do not have a current resource guide to services for children with disabilities, call a few agencies that you know deal with children's health (e.g., your county's Public Health Department, the pediatric department of a children's hospital in your state, the regional and national information and advocacy organizations listed in Chapter 3 and Appendix B at the end of this book).

7. *Seek out other families in situations similar to yours. Be sure to cultivate relationships with families who have a number of years more experience than you* do at getting information and services from agencies. Ask them to share their experiences and successful strategies with you.

8. *Take a friend or relative with you to your child's medical and related appointments. Include him or her in*

your consultations with the professional(s). Discuss the questions you want to be sure to ask about your child's treatment or progress with your companion ahead of time. A parent's concern for his or her child's condition and fear of worrisome news at such a consultation can make it difficult for the parent to gather his or her thoughts in the doctor's or other professional's office.

9.   When you are trying to solve a problem (e.g., owing $8,000 in medical debts to your child's doctor and hospital and bill collectors calling you every week), ***be sure you understand the problem. Get the facts together and find out how much time you have to consider possible solutions.*** Without talking with anyone at this point, ***think as creatively as you can about your solutions.*** Examples for a situation like this would be the following:

- Try to get the bills "written off."
- Delay paying for another few months.
- Pay a little bit each month on the bills.
- Borrow money from the bank to pay the bills.
- Increase your household income.
- Do nothing and see if the bill collector's threats are real.
- Continue to wait to pay, but talk to a lawyer about possible consequences and solutions.

Examine each possible solution. Which would be realistic for your family? With which solutions are you most comfortable? ***Then talk with others,*** such as the following:

- *Your spouse* about the different options and your feelings about each
- *A banker* about the possibility and cost of a loan
- *The business office* of another hospital about their policy of writing off or reducing bills for individuals with no health insurance, or of accepting payment plans for outstanding bills

- *Other families in similar situations* for support and to see how they have handled similar problems (Follow up on tips they offer [e.g., to check with your regional office of the Federal Trade Commission about exactly what a bill collector can and cannot do to you and what steps you can take if the bill collector is violating federal or state law].)

The advice from all of the individuals above will help you evaluate your options.

Then, rank your options, and go for the one at the top of your list. *Be assertive but respectful to those with whom you have to deal to bring about your preferred solution.* If, for example, you prefer to set up payment plans with your child's doctor, physical therapist, and clinic, *assume that you can. Don't ask for permission to do so.* Nicely, but clearly, let the person in the business office know that you can afford to pay $75 a month (or whatever you can afford) on each bill. If the business office tells you that is not enough, compromise on $100 a month.

10. **Try to meet with the people whose approval you need on a proposal in person.** You can often make a more convincing case for what your child or family needs face-to-face. Make an appointment to see the individual in charge of a particular decision on aid.

11. **If your preferred solution to a problem does not work, go for your second choice.** You will have already done your homework on this option, so you will know the advantages and drawbacks. In the example above, your second choice of outcomes might be increasing your family's income, so that you can more easily afford these and other medical bills. Can one or more adults or youths in the house seek a part-time job? Can you reduce other households expenses?

12. In researching problems and attempting solutions, **try not to take other people's abruptness or disinterest per-**

sonally. Most of the people you will call do not know you. Most likely, they are busy, were in the middle of something else when you called, or are just having a bad day. **When you are not well received on the telephone, proceed with your request anyway. If you are getting nowhere, end the conversation and call back another day.** You may get a different clerk or the same one in a more helpful mood.

Over the course of solving dozens of problems for your child or family, undoubtedly a number of doors will close and telephones will be hung up without your having solved a particular problem. However, if you keep working at it (e.g., calling another parent group, another local foundation, and another social service agency), you *will* find help that improves your child's or family's comfort, access to resources, or level of debt.

13.   *If you encounter repeated rudeness from the same person, be sure to get that individual's name, call back, and report these incidents to a supervisor or an agency's personnel department.* You will be doing other families who have called or will call this agency a service by letting someone know that you do not appreciate such treatment and expect that it will not happen again in the future. A supervisor will appreciate your call as well. Agencies are dependent on taxpayer funds and private fees and do not want people with such attitudes on their front lines.

14.   **When you call an agency or organization— particularly a large one—you may be answered by a computer instead of a person.** In many of these instances, you are asked to pick from a "menu" of choices to route your call to the department you need, or to listen to taped information messages. *If your need does not fit one of the options given, or you want to talk to a human being to clarify your question, do not push any button on your telephone.* In most cases, a human operator will answer to help

you. This is usually the case even when this procedure is not mentioned by the "computerized receptionist."

15. As mentioned previously, **when making a request of an unknown individual or organization, be sure to write down the name of the person you spoke with and the date of your call or meeting.** If you have to follow up on your request later, you will have the name of the person handy. **It is almost always most efficient and productive to talk to the same person each time you call or go to an agency for help.** Obviously, this is not true if a person has not been helpful. Otherwise, *the helpful individual becomes your contact at a particular agency and over time you develop a relationship with him or her.* Your contact comes to feel that he or she "knows" you, and often the same applies for you. *In such a situation, you will receive information and advice you would rarely receive from a person you are talking with for the first time,* no matter how friendly and helpful that first-time contact may be.

Even if future dealings with a particular agency do not concern your contact's area of responsibility, he or she can suggest the best person with whom you should talk. In these situations, *always ask your contact if you may use his or her name in approaching the new individual with whom you need to speak. You will almost never get a refusal to do that.* When you open your conversation with, "[Contact's name] suggested I call you about . . . ," you are no longer a total stranger to the person to whom you are talking. You can get more help sooner using this technique.

16. **Remember the people who have been particularly helpful** to your child, to you, and to other family members. Send notes to express appreciation, indicating what their extra effort and kindness have meant to your child's and family's well-being. Send a dozen home-baked cookies. Have your child make a picture of thanks for their office. Be

sure to include such people on your holiday card list. Include a picture of your family with the card. These are ways you can personalize your thanks.

Besides being "the right thing to do"—to acknowledge a kindness—your thoughtfulness will serve your child's and family's needs well. You have taken time out of your busy, hectic life to show appreciation. Not many individuals do that.

17.   As stated at the beginning of this chapter, **remember that the help you are seeking is needed by your child and family.** Otherwise, you would not be asking for it. Generally, people do not ask for things they truly do not need. Most people prefer to take care of themselves and their families without outside help whenever they can.

18.   *Take advantage of offers of help and ask for help when you need it.* Your church may want to send meals once a week. Neighbors may offer to babysit while you and your partner go to the movies. Ask your sister-in-law to drive a carpool for you during a particularly busy week. See if a neighbor can pick up a few groceries for you when he gets his own.

Pamper yourselves as well from time to time. Order home delivery of a pizza or go out to a neighborhood restaurant, even when it is not exactly in the month's budget. Sit by a fire. Take a long walk in the woods or soak in a hot tub. *Take time to enjoy the fortunes that you have. DO THIS WHENEVER YOU CAN, but no less often than once a month.*

All of these activities will recharge you for the next round of telephone calls, bills, trips to school, and so forth. They will help you take the edge off of your nerves and be the most effective advocate for your child while being "available" to him or her and other family members.

19.   *Tackle problems one by one, day by day.*

20.   ***When you are "on duty," and you will be a lot of the time, remember that doing as great a job as you can on almost any task brings a great reward. You both get what you were after and know that you gave your all. When things do not work out, you still have the reward of knowing that you gave it your best shot.*** For you and your family, the stakes may be higher. Your child's life may depend on your doing your best. GO FOR IT!

12

Summary:
The Outlook
for Children
with Disabilities
and Their Families

C hildren and youth with disabilities and chronic illnesses have never had better access to the opportunity
to live as typically as possible while remaining with their
families or in familial settings in their communities.

THE RESULTS OF ADVOCACY

Persistent advocacy by both families and professionals has
resulted in continued gains in the rights of children with

disabilities and chronic illnesses to live in local neighbor-
hoods and to receive health care services, public education,
life skills and job training, assistive technology services and
devices, and other related services. Many youth with disabilities or chronic illnesses now have the opportunity to
state preferences about their living situations, health care
providers, education, recreation, and job training programs.

The families of children and youth with disabilities and
chronic illnesses are also actively involved in planning a
variety of services for their children and youth. This occurs
in conferences with health care providers, teachers and other school personnel, and social service providers. Much of
this participation is now backed by legal mandate (e.g., parents' or legal guardians' active participation in the development of a child's individualized education program).

Both young people and their families are becoming better informed about their rights and how to assume these
rights. They are taking more responsibility for defining their
needs and advocating for service availability and program
funding. *The results of such advocacy on behalf of these
children has also had numerous widespread effects, including the following:*

1. Children and youth with disabilities and chronic ill-
    nesses are more visible in local communities.
2. More factual information about disabilities and chronic
    illnesses is available to the general public.
3. Developmental delays in children can be detected ear-
    lier than ever before, which provides a better chance for
    delays to be improved upon, if not eliminated, at the
    earliest possible time. (Early intervention services and
    the Early and Periodic Screening, Diagnosis, and Treat-
    ment [EPSDT] Program, for example, were created for
    this reason.)

4. Numerous legislative mandates require service coordination to plan and coordinate the variety of services that might be needed by children and youth with disabilities and chronic illnesses and their families.

5. Public and private financial assistance programs are increasingly available to more children with disabilities, helping to pay for the extra costs of their care (e.g., Supplemental Security Income [SSI] Program, Blue Cross and Blue Shield "Caring" Programs in 25 cities across the United States).

6. The public and private sectors of U.S. society are required to make their services and businesses (e.g., schools, colleges, libraries, theaters, retail stores, public transportation, telecommunications) accessible to children and youth with special health care needs. This is required by the combination of Section 504 of PL 93-112, the Rehabilitation Act of 1973, its amendments, and PL 101-336, the Americans with Disabilities Act of 1990.

7. Extensive federal and state legislation has evolved to protect the civil rights of children and youth with disabilities and chronic illnesses.

8. There is continued growth across the United States of family support programs; self-help advocacy groups; and training in community organization, lobbying skills, and the process of agency budgeting and public policy making for families with children who have special health care needs.

THE NEED FOR CONTINUED ADVOCACY

Continued efforts are required, however, to help ensure that children and youth with disabilities and chronic illnesses and their families have the support and services they need. First, with large budget deficits and a growing number of older Americans who are dependent on assistance, *it will take a lot of work to maintain the current progress and opportunities that exist for children and youth with disabilities and chronic illnesses.* Policies, laws, and court rulings must continue to be put into practice and evaluated by the persistent efforts of advocates. For example, public school systems and other service agencies will need help obtaining the level of resources needed to comply with the Individuals with Disabilities Education Act (IDEA). Advocates for children with developmental delays whose families have low incomes will need to be sure that each state's Medicaid agency is reaching out to families to enroll children in the Early and Periodic Screening, Diagnosis, and Treatment (EPSDT) Program under Medicaid, and is offering such children all medically necessary services, both of which are required by law.

Second, advocates must help to ensure that all children and youth with chronic illnesses or disabilities get health insurance coverage for their conditions, either under a parent's plan through an employer, or as individuals, without having coverage limited by "pre-existing condition" clauses.

THE CLINTON HEALTH CARE REFORM PROPOSAL

President Clinton's health care reform proposal—part of a lengthy debate on health care and health insurance reform underway in the U.S. Congress—holds promise for eliminating *some* of the concerns mentioned previously. Clinton's proposal, submitted as identical bills in both the House of Representatives (H.R. 3600) and the Senate (S. 1757), is known as *the American Health Security Act of 1993*; it proposes the following (as of March 1, 1994 revision):

1. Provides all Americans with health insurance coverage—in most cases through one of three health care plans (including one fee-for-service plan) offered by a regional health alliance or by a corporate alliance (i.e., a company employing more than 5,000 workers) that can offer its own health care plan
2. Requires all Americans to enroll in a health care plan
3. Requires that all health care plans offer a basic package of benefits that are at least as comprehensive as those offered by most large companies in 1993, but with deductibles and co-payments for all but Aid to Families with Dependent Children (AFDC) and Supplemental Security Income (SSI) recipients
4. Requires health care plans to enroll individuals without regard to their health status or history
5. Requires employers to pay as much as 80% of the cost of health insurance premiums for employees
6. Limits the out-of-pocket expenses of insured persons (in most cases to $1,500 per individual or $3,000 per family per year for the first year of the plan)
7. Includes government subsidies for the insured person's share of health insurance premiums, deductibles, and co-payments (for those earning up to $40,000 a year for a family of four)
8. Includes a new federal and state combined program for home- and community-based long-term care coverage
9. Includes a comprehensive health services program for a limited number of children from families with low incomes, but who are not necessarily welfare recipients

These provisions of Clinton's health insurance and health care reform program will be helpful to children with special health care needs, many of whom cannot qualify for any health insurance at this time or whose families cannot afford it. Pre-existing conditions will be covered, subsidies for premiums and co-payments will be available to children whose families have low incomes, and a family's total out-of-pocket cost will be capped. Additionally, a family with a child who has special health care needs no longer will need to be concerned about the loss of health insurance coverage for the child when a parent changes jobs; this is because health insurance coverage will be available to all Americans in any setting, regardless of the medical condition of the insured.

However, Clinton's plan necessitates charging higher costs (e.g., premiums, co-payments and deductibles, additional income taxes) for individuals who select health insurance benefits in excess of the "basic benefit package." *Many children with disabilities and chronic illnesses will need services that go beyond the basic benefit package to meet their basic requirements.* For example, physical, occupational, and speech-language therapies are included in Clinton's "basic benefit package" primarily on an acute care basis. Communication aids are not covered at all. Therefore, the costs to families of children who require such aids could be higher.

Furthermore, under Clinton's plan, the proposed incentives to businesses and individuals to have care offered and received in managed care settings (e.g., health maintenance organizations, preferred provider organizations) designed specifically to control costs will not be compatible with the needs of children and youth who require extensive and costly care. Cost control in these settings is achieved primarily by constantly reviewing service use, limiting access to expensive specialty care, and purchasing service provision in bulk at discounted rates. *These cost control measures are not compatible with the health service needs of children requiring frequent, expensive, specialty care.* Acknowledging that special populations have needs that are not addressed in the currently proposed reform package, there has been some discussion among the Clinton Administration of developing a special program for children with disabilities. This is *not*, however, a part of the current package, except for the limited long-term care that, as proposed, will not be able to accommodate all children in need. Furthermore, the proposed long-term care program allows states a great deal of choice in the services they offer (e.g., homemaker, chore assistance, home modification, respite services, assistive technology, rehabilitation, supported employment, service coordination).

Finally, the Clinton plan neither prescribes service coordination nor mandates involvement of families of children with special health care needs in health planning and coordination activities.

OTHER HEALTH CARE REFORM PROPOSALS

Other health insurance and health care reform proposals in Congress differ from Clinton's in the scope of benefits offered, the degree of suggested government involvement (e.g., administering health care alliances, providing subsidies for premiums and/or income tax deductions for premiums, mandating what employers offer and/or pay for in health insurance policies for their employees, treatment of pre-existing conditions, means by which access to services are increased, means by which acute and long-term care services are provided and paid for by individuals with low incomes, means by which medical malpractice is reformed, whether caps on national health care spending are proposed), and role of established businesses in the provision of, and payment for, health care (e.g., health insurance companies).

EVALUATING HEALTH CARE REFORM PROPOSALS

Each proposal for health insurance and health care reform must be evaluated on its merits from the perspective of the

*needs of a child with a disability or chronic illness and his
or her ability to gain access to needed care at reasonable
costs.* In this regard, proposals of help to children with special health care needs should do the following:

1. Offer ready access to a variety of kinds of health and
    related care needed by children and youth with disabil-
    ities and chronic illnesses, regardless of their health con-
    dition or history
2. Offer care to lessen the impact of a child's disability or
    chronic illness and improve his or her functioning in
    addition to caring for acute conditions
3. Offer access to care at a cost a family can afford, with
    limits on the family's total out-of-pocket expense tied to
    their income levels
4. Offer access to care regardless of whether a child's par-
    ents or guardians are employed or not
5. Require ongoing service coordination
6. Require the involvement of parents of children with dis-
    abilities or chronic illnesses, and their advocates, at all
    levels of health insurance, health care planning, service
    delivery, and monitoring

As discussed in Chapter 2, you can read summaries and
analyses of any proposed legislation in *Congressional Quarterly Weekly Report.* In addition, *Medicine and Health* and
Health Legislation and Regulation review proposed legislation. Furthermore, national disease- and disability-related
organizations and national and regional parent advocacy organizations listed in Chapter 3 and Appendix B at the end of
this book can provide analyses of proposed legislation from
the perspective of children with special health care needs
and their families. Finally, members of Congress can provide legislative summaries prepared by the Congressional
Research Service. The most current overview of all health
insurance and health care reform proposals as of December

3, 1993 was *CRS Issue Brief: Health Insurance* by Mark Merlis.

OTHER AREAS OF NEED—
CHILDREN WITH SOCIAL HEALTH CARE NEEDS

According to families in a number of family support and advocacy organizations for children and youth with disabilities and chronic illnesses, other areas requiring particular emphasis in the future include the following:

- Continuing the development of family and professional partnerships to plan service programs and to advocate for services and funding
- Creating planned networks of services that allow a child or youth with even a significant disability or illness to remain in a home or community setting and to function as fully as possible
- Ensuring better access to transportation of all kinds
- Ensuring the availability of a range of services in rural areas
- Developing additional sources of funding to supplement family resources in paying for needed health care, durable equipment, assistive technology services and devices, personal care services, and other supports and related services
- Developing additional psychological and material supports (e.g., respite care) for families and communities helping to raise children and youth with special health care needs in a home or small group setting
- Developing additional training opportunities in self-advocacy and the skills needed to interact with a variety of complex organizations (e.g., hospitals, specialty clinics, school systems, social service agencies, legislative bodies, private and public funding agencies) for youth with disabilities or chronic illnesses and their families

THE ROLE OF FAMILIES
AND ADVOCATES IN HEALTH CARE REFORM

It will be largely up to the families of children with disabilities or chronic illnesses, and their advocates, to help ensure that policy makers give such issues adequate attention and funding. Family members and their advocates must present themselves for positions on policy-making committees, boards, task forces, and legislative bodies whose decisions affect the well-being of children and youth with special health care needs and their families.

It will also be important for families whose children have special health care needs of any kind to join and work together for the many common concerns they share. In numbers families can advocate in an organized and effective manner. Together, they can speak for as many as one quarter of all American children and youth younger than 18 years old.

The continued and persistent efforts of families to define the full range of services needed by children and youth with special health care needs, and their well-informed and planned political activity, will increase the chance of greater service availability, new rights, and the enforcement of existing rights for such children and youth and their families. *Advocates for such families, including pediatricians and other therapists, social workers, nurses, clergy, and teachers, must join in efforts to appeal to appropriate government, nonprofit, and for-profit organizations on behalf of these children and families.* The combined efforts of youth, their families, and professionals *will* continue the significant progress that has been made in helping to ensure that all children have the chance to participate to their fullest abilities in communities across the United States— learning, living, and working with their peers.

A

Sample Letters

This appendix contains a series of sample letters to help you in writing to individuals or organizations about your child or family. The purpose of such a letter might be to request information, to share information about your child or family, to get reimbursement for an insurance claim, or to complain about or praise something or someone. You might have a reason to send a letter to one of the following individuals or organizations:

- Your child's doctor(s) or other professionals
- The clinic or hospital where your child most often receives care
- National organization(s) with information about disabilities or chronic illnesses
- Your local education agency, school board, early intervention program, or preschool or school-age program for children with special health care needs
- Disease- or disability-related organization(s)
- National advocacy or parent support groups

- Your state's Office of Maternal and Child Health (MCH) or Children's Special Health Care Needs (CSHCN) Program
- Your state's Department of Insurance
- Your state's Department of Revenue

When possible, it is best to write letters to request or communicate information, complain, or express praise. There are two exceptions. If you need something immediately or, if an organization has a toll-free telephone number, you should try a telephone call first.

If you do call, keep a record of the date of your call, the person with whom you spoke, and what was promised as a result of your call. You may need these notes for later followup. When writing a letter, try to type it. If absolutely necessary, write the letter by hand as clearly as possible. *Keep a copy of every letter you send.* Unfortunately, in a number of cases, your first telephone call or letter will not be enough to get what you need.

As an example, even though you write to a health insurance company about an unpaid claim for care for your child, your first letter may not produce the needed payment. You may want to write a second letter a month later. This time, you will also write your state's Department of Insurance and include copies of *both* of your letters to your insurance company. Being able to give the Department of Insurance proof of your efforts, including the dates of your requests, will expedite the release of the payment you or your child's caregiver is due if your insurance company is in error. *It will pay off for you in the long run!*

If your purpose is to compliment an individual who was of particular help to your child or family, sending a letter will carry more meaning. It will go to the supervisor of the individual whose contribution you want to recognize, and into that individual's personnel file. It will be more helpful to him or her than a telephone call.

When writing any kind of letter concerning your child, his or her care, a service program, financial assistance, and so forth, be sure to do the following:

- Include your name, address, home and work telephone numbers, and any identification that is relevant (e.g., account number).
- *Keep your letter as brief and to the point as possible.* Include all relevant facts and copies of letters you have sent to others that will clarify your request or concern.
- *State clearly what you want and by when.* Do not be unreasonable, but ask for what you need and in a time frame that will be helpful to you. When you request information or are following up on a problem, *2–3 weeks is generally a reasonable amount of time for the individual or organization to respond. If this is your third request for the same thing, wait no longer than 2–3 days for a response.* In the meantime, begin thinking about who else you can turn to for help.
- Be assertive, and communicate clearly what you need or feel. However, *try not to communicate anger in a way that would turn off the reader.* Remember, the person reading your letter is the person you need to help your child or family. In addition, he or she is often *not* the one causing you a problem.

If your letter is particularly important, send it "certified" mail, with a "return receipt requested." You need to go to a post office to do this. It will cost a little more to send your letter this way, but the receipt that will come back to you is evidence that your letter was received.

Do not hesitate to write a letter or make a telephone call if your child or family is in need. Disease- and disability-related, civic and social welfare, and religious organizations exist to provide help to people just like you. And they do it every day of the year.

Sarah and John Marks
3650 Michael Lane
Washington, D.C.   20016
(277) 544-0911
June 25, 1993

Dr. Janet Stone
3600 Military Road
Washington, D.C.   20016

Dear Dr. Stone:

Please send a letter to our health insurance company to justify a claim we have made for our daughter, Susan, for medical supplies used for her intermittent catheritization program. The company will only pay for items it considers "medically necessary."

The insurance company is:

    Aetna Casualty and Surety Co.
    2645 Milton Road
    Hartford, Connecticut   35624

Our group policy number listed in Sarah's name is: SLA 34 7726. Susan's birthdate is 12/31/87. Please send us a copy of your letter to Aetna. Many thanks.

                    Sincerely,

                    Sarah and John Marks

Sample letter 1. A letter to your child's doctor to ask her to write to an insurance company to justify a claim.

Matthew Robinson
2680 Cedar Lane, Apt. 2A
Minneapolis, Minnesota   26584
March 20, 1993

Dr. Robert Levy
500 Fire Oak Drive, Suite 210
St. Paul, Minnesota   26553

Dear Dr. Levy:

I feel my child Scott's teacher is having a hard time understanding the requirements of his disability. Ms. Jenks-Stone does not seem to realize that Scott needs to take medication several times while in school and to go to the restroom more often than other children. I also feel that he is not given as much choice as he needs in terms of his activity during gym.

Would you write to Ms. Jenks-Stone at Ardmore Elementary School, 2500 Bent Pine Road, Minneapolis 26435, explaining Scott's condition, the medical care he requires during school, and his need to use the restroom frequently? In your letter, could you also talk about the need to consult Scott about whether or not he feels up to participating in sports on a particular day, and why this is so? Diabetes is not as visible a chronic illness as some but, as you well know, Scott struggles to keep up a regular routine because of his illness.

Could you send Ardmore's principal, Ms. Sharon West, a copy of the letter and send one to us, too. We appreciate your time and help.

With best regards,

Matthew Robinson
(763) 322-0202

Sample letter 2.   A letter to your child's doctor to ask him to write to your child's school explaining your child's condition, medical care needed during school, and activity limitations.

Carolyn Simms
2443 East St. Louis Street
Richmond, Virginia 25982
January 6, 1993

Ms. Ellen Baker
St. Anthony's Hospital Clinic
16 W. Vincent Street
Richmond, Virginia 25962

Dear Ms. Baker:

I appreciate the time you have spent with our son, Michael, and the progress he is making in his speech. I am pleased he has come so far in the short time you have been working with him.

I wondered if I could make a special request of you. Would you and St. Anthony's be willing to accept our health insurance company's payment as "payment in full" for your services? As you may know, my husband was recently laid off from his job at Howard Mills, and I only can work part-time. We care for four other children besides Michael. We hope you will be able to help us in this way. Please let me know.

Sincerely,

Carolyn Simms
(no telephone at this time)

Sample letter 3.   A letter to your child's doctor or therapist to ask her to accept what your insurance company pays as "payment in full."

Mr. and Mrs. Samuel Sabato
Route 2, Box 4A
Pueblo, Colorado 34623
(209) 310-5676
September 2, 1993

Mr. Richard Price
Administrator, University Hospital Clinics
1437 South Lodge Boulevard
Boulder, Colorado 34667

Dear Mr. Price:

I would like to request that I set up a payment plan
for the clinic bills our family owes for the care of
our niece, Elena. We are her legal guardians and are
responsible for all of her medical bills. We have
applied for her care to be paid by Medicaid or the
Children's Special Health Care Needs Program in
Colorado. We are still waiting to hear if either
program will accept her. In the meantime, we would
like to arrange with you to make monthly payments on
her bills. Could you write us, or call me at (284)
356-4457, to let me know how we could do this? Thank
you for this consideration.

Sincerely,

Samuel Sabato and family

Sample letter 4.   A letter to the business office of the clinic where your child regularly
receives care, asking to set up a payment plan for fees.

Patsy and Don Yadov
2 West Mark Court
Kansas City, Missouri   46467
(515) 466-3949
June 18, 1993

Sr. Marguerite Olsen
Administrator, Mercy Hospital
2525 East Monroe
Kansas City, Missouri   46577

Dear Sister Olsen:

We wanted to take the time to recognize the exceptional service our child, Jason, recently received
at Mercy Hospital. Recently, he needed some surgery
on his back and was an inpatient for 2 weeks.

We cannot say enough about the care and caring he
received from the surgical team headed by Dr. Alan
Stone. They sparked friendly conversation with
Jason, explained the surgery to him in a way he
could understand at 5, and really put him at ease.
It put us as ease too, and we are really grateful.
Thanks!

Sincerely,

Patsy and Don Yadov

Sample letter 5.   A letter to the hospital where your child was recently an inpatient, to
compliment them on the care given by the surgical team.

Mark and Leah Wahl
16 N.W. Jasper Lane
Gresham, Oregon   66532
February 22, 1993

Ms. Eileen Thomas, Claims Representative
Massachusetts Mutual Insurance Co.
516 Harbor View
Boston, Massachusetts   02113

Dear Ms. Thomas:

We are writing to ask you to reconsider two claims you recently denied for the care of our daughter, Julia Megan Wahl, born 3/13/87. Due to her spina bifida, she has required *both* short-leg braces and a wheelchair. She is able to walk part of each day, but not the full day. You recently agreed to pay for one or the other, but not both. Julia's orthopedic doctor at University Hospital, Dr. Susan Parker, will be writing to you shortly to explain the medical need for both items. We would appreciate payment on our claims.

Sincerely,

Mark and Leah Wahl
(404) 334-2808

copy: Dr. Susan Parker

Sample letter 6.   A letter to your health insurance company, CHAMPUS, or local Medicaid agency to ask that a claim refused in the past be reconsidered.

Reverend Michael Carroll
St. Mark's Episcopal Church
Mesa, Arizona   34229
(406) 908-6632
August 11, 1993

Ms. Oriole Natchez
Mesa County Board of Education
16 Grand Forks Parkway
Mesa, Arizona   34120

Dear Ms. Natchez:

I am writing on behalf of my parishoners, Kathleen and Paul Smith. Their son, Todd, has a developmental disability and is taken to and from school each day by the Mesa County's transport bus for children with disabilities. The Smiths have written to Todd's principal and the county transport service, complaining that Todd gets to school 45 minutes to 1 hour late each day and leaves 30-45 minutes before the end of school. They would like to know if there is any way to avoid him losing that much school time each day? To date, no one has even answered their letters. Please answer mine.

Sincerely,

Reverend Michael Carroll

Sample letter 7.   A letter on your child's behalf to your local school board to complain about bus transportation.

Karen Johnson, J.D.
Rural Route 8
San Pedro, California   98335
May 16, 1993

Mr. Michael Stallings, Ed.D.
Principal, Caraway Middle School
Encinitas, California   98443

Dear Dr. Stallings:

I would like to request a review of my child Joseph's IEP with you and the team who developed the plan. Although I was asked for my input on the goals and objectives for Joseph this school year, I am not satisfied that the amount of physical and speech-language therapy suggested as support services will be adequate to meet his needs. Please call me so we can set up a mutually agreeable time to meet.

Sincerely,

Karen Johnson, J.D.
(469) 455-0921 (digital pager)

copy: San Diego county Education Agency

Sample letter 8.   A letter to your child's principal and local education agency to question a part of your child's IEP.

Ho and Jin-Lee Ho
44 West Broadway, Apt. 14B
New York, New York   10223
December 5, 1993

United Cerebral Palsy of New York
5202 St. Marks Place
New York, New York   10363

Dear Public Information Director:

Please send us information on the latest research findings on spastic diplegia cerebral palsy. Our 3-year old daughter, Ming, has this disease and has had it since birth. We have only recently moved to the United States and before this time have not had available to us this information.

Also, please give us names of other parents we can be in contact with who have children with the same disease as our daughter. Thank you.

The Hos
(No phone yet.)

Sample letter 9.   A letter to a disease- or disability-related organization to request information about your child's condition and support groups for family members.

Mr. and Mrs. Paul Paris
3561 The Causeway
Jacksonville, Florida   77544
October 28, 1993

Federation for Children with Special Needs
95 Berkeley Street
Boston, Massachusetts   02116

Dear Staff:

We would like a referral for care for our nephew, Simon Paris, who is in our care while his parents are overseas with the Peace Corps for 6 months. Simon was born a year ago with Down syndrome and has been treated by a general pediatrician in Boca Raton and Jacksonville. We would like him to see a pediatrician who specializes in Down syndrome and another medical specialist for consultation on his heart problem, too. Could you suggest some resources for us in Jacksonville?

Thanks a lot,

Paul and Julie Paris
(702) 565-4543

copy: John and Sari Paris, Costa Rica

Sample letter 10.   A letter to the Federation for Children with Special Needs to request a referral for care in your state.

Captain William and Marie Faulk
Meridian Naval Air Station, Box 35
Meridian, Mississippi   67433
April 3, 1993

Parent Training Center, South Region (Arc)
1851 Ram Runway, Suite 104
College Park, Georgia   30337

Dear Parents:

Could you please send us information about our child's and family's rights and responsibilities under IDEA? Our twin daughters may both qualify for services under this legislation. How much support do the girls have to need to receive services? Does IDEA apply to children attending school on a military base? Could you also send us the name of the PTI closest to our home in Meridian? Thank you.

Sincerely,

Captain William and Marie Faulk
(506) 432-4467 (Marie, before 3 P.M.)

Sample letter 11.   A letter to a Parent Training and Information (PTI) Center to request information about your child's and family's rights under the Individuals with Disabilities Education Act (IDEA).

Peggy Sue McClintock
44 West Alma Boulevard
San Antonio, Texas   48455
(417) 822-0091
February 10, 1993

Chief, Bureau of Chronically Ill
  and Disabled Children Services
Texas Department of Health
1100 West 49th Street
Austin, Texas   78756-3179

Dear Chief:

I would like to receive some information on Texas's
Children's Special Health Care Needs (CSHCN) Program. What are the services offered and would my
stepson, James Paul McClintock, be eligible for
them? He is 20 months old and has recently been diagnosed with autism. Can you refer me to other
places to look for services for him and ways to pay
for his care? My husband and I have four children,
including James Paul, and our income in 1992 was
$18,500.

Sincerely,

Peggy Sue McClintock, mother

Sample letter 12. A letter to your state's Office of Maternal and Child Health for
information about the Children's Special Health Care Needs (CSHCN) Program and your
child's eligibility for it.

Karen and Douglas Shawnee
Apt. 4, 1604 Terrace Drive
Sioux City, Iowa 35908
March 9, 1993

The Rotary Club of Iowa
14 Rotary Way
Des Moines, Iowa 35923

Dear Mr. President:

My wife and I appeal to you to help us. Our daughter, Kiosha, has had an autoimmune deficiency since her birth 4 years ago. Her condition requires daily medication that we cannot afford at this time. I have been employed as a carpenter for the last 12 years, but I am between regular jobs at this time and have no health insurance to cover my family, including Kiosha. Could your organization help us cover the cost of her medication, which is approximately $138 a month? Please help us.

Sincerely,

Douglas Shawnee
(Sorry, no phone)

Sample letter 13.   A letter to a civic, social welfare, or religious organization to request help paying for your child's medications.

Ms. Sally Fielding, M.S.W.
Bennington Area Clinic
Bennington, Vermont   25453
June 14, 1993

Ms. Ellen Janus, Supervisor
SSI Field Office, Post Office Box 35254
Burlington, Vermont   25488

Dear Ellen:

I am writing on behalf of my clients, Diedre and Carlos Janus. They made application for SSI 4 months ago for their son, Michael, who has cystic fibrosis. He also has some problems with his vision.

To date the Janus's have heard nothing about their son's SSI application. Can you give them some information on the status of Michael's application? Please write or call them directly at Rt. 4, Box 2, Bennington, Vermont 25453; telephone (867) 445-3465. My telephone number is (867) 362-8000, extension 43. Thanks very much.

Sincerely,

Sally Fielding, M.S.W.

Sample letter 14. A letter to your local Social Security Administration's SSI field office regarding a child's application for cash benefits under the SSI Program.

Paul Petersen
5656 Windsor Street
Madison, Wisconsin 53989
March 29, 1993

State of Wisconsin
Office of the Commissioner of Insurance
P.O. Box 7873
Madison, Wisconsin 53707-7873

Dear Commissioner:

Could you help me receive payment for a health insurance claim for my daughter, Olga, which was recently refused by my insurance company? The company
is Independent of Wisconsin. The policy number is
#45993, issued to me to cover my family. As I read my
policy, it should cover Olga's physical therapy for
as much as 26 sessions a year. Olga has just begun
this treatment as a part of a muscle disease she
has, and the insurance company has refused to pay my
claim. I am writing to you because I can't get anyone from the insurance company on the telephone.

                    Thank you,

                    Paul Petersen
                    (708) 355-4545 (evenings)

Sample letter 15.   A letter to your state's Department of Insurance to request help in
receiving reimbursement under your health insurance policy.

Dusty and Robin Newton
Reservation Apartments, Apt. 12
Omaha, Nebraska   24646
January 25, 1993

Nebraska Department of Revenue
Post Office Box 94818
Lincoln, Nebraska   68509-4818

Dear Commissioner:

Could you please have someone on your staff contact
us with an update on any special income tax deductions, exemptions, or credits in our state? We have
a 13-year-old daughter with a rare genetic disorder, and have only recently learned that we might be
eligible for some federal and state income tax reductions because of our daughter's health condition. Thank you.

Sincerely,

Mr. and Mrs. Dusty Newton
(608) 455-3121 (after 7 P.M.)

Sample letter 16.   A letter to your state's Department of Revenue to request an update
on your state's income tax deductions, exemptions, and credits for children with chronic
illnesses and disabilities and their families.

B

Resources to Provide Assistance

This appendix is a compilation of addresses and telephone numbers for many resources that may be helpful to you as you work to obtain and pay for quality health care and related services for your child with special needs. Resources listed here can also help your family to get services and save money. The appendix is designed to be a convenient reference for you, both as you read this book, and long after, when you need a single address or telephone number. In particular, this appendix contains the following:

1. Lists of government and independent agencies important in getting services for you child and in paying for them.
2. Lists of miscellaneous resources, most of which have toll-free telephone numbers, that can be of help with obtaining or financing services.

Agencies are listed alphabetically under the topical headings that best describe their purpose(s). For example, the Judge David L. Bazelon Center for Mental Health Law appears under both "Advocacy" and "Legal Services" headings, with references to Chapters 2 and 3 where fuller discussions of this organization fall.

A listing of miscellaneous useful telephone numbers appears after the alphabetical topic headings.

ADVOCACY AND FAMILY SUPPORT
FOR CHILDREN WITH SPECIAL HEALTH CARE NEEDS

Association for the Care of
  Children's Health, National
  Center for Family-Centered
  Care
7910 Woodmont Avenue
Suite 300
Bethesda, Maryland 20814-3015
(301) 654-6549

Family Voices
c/o Polly Arango
Post Office Box 769
Algondones, New Mexico 87001
(See Chapter 3)

Federation for Children with
  Special Needs
95 Berkeley Street
Boston, Massachusetts 02116
(617) 482-2915 (Voice and TT)
(See Chapter 3)

Federation of Families for
  Children's Mental Health
1021 Prince Street
Alexandria, Virginia
  22314-2971
(703) 684-7710 (Voice only)
(See Chapter 3)

National Parent Network on
  Disability (NPND)
1600 Prince Street
Suite 115
Alexandria, Virginia 22314
(703) 684-6763 (Voice only)
(See Chapter 3)

Disease and Disability-Related Organizations

Alliance of Genetic Support
  Groups
1001 22nd Street, Northwest
Suite 800
Washington, D.C. 20037
1-800-336-GENE (toll-free)
(202) 331-0942

American Council of the Blind
115 15th Street, Northwest
Suite 720
Washington, D.C. 20005
1-800-426-8666 (toll-free)
(202) 424-8666

American Foundation for the
  Blind
15 West 16th Street
New York, New York 10011
1-800-232-5463 (toll-free)

American Heart Association
7272 Greenville Avenue
Dallas, Texas 75231-4596
1-800-242-8721 (toll-free)
(214) 373-6300

American Juvenile Arthritis
  Organization
1314 Spring Street, Northwest
Atlanta, Georgia 30309
(404) 872-7100

American Lung Association
1740 Broadway
New York, New York 10019
(212) 315-8700

American Lupus Society
3914 Del Amo Boulevard
Suite 922
Torrance, California 90503
1-800-331-1802 (toll-free)
(310) 542-8891

American Society for Deaf
  Children
814 Thayer Avenue
Silver Spring, Maryland 20910
1-800-942-ASDC (Voice and
  TT) (toll-free)

The Arc
500 East Border Street
Suite 300
Arlington, Texas 76006
1-800-433-5255 (toll-free)

Asthma and Allergy
  Foundation of America
1125 15th Street, Northwest
Suite 502
Washington, D.C. 20005
1-800-7-ASTHMA (toll-free)
(202) 466-7643

Autism Society of America
8601 Georgia Avenue
Suite 503
Silver Spring, Maryland 20910
(301) 565-0433

Candlelighters Childhood
  Cancer Foundation
1312 18th Street, Northwest
Suite 200
Washington, D.C. 20036
1-800-366-2223 (toll-free)
(202) 659-5136

Children and Adults with
  Attention Deficit Disorders
499 Northwest 70th Avenue
Suite 308
Plantation, Florida 33317
(305) 587-3700

Cleft Palate Foundation
1218 Grandview Avenue
Pittsburgh, Pennsylvania 15211
1-800-24-CLEFT (toll-free)
(412) 481-1376

Crohn's and Colitis
  Foundation of America, Inc.
386 Park Avenue South
New York, New York
  10016-7374
1-800-343-3637 (toll-free)
(212) 685-3440

Cystic Fibrosis Foundation
6931 Arlington Road
Bethesda, Maryland
  29814-5200
1-800-FIGHT CF (toll-free)
(301) 951-4442

Epilepsy Foundation of
  America
4351 Garden City Drive
Suite 406
Landover, Maryland 20785
1-800-EFA-1000 (toll-free)
(301) 459-3700

Federation of Families for
  Children's Mental Health
1021 Prince Street
Alexandria, Virginia
  22314-2971
(703) 684-7710

Juvenile Diabetes Foundation
  International
432 Park Avenue South
New York, New York 10016
1-800-JDF-CURE (toll-free)

Learning Disability
  Association of America
4156 Library Road
Pittsburgh, Pennsylvania 15234
(412) 341-1515 or (412) 341-8077

Leukemia Society of America
600 Third Avenue
New York, New York 10016
1-800-955-4LSA (toll-free)
(212) 573-8484

Lupus Foundation of America
4 Research Place
Suite 180
Rockville, Maryland
    20850-3226
1-800-670-9292 (toll-free)
(301) 670-9292

March of Dimes Birth Defects
    Foundation
1275 Mamaroneck Avenue
White Plains, New York 10605
(914) 428-7100

Muscular Dystrophy
    Association, Inc.
3300 East Sunrise Drive
Tucson, Arizona 85718
(602) 529-2000

The National Alliance for the
    Mentally Ill, Children and
    Adolescent Network (CAN)
2101 Wilson Boulevard
Suite 302
Arlington, Virginia 22201
(703) 524-7600
1-800-950-NAMI (toll-free)

National Association of the
    Deaf
814 Thayer Avenue
Silver Spring, Maryland 20910
(301) 587-1788 (Voice and TT)

National Association for Sickle
    Cell Disease, Inc.
3345 Wilshire Boulevard
Suite 1106
Los Angeles, California
    90010-1880
1-800-421-8453 (toll-free)
(213) 736-5455

National Association for the
    Visually Handicapped
22 West 21st Street, 6th Floor
New York, New York 10010
(212) 889-3141

National Down Syndrome
    Congress
1800 Dempster Street
Park Ridge, Illinois 60068-1146
1-800-232-6372 (toll-free
    outside Illinois)
1-800-823-7550 (toll-free in
    Illinois)

National Down Syndrome
    Society
666 Broadway
Suite 810
New York, New York 10012
1-800-221-4602 (toll-free)

National Easter Seal Society
70 East Lake Street
Chicago, Illinois 60601
1-800-221-6827 (toll-free)
(312) 726-6200
(312) 726-4258 (TT)

National Fragile X Foundation
1441 York Street
Suite 215
Denver, Colorado 80206
1-800-688-8765 (toll-free)

National Head Injury
  Foundation
1140 Connecticut Avenue,
  Northwest
Suite 812
Washington, D.C. 10026
1-800-444-NHIF (toll-free
  "Family Helpline")
(202) 296-6443

National Hemophilia
  Foundation
The Soho Building
110 Greene Street
Suite 406
New York, New York 10012
(212) 219-8180

National Kidney Foundation
30 East 33rd Street, 11th Floor
New York, New York 10016
1-800-622-9010 (toll-free)

National Mental Health
  Association
1021 Prince Street
Alexandria, Virginia 22314-2971
(703) 684-7722

National Organization for Rare
  Disorders, Inc.
Post Office Box 8923
New Fairfield, Connecticut
  06182-1783
1-800-937-NORD (toll-free)

National Spinal Cord Injury
  Association
600 West Cummings Park
Suite 2000
Woburn, Massachusetts
  01801-6379
1-800-962-9629 (toll-free)
(617) 962-9629

Spina Bifida Association of
  America
4590 MacArthur Boulevard
Suite 250
Washington, D.C. 20007
1-800-621-3141 (toll-free)
(202) 944-3285

United Cerebral Palsy
  Association
1522 K Street, Northwest
Washington, D.C. 20005
1-800-872-5827 (toll-free)
(202) 842-1266 (Voice or TT)

Judge David L. Bazelon Center
  for Mental Health Law
1101 15th Street, Northwest
Washington, D.C. 20005
(202) 467-5730 (toll-free)
(202) 467-4232 (TT)
(See Chapters 2 and 3)

Protection and Advocacy (P & A) Agencies

Protection and Advocacy (P & A) Agencies are largely government-funded but operate independently. There is one in each state *to help ensure that the civil rights of individuals with chronic illnesses or disabilities are protected, both in institutional and community settings.* P & A Agencies can also serve as lawyers for individuals with disabilities or chronic illnesses. They are good *sources of information about the rights of children with disabilities and background on related federal and state law and court rulings* (see Chapters 2 and 5 for more information).

Alabama
Director
Alabama Disabilities Advocacy
    Program
The University of Alabama
Post Office Drawer 870395
Tuscaloosa, Alabama
    35487-0395
(205) 348-4928

Alaska
Executive Director
Advocacy Services of Alaska
615 East 82nd Avenue
Suite 101
Anchorage, Alaska 99518
(907) 344-1002
1-800-478-1234

Arizona
Executive Director
Arizona Center for Law in the
    Public Interest
3724 North Third Street
Suite 300
Phoenix, Arizona 85012
(602) 274-6287
(602) 327-9547

Arkansas
Executive Director
Advocacy Services, Inc.
1120 Marshall Street
Suite 311
Little Rock, Arkansas 72202
(501) 324-9215

California
Executive Director
Protection & Advocacy, Inc.
100 Howe Street
Suite 185N
Sacramento, California 95825
(916) 488-9950
1-800-952-5746

Colorado
Executive Director
The Legal Center
455 Sherman Street
Suite 130
Denver, Colorado 80203
(303) 722-0300

Connecticut
Executive Director
Office P & A for Handicapped
    & DD Persons
60 Weston Street
Hartford, Connecticut
    06120-1551
(203) 297-4300
(203) 566-2102
1-800-842-7303 (statewide)

Delaware
DD Administrator
Disabilities Law Program
144 East Market Street
Georgetown, Delaware 19947
(302) 856-0038

MI Director
Disabilities Law Program
144 East Market Street
Georgetown, Delaware 19947
(302) 856-0038

District of Columbia
Executive Director
I.P.A.C.H.I.
4455 Connecticut Avenue,
    Northwest
Suite B100
Washington, D.C. 20008
(202) 966-8081

Florida
Executive Director
Advocacy Center for Persons
   with Disabilities
2671 Executive Center, Circle W
Suite 100
Tallahassee, Florida
   32301-5024
(904) 488-9071
1-800-342-0823
1-800-346-4127

PAIMI Director
Advocacy Center for Persons
   with Disabilities
2671 Executive Center, Circle W
Suite 100
Tallahassee, Florida
   32301-5024
(904) 488-9071
1-800-342-0823
1-800-346-4127

Georgia
Executive Director
Georgia Advocacy Office
1708 Peachtree Street,
   Northwest
Suite 505
Atlanta, Georgia 30309
(404) 885-1234
1-800-537-2329

Hawaii
Executive Director
Protection & Advocacy Agency
1580 Makaloa Street
Suite 1060
Honolulu, Hawaii 96814
(808) 949-2922

Idaho
Director
Co-Ad, Inc.
1409 West Washington
Boise, Idaho 83702
(208) 336-5353

Illinois
Director
P & A, Inc.
11 East Adams
Suite 1200
Chicago, Illinois 60603
(312) 341-0295

Indiana
Executive Director
Indiana Advocacy Services
850 North Meridian Street
Suite 2-C
Indianapolis, Indiana 46204
(317) 232-1150
1-800-622-4845

Iowa
Director
Iowa P & A Service, Inc.
3015 Merle Hay Road
Suite 6
Des Moines, Iowa 50310
(515) 278-2502

Kansas
Executive Director
Kansas Advocacy & Protective
   Services
513 Leavenworth Street
Suite 2
Manhattan, Kansas 66502
(913) 776-1541
1-800-432-8276

Kentucky
Director
Office of Public Advocacy—
   Division for P & A
Perimeter Park West
1264 Louisville Road
Frankfort, Kentucky 40601
(502) 564-2967
1-800-372-2988

Louisiana
Executive Director
Advocacy Center for the
   Elderly and Disabled
210 O'Keefe
Suite 700
New Orleans, Louisiana 70112
(504) 522-2337
1-800-662-7705

Maine
Executive Director
Maine Advocacy Services
One Grandview Place
Suite 1
Post Office Box 445
Winthrop, Maine 04364
(207) 377-6202
1-800-452-1948

Maryland
Executive Director
Maryland Disability Law
   Center
2510 St. Paul Street
Baltimore, Maryland 21218
(410) 333-7600

Massachusetts
DD Director
Disability Law Center, Inc.
11 Beacon Street
Suite 925
Boston, Massachusetts 02108
(617) 723-8455

PAIMI Director
Center for Public
   Representation
22 Green Street
Northampton, Massachusetts
   01060
(413) 584-1644

Michigan
Executive Director
Michigan P & A Service
106 West Allegan
Suite 211
Lansing, Michigan 48933-1706
(517) 487-1755

Minnesota
Deputy Director
Minnesota Disability Law
   Center
430 First Avenue, North
Suite 300
Minneapolis, Minnesota
   55401-1780
(612) 332-1441

Coordinator MI P & A
Minnesota Disability Law
   Center
430 First Avenue, North
Suite 300
Minneapolis, Minnesota
   55401-1780
(612) 332-1441

Mississippi
Executive Director
Mississippi P & A System for
   Developmental Disabilities
5330 Executive Place
Suite A
Jackson, Mississippi 39206
(601) 981-8207

Missouri
Director
Missouri P & A Service
925 South Country Club Drive
Unit B-1
Jefferson City, Missouri 65109
(314) 893-3333
1-800-392-8667

Montana
Executive Director
Montana Advocacy Program
1410 8th Avenue
Helena, Montana 59601
(406) 444-3889

Nebraska
Executive Director
Nebraska Advocacy Services,
   Inc.
522 Lincoln Center Building
215 Centennial Mall South
Lincoln, Nebraska 68508
(402) 474-3183

Nevada
Executive Director
Office of Protection &
   Advocacy, Inc.
2105 Capurro Way
Suite B
Sparks, Nevada 89431
(702) 688-1233
1-800-992-5715

New Hampshire
Director
Disabilities Rights Center
Post Office Box 19
Concord, New Hampshire
   03302-0019
(603) 228-0432

New Jersey
Director
New Jersey Department of
   Public Advocate
Office of Advocacy for the DD
Hughes Justice Complex
   CN850
Trenton, New Jersey 08625
(609) 292-9742
1-800-792-8600

Director
New Jersey Department of
   Public Advocate
Division of Mental Health
   Advocacy
Hughes Justice Complex
   CN850
Trenton, New Jersey 08625
(609) 292-1780
1-800-792-8600

New Mexico
Executive Director
Protection & Advocacy
   System, Inc.
1720 Louisiana Boulevard,
   Northeast
Suite 204
Albuquerque, New Mexico
   87110
(505) 256-3100
1-800-432-4682

New York
Commissioner
New York Commission on
   Quality of Care for the
   Mentally Disabled
99 Washington Avenue
Albany, New York 12210
(518) 473-4057

North Carolina
Executive Director
Governor's Advocacy Council
  for Persons with Disabilities
1318 Dale Street
Suite 100
Raleigh, North Carolina 27605
(919) 733-9250

North Dakota
Director
North Dakota Protection &
  Advocacy Project
400 East Broadway
Suite 515
Bismarck, North Dakota 58501
(701) 224-2972
1-800-472-2670

North Mariana Islands
Executive Director
Karidat, Box 745
Saipan, Commonwealth of the
  Northern Mariana Islands
  96950
(670) 234-6981

Ohio
Executive Director
Ohio Legal Rights Service
8 East Long Street
6th Floor
Columbus, Ohio 43215
(614) 466-7264
1-800-282-9181

Oklahoma
Executive Director
Protection & Advocacy Agency
  for DD
9726 East 42nd, Osage
  Building, Room 133
Tulsa, Oklahoma 74146
(918) 664-5883

Oregon
Executive Director
Oregon Advocacy Center
625 Board of Trade Building
310 Southwest 4th Avenue
Portland, Oregon 97204-2309
(503) 243-2081

Pennsylvania
Executive Director
Pennsylvania P & A, Inc.
116 Pine Street
Harrisburg, Pennsylvania 17101
(717) 236-8110
1-800-692-7443
1-800-238-6222

Rhode Island
Executive Director
Rhode Island P & A System,
  Inc. (RIPAS)
55 Bradford Street, 2nd Floor
Providence, Rhode Island
  02903
(401) 831-3150

South Carolina
Executive Director
South Carolina P & A System
  for the Handicapped, Inc.
3710 Landmark Drive
Suite 204
Columbia, South Carolina
  29204
(803) 782-0639
1-800-922-5225

South Dakota
Executive Director
South Dakota Advocacy
  Services
221 South Central Avenue
Pierre, South Dakota 57501
(605) 224-8294
1-800-658-4782

Tennessee
Executive Director
Tennessee Protection &
   Advocacy, Inc.
Post Office Box 121257
Nashville, Tennessee 37212
(615) 298-1080
1-800-342-1660

Texas
Executive Director
Advocacy, Inc.
7800 Shoal Creek Boulevard
Suite 171-E
Austin, Texas 78757
(512) 454-4816
1-800-252-9108

Utah
Executive Director
Legal Center for People with
   Disabilities
455 East 400 South
Suite 201
Salt Lake City, Utah 84111
(801) 363-1347
1-800-662-9080

Vermont
Vermont DD Law Project
12 North Street
Burlington, Vermont 05401
(802) 863-2881

RR1 Box 1436
Waterbury, Vermont, 05676
(802) 244-5126

Citizen Advocacy, Inc.
Chase Mill
1 Mill Street
Burlington, Vermont 05410
(802) 860-1823

PAIMI
Vermont Advocacy Network
65 South Main Street
Waterbury, Vermont 05676
(802) 244-7868

Virginia
Director
Department for Rights of the
   Disabled
James Monroe Building
101 North 14th Street, 17th
   Floor
Richmond, Virginia 23219
(804) 225-2042
1-800-552-3962 (DD and Voice)

Washington
Executive Director
Washington P & A System
1401 East Jefferson, #506
Seattle, Washington 98122
(206) 324-1521

West Virginia
Executive Director
West Virginia Advocates
1524 Kanawha Boulevard, East
Charleston, West Virginia
   24311
(304) 346-0847
1-800-950-5250

Wisconsin
PAIMI Coordinator
WI Coalition for Advocacy,
   Inc.
16 North Carroll Street
Suite 400
Madison, Wisconsin 53703
(608) 267-0214

Wyoming
Executive Director
Wyoming P & A System, Inc.
2424 Pioneer Avenue, #101
Cheyenne, Wyoming 82001
(307) 638-7668
(307) 632-3496
1-800-624-7648

Developmental Disabilities Planning Councils

For referral to the Council in your state, contact:

National Association of
  Developmental Disabilities
  Planning Councils
1234 Massachusetts Avenue,
  Northwest
Suite 103
Washington, D.C. 20005
(202) 347-1234

For information about services offered by Developmental Disabilities Planning Councils, see Chapters 2 and 5.

Parent Training and Information (PTI) Centers

Midwest Region (Pacer Center)
4826 Chicago Avenue, South
Minneapolis, Minnesota 55417
(612) 827-2966 (Voice and TT)

Northwest Region (Parent
  Information Center)
151A Manchester Street
Post Office Box 1422
Concord, New Hampshire
  03302
(603) 224-6299 (Voice)
(603) 224-7005 (TT)

South Region (The Arc)
1851 Ram Runway
Suite 104
College Park, Georgia 30337
(404) 761-3150 (Voice and TT)

West Region (Washington State
  PAVE)
6316 South 12th Street
Tacoma, Washington 98465
(206) 565-2266 (Voice and TT)

DEBT MANAGEMENT

National Foundation for
  Consumer Credit
1-800-388-CCCS
(See Chapter 9)

Federal Trade Commission Regional Offices

For information about how these offices can be helpful, see Chapter 9.

1718 Peachtree Street,
  Northwest
Suite 1000
Atlanta, Georgia 30367
(404) 347-4836

10 Causeway Street
Suite 1184
Boston, Massachusetts
  02222-1073
(617) 565-7240

55 East Monroe Street
Suite 1437
Chicago, Illinois 60603
(312) 353-4423

668 Euclid Avenue
Suite 520-A
Cleveland, Ohio 44114
(216) 522-4207

100 North Central Expressway
Suite 500
Dallas, Texas 75201
(214) 767-5501

1405 Curtis Street
Suite 2900
Denver, Colorado 80202-2393
(303) 844-2271

11000 Wilshire Boulevard
Suite 13209
Los Angeles, California 90024
(213) 209-7575

150 William Street
Suite 1300
New York, New York 10038
(212) 264-1207

901 Market Street
Suite 570
San Francisco, California
  94103
(415) 744-7920

2806 Federal Building
Seattle, Washington 98174
(206) 553-4656

County Agricultural Extension Services, United States Department of Agriculture

For more information about the County Agricultural Extension Services of the U.S. Department of Agriculture, see Chapter 9.

EDUCATION AND TRAINING OF CHILDREN
AND YOUTH WITH SPECIAL HEALTH CARE NEEDS

Part H Lead Agencies—Early Intervention
Programs for Children (Birth Through 2 Years of Age)

Part H lead agencies in each state administer the early intervention program *for children from birth through two years old with special health care needs.* Part H is a federal and state combined program (part of the Individuals with Disability Education Act [IDEA]) to be sure that infants and toddlers "with a developmental delay" or with a condition with a "high probability of resulting in delay" receive needed services. *Services are offered to all such children on a free or low-cost basis.* Call your state Part H agency for *any* information relating to your infant's or toddler's problems and available evaluative and treatment services (See Chapters 2 and 5 in this book for more information about IDEA's eligibility guidelines and required minimum services.)

Alabama
Director
Division of Rehabilitative
  Services
Department of Education
2129 East South Boulevard
Montgomery, Alabama 36111
(205) 281-8780

Alaska
Section of Maternal, Child,
  and Family Health
1231 Gambell Street
Anchorage, Alaska 99501
(907) 274-7626

Arizona
Director
Department of Economic
  Security
1717 West Jefferson Street
Post Office Box 6123
Phoenix, Arizona 85005
(602) 542-5678

Arkansas
Director
Division of DD Services
Director
Department of Human
  Services
Donaghey Plaza South, Slot
  329
Post Office Box 1437
Little Rock, Arkansas
  72203-1437
(501) 682-8662 (DD Services)
(501) 682-8650 (Human
  Services)
Fax: (501) 682-6571

California
Director
Department of Developmental
  Services
1600 9th Street
Sacramento, California 95814
(916) 654-1897

Colorado
Director
Special Education Services
State Department of Education
201 East Colfax Street
Denver, Colorado 80203
(303) 866-6694
Fax: (303) 830-0793

Connecticut
Bureau Chief
Bureau of Early Childhood
Education and Social
Services
State Department of Education
25 Industrial Park Road
Middletown, Connecticut
06457
(203) 638-4204
Fax: (203) 638-4218

Delaware
Deputy Director
Bureau of Human Services
Planning
Division of Planning,
Research, & Evaluation
Department of Health & Social
Services
1901 North Dupont Highway
Newcastle, Delaware 19720
(302) 577-4632
Fax: (302) 577-4510

District of Columbia
Director
Department of Human
Services
801 North Capitol Street,
Northeast
Suite 700
Washington, D.C. 20002
(202) 727-0310

Florida
Commissioner
State Department of Education
Capitol Building, Room PL 116
Tallahassee, Florida 32399
(904) 487-1785

Georgia
Commissioner
Department of Human
Resources/Division of
Health
47 Trinity Avenue, Southwest
Atlanta, Georgia 30334-1202
(404) 656-5680
Fax: (404) 651-8669

Hawaii
Director
Department of Health
Post Office Box 3378
Honolulu, Hawaii 96816
(808) 548-6505
Fax: (808) 548-3263 Code #15

Idaho
Director
Department of Health and
Welfare
450 West State Street
Boise, Idaho 83720
(208) 334-5500

Illinois
Superintendent
State Board of Education
100 North First Street
Springfield, Illinois 62777
(217) 782-2221

Indiana
Secretary
Family and Social Services
  Administration
402 West Washington Street
Post Office Box 7083
Indianapolis, Indiana
  46207-7083
(317) 233-4454
Fax: (317) 232-7948

Iowa
Director of Education
State Department of Education
Grimes State Office Building
Des Moines, Iowa 50319-0146
(515) 281-5294

Kansas
Secretary
Kansas Department of Health
  and Environment
Landon State Office Building
900 Southwest Jackson
Suite 901
Topeka, Kansas 66612-1250
(913) 296-0461
Fax: (913) 296-7119

Kentucky
Part H Coordinator
Infant/Toddler Program
Division of Mental Retardation
Department of MH/MR
  Services
275 East Main Street
Frankfort, Kentucky 40621
(502) 564-7700
Fax: (502) 546-3844

Louisiana
Assistant Superintendent
Office of Special Education
  Services
State Department of Education
Post Office Box 94064
Baton Rouge, Louisiana
  70804-9064
(504) 342-3633

Maine
Commissioner
Department of Mental Health/
  Mental Retardation
State House Station #40
Augusta, Maine 04333
(207) 287-4220

Maryland
Governor's Office for Children,
  Youth, and Families
301 West Preston, Room 1502
Baltimore, Maryland 21201
(410) 225-4160

Massachusetts
Commissioner
State Department of Public
  Health
150 Tremont Street
Boston, Massachusetts 02111
(617) 727-2700
Fax: (617) 727-6496

Michigan
Superintendent of Education
State Department of Education
Post Office Box 30008
Lansing, Michigan 48909
(517) 373-3354
Fax: (517) 373-2537

Minnesota
Deputy Commissioner
State Department of Education
712 Capitol Square Building
550 Cedar Street
St. Paul, Minnesota 55101
(612) 296-2358

Mississippi
State Health Officer
State Board of Health
Post Office Box 1700
Jackson, Mississippi
  39215-1700
(601) 960-7634
Fax: (601) 960-7948

Missouri
Commissioner
Department of Elementary and
  Secondary Education
Post Office Box 480
Jefferson City, Missouri 65102
(314) 751-444-2995

Montana
Administrator
Developmental Disabilities
  Division
Department of Social &
  Rehabilitation Services
Post Office Box 4210
Helena, Montana 59604
(406) 444-2995

Nebraska
Commissioner of Education
State Department of Education
Post Office Box 94987
Lincoln, Nebraska 68509
(402) 471-2465

Director
Nebraska Department of Social
  Services
Post Office Box 95026
Lincoln, Nebraska 68509-5026
(402) 471-9105
Fax: (402) 471-9455

Nevada
Director
Department of Human
  Resources
505 East King Street
Carson City, Nevada 98710
(702) 885-4400

New Hampshire
Director
Part H Infant and Toddler
  Project
Division of Mental Health and
  Developmental Services
State Department of Health
  and Human Services
New Hampshire Hospital
  Administration Building
105 Pleasant Street
Concord, New Hampshire
  03301
(603) 271-5007
Fax: (603) 271-5058

New Jersey
Director
Division of Special Education
State Department of Education
225 West State Street, CN 500
Trenton, New Jersey
  08625-0001
(609) 633-6833
Fax: (609) 984-8422

New Mexico
Secretary
Department of Health
Post Office Box 968
Santa Fe, New Mexico
    87504-0968
(505) 827-2623
Fax: (505) 827-2530

New York
Director
Division of Family Health
Department of Health
Corning Tower, Room 890
Empire State Plaza
Albany, New York 12237
(518) 474-2084

North Carolina
Secretary
Department of Human
    Resources
325 North Salisbury Street
Raleigh, North Carolina 27611
(919) 733-4534

North Dakota
Executive Director
Department of Human
    Services
State Capitol
Bismarck, North Dakota 58505
(701) 224-2310

Ohio
Director
State Department of Health
Post Office Box 118
Columbus, Ohio 43266-0118
(614) 466-2253

Oklahoma
Director
Special Education Section
Oliver Hodge Memorial
    Building, Room 215
2500 North Lincoln Boulevard
Oklahoma City, Oklahoma
    73105-4599
(405) 521-3352
Fax: (405) 521-6265

Oregon
Superintendent of Public
    Instruction
Oregon Department of
    Education
700 Pringle Parkway, Southeast
Salem, Oregon 97301
(503) 378-3573
Fax: (503) 378-4772
    or (503) 378-8434

Pennsylvania
Secretary
Department of Public Welfare
Health and Welfare Building,
    Room 333
Harrisburg, Pennsylvania 17120
(717) 787-2600
Fax: (717) 772-2062
    or (717) 787-1229

Rhode Island
Commissioner
Division of Family Health
State Department of Health
3 Capitol Hill, Room 302
Providence, Rhode Island
    02908-5097
(401) 277-2313
(401) 277-2312
Fax: (401) 277-1442

South Carolina
Director—CRS
Department of Health &
Environmental Control
2600 Bull Street
Columbia, South Carolina
29201
(803) 737-4050
Fax: (803) 737-4078

South Dakota
Secretary
Division of Education
Department of Education and
Cultural Affairs
700 Governors Drive
Pierre, South Dakota
57501-3133
(605) 773-3243

Tennessee
Commissioner of Education
State Department of Education
100 Cordell Hull Building
Nashville, Tennessee 37219
(615) 741-2731

Texas
Chair
Texas Interagency Council on
Early Childhood
Intervention
State Department of Health
Division of Personal Health
Services
1100 West 49th Street
Austin, Texas 78756
(512) 458-7111
Fax: (512) 458-7358

Administrator
Texas Early Childhood
Intervention Program
State Department of Health
1100 West 49th Street
Austin, Texas 78756
(512) 465-2671
Fax: (512) 458-7446

Utah
Director
Family Health Services
Division
State Department of Health
Post Office Box 16650-20FHS
Salt Lake City, Utah
84116-0650
(801) 538-6161

Vermont
Commissioner of Education
State Department of Education
120 State Street
Montpelier, Vermont
05602-2703
(802) 828-3135
Fax: (802) 828-3140

Virgin Islands
Commissioner
Department of Health
St. Thomas Hospital
48 Sugar Estate
St. Thomas, Virgin Islands
00802
(809) 774-0117
or (809) 774-8311

Virginia
Commissioner
Department of
  MH/MR/Substance Abuse
  Services
Post Office Box 1797
Richmond, Virginia 23214
(804) 786-3921
Fax: (804) 371-6984

Washington
Secretary
Department of Social & Health
  Services
12th & Franklin Streets
MS: OB-44
Olympia, Washington
  98504-0095
(206) 753-3395
Fax: (206) 586-5874

West Virginia
Secretary
Department of Health &
  Human Services
Capitol Complex
Building 6, Room 637
1800 Washington Street, East
Charleston, West Virginia
  25305
(304) 558-2971

Wisconsin
Secretary
Department of Health & Social
  Services
Post Office Box 7850
Madison, Wisconsin 53707
(608) 266-3681

Wyoming
Administrator
Division of Developmental
  Disabilities
Department of Health
2020 Capitol Avenue
Cheyenne, Wyoming 82002
(307) 777-7115
Fax: (307) 777-6047

Part B Lead Agencies—Preschool and School-Age Programs for Children 3 Through 5 and 6 Through 21 Years of Age (Office of State Special Education Directors)

Part B lead agencies are responsible for the administration of the *preschool (3 through 5 years old) and school-age (6 through 21)* programs, according to the Individuals with Disabilities Education Act (IDEA). Children and youth with certain disabilities or chronic illnesses, or in the case of preschoolers "with a developmental delay," are eligible for a number of services including a "free and appropriate public education in the least restrictive environment" possible. (See Chapters 2 and 5 for a fuller discussion of Part B Programs.) Call this agency for information on Part B programs in your state and to see if your child qualifies for services.

Alabama
Assistant Director
Division of Special Education
  Services
State Department of Education
3346 Gordon Persons Building
50 North Ripley Street
Montgomery, Alabama
  36130-3901
(205) 242-8114
Fax: (205) 242-9708

Alaska
Director
Office of Special and
  Supplemental Services
State Department of Education
Post Office Box F
Juneau, Alaska 99811
(907) 465-2970
Fax: (907) 463-5279

Arizona
Deputy Associate
  Superintendent
Special Education Section
State Department of Education
1535 West Jefferson
Phoenix, Arizona 85007-3280
(602) 542-3084
Fax: (602) 542-5404

Arkansas
Associate Director
Special Education
State Department of Education
Education Building, Room 105-C
#4 Capitol Mall
Little Rock, Arkansas
  72201-1071
(501) 682-4221
Fax: (501) 682-4313

California
Director
Special Education Division
State Department of Education
721 Capitol Mall
Sacramento, California 95614
(916) 657-3567
Fax: (916) 657-4770

Colorado
Director
Special Education Services Unit
State Department of Education
201 East Colfax Avenue
Denver, Colorado 80203
(303) 866-6695
Fax: (303) 830-0793

Connecticut
Bureau Chief
Bureau of Special Education &
  Pupil Personnel Services
State Department of Education
25 Industrial Park Road
Middletown, Connecticut 06457
(203) 638-4265
Fax: (203) 638-1854

Delaware
Director
Division for Exceptional
  Children
Department of Public
  Instruction
Post Office Box 1402
Dover, Delaware 19903-1402
(302) 739-5471
Fax: (302) 739-3092

District of Columbia
Assistant Superintendent
Division of Special Education
  & Pupil Personnel Services
D.C. Public Schools
Webster Administration
  Building
10th and H Streets,
  Northwest
Washington, D.C. 20001
(202) 724-4178
Fax: (202) 724-5094

Chief
Branch of Exceptional Education
Bureau of Indian Affairs
MS #3530
1951 Constitution Avenue,
  Northwest
Washington, D.C. 20245
(202) 208-6675
Fax: (202) 208-3312

Florida
Bureau Chief
Bureau of Education for
  Exceptional Students
Florida Education Center
325 West Gaines Street
Suite 614
Tallahassee, Florida 32399-0400
(904) 488-1570
Fax: (904) 487-2194

Georgia
Director
Division for Exceptional
  Students
State Department of Education
1952 Twin Towers East
205 Butler Street
Atlanta, Georgia 39334-5040
(404) 656-3963
Fax: (404) 651-6457

Hawaii
State Administrator
Special Education Section
State Department of Education
3430 Leahi Avenue
Honolulu, Hawaii 96815
(808) 737-3720
Fax: (808) 732-3701

Idaho
Supervisor
Special Education Division
State Department of Education
Len B. Jordan Building
650 West State Street
Boise, Idaho 83720-3650
(208) 334-3940
Fax: (208) 334-2228

Illinois
Assistant Superintendent
Department of Special Education
State Board of Education
Mail Code E-216
100 North First Street
Springfield, Illinois 62777-0001
(217) 782-6601
Fax: (217) 782-0679

Indiana
Director
Division of Special Education
State Department of Education
229 State House
Indianapolis, Indiana 46204-2798
(317) 232-0570
Fax: (317) 232-9121

Iowa
Chief
Bureau of Special Education
Department of Public Instruction
Grimes State Office Building
Des Moines, Iowa 50319-0146
(515) 281-3176
Fax: (515) 242-5988

Kansas
Team Leader
Special Education Outcomes
 Team
State Board of Education
120 Southeast 10th Avenue
Topeka, Kansas 66612-1182
(913) 296-3869
Fax: (913) 296-7933

Kentucky
State Director
Division of Exceptional
 Children Services
State Department of Education
500 Mero Street, Room 805
Frankfort, Kentucky 40601
(502) 564-4970
Fax: (502) 564-6771

Louisiana
Director
Office of Special Education
 Services
State Department of
 Education, 9th Floor
Post Office Box 94064
Baton Rouge, Louisiana
 70804-9064
(504) 342-3633
Fax: (504) 342-7316

Maine
Director
Division of Special Education
Department of Education and
 Cultural Services
State House, Station #23
Augusta, Maine 04333
(207) 289-5953
Fax: (207) 289-5900

Maryland
Director
Division of Special Education
State Department of Education
200 West Baltimore Street
Baltimore, Maryland 21201-2595
(410) 333-2490
Fax: (410) 333-8165

Massachusetts
Associate Commissioner
Division of Special Education
State Department of Education
1385 Hancock Street, 3rd Floor
Quincy, Massachusetts
 02169-5183
(617) 770-7468
Fax: (617) 770-7332

Michigan
State Director
Special Education Services
State Department of Education
Post Office Box 30008
Lansing, Michigan 48909-7508
(517) 373-9433
Fax: (517) 373-7504

Minnesota
Manager
Special Education Section
State Department of Education
812 Capitol Square Building
550 Cedar Street
St. Paul, Minnesota 55101-2233
(612) 296-1793
Fax: (612) 296-3272

Mississippi
Director
Bureau of Special Services
State Department of Education
Post Office Box 771
Jackson, Mississippi 39205-0771
(601) 359-3490
Fax: (601) 359-2326

Missouri
Coordinator
Special Education Programs
Department of Elementary &
  Secondary Education
Post Office Box 480
Jefferson City, Missouri
  65102-0480
(314) 751-2965
Fax: (314) 526-4404

Montana
Director
Office of Public Instruction
Division of Special Education
State Capitol, Room 106
Helena, Montana 59620
(406) 444-4429
Fax: (406) 444-3924

Nebraska
Director
Special Education Office
State Department of Education
301 Centennial Mall South
Post Office Box 94987
Lincoln, Nebraska 68509-4987
(402) 471-2471
Fax: (402) 471-2701

Nevada
Director
Special Education
State Department of Education
Capitol Complex
440 West King Street
Carson City, Nevada
  89710-0004
(702) 687-3140
Fax: (702) 687-5660

New Hampshire
Director
Bureau for Special Education
  Services
State Department of Education
State Office Park, South
101 Pleasant Street
Concord, New Hampshire
  03301-3860
(603) 271-3741
Fax: (603) 271-1953

New Jersey
Director
Division of Special Education
State Department of Education
225 West State Street
Post Office Box CN 500
Trenton, New Jersey
  08625-0001
(609) 633-6833
Fax: (609) 984-8422

New Mexico
Director
Division of Special Education
State Department of Education
300 Don Gaspar Avenue
Santa Fe, New Mexico
  87501-2786
(505) 827-6541
Fax: (505) 827-6696

New York
Assistant Commissioner
Office for Special Education
  Services
State Education Department
Education Building Annex,
  Room 1073
Albany, New York 12234-0001
(518) 474-5548
Fax: (518) 473-2917

North Carolina
Director
Division for Exceptional
  Children's Services
Department of Public
  Instruction
Education Building, #442
116 West Edenton
Raleigh, North Carolina
  27603-1712
(919) 733-3921
Fax: (919) 733-9568

North Dakota
Director
Special Education Division
Department of Public
  Instruction
State Capitol, 10th Floor
600 East Boulevard
Bismarck, North Dakota
  58505-0440
(701) 224-2277
Fax: (701) 224-2461

Ohio
Director
Division of Special Education
State Department of Education
933 High Street
Worthington, Ohio 43085-4087
(614) 466-2650
Fax: (614) 436-9496

Oklahoma
Executive Director
Special Education Section
State Department of Education
Oliver Hodge Memorial
  Building, Room 215
2500 North Lincoln Boulevard
Oklahoma City, Oklahoma
  73105-4599
(405) 521-3351
Fax: (405) 521-6205

Oregon
Associate Superintendent
Special Education & Student
  Services Division
State Department of Education
700 Pringle Parkway,
  Southeast
Salem, Oregon 97310-0290
(503) 378-3598
Fax: (503) 378-8434

Pennsylvania
Director
Bureau of Special Education
State Department of Education
333 Market Street
Harrisburg, Pennsylvania
  17126-0333
(717) 783-6913
Fax: (717) 783-6139

Rhode Island
Coordinator
Special Education Programs
State Department of Education
Roger Williams Building,
  Room 209
22 Hayes Street
Providence, Rhode Island
  02908-5025
(401) 277-3505
Fax: (401) 277-6178

South Carolina
Director
Office of Programs for
  Exceptional Children
State Department of Education
Rutledge Building, Room 505
1429 Senate
Columbia, South Carolina
  29201
(803) 734-8353
Fax: (803) 734-8624

South Dakota
Director
Office of Special Education
State Department of Education
Richard F. Kneip Building
700 North Illinois Street
Pierre, South Dakota
   57501-2293
(605) 773-3315
Fax: (605) 773-4855

Tennessee
Associate Commissioner
Special Education Programs
State Department of Education
Cordell Hull Building
Room 132
Nashville, Tennessee 37219
(615) 741-2851
Fax: (615) 741-6236

Texas
Senior Director
Special Education Unit
Texas Education Agency
William B. Travis Building,
   Room 5-120
1701 North Congress Avenue
Austin, Texas 78701-2486
(512) 463-9414
Fax: (512) 463-9838

Utah
Director
At-Risk & Special Education
   Services
Special Education Services
   Unit
State Office of Education
250 East 500 South
Salt Lake City, Utah
   84111-3204
(801) 538-7706
Fax: (801) 538-7701

Vermont
Director
Division of Special Education
State Department of Education
State Office Building
120 State Street
Montpelier, Vermont
   05602-3403
(802) 828-3141
Fax: (802) 828-3140

Virginia
Lead Specialist for Special
   Education
Division of Pre & Early
   Adolescent Education
State Department of Education
Post Office Box 6Q
Richmond, Virginia 23216-2060
(804) 225-2847
Fax: (804) 371-2456

Washington
Director
Special Education Section
Department of Public
   Instruction
Old Capitol Building FG-11
Olympia, Washington
   98504-0001
(206) 753-6733
Fax: (206) 586-0247

West Virginia
Director
Office of Special Education
State Department of Education
Building 6, Room B-304
Capitol Complex
Charleston, West Virginia
   25305
(304) 558-2696
Fax: (304) 558-0048

Wisconsin
Division of Handicapped
 Children and Pupil Services
Department of Public
 Instruction
128 South Webster
Post Office Box 7841
Madison, Wisconsin
 53707-7841
(608) 266-1649
Fax: (608) 267-1052

Wyoming
Director
Special Education Unit
State Department of Education
Hathaway Building, 2nd Floor
2300 Capitol Avenue
Cheyenne, Wyoming
 82002-0050
(307) 777-7417
Fax: (307) 777-6234

Parent Training and Information (PTI) Centers

For information about PTI Centers, see "Advocacy and Family
Support for Children with Special Health Care Needs and Their
Families," page 378.

State Vocational Rehabilitation (VR) Programs

State Vocational Rehabilitation (VR) programs *administer educa-*
tion and training programs for individuals with disabilities (in-
cluding young adults) who have some potential of working. If an
individual is accepted into VR, VR can pay some of his or her
medical and educational expenses as the individual trains for employment and begins working. Call VR as your youth approaches 14
years old to see what services are available in your state and how
your young adult can apply (see Chapter 5 for more information).

Alabama
Director
Rehabilitation Services
Post Office Box 11586
Montgomery, Alabama
 36111-0586
(205) 201-8780

American Samoa
Director
Vocational Rehabilitation
Department of Manpower
 Resources
Pago Pago, American Samoa
 96799
011 (684) 633-2336

Alaska
Director
Division of Vocational
 Rehabilitation
Box F, M.S. 0581
Juneau, Alaska 99811-0500
(907) 465-2814
(907) 465-2440 (TT)

Arizona
Administrator
Rehabilitation Services
 Administration
1789 West Jefferson
North Wing
Phoenix, Arizona 85007
(602) 542-3332
(602) 542-6049 (Voice and TT)

Arkansas
Director
Division of Rehabilitation
  Services
Department of Human
  Services
Post Office Box 3781
Little Rock, Arkansas 72203
(501) 682-6709
(501) 682-6669 (TT)

Commissioner
Division of Services for the
  Blind
Department of Human Services
Post Office Box 3237
Little Rock, Arkansas 72203
(501) 324-9270

California
Director
Department of Rehabilitation
830 K Street Mall
Sacramento, California 95814
(916) 445-3971 (Voice and TT)

Colorado
Manager
Department of Social and
  Rehabilitation Services
1575 Sherman Street, 4th Floor
Denver, Colorado 80203-1714
(303) 866-2866 (Voice and TT)

Connecticut
Bureau Chief
Bureau of Client Services
State Department of Education
Division of Rehabilitation
  Services
10 Griffin Road North
Windsor, Connecticut 06095
(203) 298-2000
1-800-537-2549 (in
  Connecticut)

Delaware
Director
Division of Vocational
  Rehabilitation
Delaware Elwyn Institutes
321 East 11th Street, 4th Floor
Wilmington, Delaware 19801
(302) 577-2851 (Voice and TT)

Director
Division for the Visually
  Impaired
Department of Health and
  Social Services
305 West 8th Street
Wilmington, Delaware 19801
(302) 421-5730

District of Columbia
Administrator
District of Columbia
  Rehabilitation Services
  Administration
Department of Human
  Services
605 G Street, Northwest
Suite 1111
Washington, D.C. 20001
(202) 727-3227
(202) 727-0981 (TT)

Florida
Director
Division of Vocational
  Rehabilitation
Department of Labor and
  Employment Security
1709 A Mahan Drive
Tallahassee, Florida
  32399-0696
(904) 488-6210
(904) 488-2867 (Voice and TT)

Georgia
Director
Division of Rehabilitation
  Services
Department of Human
  Resources
878 Peachtree Street,
  Northeast
Room 706
Atlanta, Georgia 30309
(404) 894-6670
(404) 894-8558 (Voice and TT)
1-800-822-9727 (in Georgia)

Hawaii
Administrator
Division of Vocational
  Rehabilitation and Services
  for the Blind
Department of Human
  Services
Post Office Box 339
Honolulu, Hawaii 96809
(808) 586-5355
1-800-586-5366 (in Hawaii)

Idaho
Administrator
Division of Vocational
  Rehabilitation
Len B. Jordan Building
Room 150
650 West State
Boise, Idaho 83720-3650
(208) 334-3390
(208) 334-2520 (Voice and TT)

Illinois
Director
Department of Rehabilitation
  Services
623 East Adams Street
Springfield, Illinois 62794
(217) 785-0218
(217) 782-5734 (TT)

Indiana
Commissioner
Department of Human
  Services
402 West Washington Street
Post Office Box 7083
Indianapolis, Indiana
  46207-7083
(317) 232-6500
(317) 232-1427 (TT)
1-800-545-7763 (in Indiana)

Iowa
Administrator
Division of Vocational
  Rehabilitation Services
Department of Education
510 East 12th Street
Des Moines, Iowa 50319
(515) 281-4311 (Voice and TT)

Kansas
Commissioner
Rehabilitation Services
Department of Social and
  Rehabilitation Services
300 Southwest Oakley
Biddle Building, 1st Floor
Topeka, Kansas 66606
(913) 296-3911
(913) 296-7029 (TT)

Kentucky
Commissioner
Department of Vocational
  Rehabilitation
Capital Plaza Tower, 9th Floor
Frankfort, Kentucky 40601
(502) 564-4566
(502) 564-4440 (Voice and TT)
1-800-372-7172 (in Kentucky)

Louisiana
Director
Louisiana Rehabilitation
    Services
Department of Social Services
Post Office Box 94371
Baton Rouge, Louisiana
    70804-9071
(504) 342-2285
(504) 342-2266 (Voice and TT)

Maine
Director
Bureau of Rehabilitation
    Services
Department of Human
    Services
35 Anthony Avenue
Augusta, Maine 04333-0011
(207) 626-5300
(207) 626-5321 (Voice and TT)

Maryland
Assistant State Superintendent
Division of Vocational
    Rehabilitation
State Department of Education
2301 Argonne Drive
Baltimore, Maryland 21218
(410) 554-3276
(410) 554-3277 (TT)

Massachusetts
Commissioner
Rehabilitation Commission
4 Point Place
27-43 Wormwood Street
Boston, Massachusetts 02210
(617) 727-2172
(617) 727-9063 (TT)

Michigan
State Director
Michigan Rehabilitation
    Services
Department of Education
Post Office Box 30010
Lansing, Michigan 48909
(517) 373-3391
(517) 373-4031 (Voice and TT)
1-800-292-5896 (in Michigan)

Minnesota
Assistant Commissioner
Department of Jobs and
    Training
Division of Rehabilitation
    Services
390 North Robert Street
5th Floor
St. Paul, Minnesota 55101
(612) 296-1822
(612) 296-3900 (TT)

Mississippi
Director
Vocational Rehabilitation
    Division
Department of Rehabilitation
    Services
Post Office Box 1698
Jackson, Mississippi 39215
(601) 354-6825
(601) 354-6830 (Voice and TT)
1-800-943-1000 (in Mississippi)

Missouri
Assistant Commissioner
Division of Vocational
    Rehabilitation
State Department of Education
2401 East McCarty
Jefferson City, Missouri 65101
(314) 751-3251 (Voice and TT)

Montana
Administrator
Department of Social and
　Rehabilitation Services
Rehabilitative/Visual Services
　Divisions
Post Office Box 4210
Helena, Montana 59604
(406) 444-2590 (Voice and TT)

Nebraska
Commissioner
Division of Rehabilitation
　Services
State Department of Education
Post Office Box 94987
Lincoln, Nebraska 68509
(402) 471-3649
(402) 471-3659 (Voice and TT)

Nevada
Administrator
Department of Human
　Resources
Rehabilitation Division
505 East King Street
Room 502
Carson City, Nevada 89710
(702) 687-4440 (Voice and TT)

New Hampshire
Director
Division of Vocational
　Rehabilitation
State Department of Education
78 Regional Drive
Concord, New Hampshire
　03301
(603) 271-3800
(603) 271-3471 (Voice and TT)

New Jersey
Director
Division of Vocational
　Rehabilitation Services
Labor Building
CN 398—Room 612
Trenton, New Jersey 08625
(609) 292-5987
(609) 292-2919 (Voice and TT)

New Mexico
Director
Department of Education
Division of Vocational
　Rehabilitation
604 West San Mateo
Santa Fe, New Mexico 87503
(505) 827-3500 (Voice and TT)
1-800-235-5387 (complaints)

New York
Commissioner
Office of Vocational and
　Educational Services for
　Individuals with Disabilities
New York State Education
　Department
One Commerce Plaza
Room 1606
Albany, New York 12234
(518) 474-2714
(518) 473-9333 (Voice and TT)

North Carolina
Director
Division of Vocational
　Rehabilitation Services
Department of Human
　Resources
State Office
Post Office Box 26053
Raleigh, North Carolina 27611
(919) 733-3364
(919) 733-5920 (Voice and TT)

North Dakota
Director
Office of Vocational
  Rehabilitation
Department of Human Services
600 East Boulevard
State Capitol Building
Bismarck, North Dakota 58505
(701) 224-2907
(701) 224-2699 (Voice and TT)
1-800-472-2622 (in North
  Dakota)

Ohio
Administrator
Rehabilitation Services
  Commission
400 East Campus View
  Boulevard
Columbus, Ohio 43235-4604
(614) 438-1210 (Voice and TT)
1-800-282-4536, ext. 1210 (in
  Ohio)

Oklahoma
Administrator
Department of Human
  Services
Division of Rehabilitation
  Services
Post Office Box 25352
Oklahoma City, Oklahoma
  73125
(405) 424-6647
(405) 424-2794 (Voice and TT)

Oregon
Administrator
Division of Vocational
  Rehabilitation
Department of Human
  Resources
2045 Silverton Road Northeast
Salem, Oregon 97310
(503) 378-3850 (Voice and TT)

Pennsylvania
Executive Director
Office of Vocational
  Rehabilitation
Labor and Industry Building
7th and Forster Streets
Harrisburg, Pennsylvania 17120
(717) 787-5244
(717) 783-8917 (Voice and TT)
1-800-442-6351 (in Pennsylvania)

Rhode Island
Administrator
Department of Human Services
Division of Community Services
Vocational Rehabilitation
  Services
40 Fountain Street
Providence, Rhode Island
  02903
(401) 421-7005
(401) 421-7016 (TT)

South Carolina
Commissioner
Vocational Rehabilitation
  Department
1410 Boston Avenue
Post Office Box 15
West Columbia, South
  Carolina 29171
(803) 822-4300
(803) 822-5313 (Voice and TT)

South Dakota
Division Director
Division of Rehabilitation
  Services
Department of Human
  Services
700 Governors Drive
Pierre, South Dakota
  57501-2291
(605) 773-3195
(605) 773-4544 (TT)

Tennessee
Commissioner
Rehabilitation Services
Department of Human
  Services
Citizens Plaza State Office
  Building
15th Floor
400 Deaderick Street
Nashville, Tennessee
  37248-0060
(615) 741-2019
(615) 741-5644 (Voice and TT)

Texas
Commissioner
Rehabilitation Commission
4900 North Lamar
Austin, Texas 78751
(512) 445-8100
1-800-735-2988 (Voice)
1-800-735-2989 (TT)
1-800-628-5115 (in Texas)

Utah
Director
Division of Rehabilitation
  Services
State Office of Education
250 East Fifth South
Salt Lake City, Utah 84111
(801) 538-7530 (Voice and TT)

Vermont
Director
Vocational Rehabilitation
  Division
103 South Main Street
Waterbury, Vermont
  05671-2303
(802) 241-2189 (Voice and TT)

Virginia
Commissioner
Department of Rehabilitative
  Services
4901 Fitzhugh Avenue
Post Office Box 11045
Richmond, Virginia 23230
(804) 367-0316
(804) 367-0315 (Voice and TT)
1-800-552-5019 (in Virginia)

Washington
Director
Division of Vocational
  Rehabilitation
Department of Social and
  Health Services
OB 21-C
Olympia, Washington 98504
(206) 753-0293
(206) 753-5473 (Voice and TT)
1-800-637-5627 (in
  Washington)

West Virginia
Director
Division of Rehabilitation
  Services
State Board of Rehabilitation
State Capitol
Charleston, West Virginia
  25305
(304) 766-4600
(304) 766-4970 (Voice and TT)
1-800-642-3021 (in West
  Virginia)

Wisconsin
Administrator
Division of Vocational
  Rehabilitation
Department of Health and
  Social Services
1 West Wilson, 8th Floor
Madison, Wisconsin
  53707-7852
(608) 266-5466
(608) 266-9599 (Voice and TT)
1-800-362-7433 (in Wisconsin)

Wyoming
Administrator
Division of Rehabilitation
  Services
Department of Employment
1 East Herschler Building
Cheyenne, Wyoming 82002
(307) 777-7385
(307) 777-7389 (Voice and TT)

Client Assistance Programs (CAP)

Client Assistance Programs (CAP) are independent state agencies designed to assist individuals inquiring about Vocational Rehabilitation programs, applying for VR programs, or having any problem with a Vocational Rehabilitation program or service. They are also required to provide outreach to individuals with disabilities who may qualify for VR services.

Alabama
Division of Rehabilitation
  Services and Children's
  Rehabilitation Services
2129 East South Boulevard
Post Office Box 11586
Montgomery, Alabama 36111
(205) 281-8780

Alaska
CAP Director
ASIST
2900 Boniface Parkway, #100
Anchorage, Alaska 99504-3195
(907) 333-2211

Arizona
CAP Director
Arizona Center for Law in the
  Public Interest
3208 East Fort Lowell
Suite 106
Tucson, Arizona 85716
(602) 327-9547

Arkansas
CAP Director
Advocacy Services, Inc.
Evergreen Place
Suite 201
1100 North University
Little Rock, Arkansas 72207
(501) 324-9215
1-800-482-1174

California
Director
Client Assistance Program
830 K Street Mall, Room 220
Sacramento, California 95814
(916) 322-5066

Colorado
CAP Coordinator
The Legal Center
455 Sherman Street
Suite 130
Denver, Colorado 80203
(303) 722-0300

Connecticut
Director
Client Assistance Program
Office of P & A for
  Handicapped and
  Developmentally Disabled
  Persons
60 Weston Street
Hartford, Connecticut
  06120-1551
(203) 297-4300

Delaware
Director
Client Assistance Program
United Cerebral Palsy, Inc.
254 Camden-Wyoming Avenue
Camden, Delaware 19934
(302) 698-9336
1-800-640-9336

District of Columbia
Coordinator
Client Assistance Program
I.P.A.C.H.I.
4455 Connecticut Avenue,
  Northwest
Suite B100
Washington, D.C. 20008
(202) 966-8081

Florida
CAP Program Director
Advocacy Center for Persons
  with Disabilities
2671 Executive Center
Circle West
Webster Building
Suite 100
Tallahassee, Florida
  32301-5024
(904) 488-9070

Georgia
CAP Director
Department of Human
  Resources
Division of Rehabilitation
  Services
2 Peachtree Street, Northwest,
  Room 23-307
Atlanta, Georgia 30303
(404) 657-3012

Hawaii
Executive Director
Protection & Advocacy Agency
1580 Makaloa Street
Suite 1060
Honolulu, Hawaii 96814
(808) 949-2922

Idaho
Executive Director
Co-Ad, Inc.
4477 Emerald
Suite B-100
Boise, Idaho 83706
(208) 336-5353

Illinois
Manager
Illinois Client Assistance
  Project
100 North First Street
1st Floor
Springfield, Illinois 62702
(217) 782-5374

Indiana
Executive Director
Indiana Advocacy Services
850 North Meridian Street
Suite 2-C
Indianapolis, Indiana 46204
(317) 232-1150

Iowa
CAP Director
Division on Persons with
    Disabilities
Lucas State Office Building
Des Moines, Iowa 50319
(515) 281-3957

Kansas
Director
Client Assistance Program
Biddle Building, 2nd Floor
2700 West 6th Street
Topeka, Kansas 66606
(913) 296-1491

Kentucky
Client Assistance Program
Capitol Plaza Tower
Frankfort, Kentucky 40601
(502) 564-8035
1-800-633-6283

Louisiana
Director
Client Assistance Program
Advocacy Center for the
    Elderly and Disabled
210 O'Keefe
Suite 700
New Orleans, Louisiana 70112
(504) 522-2337

Maine
Executive Director
CARES, Inc.
4-C Winter Street
August, Maine 04330
(207) 622-7055

Maryland
Program Director
Client Assistance Program
MD State Department of
    Education
Division of Vocational
    Rehabilitation
300 West Preston Street
Suite 205
Baltimore, Maryland 21201
(410) 333-7251

Massachusetts
Director
Client Assistance Program
MA Office on Disability
One Ashburton Place
Room 303
Boston, Massachusetts 02108
(617) 727-7440

Michigan
Director
Client Assistance Program
Department of Rehabilitation
    Services
Post Office Box 30008
Lansing, Michigan 48909
(517) 373-8193

Minnesota
CAP Project Coordinator
Minnesota Disability Law
    Center
430 First Avenue North
Suite 300
Minneapolis, Minnesota
    55401-1780
(612) 332-1441

Mississippi
Director
Client Assistance Program
Blind and Visually Impaired
Easter Seal Society
3226 North State Street
Jackson, Mississippi 39216
(601) 982-7051

Missouri
Executive Director
Missouri P & A Services
925 South Country Club
   Drive, Unit B-1
Jefferson City, Missouri 65109
(314) 893-3333

Montana
Executive Director
Montana Advocacy Program
316 North Park, Room 211
Post Office Box 1680
Helena, Montana 59624
(406) 444-3889
1-800-245-4743

Nebraska
CAP Director
Division of Rehabilitation
   Services
Nebraska Department of
   Education
301 Centennial Mall South
Lincoln, Nebraska 68509
(402) 471-3656

Nevada
Director
Client Assistance Program
1755 East Plumb Lane, #128
Reno, Nevada 89502
(702) 688-1440
1-800-633-9879

New Hampshire
CAP Ombudsman
Governor's Commission on
   Disability
57 Regional Drive
Concord, New Hampshire
   03301-8506
(603) 271-2773

New Jersey
CAP Coordinator
Department of Public
   Advocate
Office of Advocacy for the DD
Hughes Justice Complex,
   CN 850
Trenton, New Jersey 08625
(609) 292-9742
1-800-792-8600

New Mexico
CAP Coordinator
Protection & Advocacy
   System, Inc.
1720 Louisiana Boulevard,
   Northeast
Suite 204
Albuquerque, New Mexico
   87110
(505) 256-3100

New York
Director
Client Assistance Program
New York State Commission
   on Quality of Care for the
   Mentally Disabled
99 Washington Avenue
Suite 1002
Albany, New York 12210
(518) 473-7378

North Carolina
Director
Client Assistance Program
North Carolina Division of
    Vocational Rehabilitation
    Services
Post Office Box 26053
Raleigh, North Carolina 27611
(919) 733-3364

North Dakota
Director
North Dakota Client
    Assistance Program
400 East Broadway
Suite 303
Bismarck, North Dakota
    58501-4038
(701) 224-3970
(701) 224-3975

Ohio
CAP Administrator
Governor's Office of Advocacy
    for People with Disabilities
30 East Broad Street, Room 1201
Columbus, Ohio 43266-0400
(614) 466-9956

Oklahoma
Director
Client Assistance Program
Oklahoma Office of
    Handicapped Concerns
4300 North Lincoln Boulevard
Suite 200
Oklahoma City, Oklahoma
    73105
(405) 521-3756

Oregon
CAP Director
Oregon Disabilities
    Commission
1257 Ferry Street, Southeast
Salem, Oregon 97310
(503) 378-3142

Pennsylvania
Statewide Director
Client Assistance Program
    (SEPLS)
1650 Arch Street
Suite 2310
Philadelphia, Pennsylvania
    19103
(215) 557-7112

Rhode Island
CAP Director
Rhode Island Protection &
    Advocacy System
151 Broadway
Providence, Rhode Island
    02903
(401) 831-3150
(401) 831-5335 (TT)

South Carolina
Director
Office of the Governor,
    Division of Ombudman &
    Citizen Services
Post Office Box 11369
Columbia, South Carolina
    29211
(803) 734-0457

South Dakota
Director
Client Assistance Program
South Dakota Advocacy
    Services
221 South Central Avenue
Pierre, South Dakota 57501
(605) 224-8294
1-800-658-4782

Tennessee
CAP Director
Tennessee P & A, Inc.
Post Office Box 121257
Nashville, Tennessee 37212
(615) 298-1080

Texas
CAP Coordinator
Advocacy, Inc.
7800 Shoal Creek Boulevard
Suite 171-E
Austin, Texas 78757
(512) 454-4816

Utah
Director
Client Assistance Program
Legal Center for People with
    Disabilities
455 East 400 South
Suite 201
Salt Lake City, Utah 84101
(801) 363-1347
1-800-662-9080

Vermont
Director
Client Assistance Program
Ladd Hall
103 South Main Street
Waterbury, Vermont 05676
(802) 241-2641

Virginia
Manager
Department for Rights of
    Virginians with Disabilities
101 North 14th Street
17th Floor
Richmond, Virginia 23219
(804) 225-2042
1-800-552-3962

Washington
Director
Client Assistance Program
Post Office Box 22510
Seattle, Washington 98122
(206) 721-4049
(206) 721-4575

West Virginia
Director
Client Assistance Program
West Virginia Advocates
1524 Kanawha Boulevard, East
Charleston, West Virginia 25311
(304) 346-0847
1-800-950-5250

Wisconsin
CAP Director
Governor's Commission for
    People with Disabilities
1 West Wilson Street, Room 558
Post Office Box 7852
Madison, Wisconsin
    53707-7852
(608) 267-7422
1-800-362-1290

Wyoming
Director
Client Assistance Program
Wyoming P & A System, Inc.
2424 Pioneer Avenue
Suite 101
Cheyenne, Wyoming 82001
(307) 638-7668
(307) 632-3496
1-800-821-3091

FINANCIAL AND RELATED ASSISTANCE
Social Security Administration

For information about Supplemental Security Income (SSI), contact:

1-800-772-1213 (Voice)
1-800-325-0778 (TT)

County Departments of Human Resources or Social Services

For information about assistance offered by County Departments of Human Resources or County Departments of Social Services, see Chapters 5 and 7.

State Community Service Block Grant Agencies (for Community Action Agencies/County Commissions on Economic Opportunity)

State Community Service Block Grant Agencies administer a large number of federal funds given to states for a variety of community programs. Included in these programs are the Community Action Agencies (CAAs) (known in some places as County Commissions on Economic Opportunity [CCEOs]). One of the services CAAs/CCEOs provide is *emergency financial assistance for medication, rent, rent deposits, and so forth.* Call this state agency for a referral to a local CAA or CCEO if the strategies suggested in Chapter 7 of this book do not work.

Alabama
CSBG Program Director
Alabama Department of
  Economic & Community
  Affairs
401 Adams Avenue
Post Office Box 5690
Montgomery, Alabama
  36103-5690
(205) 242-5369
Fax: (205) 242-5515

Alaska
Administrator
Department of Community &
  Regional Affairs
1001 Noble Street
Suite 430
Fairbanks, Alaska 99701
(907) 452-4468

Arkansas
Assistant Deputy Director
Office of Community Services
Post Office Box 1437/Slot 1330
Little Rock, Arkansas
  72203-1437
(501) 682-8715
Fax: (501) 682-6736

Arizona
Program Administrator
Department of Economic
  Security
Post Office Box 6123
1789 West Jefferson Street
Phoenix, Arizona 85005
(602) 542-6600
Fax: (602) 542-6655

California
Director
Department of Economic
   Opportunity
700 North 10th Street
Room 258
Sacramento, California 95814
(916) 323-8694
Fax: (916) 327-3153

Colorado
Director
Department of Local Affairs
1575 Sherman Street
Denver, Colorado 80203
(303) 866-5700
Fax: (303) 866-4214

Weatherization Program Manager
Division of Housing
1313 Sherman Street
Room #623
Denver, Colorado 80203
(303) 866-2033
Fax: (303) 866-2251

Connecticut
Chief
Connecticut Department of
   Human Resources
1049 Asylum Avenue
3rd Floor
Hartford, Connecticut 06105
(203) 566-7890
Fax: (203) 566-7613

Delaware
Program Manager
Department of Community
   Affairs
820 North French Street
Post Office Box 1401
Wilmington, Delaware 19801
(302) 577-3491
Fax: (302) 577-2383

Director
Division of Community
   Service
820 North French Street
4th Floor
Wilmington, Delaware 19801
(302) 577-3491
Fax: (302) 577-2383

District of Columbia
Chief
District of Columbia
   Department of Human
   Service
625 H Street, Northeast
5th Floor
Washington, D.C. 20002
(202) 727-5951
Fax: (202) 727-1687

Florida
Community Program
   Administrator
Department of Community
   Affairs
2740 Centerview Drive
Tallahassee, Florida
   32399-2100
(904) 488-7541
Fax: (904) 922-5623

Georgia
CSBG Program Manager
Office of Community and
   Intergovernmental Affairs
Georgia Department of Human
   Resources
Room 315-H, 47 Trinity
   Avenue, Southwest
Atlanta, Georgia 30334-5600
(404) 656-6697
Fax: (404) 651-6884

Director
Office of Community Services
47 Trinity Avenue, Southwest,
    Room 315 H
Atlanta, Georgia 30334-1202
(404) 656-4497
Fax: (404) 651-6884

Hawaii
Executive Director
Office of Community Services
335 Merchant Street
Room 101
Honolulu, Hawaii 96813
(808) 586-8675
Fax: (808) 586-8685

Idaho
Director
Department of Health &
    Welfare
405 West State Street
Boise, Idaho 83720
(208) 554-5730
Fax: (208) 334-5817

Illinois
Chief
Department of Commerce &
    Community Affairs
620 East Adams, 4th Floor
Springfield, Illinois 62701
(217) 785-3203
Fax: (217) 785-1206

Indiana
Secretary
Indiana Department of Human
    Services
402 West Washington Street
Post Office Box 7083
Indianapolis, Indiana
    46207-7083
(317) 233-4690
Fax: (317) 233-4693

Iowa
Chief
Bureau of Community
    Services
Lucas State Office Building
Des Moines, Iowa 50319
(515) 281-3951
Fax: (515) 242-6119

Program Manager
Iowa Energy Policy Council
Lucas State Office Building
Des Moines, Iowa 50319
(515) 281-3855

Kansas
Director
Department of Commerce
700 Southwest Harrison Street
Suite 1300
Topeka, Kansas 66603-3755
(913) 296-2686
Fax: (913) 296-6988

Kentucky
Manager
Department of Social Services
275 East Main Street 6-West
Frankfort, Kentucky 40621
(502) 564-6750
Fax: (502) 564-2467

Louisiana
Director of CSBG
Louisiana Department of
    Labor
1001 North 23rd Street, 3rd
    Floor Annex
Baton Rouge, Louisiana
    70804
(504) 342-3053
Fax: (504) 342-7664

Massachusetts
Director
Office of Community Action
100 Cambridge Street, #1103
Boston, Massachusetts 02202
(617) 727-0050
Fax: (617) 727-4259

Maryland
Director
Office of Community Services
100 Community Place
Crownsville, Maryland
    21032-2023
(410) 514-7229
Fax: (410) 987-4660

Maine
Director
Division of Community
    Services
State House Station #73
Augusta, Maine 04333
(207) 287-5060
Fax: (207) 626-5555

Michigan
Deputy Director
Bureau of Community Services
201 North Washington
3rd Floor
Lansing, Michigan 48909
(517) 335-5953
Fax: (517) 335-6965

Minnesota
Assistant Commissioner
Economic Opportunity,
    Department of Jobs &
    Training
390 North Robert Street
St. Paul, Minnesota 55101
(612) 296-3700
Fax: (612) 297-5820

Mississippi
Director
Department of Human
    Development
421 West Pascagoula Street
Jackson, Mississippi
    39203-3094
(601) 949-2041
Fax: (601) 354-6988

Missouri
Program Manager
Division of Energy
Post Office Box 176
Jefferson City, Missouri 65102
(314) 751-4422

Special Projects Coordinator
State of Missouri/CSBG Unit
2705 West Main Street
Jefferson City, Missouri 65103
(314) 751-6789
Fax: (314) 526-5592

Montana
CSBG Director
Department of Social &
    Rehabilitation Services
Post Office Box 4210, 111
    Sanders, Cap. Station
Helena, Montana 59604
(406) 444-4545
Fax: (406) 444-1970

North Carolina
Director
Department of Human
    Resources, OEO
2413 Crabtree Boulevard
Suite 119
Raleigh, North Carolina 27610
(919) 733-2633
Fax: (919) 733-1229

Program Manager
North Carolina Department of
  Commerce
Post Office Box 25249
Raleigh, North Carolina
  27611
(919) 733-2230

North Dakota
Director
Office of Intergovernmental
  Assistance
State Capitol Building
600 East Boulevard, 14th Floor
Bismarck, North Dakota
  58505
(701) 224-4499
Fax: (701) 224-2308

Nebraska
Program Manager
Nebraska State Energy Office
9th Floor—State Capitol
Post Office Box 95085
Lincoln, Nebraska 68509
(402) 471-3347

Director
Nebraska Department of Social
  Services
Post Office Box 95026
Lincoln, Nebraska 68509
(402) 471-9370
Fax: (402) 471-9455

New Hampshire
Director
Governor's Office of Energy &
  Community Services
57 Regional Drive
Concord, New Hampshire
  03301-8506
(603) 271-2611
Fax: (603) 271-2615

New Jersey
Director
New Jersey Department of
  Community Affairs
101 South Broad CN-814
Trenton, New Jersey 08625
(609) 292-6212
Fax: (609) 984-0386

New Mexico
Planner Director
Human Services Department
Post Office Box 2348
Santa Fe, New Mexico
  87504-2348
(505) 827-7264
Fax: (505) 827-8480

Nevada
CSBG Program Manager
Office of Community Services
400 West King Street, #400
Capitol Complex
Carson City, Nevada 89710
(702) 687-4990
Fax: (702) 687-4914

New York
Executive Director
Division of Economic
  Opportunity
New York State Department of
  State
162 Washington Avenue
Albany, New York 12231
(518) 474-5700
Fax: (518) 486-4663

Executive Director
Division of Economic
  Opportunity
162 Washington Avenue
7th Floor
Albany, New York 12231
(518) 474-5741
Fax: (518) 474-4663

Ohio
Chief
Office of Community Services
Post Office Box 2668
Columbus, Ohio 43216
(614) 644-6858
Fax: (614) 466-4708

Oklahoma
Director
Oklahoma Department of
  Commerce
Post Office Box 26980
Oklahoma City, Oklahoma
  73126-0980
(405) 841-9326
Fax: (405) 841-5199

Oregon
Director
Department of Human
  Resources
1600 State Street
Salem, Oregon 97310
(503) 378-4729
Fax: (503) 378-3465

Pennsylvania
Director
Bureau of Human Resources
358 Forum Building
Harrisburg, Pennsylvania
  17120
(717) 787-1984
Fax: (717) 787-6074

Rhode Island
Principal Resource Specialist
Department of Human
  Services
600 New London Avenue
Cranston, Rhode Island 02920
(401) 464-2421
Fax: (401) 464-1876

South Carolina
Director
Division of Economic
  Opportunity
1205 Pendleton Street
Columbia, South Carolina
  29201
(803) 734-0662
Fax: (803) 734-0356

South Dakota
Director
Department of Community &
  Regional/Community
  Assistance
500 East Capitol
Pierre, South Dakota 57501
(605) 773-3178
Fax: (605) 773-5369

Tennessee
Program Director
Department of Human
  Services
400 Deaderick Street
Nashville, Tennessee 37248
(615) 741-4983
Fax: (615) 741-4165

Texas
Executive Director
Texas Department of Housing
  & Community Affairs
Post Office Box 13941
Austin, Texas 78701-3941
(512) 475-3950
Fax: (512) 475-3935

Utah
Director
Department of Community &
  Economic Development
324 South State Street, Suite 500
Salt Lake City, Utah 84111
(801) 538-8731
Fax: (801) 538-8888

Virginia
Director
Virginia Department of Social
  Services
730 East Broad Street
Richmond, Virginia 23219
(804) 692-1898
Fax: (804) 662-9109

Vermont
Executive Director
Office of Economic
  Opportunity
103 South Main Street
Waterbury, Vermont 05676
(802) 241-2450
Fax: (802) 244-8103

Washington
Assistant Director
Department of Community
  Development
906 Columbia Street,
  Southwest
Post Office Box 48300
Olympia, Washington
  98504-8300
(206) 753-4979
Fax: (206) 586-5880

West Virginia
Manager
Office of Community &
  Industrial Development
1204 Kanawha Boulevard, East,
  2nd Floor
Charleston, West Virginia
  25301
(304) 558-8860

Wisconsin
Director
Department of Health & Social
  Services
Post Office Box 7935
Madison, Wisconsin 53707
(608) 266-0073
Fax: (608) 267-3240

Wyoming
CSBG Administrator
Community Services
US West Building, 259 B,
6101 Yellowstone
Cheyenne, Wyoming 82002
(307) 777-6779
Fax: (307) 777-6964

Church Ministries

For information about the assistance offered by various church ministries, see Chapter 6.

Health, Social Service, and Religious Organizations

For information about the assistance offered by various health, social service, and religious organizations, see Chapter 6 and its appendices.

Civic and Social Welfare Organizations

For information about the assistance offered by various civic and social welfare organizations, see Chapter 6 and Appendix 6B.

Hill-Burton Hotline

For information about how this hotline can be helpful, see Chapter 5 or call:

1-800-638-9742
1-800-492-0359 (in Maryland only)

Caring Programs for Children

For information about how these programs can be helpful, see Chapter 6.

Alabama
Alabama Child Caring
  Foundation
Blue Cross and Blue Shield of
  Alabama
936 South 19th Street
Birmingham, Alabama 35205
(205) 985-5640

California
California Kids
Blue Cross of California
Work State WH 1-F
21555 Oxnard Street
Woodland Hills, California
  91367
(818) 703-4947

Georgia
Caring Program for Children
Blue Cross and Blue Shield of
  Georgia
Post Office Box 4445
Atlanta, Georgia 30302-4445
(404) 842-8172

Idaho
Idaho Caring Program for
  Children
1408 West State Street
Boise, Idaho 83702
(208) 336-2420

Iowa
Caring Program for Children
Blue Cross and Blue Shield of
  Iowa
636 Grand Avenue, Station 150
Des Moines, Iowa 50309
(515) 245-4691

Kansas
Caring Program for Children
Blue Cross and Blue Shield of
  Kansas
1133 Topeka Boulevard
Topeka, Kansas 66629
(913) 291-8203

Louisiana
Louisiana Caring Program for
Children
Post Office Box 98022
Baton Rouge, Louisiana
70898-9022
(504) 295-2340

Maryland
Caring Program for Children
Blue Cross and Blue Shield of
Maryland
10455 Mill Run Circle
Owings Mills, Maryland 21117
(410) 998-5823

Massachusetts
Massachusetts Caring for
Children Foundation
Blue Cross and Blue Shield of
Massachusetts
100 Summer Street, 15th Floor
Boston, Massachusetts 02110
(617) 956-2615

Michigan
Caring Program for Children
Blue Cross and Blue Shield of
Michigan—B241
600 Lafayette East
Detroit, Michigan 48226
(313) 225-0111

Mississippi
Caring Program for Children
Blue Cross and Blue Shield of
Mississippi
Post Office Box 3338
Jackson, Mississippi 39207
(601) 932-3704

Missouri
Caring Foundation
Blue Cross and Blue Shield of
Missouri
4444 Forest Park
St. Louis, Missouri 63108
(314) 658-4766

Missouri Valley Caring
Program for Children
Post Office Box 419071
Kansas City, Missouri 64179
(816) 395-2215

Montana
Caring Program for Children
Blue Cross and Blue Shield of
Montana
404 Fuller Avenue
Helena, Montana 59601
(406) 447-8600

New York
Caring Program for Children
Foundation
Blue Cross and Blue Shield of
Central New York
344 South Warren Street
Syracuse, New York 13202
(315) 424-3893

North Carolina
Caring Program
Blue Cross and Blue Shield of
North Carolina
Post Office Box 610
Durham, North Carolina
27702
(919) 490-2798
    or (919) 490-2478

North Dakota
Caring Program for Children
Blue Cross and Blue Shield of
North Dakota
4510 13th Avenue,
Southwest
Fargo, North Dakota 58121
(701) 282-1184

Ohio
Caring Program for Children
Community Mutual Insurance
Company
2810 Victory Parkway
Cincinnati, Ohio 45206
(513) 872-6405

Pennsylvania
Caring Program for Children
Blue Cross of Western
Pennsylvania
Suite 600
500 Wood Street
Pittsburgh, Pennsylvania
14222
(412) 645-6202

Caring Program for Children
Independence Blue Cross
1901 Market Street,
38th Floor
Philadelphia, Pennsylvania
19103
(215) 241-3444

South Dakota
Caring Program for Children
1601 West Madison Street
Sioux Falls, South Dakota
57104
(605) 336-1976

Texas
Caring Program for Children
Blue Cross and Blue Shield of
Texas
Post Office Box 655488
Dallas, Texas 75265
(214) 669-7190

Utah
Caring Program for Children
Blue Cross and Blue Shield of
Utah
Post Office Box 25185
Salt Lake City, Utah 84125
(801) 481-6615

Virginia
Caring Program for Children
Blue Cross and Blue Shield of
Virginia
Post Office Box 27401
Richmond, Virginia 23279
(804) 354-2618

Wyoming
Caring Program for Children
Blue Cross and Blue Shield of
Wyoming
231 East Midwest
Casper, Wyoming 82602
(307) 234-2649

Aid to Families with Dependent Children (AFDC)

For information about AFDC, see Chapter 7.

State and County General Assistance
Programs and General Assistance–Medical Programs

For information about General Assistance Programs and General Assistance–Medical Programs, see Chapter 5.

Regional Offices of the Food and Nutrition Service, the U.S. Department of Agriculture (U.S.D.A.) (for State Distribution Agencies for Surplus and Other Food)

The regional offices of the Food and Nutrition Service *distribute food* for a number of U.S. Department of Agriculture (U.S.D.A.) programs. Included are the Temporary Emergency Food Assistance Program (TEFAP) and the Soup Kitchens and Food Banks (SKFB) programs. If you cannot get information on where to get food under one of these programs from your local television station, newspaper, or social service agency, call the regional agency closest to your home for a local referral. (See Chapter 7 for additional information.)

Mid-Atlantic Regional Office (for Delaware, Maryland, New Jersey, Pennsylvania, Puerto Rico, Virgin Islands, Washington, D.C., and West Virginia)

Food and Nutrition Service
U.S. Department of Agriculture
Mercer Corporate Park
CN 02150
Trenton, New Jersey 08650
(609) 259-5025

Midwest Regional Office (for Illinois, Indiana, Michigan, Minnesota, Ohio, and Wisconsin)

Food and Nutrition Service
U.S. Department of Agriculture
50 East Washington Street
Chicago, Illinois 60602
(312) 353-6664

Mountain Plains Regional Office (for Colorado, Iowa, Kansas, Missouri, Montana, Nebraska, North Dakota, South Dakota, Utah, and Wyoming)

Food and Nutrition Service
U.S. Department of Agriculture
1244 Speer Boulevard
Suite 903
Denver, Colorado 80204
(303) 844-0300

Northeast Regional Office (for Connecticut, Maine, Massachusetts, New Hampshire, New York, Rhode Island, and Vermont)

Food and Nutrition Service
U.S. Department of Agriculture
10 Causeway Street
Boston, Massachusetts 02222
(617) 565-6370

Southeast Regional Office (for Alabama, Florida, Georgia, Kentucky, Mississippi, North Carolina, South Carolina, and Tennessee)

Food and Nutrition Service
U.S. Department of Agriculture
77 Forsyth Street, Southwest
Suite 112
Atlanta, Georgia 30303
(404) 730-2566

Southwest Regional Office (for Arkansas, Louisiana, New Mexico, Oklahoma, and Texas)

Food and Nutrition Service
U.S. Department of Agriculture
1100 Commerce Street
Room 5-C-30
Dallas, Texas 75242
(214) 767-0222

Western Regional Office (for Alaska, American Samoa, Arizona, California, Guam, Hawaii, Idaho, Nevada, Oregon, Trust Territories, and Washington)

Food and Nutrition Service
U.S. Department of Agriculture
550 Kearney Street, Room 400
San Francisco, California 94108
(415) 465-1310

HEATH (Higher Education and Adult Training for Individuals with Disabilities) Resource Center

1 DuPont Circle
Washington, D.C. 20036-1193
1-800-544-3284 (Voice and TT)
(202) 939-9320 (Voice and TT, in Washington, D.C. area)

For information about the assistance offered by this organization, see Chapter 3.

Internal Revenue Service (IRS)

1-800-829-1040 (Voice)
1-800-829-4059 (TT)
1-800-829-4477 (TELETAX)
1-800-TAX-FORM (1-800-829-3676)

For information on the assistance offered by the IRS, see Chapter 8.

Indiana
Commissioner
Indiana Department of
    Revenue
100 North Senate Avenue
Indianapolis, Indiana 46204
(317) 232-2101

Iowa
Director
Iowa Department of Revenue
    & Finance
Hoover State Office Building
Des Moines, Iowa 50319
(515) 281-3204

Kansas
Secretary of Revenue
Kansas Department of
    Revenue
Docking State Office Building
Topeka, Kansas 66625
(913) 296-3041

Kentucky
Secretary
Kentucky Revenue Cabinet
New Capitol Annex
Frankfort, Kentucky 40620
(502) 564-3226

Louisiana
Secretary of Revenue &
    Taxation
Louisiana Department of
    Revenue & Taxation
Post Office Box 201
Baton Rouge, Louisiana 70821
(504) 925-7680

Maine
State Tax Assessor
Maine Bureau of Taxation
State Office Building
Augusta, Maine 04333
(207) 289-2076

Maryland
Comptroller of the Treasury
Maryland Comptroller of the
    Treasury
Post Office Box 466
Annapolis, Maryland 21404
(410) 974-3801

Chief Deputy Comptroller
Maryland Comptroller of the
    Treasury
Goldstein Treasury Building
Post Office Box 466
Annapolis, Maryland 21404
(410) 974-3805

Massachusetts
Commissioner
Massachusetts Department of
    Revenue
100 Cambridge Street
Boston, Massachusetts
    02204
(617) 727-4201

Michigan
Commissioner
Michigan Bureau of Revenue
Department of Treasury,
    Treasury Building
Lansing, Michigan 48922
(517) 373-3196

Minnesota
Commissioner of Revenue
Minnesota Department of
    Revenue
10 River Park Plaza, Mail
    Station 7100
St. Paul, Minnesota
    55146-7100
(612) 296-3403

Mississippi
Chairman
Mississippi State Tax
 Commission
Post Office Box 1033
Jackson, Mississippi 39215
(601) 359-1100

Missouri
Director of Revenue
Missouri Department of
 Revenue
Post Office Box 311
Jefferson City, Missouri
 65105-0311
(314) 751-7227

Montana
Director
Montana Department of
 Revenue
Mitchell Building
Helena, Montana 59620
(406) 444-2460

Nebraska
State Tax Commissioner
Nebraska Department of
 Revenue
Post Office Box 94818—301
 Centennial Mall South
Lincoln, Nebraska 68509
(402) 471-5604

Nevada
Executive Director
Nevada Department of
 Taxation
Capitol Complex
Carson City, Nevada 89710
(702) 687-4892

New Hampshire
Commissioner
New Hampshire Department
 of Revenue Administration
61 South Spring Street
Concord, New Hampshire
 03301
(603) 271-2191

New Jersey
Director
New Jersey Division of
 Taxation
50 Barrack Street, CN269
Trenton, New Jersey 08646
(609) 292-5185

New Mexico
Secretary
New Mexico Taxation &
 Revenue Department
Post Office Box 630
Santa Fe, New Mexico
 87509-0630
(505) 827-0341

New York
Commissioner
New York City Department of
 Finance
1 Centre Street, Municipal
 Building, #500
New York, New York 10007
(212) 669-4855

Commissioner
New York State Department of
 Taxation & Finance
W.A. Harriman Campus,
 Building #9
Albany, New York 12227-0125
(518) 457-2244

North Carolina
Secretary
North Carolina Department of
Revenue
Post Office Box 25000
Raleigh, North Carolina
27640
(919) 733-7211

North Dakota
Commissioner
Office of State Tax
Commissioner
State Capitol, 600 East
Boulevard Avenue
Bismarck, North Dakota
58505
(701) 224-2770

Ohio
Commissioner
Ohio Department of
Taxation
Post Office Box 530
Columbus, Ohio 43266-0030
(614) 466-2166

Oklahoma
Chairman
Oklahoma Tax Commission
2501 Lincoln Boulevard
Oklahoma City, Oklahoma
73194-0001
(405) 521-3115

Oregon
Director
Oregon Department of
Revenue
955 Center Street, Northeast,
Revenue Building
Salem, Oregon 97310
(503) 378-3363

Pennsylvania
Secretary of Revenue
Pennsylvania Department of
Revenue
11 Strawberry Square
Harrisburg, Pennsylvania
17128-1100
(717) 783-3680

Rhode Island
Tax Administrator
Rhode Island Division of
Taxation
One Capitol Hill
Providence, Rhode Island
02908-5800
(401) 277-3050

South Carolina
Chairman
South Carolina Tax
Commission
Post Office Box 125
Columbia, South Carolina
29214
(803) 737-9850

South Dakota
Secretary of Revenue
South Dakota Department of
Revenue
700 Governor's Drive
Pierre, South Dakota
57501-2276
(605) 773-5131

Tennessee
Commissioner
Tennessee Department of
Revenue
Andrew Jackson State Office
Building
Nashville, Tennessee 37242
(615) 741-2461

Texas
Comptroller of Public
  Accounts
Texas Comptroller of Public
  Accounts
111 East 17th Street, LBJ State
  Office Building
Austin, Texas 78774
(512) 463-4000

Utah
Chairman
Utah State Tax Commission
160 East 300 South
Salt Lake City, Utah 84134
(801) 530-6088

Vermont
Commissioner of Taxes
Vermont Department of
  Taxes
109 State Street, Pavilion
  Office Building
Montpelier, Vermont
  05602
(802) 828-2505

Virginia
Commissioner
Virginia Department of
  Taxation
Post Office Box 6-L
Richmond, Virginia 23282
(804) 367-8005

Washington
Director
Washington Department of
  Revenue
Post Office Box 47450 (General
  Administration Building)
Olympia, Washington
  98504-7450
(206) 753-5574

Wisconsin
Secretary of Revenue
Wisconsin Department of
  Revenue
Post Office Box 8933
Madison, Wisconsin 53708
(608) 266-6466

West Virginia
Secretary
West Virginia Department of
  Tax & Revenue
Post Office Box 963 (Building
  1, Room WW-300)
Charleston, West Virginia
  25324-0963
(304) 348-2500

Wyoming
Director
Wyoming Department of
  Revenue
122 West 25th Street
  (Herschler Building)
Cheyenne, Wyoming
  82002-0110
(307) 777-5287

HEALTH INSURANCE

State Departments of Insurance

State Departments of Insurance *regulate all insurance companies doing business in the state,* including those selling health insurance policies. They also are *concerned with individuals who can-*

not get health insurance, and play a major role in setting up and administering "risk pools" and other programs for individuals who are medically uninsurable.

Contact your state's Department of Insurance, Office of Consumer Affairs, if: 1) you have a dispute with your insurance company over an unpaid claim (after you have tried to settle it yourself), 2) you want to find out if there is a "risk pool" in your state and you want information about it, or 3) you want to find out about any insurance reform proposals in your state that will make it easier for your child to be insured (see Chapter 6 for additional information).

Alabama
Insurance Commissioner
135 South Union Street
  #181
Montgomery, Alabama
  36130
(205) 269-3550

Alaska
Director of Insurance
Post Office Box D
Juneau, Alaska 99811
(907) 465-2515

Arizona
Director of Insurance
3030 North Third Street
Suite 1100
Phoenix, Arizona 85012
(602) 255-5400

Arkansas
Insurance Commissioner
400 University Tower
  Building
Little Rock, Arkansas
  72204-1699
(501) 371-1325

California
Commissioner of Insurance
100 Van Ness Avenue
San Francisco, California
  94102
(415) 557-3245 (San Francisco)
(213) 736-2551 (Los Angeles)
1-800-233-9045 (in California
  for complaints)
1-800-927-HELP (in California
  for complaints)

Colorado
Commissioner of Insurance
303 West Colfax Avenue
Suite 500
Denver, Colorado 80204
(303) 866-6400

Connecticut
Insurance Commissioner
Post Office Box 816
Hartford, Connecticut
  06142-0816
(203) 297-3800

Delaware
Insurance Commissioner
841 Silver Lake Boulevard
Dover, Delaware 19901
(302) 739-4251
1-800-282-8611 (in Delaware)

District of Columbia
Superintendent of Insurance
614 H Street, Northwest
North Potomac Building
Suite 516
Washington, D.C. 20001
(202) 727-7424

Florida
Insurance Commissioner
Plaza Level Eleven—The
  Capitol
Tallahassee, Florida
  32399-0300
(904) 488-3440
1-800-342-2762 (in Florida)

Georgia
Insurance Commissioner
2 Martin L. King, Jr. Drive
Atlanta, Georgia 30334
(404) 656-2056

Hawaii
Insurance Commissioner
Post Office Box 3614
Honolulu, Hawaii 96811
(808) 586-2790

Idaho
Acting Director of Insurance
500 South 10th Street
Boise, Idaho 83720
(208) 334-2250

Illinois
Acting Director of Insurance
320 West Washington Street
Springfield, Illinois 62767
(217) 524-4872 (TT)

Indiana
Commissioner of Insurance
311 West Washington Street
Suite 300
Indianapolis, Indiana
  46204-2787
(317) 232-2385
1-800-622-4461 (in Indiana for
  complaints)

Iowa
Insurance Commissioner
Lucas State Office Building,
  6th Floor
Des Moines, Iowa 50319
(515) 281-5705

Kansas
Commissioner of Insurance
420 Southwest 9th Street
Topeka, Kansas 66612
(913) 296-7801
1-800-432-2484 (in Kansas)

Kentucky
Insurance Commissioner
229 West Main Street
Post Office Box 517
Frankfort, Kentucky 40602
(502) 564-3630

Louisiana
Commissioner of Insurance
Post Office Box 94214
Baton Rouge, Louisiana
  70804-9214
(504) 342-5900

Maine
Superintendent of Insurance
State House Station 34
Augusta, Maine 04333-0034
(207) 582-8707

Maryland
Insurance Commissioner
501 St. Paul Place
7th Floor South
Baltimore, Maryland 21202
(410) 333-2520
(410) 383-7555 (TT)
1-800-492-7521 (in Maryland)

Massachusetts
Commissioner of Insurance
280 Friend Street
Boston, Massachusetts 02114
(617) 727-7189, ext. 300

Michigan
Commissioner of Insurance
Insurance Bureau
Post Office Box 30220
Lansing, Michigan 48909

Minnesota
Commissioner of Commerce
133 East 7th Street
St. Paul, Minnesota 55101
(612) 296-2594

Mississippi
Commissioner of Insurance
1804 Walter Sillers Building
Jackson, Mississippi 39201
(601) 359-3569
1-800-562-2957 (in
    Mississippi—claims only)

Missouri
Director of Insurance
301 West High Street
Room 630
Post Office Box 690
Jefferson City, Missouri 65102
(314) 751-4126
1-800-726-7390 (in Missouri)

Montana
Commissioner of Insurance
Post Office Box 4009
Helena, Montana 59604-4009
(406) 444-2040
1-800-332-6148

Nebraska
Director of Insurance
941 O Street
Suite 400
Lincoln, Nebraska 68508
(402) 471-2201

Nevada
Commissioner of Insurance
1665 Hot Springs Road
Capitol Complex 152
Carson City, Nevada
    89710
(702) 687-4270
1-800-992-0900
    (in Nevada)

New Hampshire
Insurance Commissioner
169 Manchester Street
Concord, New Hampshire
    03301
(603) 271-2261
1-800-852-3416 (in New
    Hampshire for consumer
    services)

New Jersey
Commissioner
Department of Insurance
20 West State Street
CN325
Trenton, New Jersey 08625
(609) 292-5363

New Mexico
Superintendent of Insurance
PERA Building, Room 428
Post Office Drawer 1269
Santa Fe, New Mexico
    87504-1269
(505) 827-4500

New York
Superintendent of Insurance
160 West Broadway
New York, New York
    10013-3393
(212) 602-0429
1-800-342-3736 (in New York
    for consumer services)

North Carolina
Commissioner of Insurance
Dobbs Building
Post Office Box 26387
Raleigh, North Carolina
    27611
(919) 733-7343
1-800-662-7777 (in North
    Carolina)

North Dakota
Commissioner of Insurance
Capitol Building, 5th Floor
600 East Boulevard Avenue
Bismarck, North Dakota
    58505-0320
(701) 224-2440
1-800-247-0560 (in North
    Dakota)

Ohio
Director of Insurance
2100 Stella Court
Columbus, Ohio 43266-0566
(614) 644-2651
(614) 644-2673 (Consumer
    Services)
1-800-686-1526 (Consumer
    Services)
(614) 644-2671 (Fraud)
1-800-686-1527 (Fraud)

Oklahoma
Insurance Commissioner
Post Office Box 53408
Oklahoma City, Oklahoma
    73152
(405) 521-2828
1-800-522-0071 (in Oklahoma)

Oregon
Insurance Commissioner
21 Labor and Industries Building
Salem, Oregon 97310-0765
(503) 378-4271

Pennsylvania
Insurance Commissioner
Strawberry Square, 13th Floor
Harrisburg, Pennsylvania
    17120
(717) 787-5173

Rhode Island
Insurance Commissioner
233 Richmond Street
Providence, Rhode Island
    02903
(401) 277-2246

South Carolina
Chief Insurance Commissioner
Post Office Box 100105
Columbia, South Carolina
    29202-3105
(803) 737-6117
1-800-768-3467 (in South
    Carolina)

South Dakota
Director of Insurance
Insurance Building
910 East Sioux Avenue
Pierre, South Dakota
    57501-3940
(605) 773-3563

Tennessee
Commissioner of Insurance
500 James Robertson Parkway
Nashville, Tennessee
    37243-0565
(615) 741-2241
1-800-342-4029 (in Tennessee)

Texas
Director
Claims and Compliance
    Division
State Board of Insurance
Post Office Box 149091
Austin, Texas 78714-9091
(512) 463-6501
1-800-252-3439 (in Texas for
    complaints)

Utah
Commissioner of Insurance
3110 State Office Building
Salt Lake City, Utah 84114
(801) 530-6400

Vermont
Commissioner of Banking and
    Insurance
120 State Street
Montpelier, Vermont
    05620-3101
(802) 828-3301

Virginia
Commissioner of Insurance
700 Jefferson Building
Post Office Box 1157
Richmond, Virginia 23209
(804) 786-3741
(804) 225-3806 (TT)
1-800-552-7945 (in Virginia)

Washington
Insurance Commissioner
Insurance Building AQ21
Olympia, Washington
    98504-0321
(206) 753-7301
1-800-562-6900 (in
    Washington)

West Virginia
Insurance Commissioner
2019 Washington Street, East
Charleston, West Virginia
    25305
(304) 348-3394
1-800-642-9004 (in West
    Virginia)

Wisconsin
Commissioner of Insurance
Post Office Box 7873
Madison, Wisconsin
    53707-7873
(608) 266-3585
1-800-236-8517 (in Wisconsin
    for complaints)

Wyoming
Commissioner of Insurance
Herschler Building
122 West 25th Street
Cheyenne, Wyoming
    82002-0440
(307) 777-7401
1-800-442-4333 (in Wyoming)

State Medicaid Agencies

One State Medicaid agency is located in each state *to administer* the federal and state combined Medicaid public health insurance program and *to help ensure that children and adults with low incomes receive the health and related care* they require. Your state's Medicaid agency develops and recommends changes to your state's Medicaid program. It advises your state legislature about which optional eligibility groups and optional services to include. If you cannot obtain clear information from your local Medicaid agency about your state's Medicaid program, including covered services, eligibility requirements, and how to apply, contact your state's Medicaid agency for the information (see Chapter 5 for more information).

Alabama
Commissioner
Alabama Medicaid
    Agency
2500 Fairlane Drive
Montgomery, Alabama
    36130
(205) 277-2710, ext. 200
Fax: (205) 272-6364

Alaska
Director
Division of Medical
    Assistance
Department of Health and
    Social Services
Post Office Box 110660
Juneau, Alaska 99811-0660
(907) 465-3355
Fax: (907) 463-5154

Arizona
Director
Arizona Health Care Cost
    Containment System
    (AHCCCS)
801 East Jefferson
Phoenix, Arizona 85034
(602) 234-3655, ext. 4053
Fax: (602) 256-6756

Arkansas
Director
Office of Medical Services
Arkansas Department of
    Human Services
Post Office Box 1437
Slot 1100
Little Rock, Arkansas
    72203-1437
(507) 682-8292
Fax: (501) 682-8013

Director
Office of Long-Term Care
Arkansas Department of
    Human Services
Post Office Box 1437
Slot 400
Little Rock, Arkansas
    72203-1437
(501) 682-8487
Fax: (501) 682-6171

California
Director
Medical Care Services
Department of Health
    Services
714 P Street, Room 1253
Sacramento, California
    95814
(916) 657-1496
Fax: (916) 657-1156

Colorado
Manager
Health and Medical Services
Department of Social
    Services
1575 Sherman Street
10th Floor
Denver, Colorado 80203-1714
(303) 866-5901
Fax: (303) 866-4214

Connecticut
Director
Medical Care Administration
Department of Income
    Maintenance
110 Bartholomew Avenue
Hartford, Connecticut 06106
(203) 566-2934
Fax: (203) 566-7881

Delaware
Medicaid Director
Department of Health and
    Social Services
Delaware State Hospital
1901 North DuPont Highway
New Castle, Delaware 19720
(302) 577-4400
Fax: (302) 577-4899

District of Columbia
Chief
Office of Health Care
    Financing
D.C. Dept. of Human Services
2100 M. L. King, Jr., Avenue
    Southeast
Suite 302
Washington, D.C. 20023
(202) 727-0735
Fax: (202) 610-3209

Florida
Assistant Secretary for
    Medicaid
Department of Health &
    Rehabilitation Services
1317 Winewood Boulevard
Building 6, Room 233
Tallahassee, Florida
    32399-0700
(904) 488-3560
Fax: (904) 488-2520

Georgia
Commissioner
Georgia Department of
    Medical Assistance
2 M.L. King, Jr., Drive,
    Southeast
1220-C West Tower
Atlanta, Georgia 30334
(404) 656-4479
Fax: (404) 651-9496

Hawaii
Administrator
Health Care Administration
Department of Human
  Services
Post Office Box 339
Honolulu, Hawaii 96809-0339
(808) 586-5392
Fax: (808) 586-5389

Idaho
Bureau of Medicaid Policy and
  Reimbursement
Department of Health and
  Welfare
450 West State Street
2nd Floor
Boise, Idaho 83720-5450
(208) 334-5795
Fax: (208) 334-0657

Illinois
Deputy Director
Medical Operations
Illinois Department of Public
  Aid
201 South Grand Avenue, East
Springfield, Illinois 62763-0001
(217) 782-2570
Fax: (217) 524-7232

Indiana
Assistant Secretary
Medicaid Policy and Planning
Indiana Family and Social
  Services Administration
Room W341
402 West Washington Street
Post Office Box 7083
Indianapolis, Indiana
  46207-7083
(317) 233-4448
Fax: (317) 233-3472

Iowa
Administrator
Division of Medical Services
Department of Human
  Services
Hoover Street Office Building,
  5th Floor
Des Moines, Iowa 50319
(515) 281-8794
Fax: (515) 281-4597

Kansas
Director
Medical Services
Department of Social and
  Rehabilitation Services
Docking State Office Building
Room 628-S
915 Harrison Street
Topeka, Kansas 66612
(913) 296-3981
Fax: (913) 296-4813

Kentucky
Commissioner
Department of Medicaid
  Services
275 East Main Street
3rd Floor
Frankfort, Kentucky 40621
(502) 564-4321
Fax: (502) 564-3232

Louisiana
Director
Bureau of Health Services
  Financing
Post Office Box 91030
Baton Rouge, Louisiana
  70821-9030
(504) 342-3891
Fax: (504) 342-9508

Maine

Director
Bureau of Medical Services
Department of Human
  Services
State House Station 11
Augusta, Maine 04333
(207) 289-2674
Fax: (207) 289-2675

Maryland

Deputy Secretary
Health Care Policy, Finance
  and Regulation
Department of Health &
  Mental Hygiene
Herbert R. O'Connor Building
201 West Preston Street
5th Floor
Baltimore, Maryland 21201
(410) 225-6535
Fax: (410) 225-6489

Massachusetts

Deputy Commissioner for
  Medical Services
Department of Public Welfare
600 Washington Street
Boston, Massachusetts 02111
(617) 348-5691
Fax: (617) 727-0166

Michigan

Director
Medical Services
  Administration
Department of Social Services
Post Office Box 30037
Lansing, Michigan 48909
(517) 335-5001
Fax: (517) 335-5007

Minnesota

Deputy Assistant
  Commissioner
Health Care Administration
Department of Human
  Services
444 Lafayette Road, 6th Floor
St. Paul, Minnesota
  55155-3848
(612) 296-2766
Fax: (612) 297-3230

Mississippi

Executive Director
Division of Medicaid
Office of the Governor
Suite 801, Robert E. Lee
  Building
239 North Lamar Street
Jackson, Mississippi
  39201-1399
(601) 359-6050
Fax: (601) 359-6048

Missouri

Director
Division of Medical Services
Department of Social Services
Post Office Box 6500
Jefferson City, Missouri 65102
(314) 751-6922
Fax: (314) 751-7753

Montana

Administrator
Medicaid Services Division
Department of Social and
  Rehabilitation Services
Post Office Box 4210
Helena, Montana 59604
(406) 444-4540
Fax: (406) 444-1970

Nebraska
Administrator
Medical Services Division
Department of Social Services
301 Centennial Mall South
5th Floor
Lincoln, Nebraska 68509
(402) 471-9147
Fax: (402) 471-9455

Nevada
Deputy Administrator
Nevada Medicaid
Welfare Division,
  Department of Human
  Resources
2527 North Carson Street
Carson City, Nevada 89710
(702) 687-4378
Fax: (702) 687-5080

New Hampshire
Administrator
Office of Medical Services
Division of Human Services
6 Hazen Drive
Concord, New Hampshire
  03301-6521
(603) 271-4314
Fax: (603) 271-2896

New Jersey
Director
Division of Medical
  Assistance and Health
  Services
Department of Human
  Services
CN-712, 7 Quakerbridge
  Plaza
Trenton, New Jersey 08625
(609) 588-2600
Fax: (609) 588-3583

New Mexico
Director
Medical Assistance Division
Human Services Department
Post Office Box 2348
Santa Fe, New Mexico
  87504-2348
(505) 827-4315
Fax: (505) 827-4002

New York
Deputy Commissioner
Division of Medical Assistance
New York State Department of
  Social Services
40 North Pearl Street
Albany, New York 12243
(518) 474-9132
Fax: (518) 473-4232

North Carolina
Director
Division of Medical Assistance
Department of Human
  Resources
1985 Umstead Drive
Post Office Box 29529
Raleigh, North Carolina
  27626-0529
(919) 733-2060
Fax: (919) 733-6608

North Dakota
Director
Medicaid Operations
North Dakota Department of
  Human Services
State Capitol—Judicial Wing
600 East Boulevard Avenue
Bismarck, North Dakota
  58505-0261
(701) 224-2321
Fax: (701) 224-2359

Ohio

Medicaid Director
Administration
Department of Human
   Services
30 East Broad Street
31st Floor
Columbus, Ohio 43266-0423
(614) 644-0140
Fax: (614) 466-1504

Oklahoma

Division Administrator
Division of Medical Services
Department of Human
   Services
Post Office Box 25352
Oklahoma City, Oklahoma
   73125
(405) 557-2539
Fax: (405) 528-4786

Oregon

Director
Office of Medical Assistance
   Programs
Department of Human
   Resources
203 Public Service Building
Salem, Oregon 97310
(503) 378-2263
Fax: (503) 373-7689

Pennsylvania

Deputy Secretary for Medical
   Assistance Programs
Department of Public Welfare
Room 515
Post Office Box 2675
Health and Welfare Building
Harrisburg, Pennsylvania
   17105-2675
(717) 787-1870
Fax: (717) 787-4639

Rhode Island

Associate Director for Medical
   Services
Department of Human
   Services
600 New London Avenue
Cranston, Rhode Island
   02920
(401) 464-3575
Fax: (401) 464-1876

South Carolina

Deputy Executive Director for
   Programs
South Carolina State Health
   and Human Services Finance
   Commission
Post Office Box 8206
Columbia, South Carolina
   29202-8206
(803) 253-6100
Fax: (803) 253-4137

South Dakota

Program Administrator
Medical Services
Department of Social Services
Kneip Building
700 Governors Drive
Pierre, South Dakota
   57501-2291
(605) 773-3495
Fax: (605) 773-4855

Tennessee

Assistant Commissioner
Bureau of Medicaid
729 Church Street
Nashville, Tennessee
   37247-6501
(615) 741-0213
Fax: (615) 741-0882

Texas
State Medicaid Director
Department of Human
 Services
Post Office Box 149030
Austin, Texas 78714-9030
(512) 450-3050
Fax: (512) 450-4176

Utah
Director
Division of Health Care
 Financing
Utah Department of Health
Post Office Box 16580
Salt Lake City, Utah
 84116-0580
(801) 538-6406
Fax: (801) 538-6478

Vermont
Director, Division of
 Medicaid
Department of Social
 Welfare
Vermont Agency of Human
 Services
103 South Main Street
Waterbury, Vermont
 05671-1102
(802) 241-2880
Fax: (802) 241-2974

Virginia
Director
Virginia Department of
 Medical Assistance
 Services
600 East Broad Street
Suite 1300
Richmond, Virginia 23219
(804) 786-7933
Fax: (804) 371-4981

Washington
Assistant Secretary
Medical Assistance
Post Office Box 45080
Olympia, Washington
 98504-5080
(206) 753-1777
Fax: (206) 586-7498

West Virginia
Director
Office of Medical Services
Bureau of Administration and
 Finance
Department of Health and
 Human Resources
Building 6, State Capitol
 Complex
Room 717B
Charleston, West Virginia
 25305
(304) 926-1700
Fax: (304) 926-1776

Wisconsin
Director
Bureau of Health Care
 Financing
Division of Health
Wisconsin Department of
 Health and Social Services
Post Office Box 309
Madison, Wisconsin
 53701-0309
(608) 266-2522
Fax: (608) 267-2832

Wyoming
Administrator
Division of Health Care
 Financing
6101 Yellowstone Road
Cheyenne, Wyoming 82002
(307) 777-7531
Fax: (307) 777-6964

Children's Special
Health Care Needs (CSHCN) Program

The Children's Special Health Care Needs (CSHCN) Program *is designed to serve children with special health needs from families with low to middle incomes.* There is one CSHCN Program in each state, but the extent of services and eligibility varies widely from state to state. Some or all of a child's health and related care *due to his or her chronic illness or disability* is paid for by this program, depending on the state in which you live. Call this program to see what services are offered in your state and whether your child qualifies for participation in the program (see Chapters 2 and 5 for more information).

Alabama
Coordinator
Children's Rehabilitation
  Services
Post Office Box 11586
Montgomery, Alabama
  36111-0586
(205) 288-0220
Fax: (205) 281-1973

Alaska
Program Manager
Handicapped Children's
  Program
Alaska Department of Health
  and Social Services
1231 Gambell
Anchorage, Alaska 99501-4627
(907) 274-7626
Fax: (907) 586-1877

Arizona
Chief
Office of Children's
  Rehabilitative Services
Arizona Department of Health
1740 West Adams
Phoenix, Arizona 85007
(602) 542-1860
Fax: (602) 542-2789

Arkansas
Administrator
Children's Medical Service
Department of Human Service
Post Office Box 1437
Slot #526
Little Rock, Arkansas 72203
(501) 682-2277
Fax: (501) 682-6571

California
Chief
California Children's Medical
  Services Branch
714 P Street, Room 323
Sacramento, California 95814
(916) 654-0499
Fax: (916) 657-0796

Colorado
Director
Handicapped Children's
  Program
FCHSD-HCP-A4
Colorado Department of
  Health
4300 Cherry Creek Drive,
  South
Denver, Colorado 80220
(303) 692-2370
Fax: (303) 782-5576

Connecticut
Director
Division of Child &
   Adolescent Health
Bureau of Community Health
150 Washington Street
Hartford, Connecticut 06106
(203) 566-2520
Fax: (203) 566-8401

Delaware
Director
Child Health/CSHN
Division of Public Health
Jesse Cooper Building
Post Office Box 637
Dover, Delaware 19903
(302) 739-4735
Fax: (302) 735-6617

District of Columbia
Director
Health Services for Children
   with Special Needs
D.C. General Hospital,
   Building 1 East
19th & Massachusetts Avenue,
   Southeast
Washington, D.C. 20003
(202) 675-5214
Fax: (202) 675-7694

Florida
Director
Children's Medical Services
   Program
Florida Department of Health
   and Rehabilitation Services
Building 5, Room 129
1317 Winewood Boulevard
Tallahassee, Florida
   32399-0700
(904) 487-2690
Fax: (904) 488-3813

Georgia
Acting Chief
Children's Health Services
   Sections
Georgia Department of Human
   Resources
Division of Physical Health
2600 Skyland Drive,
   Northeast, Lower Level
Atlanta, Georgia 30319
(404) 679-0547
Fax: (404) 679-0537

Hawaii
Chief
Children with Special Health
   Needs
741 Sunset Avenue
Honolulu, Hawaii 96816
(808) 733-9070
Fax: (808) 733-9068

Idaho
Coordinator
Children with Special Health
   Needs Program
Bureau of Maternal and Child
   Health
Idaho Department of
   Health/Welfare
450 West State Street
Boise, Idaho 83720
(208) 334-5963
Fax: (208) 334-5964

Illinois
Director
Division of Specialized Care
   for Children
University of Illinois at
   Chicago
2815 West Washington
Suite 300
Post Office Box 19481
Springfield, Illinois 62794-9481
(217) 793-2340
Fax: (217) 793-0773

Indiana
Director
Children's Special Health Care
  Services Division
Indiana Board of Health
1330 West Michigan Street
Post Office Box 1964
Indianapolis, Indiana
  46206-1964
(317) 633-8522
Fax: (317) 232-4331

Iowa
Director
Child Health Specialty Clinic
University of Iowa, Room 247
University Hospital Schools
Iowa City, Iowa 52242
(319) 356-1118
Fax: (319) 356-8284

Kansas
Director
Services for Children with
  Special Health Care Needs
Kansas Department of Health
  and Environment
Landon State Office Building
900 Southwest Jackson
10th Floor
Topeka, Kansas 66612-1290
(913) 296-1313
Fax: (913) 296-4166

Kentucky
Executive Director
Kentucky Commission for
  Handicapped Children
Kentucky Department of
  Human Resources
982 Eastern Parkway
Louisville, Kentucky
  40217-7566
(502) 588-3264
Fax: (502) 588-4673

Louisiana
Administrator
Handicapped Children's
  Services
Office of Public Health
Louisiana Department of
  Health and Hospitals
Post Office Box 60630
New Orleans, Louisiana 70160
(504) 568-5055
Fax: (504) 568-5507

Maine
Director
Coordinated Care Service for
  Children with Special
  Health Needs
Maine Department of Human
  Services
State House Station 11
151 Capital Street
Augusta, Maine 04333
(207) 289-3311
Fax: (207) 289-4172

Maryland
Director
Children's Medical Services
Maryland Department of
  Health
201 West Preston Street
4th Floor
Baltimore, Maryland 21201
(410) 225-5580
Fax: (410) 333-5995

Massachusetts
Director
Division for Children with
  Special Health Care Needs
Massachusetts Department of
  Public Health
150 Tremont Street, 7th Floor
Boston, Massachusetts 02111
(617) 727-6941
Fax: (617) 727-6496

Michigan
Chief
Children's Special Health Care
   Services
Child and Family Services
Michigan Department of
   Public Health
Post Office Box 30195
Lansing, Michigan 48909
(517) 335-8961
Fax: (517) 335-8560

Minnesota
Director
Services for Children with
   Handicaps
Minnesota Department of
   Health
717 Delaware Street, Southeast
Post Office Box 9441
Minneapolis, Minnesota 55440
(612) 623-5150
Fax: (612) 623-5043

Mississippi
Director
Children's Medical Program
Mississippi Department of
   Health
2433 North State Street
Post Office Box 1700
Jackson, Mississippi
   39215-1700
(601) 987-3965
Fax: (601) 987-5560

Missouri
Bureau Chief
Bureau of Special Health Care
   Needs
1730 East Elm Street
Post Office Box 570
Jefferson City, Missouri 65102
(314) 751-6246

Montana
Program Manager
Children's Special Services
   Program
Montana Department of
   Health and Environmental
   Sciences
1400 Broadway, Room C314
Cogswell Building
Helena, Montana 59620
(406) 444-3622

Nebraska
Administrator
Special Services for Children
   and Adults
Nebraska Department of
   Health
301 Centennial Mall, South
5th Floor
Lincoln, Nebraska 68509-5026
(402) 471-9345
Fax: (402) 471-9455

Nevada
Acting Chief
Bureau of Family Health
   Services
Nevada State Health Division
505 East King Street
Room 205
Carson City, Nevada 98710
(702) 687-4885
Fax: (702) 687-3859

New Hampshire
Chief
Bureau of Special Medical
   Services
New Hampshire Division of
   Public Health Services
6 Hazen Drive
Concord, New Hampshire
   03301-6527
(603) 271-4596
Fax: (603) 271-3745

New Jersey
Director
Special Child Health Services
New Jersey Department of
    Health
363 West State Street, CN 364
Trenton, New Jersey
    08625-0364
(609) 984-0755
Fax: (609) 292-3580

New Mexico
Program Manager
Children's Medical Services
New Mexico Department of
    Health and Environment
1190 St. Francis Drive
Post Office Box 968
Santa Fe, New Mexico
    87504-0968
(505) 827-2548
Fax: (505) 827-2329

New York
Director
Bureau of Child/Adolescent
    Health
New York Department of
    Health
Empire State Plaza
Corning Tower Building
Room 780
Albany, New York 12237
(518) 474-2084
Fax: (518) 474-4471

North Carolina
Chief
Child and Youth Section
North Carolina Department of
    Environment, Health, and
    Natural Resources
Post Office Box 27687
Raleigh, North Carolina
    27611-7687
(919) 733-7437
Fax: (919) 733-2997

North Dakota
Administrator
Crippled Children's Services
North Dakota Department of
    Health
State Capitol Building
Judicial Wing
600 East Boulevard Avenue
Bismarck, North Dakota
    58505
(701) 224-2436
Fax: (701) 224-2359

Ohio
Chief
Division of Maternal and
    Child Health
Ohio Department of Health
246 North High Street
7th Floor
Post Office Box 118
Columbus, Ohio 43266-0118
(614) 466-3263
Fax: (614) 644-8526

Oklahoma
Director
Children's Medical Services
    Division
4545 North Lincoln Boulevard,
    4th Floor
Oklahoma City, Oklahoma
    73103
(405) 557-2539
Fax: (405) 528-4786

Oregon
Director
Child Development/
    Rehabilitation Center
Oregon Health Sciences
    University
Post Office Box 574
Portland, Oregon 97207
(503) 494-8362
Fax: (503) 279-4447

Pennsylvania
Director
Division of Rehabilitative
  Services
Pennsylvania Department of
  Health
Health and Welfare Building,
  Room 724
Post Office Box 90
Harrisburg, Pennsylvania 17108
(717) 783-5436
Fax: (717) 772-0323

Rhode Island
Assistant Medical Director
Division of Family Health
Rhode Island Department of
  Health
3 Capital Hill, Room 302
Providence, Rhode Island
  02908-5098
(401) 277-2312
Fax: (401) 277-1442

South Carolina
Director
Division of Children's
  Rehabilitative Services
South Carolina Department of
  Health and Environmental
  Control
Robert Mills Complex
Post Office Box 101106
Columbia, South Carolina
  29211
(803) 737-4050
Fax: (803) 737-4078

South Dakota
Director
Preventive Health Services
South Dakota Department of
  Health
118 West Capitol
Pierre, South Dakota 57501
(605) 773-3737
Fax: (605) 773-3683

Tennessee
Coordinator
Children's Special Services
Tennessee Department of
  Health and Environment
525 Cordell Hull Building
Nashville, Tennessee
  37247-4701
(615) 741-7353
Fax: (615) 741-2491

Texas
Chief
Bureau of Chronically Ill
  and Disabled Children
  Services
Texas Department of
  Health
1100 West 49th Street
Austin, Texas 78756-3179
(512) 458-7355
Fax: (512) 458-7417

Utah
Director
Children with Special Health
  Care Needs
Utah Department of Health
288 North 1460 West
Salt Lake City, Utah
  84116-0650
(801) 538-6165

Vermont
Director
Children with Special Health
  Needs
Vermont Department of
  Health
108 Cherry Street
Post Office Box 70
Burlington, Vermont 05402
(802) 863-7338
Fax: (802) 863-7425

Virginia
Director
Children's Specialty Services
Virginia Department of Health
1500 East Main Street
Room 135
Post Office Box 2448
Richmond, Virginia 23218
(804) 786-3691
Fax: (804) 371-6032

Washington
Program Manager
Children with Special Health
  Needs
Division of Parent Health
  Services
Washington Department of
  Health
Post Office Box 47880
Olympia, Washington
  98504-7880
(206) 753-0908
Fax: (206) 586-3890

West Virginia
Director
Division of Handicapped
  Children
West Virginia Department of
  Health & Human Services
1116 Quarrier Street
Charleston, West Virginia
  25301
(304) 558-3071
Fax: (304) 348-2183

Wisconsin
Supervisor
Program for Children with
  Special Health Care Needs
Wisconsin Division of Health
Post Office Box 309
Madison, Wisconsin 53701-0309
(608) 266-3886
Fax: (608) 267-1052

Wyoming
Manager
Children's Health Services
Division of Health and
  Medical Services
Wyoming Department of
  Health
Hathaway Building
4th Floor
Cheyenne, Wyoming
  82002-0710
(307) 777-7941
Fax: (307) 777-5402

State Offices of Maternal and Child Health (MCH)

The office of Maternal and Child Health (MCH) in each state administers federal and state funds and programs for health care for infants and young children and their mothers. There is an emphasis on preventative care. The Children's Special Health Care Needs (CSHCN) Program falls under the overall administration of

MCH. Call MCH for leads to any information or services relating to your child with a chronic illness or a disability (see Chapter 4 for additional information).

Alabama
Director
Bureau of Family Health
  Services
Alabama Department of Public
  Health
434 Monroe Street
Room 381
Montgomery, Alabama
  36130-170!
(205) 242-5661
1-800-568-9034
Fax: (205) 269-4865

Alaska
Chief
Section of Maternal, Child &
  Family Health
Alaska Department of Health
  and Social Services
1231 Gambell, Room 314
Anchorage, Alaska 99501-4657
(907) 274-7626
Fax: (907) 586-1877

Arizona
Acting Director
Office of Women and
  Children's Health
Division of Family Health
  Services
Arizona Department of Health
1740 West Adams, Room 200
Phoenix, Arizona 85007
(602) 542-1870
1-800-232-1676
Fax: (602) 542-2789

Arkansas
Administrative Director
Section of Maternal and Child
  Health
Arkansas Department of
  Health
4815 West Markham, Slot #41
Little Rock, Arkansas 72205
(501) 661-2199
1-800-482-5850
Fax: (501) 661-2055

California
Chief
Maternal and Child Health
  Branch
California Department of
  Health Services
714 P Street, Room 750
Sacramento, California 95814
(916) 667-1347
Fax: (916) 657-0796

Colorado
Director
Family Health Services
  Division
Colorado Department of
  Health
4210 East 11th Avenue
Denver, Colorado 80220
(303) 692-2315
1-800-688-7777 (baby care)
1-800-255-3477 (disability
  referral services)
Fax: (303) 782-5576

Connecticut
Chief
Bureau of Community Health
150 Washington Street
Hartford, Connecticut 06106
(203) 566-4282
1-800-286-2229
Fax: (203) 566-8401

Delaware
Director
Maternal and Child Health
Division of Public Health
Jesse Cooper Building
Post Office Box 637
Dover, Delaware 19903
(302) 739-4726
1-800-464-4357
Fax: (302) 735-6617

District of Columbia
Chief
Office of Maternal and Child
   Health
Commission of Public Health
1660 L Street, Northwest
Suite 907
Washington, D.C. 20036
(202) 673-4551
Fax: (202) 737-2386

Florida
Chief
Health Program Policy and
   Development
Florida Department of Health
   and Rehabilitation Services
Family Health Services
1317 Winewood Street
Tallahassee, Florida
   32399-0700
(904) 487-1321
Fax: (904) 488-2341

Georgia
Director
Maternal and Child Health
   Branch
Georgia Department of Human
   Resources
Division of Public Health
878 Peachtree Street, Northeast
Suite 217
Atlanta, Georgia 30309
(404) 894-6622
1-800-822-2539
Fax: (404) 894-7799

Hawaii
Chief
Maternal and Child Health
   Branch
741-A Sunset Avenue
Honolulu, Hawaii 98616
(808) 733-9022
1-800-235-5477
Fax: (808) 733-9032

Idaho
Chief
Bureau of Maternal and Child
   Health
Idaho Department of
   Health/Welfare
450 West State Street
Boise, Idaho 83720
(208) 334-5965
1-800-926-2588
Fax: (208) 334-5694

Illinois
Chief
Division of Family Health
Illinois Department of Public
   Health
535 West Jefferson Street
Springfield, Illinois 62761
(217) 782-2736
1-800-322-3722
Fax: (217) 782-3987

Indiana
Director
Division of Maternal and
  Child Health
Indiana Board of Health
1330 West Michigan Street
Post Office Box 1954
Indianapolis, Indiana
  46204-1954
(317) 633-8451
1-800-433-0746
Fax: (317) 633-0776

Iowa
Chief
Bureau of Family Services
Iowa Department of Public
  Health
Lucas State Office Building
Des Moines, Iowa 50319-0075
(515) 281-4911
1-800-779-2001
Fax: (515) 281-4958

Kansas
Director
Bureau of Family Health
Kansas Department of Health
  and Environment
Landon State Office Building
900 Southwest Jackson
10th Floor
Topeka, Kansas 66612-1290
(913) 296-1303
1-800-332-6262
Fax: (913) 296-4166

Kentucky
Director
Division of Maternal and
  Child Health
Kentucky Department of
  Human Resources
275 East Main Street
Frankfort, Kentucky 40621
(502) 564-4830
1-800-232-1160
Fax: (502) 564-8389

Louisiana
Administrator
Maternal and Child Health
  Section
Louisiana Department of
  Health and Hospitals
Post Office Box 60630
New Orleans, Louisiana 70160
(504) 568-5073
1-800-922-3425
Fax: (504) 568-8162

Maine
Director
Division of Maternal and
  Child Health
Maine Department of Human
  Services
State House Station 11
151 Capital Street
Augusta, Maine 04333
(207) 289-3311
1-800-698-3624
Fax: (207) 289-4172

Maryland
Director
Child & Adolescent Health
Maryland Department of
  Health
201 West Preston Street
Baltimore, Maryland 21201
(410) 225-6749
1-800-456-8900
Fax: (410) 333-5995

Massachusetts
Assistant Commissioner
Bureau of Family and
  Community Health
Massachusetts Department of
  Public Health
150 Tremont Street, 4th Floor
Boston, Massachusetts 02111
(617) 727-3372
1-800-882-1435
1-800-462-5015
Fax: (617) 727-6496

Michigan
Chief
Bureau of Child and Family
  Services
Michigan Department of
  Public Health
3423 North Logan/Martin
  Luther King Jr. Boulevard
Post Office Box 30195
Lansing, Michigan 48909
(517) 335-8955
1-800-359-3722
1-800-788-7889 (TT)
Fax: (517) 335-8560

Minnesota
Director
Division of Maternal and
  Child Health
Minnesota Department of
  Health
717 Delaware Street,
  Southeast
Post Office Box 9441
Minneapolis, Minnesota 55440
(612) 623-5166
1-800-728-5420
Fax: (612) 623-5043

Mississippi
Acting Director
Bureau of Health Services
Mississippi Department of
  Health
2433 North State Street
Post Office Box 1700
Jackson, Mississippi
  39215-1700
(601) 960-7463
1-800-844-0898
Fax: (601) 960-7852

Missouri
Director
Division of Maternal, Child
  and Family Health
Missouri Department of
  Health
1738 East Elm Street
Post Office Box 570
Jefferson City, Missouri 65102
(314) 751-6174
1-800-878-6246
Fax: (314) 751-6010

Montana
Bureau Chief
Family/Maternal and Child
  Health Bureau
Montana Department of
  Health and Environmental
  Sciences
1400 Broadway, Room C314
Cogswell Building
Helena, Montana 59620
(406) 444-4753
1-800-762-9891
Fax: (406) 444-2606

Nebraska
Director
Division of Maternal and
  Child Health
Nebraska Department of
  Health
301 Centennial Mall, South
3rd Floor/Post Office
Box 95007
Lincoln, Nebraska 68509-5007
(402) 471-2907
1-800-358-8802
Fax: (402) 471-0383

Nevada
Chief
Bureau of Family Health
  Services
Nevada State Health Division
505 East King Street, Room 205
Carson City, Nevada 98710
(702) 687-4885
1-800-992-0900, ext. 4885
Fax: (702) 687-3859

New Hampshire
Director
Office of Family and
  Community Health
New Hampshire Division of
  Public Health Services
6 Hazen Drive
Concord, New Hampshire
  03301-6527
(603) 271-4726
1-800-852-3345, extension 4488
Fax: (603) 271-3745

New Jersey
Director
Parental and Child Health
  Services
New Jersey Department of
  Health
363 West State Street, CN 364
Trenton, New Jersey 08625-0360
(609) 292-5656
Fax: (609) 292-3580

New Mexico
Chief
Bureau of Maternal and Child
  Health
New Mexico Department of
  Health and Environment
1190 St. Francis Drive
Post Office Box 968
Santa Fe, New Mexico
  87504-0968
(505) 827-2350
1-800-552-8195
Fax: (505) 827-2329

New York
Director
Division of Family Health
Center for Community Health
New York Department of
  Health
Bureau of Child and
  Adolescent Health
Empire State Plaza
Corning Tower Building
Room 780
Albany, New York 12237
(518) 474-7922
1-800-522-5006
Fax: (518) 474-4471

North Carolina
Director
Division of Maternal and
  Child Health
North Carolina Department of
  Environment, Health, and
  Natural Resources
Post Office Box 27687
Raleigh, North Carolina
  27611-7687
(919) 733-3816
1-800-TLC-0042
Fax: (919) 733-2997

North Dakota
Director
Division of Maternal and
  Child Health
North Dakota Department of
  Health
State Capitol Building
600 East Boulevard Avenue
Bismarck, North Dakota 58505
(701) 224-2493
1-800-472-2436
Fax: (701) 224-3000

Ohio
Chief
Division of Maternal and
   Child Health
Ohio Department of Health
246 North High Street
7th Floor
Post Office Box 118
Columbus, Ohio 43266-0118
(614) 466-3263
Fax: (614) 644-8526

Oklahoma
Chief
Maternal and Child Health
   Medical Services
Oklahoma Department of
   Health
1000 Northeast 10th Street,
   Room 703
Post Office Box 53551
Oklahoma City, Oklahoma
   73152
(405) 271-4476
1-800-522-0323

Oregon
Assistant Administrator
Office of Health Services
Oregon State Health Division
800 Northeast Oregon Street,
   #21
Portland, Oregon 97214-0450
(503) 731-4016
1-800-452-3563
Fax: (503) 229-6519

Pennsylvania
Director
Division of Maternal and
   Child Health
Pennsylvania Department of
   Health
Health and Welfare Building,
   Room 725
Post Office Box 90
Harrisburg, Pennsylvania
   17108
(717) 787-7440
1-800-852-4453
Fax: (717) 772-0323

Rhode Island
Medical Director
Division of Family Health
Rhode Island Department of
   Health
3 Capitol Hill, Room 302
Providence, Rhode Island
   02908-5098
(401) 277-2312
1-800-346-1004 (Family Health
   Information Line)
Fax: (401) 277-1442

South Carolina
Director
Bureau of Maternal and Child
   Health
South Carolina Department of
   Health and Environmental
   Control
Robert Mills Complex
Post Office Box 101106
Columbia, South Carolina
   29211
(803) 737-4190
1-800-868-0404
Fax: (803) 734-4442

South Dakota
Director
Preventive Health Services
South Dakota Department of
    Health
118 West Capitol
Pierre, South Dakota 57501
(605) 773-3737
1-800-658-3080
Fax: (605) 773-3683

Utah
Director
Division of Family Health
    Services
Utah Department of Health,
    Cannon Building
288 North 1460 West
Post Office Box 16650
Salt Lake City, Utah
    84116-0650
(801) 538-6161
1-800-826-9662
Fax: (801) 538-6510

Tennessee
Director
Maternal and Child Health
    Programs
Tennessee Department of
    Health and Environment
525 Cordell Hull Building
Nashville, Tennessee
    37247-4701
(615) 741-0323
1-800-428-2229
1-800-852-7517 (Early
    Intervention System)
Fax: (615) 741-2491

Vermont
Director
Maternal and Child Health
Vermont Department of
    Health
108 Cherry Street
Post Office Box 70
Burlington, Vermont 05402
(802) 863-7333
1-800-660-4427
Fax: (802) 863-7425

Virginia
Director
Bureau of Maternal and Child
    Health
Virginia Department of Health
1500 East Main Street
Post Office Box 2448
Richmond, Virginia 23218
(804) 786-7367
1-800-523-4019
Fax: (804) 371-6031

Texas
Chief
Bureau of Maternal and Child
    Health
Texas Department of Health
1100 West 49th Street
Austin, Texas 78756-3179
(512) 458-7700
1-800-252-8823
Fax: (512) 458-7350

Washington

Assistant Secretary
Division of Parent Child
    Health Services
Washington Department of
    Health
Post Office Box 47880
Olympia, Washington
    98504-7880
(206) 753-7021
1-800-841-1410
Fax: (206) 586-3890

Wisconsin

Chief Medical Officer
Division of Maternal and
    Child Health
Bureau of Public Health
Wisconsin Division of Health
Post Office Box 309
Madison, Wisconsin
    53701-0309
(608) 266-5818
1-800-441-4576
Fax: (608) 267-3824

West Virginia

Director
Division of Maternal and
    Child Health
West Virginia Department of
    Health & Human Services
1411 Virginia Street, East
Charleston, West Virginia
    25301-3013
(304) 558-3071
1-800-642-8522
Fax: (304) 348-2183

Wyoming

Administrator
Family Health Services
Division of Health and
    Medical Services
Wyoming Department of
    Health
Hathaway Building, 4th Floor
Cheyenne, Wyoming
    82002-0710
(307) 777-6186
1-800-842-8333
Fax: (307) 777-5402

Civilian Health and Medical
Program of the Uniformed Services (CHAMPUS)

CHAMPUS
Aurora, Colorado 80045-6900

For more information about assistance and services available from
CHAMPUS, see Chapter 6.

Communicating for Agriculture

Communicating for
  Agriculture
2626 East 82nd Street
Suite 325
Bloomington, Minnesota 55425
(612) 854-9005
1-800-445-1525

For information about services offered by Communicating for Agriculture, see Chapter 6.

U.S. Department of Labor

U.S. Department of Labor
Pension and Welfare Benefits
  Administration
Division of Technical
  Assistance and Inquiries
200 Constitution Avenue,
  Northwest
Room N-5658
Washington, D.C. 20210

For information about assistance available from the U.S. Department of Labor, see Chapter 6.

U.S. Public Health Service

U.S. Public Health Service
Office of the Assistant
  Secretary for Health
Grants Policy Branch (COBRA)
5600 Fishers Lane
Room 17A-45
Rockville, Maryland 20857

For information about assistance available from the U.S. Public Health Service, see Chapter 6.

HEALTH AND RELATED SERVICES
FOR CHILDREN AND YOUTH WITH DISABILITIES

State Offices of Maternal and Child Health (MCH)

For information about State Offices of Maternal and Child Health (MCH), see under "Health Insurance," pages 442–450.

Children's Special Health Care Needs (CSHCN) Programs

For information about Children's Special Health Care Needs (CSHCN) Programs, see under "Health Insurance," pages 436–442.

State Departments of Developmental Disabilities

State Departments of Developmental Disabilities administer a number of *institutional and community programs for individual of all ages with developmental disabilities* (e.g., mental retardation). The agency may be a separate department or combined with your state's Department of Mental Health and/or Department of Substance Abuse. Call your state's Department of Developmental Disabilities' *Community Services Division* to find out about service programs for your child, including evaluation (see Chapter 5 for more information).

Alabama
Associate Commissioner
Department of Mental Health
200 Interstate Park Drive
Post Office Box 3710
Montgomery, Alabama 36193
(205) 271-9287

Alaska
Developmental Disabilities
  Program Administrator
Developmental Disabilities
  Section
Division of Mental Health and
  Developmental Disabilities
Department of Health and
  Social Services
Post Office Box 110620
Juneau, Alaska 99811
(907) 465-3370

Arizona
Assistant Director
Division of Developmental
  Disabilities
Department of Economic
  Security
1789 West Jefferson—791A
Phoenix, Arizona 85007
(602) 542-6853

Arkansas
Director
Developmental Disabilities
  Services
Department of Human Services
Post Office Box 1437, Slot #2500
7th and Main Streets, 5th Floor
Little Rock, Arkansas
  72203-1437
(501) 682-8662

California
Director
Department of Developmental
  Services
1600 9th Street
Room 240
Sacramento, California 95814
(916) 654-1897

Colorado
Director
Division for Developmental
  Disabilities
Department of Institutions
3824 West Princeton Circle
Denver, Colorado 80236
(303) 762-4560

Connecticut
Commissioner
Department of Mental
  Retardation
90 Pitkin Street
East Hartford, Connecticut
  06108
(203) 725-3860

Delaware
Director
Division of Mental Retardation
Department of Health and
  Social Services
Jesse Cooper Building
Post Office Box 637
Federal Street
Dover, Delaware 19903
(302) 739-4452

District of Columbia
Director
Developmental Disabilities
  Administration
Commission on Social Services
Department of Human Services
429 O Street, Northwest, #202
Washington, D.C. 20001
(202) 673-7633

Florida
Director
Department of Health and
  Rehabilitative Services
Developmental Services
  Program Office
1311 Winewood Boulevard
Building 5, Room 215
Tallahassee, Florida 32301
(904) 488-4257

Georgia
Assistant Director for MR
  Services
Division of Mental Health,
  Mental Retardation and
  Substance Abuse
Department of Human
  Resources
2 Peachtree Street, 4th Floor,
  Suite 130
Atlanta, Georgia 30303
(404) 657-2110

Hawaii
Director
Developmental Disabilities
  Division
2201 Waimano Home Road
Hale Ola "D"
Honolulu, Hawaii 96782
(808) 453-6404

Idaho
Director
Bureau of Developmental
  Disabilities
Division of Community
  Rehabilitation
Department of Health and
  Welfare
450 West State, 10th Floor
Boise, Idaho 83720
(208) 334-5512

Illinois
Associate Director
Division of Developmental
   Disabilities
Department of Mental Health
   and Developmental
   Disabilities
402 Stratton Office Building
Springfield, Illinois 62706
(217) 782-2442

Indiana
Director
Indiana Family Social Services
Aging and Rehabilitation
   Division
Indiana Government Center
402 West Washington Street
Room W353
Indianapolis, Indiana 46204
(317) 232-7830

Iowa
Administrator
Division of Mental Health,
   Mental Retardation and
   Developmental Services
Iowa Department of Human
   Services
Hoover State Office Building
Des Moines, Iowa 50319-0114
(515) 281-5874

Kansas
Director of Mental
   Retardation/Developmental
   Disabilities Services
Department of Social and
   Rehabilitative Services
State Office Building, 5th Floor
Topeka, Kansas 66612
(913) 296-3561

Kentucky
Director
Division of Mental Retardation
Department for Mental Health
   and Mental Retardation
   Services
275 East Main
Frankfort, Kentucky 40621
(502) 564-7702

Louisiana
Assistant Secretary
Office of Mental Retardation/
   Developmental Disabilities
Department of Human
   Services
Box 3117, Bin 21
Baton Rouge, Louisiana
   70821-3117
(504) 342-0095

Maine
Director
Bureau of Mental Retardation
Maine Department of Mental
   Health and Mental
   Retardation
411 State Office Building
Station 40
Augusta, Maine 04333
(207) 289-4242

Maryland
Director
Developmental Disabilities
   Administration
Department of Health and
   Mental Hygiene
201 West Preston Street
4th Floor, O'Conner Building
Baltimore, Maryland 21201
(410) 225-5600

Massachusetts
Commissioner
Department of Mental
    Retardation
160 North Washington Street
Boston, Massachusetts 02114
(617) 727-5608

Michigan
Director
Office of Federal Liaison and
    Entitlements
Department of Mental Health
6th Floor, Lewis Cass Building
Lansing, Michigan 48913
(517) 373-6440

Minnesota
Director
Division for Persons with
    Developmental Disabilities
Department of Human Services
Human Services Building
444 Lafayette Road
St. Paul, Minnesota 55155-3825
(612) 296-9139

Mississippi
Director
Bureau of Mental Retardation
Department of Mental Health
1100 Robert East Lee Building
239 North Lamar Street
Jackson, Mississippi 39201
(601) 359-1288

Missouri
Director
Division of Mental Retardation
    and Developmental
    Disabilities
Department of Mental Health
1706 East Elm Street
Post Office Box 687
Jefferson City, Missouri 65102
(314) 751-8215

Montana
Director
Division of Developmental
    Disabilities
Department of Social and
    Rehabilitation Services
Post Office Box 4210
111 Sanders, Room 202
Helena, Montana 59604
(406) 444-2995

Nebraska
Director
Developmental Disabilities
    Division
Department of Public
    Institutions
Post Office Box 94728
Lincoln, Nebraska 68509
(402) 471-2851

Nevada
Director
Division of Mental Hygiene
Department of Human
    Services
Kinkead Building, Room 403
505 E. King Street
Carson City, Nevada 89710
(702) 687-5943

New Hampshire
Director
Bureau of Community
    Developmental Services
Division of Mental Health and
    Developmental Services
State Office Park South
105 Pleasant Street
Concord, New Hampshire
    03301
(603) 271-5013

New Jersey
Director
Division of Developmental
   Disabilities
Department of Human
   Services
2-98 East State Street
CN 726
Trenton, New Jersey 08625
(609) 292-7260

New Mexico
Director of Developmental
   Disabilities Division
Department of Health
1190 St. Francis Drive
Santa Fe, New Mexico 87503
(505) 827-2574

New York
Commissioner
New York State Office of
   Mental Retardation and
   Developmental Disabilities
44 Holland Avenue
Albany, New York 12229
(518) 473-1997

North Carolina
Deputy Directory for
   Developmental Disabilities
   Services
Division of Mental Health/
   Developmental Disabilities
   and Substance Abuse
   Services
325 North Salisbury Street
Raleigh, North Carolina 27603
(919) 733-3654

North Dakota
Director
Developmental Disabilities
   Division
North Dakota Department of
   Human Services
600 East Boulevard Avenue
State Capitol-Judicial Wing
Bismarck, North Dakota
   58505-0270
(701) 224-2768

Ohio
Director
Ohio Department of Mental
   Retardation and
   Developmental Disabilities
30 East Broad Street
Room 1280
Columbus, Ohio 43215
(614) 466-5214

Oklahoma
Director of Community Services
Developmental Disabilities
   Services Division
Department of Human Services
Post Office Box 25352
Sequoyah Memorial Office
   Building
Oklahoma City, Oklahoma
   73125
(405) 521-4979

Oregon
Assistant Administrator for
   Developmental Disabilities
Mental Health and
   Developmental Disability
   Services Division
Department of Human
   Resources
2575 Bittern Street, Northwest
Salem, Oregon 97310
(503) 378-2429

Pennsylvania
Director for Mental
  Retardation
Department of Public Welfare
Room 512, Health and Welfare
  Building
Post Office Box 2675
Harrisburg, Pennsylvania
  17105-2675
(717) 787-3700

Rhode Island
Executive Director
Division of Retardation
Department of Mental Health,
  Mental Retardation and
  Hospitals
Aimee J. Forand Building
600 New London Avenue
Cranston, Rhode Island 02920
(401) 464-3234

South Carolina
Commissioner
South Carolina Department of
  Disabilities and Special
  Needs
3440 Harden Street Extension
Post Office Box 4706
Columbia, South Carolina
  29240
(803) 737-6444

South Dakota
Director
Division of Developmental
  Disabilities
Department of Human
  Services
Hillsview Plaza, East
  Highway 34
500 East Capitol
Pierre, South Dakota
  57501-5070
(605) 773-3438

Tennessee
Director
Division of Mental Retardation
Department of Mental Health
  and Mental Retardation
Doctor's Building
706 Church Street
Nashville, Tennessee
  37219-5393
(615) 741-3803

Texas
Deputy Commissioner for
  Mental Retardation Services
Department of Mental Health
  and Mental Retardation
Box 12668, Capitol Station
Austin, Texas 78711-2668
(512) 465-4520

Utah
Director
Division of Services for People
  with Disabilities
Department of Human
  Services
120 North, 200 West, #201
Salt Lake City, Utah 84103
(801) 538-4200

Vermont
Director, Division of Mental
  Retardation Programs
Vermont Department of
  Mental Health and Mental
  Retardation
103 South Main Street
Waterbury, Vermont 05676
(802) 241-2729

Virginia
Director
Office of Mental Retardation
  Services
Department of Mental Health,
  Mental Retardation and
  Substance Abuse
Post Office Box 1797
Richmond, Virginia 23214
(804) 786-1746

Washington
Director
Division of Developmental
  Disabilities
Department of Social and
  Health Services
Post Office Box 45310
Olympia, Washington 98504
(206) 753-3900

West Virginia
Director
Division of Developmental
  Disabilities
OBHS—Capitol Complex,
  Building 6
Room B717
Charleston, West Virginia
  25305
(304) 558-0627

Wisconsin
Bureau Director
Developmental Disabilities
  Office
Department of Health and
  Social Services
Post Office Box 7851
Madison, Wisconsin 53707
(608) 266-9329

Administrator
Division of Community
  Services
Department of Health and
  Social Services
Post Office Box 7851
Madison, Wisconsin 53707
(608) 266-0554

Wyoming
Administrator
Division of Community
  Programs
Department of Health
Herschler Building
1st Floor West
Cheyenne, Wyoming 82002
(307) 777-7115

State Departments of Mental Health, Children and Youth Services

A State Department of Mental Health (which may be combined in your state with the Department of Developmental Disabilities and/or the Department of Substance Abuse) *administers institutional and community programs for individuals of all ages with emotional, behavior, or mental disorders.* Call the *Children and Youth Division* for information about services for your child, including evaluation (see Chapter 5 for additional information).

Alabama
CASSP Coordinator
Bureau of Mental Illness
 Community Programs
Department of Mental Health
 & Mental Retardation
200 Interstate
Post Office Box 3710
Montgomery, Alabama
 36193-5001
(205) 271-9249
Fax: (205) 271-2623

Alaska
Coordinator, Child &
 Adolescent Mental Health
Division of Mental Health &
 Developmental Disabilities
Department of Health & Social
 Services
Pouch H-04
Juneau, Alaska 99811
(907) 465-3370
Fax: (907) 465-2668

Arizona
Director, CASSP Program
Division of Behavioral Health
 Services
Department of Health Services
2122 East Highland
Phoenix, Arizona 85016
(602) 255-1743
Fax: (602) 553-9141

Arkansas
Assistant Director
Children's Services
Division of Mental Health
 Services
4313 West Markam Street
Little Rock, Arkansas
 72205-4096
(501) 686-9166
Fax: (501) 686-9182

California
Chief
Children, Youth & Families
 Branch
Department of Mental Health
1600 9th Street
Sacramento, California 95814
(916) 654-2147
Fax: (916) 654-1732

Colorado
Child & Adolescent Program
 Specialist
Division of Mental Health
Department of Institutions
3520 West Oxford Avenue
Denver, Colorado 80236
(303) 762-4076
Fax: (303) 762-4373

Connecticut
Director of Mental Health
 Services
Department of Children &
 Youth Services
170 Sigourney Street
Hartford, Connecticut 06105
(203) 566-2087
Fax: (203) 566-7947

Delaware
Director, Division of Child
 Mental Health Services
Department of Services for
 Children, Youth & Families
Delaware Youth & Family
 Center
Center & Faulklands Roads
Wilmington, Delaware
 19805-1195
(302) 633-2600
Fax: (302) 633-2614

District of Columbia
Administrator, Children &
   Youth Services
D.C. Commission on Mental
   Health Services
Child, Youth Services
   Administration
2700 Martin Luther King
   Avenue, Southeast
Building L, SEH Campus
Washington, D.C. 20032
(202) 373-7225
Fax: (202) 373-7224

Florida
Chief, Children's Programs
Mental Health Services
   Division
Alcohol, Drug Abuse &
   Mental Health Program
   Office
1317 Winewood Boulevard
Tallahassee, Florida 32301
(904) 487-2415
Fax: (904) 487-2239

Georgia
Director, Child & Adolescent
   Mental Health Services
Division of Mental Health,
   Mental Retardation &
   Substance Abuse
Department of Human
   Resources
2 Peachtree Street
3rd Floor West
Atlanta, Georgia 30309-3999
(404) 894-6559
Fax: (404) 657-2187

Hawaii
Chief
Child & Adolescent Mental
   Health Division
Department of Health
3627 Kilauea Avenue, Room 101
Honolulu, Hawaii 96816
(808) 735-5242
Fax: (808) 733-9357

Idaho
Child Mental Health
   Coordinator
Division of Community
   Rehabilitation
Bureau of Mental Health
Department of Health & Welfare
450 West State Street
Statehouse Mail
Boise, Idaho 83720
(208) 334-5525
Fax: (208) 334-6699

Illinois
Associate Director
Division of Mental Health
Department of Mental Health
   & Developmental
   Disabilities
400 William G. Stratton
   Building
Springfield, Illinois 62765
(217) 782-7555
Fax: (217) 782-9535

Indiana
Chief
Bureau of Children's Services
Division of Mental Health
402 West Washington Street,
   W353
Indianapolis, Indiana
   46204-2739
(317) 232-7934
Fax: (317) 233-3472

Iowa
CASSP Project Director
Division of Mental Health,
  Mental Retardation &
  Developmental Disabilities
Department of Human
  Services
Hoover State Office Building
Des Moines, Iowa 50319-0114
(515) 281-6098
Fax: (515) 281-4597

Louisiana
Director of Child &
  Adolescent Services
Office of Mental Health
Department of Health &
  Hospitals
Post Office Box 4049
Baton Rouge, Louisiana
  70821-4049
(504) 342-2548
Fax: (504) 342-5066

Kansas
Director, Child & Adolescent
  Mental Health Services
Department of Social &
  Rehabilitation Services
Division of Mental Health &
  Retardation Services
506 Number Docking State
  Office Building
Topeka, Kansas 66612
(913) 296-3471
Fax: (913) 296-6142

Maine
Director, Bureau of Children
  with Special Needs
Department of Mental Health
  & Mental Retardation
411 State Office Building,
  Room 424
Augusta, Maine 04333
(207) 287-4250
Fax: (207) 287-4268

Kentucky
Manager
Children & Youth Services
  Branch
Department for Mental Health
  & Mental Retardation
  Services
Health Services Building
275 East Main Street
Frankfort, Kentucky 40621
(502) 564-7610
Fax: (502) 564-3844

Maryland
Assistant Director for Child &
  Adolescent Services Unit
Mental Hygiene
  Administration
Department of Health &
  Mental Hygiene
201 West Preston Street
Baltimore, Maryland 21201
(410) 225-6639
Fax: (410) 333-5402

Massachusetts
Assistant Commissioner for
    Child–Adolescent Services
Department of Mental Health
25 Staniford Street, Central
    Office
Boston, Massachusetts 02114
(617) 727-5600, ext. 543
Fax: (617) 727-5500, ext. 474

Michigan
Director
Office of Children's Services
Department of Mental Health
320 Walnut Boulevard
Lewis Cass Building
Lansing, Michigan 48913
(517) 373-1839
Fax: (517) 373-8074

Minnesota
Children's Mental Health
    Manager
Mental Health Division
Department of Human
    Services
Human Services Building
444 Lafayette Road
St. Paul, Minnesota
    55155-3828
(612) 296-6046
Fax: (612) 296-6244

Mississippi
Director
Division of Children & Youth
    Services
Department of Mental Health
1101 Robert E. Lee Building
239 North Lamar Street
Jackson, Mississippi 39201
(601) 359-1288
Fax: (601) 359-6295

Missouri
Acting Director
Children & Youth Services
Department of Mental Health
Post Office Box 687
1706 East Alm Street
Jefferson City, Missouri 65102
(314) 751-9485
Fax: (314) 751-7815

Montana
CASSP Project Director
Mental Health Division
Department of Correction &
    Human Services
1539 Eleventh Avenue
Helena, Montana 59620
(406) 444-1290
Fax: (406) 444-4920

Nebraska
Director
Office of Community Mental
    Health
Department of Public
    Institutions
Post Office Box 94728, State
    Capitol
Lincoln, Nebraska 68509-4728
(402) 471-2851
Fax: (402) 479-5145

Nevada
Deputy Administrator
Department of Human
    Resources
Division of Child & Family
    Services
6171 West Charleston
    Boulevard
Las Vegas, Nevada 89158
(702) 486-6190
Fax: (702) 486-7626

New Hampshire
Administrator, Children's
  Mental Health Services
Division of Mental Health &
  Developmental Services
State Office Park South
105 Pleasant Street
Concord, New Hampshire
  03301
(603) 271-5095
Fax: (603) 271-5058

New Jersey
Assistant Director
Office of Children's Services
Division of Mental Health &
  Hospitals
50 East State Street
Trenton, New Jersey 08625
(609) 777-0707
Fax: (609) 777-0835

New Mexico
CASSP Director
Division of Mental Health
Department of Health
Post Office Box 26110
1190 St. Francis Drive
Santa Fe, New Mexico 87502
(505) 827-2640
Fax: (505) 827-2695

New York
Associate Commissioner for
  Children & Families
Office of Mental Health
44 Holland Avenue
Albany, New York 12229
(518) 473-6902
Fax: (518) 473-7926

North Carolina
Head, Child & Family Services
  Branch
Division of Mental Health,
  Developmental Disabilities
  & Substance Abuse Services
Department of Human
  Resources
325 North Salisbury Street
Raleigh, North Carolina 27603
(919) 733-0598
Fax: (919) 733-8259

North Dakota
Director, CASSP Program
Division of Mental Health
Department of Human
  Services
600 East Boulevard Avenue
Bismarck, North Dakota
  58505-0271
(701) 224-2766
Fax: (701) 224-2359

Ohio
Chief
Office of Children's Services
Department of Mental Health
30 East Broad Street
Room 1135
Columbus, Ohio 43215
(614) 466-1984
Fax: (614) 466-1571

Oklahoma
Director of Services to
  Children & Youth
Department of Mental Health
Post Office Box 53277
Capitol Station
Oklahoma City, Oklahoma
  73152
(405) 271-8653
Fax: (405) 271-7413

Oregon
Coordinator, Child &
 Adolescent Services
Mental Health &
 Developmental Disability
 Services Division
Department of Human
 Resources
2575 Bittern Street, Northeast
Salem, Oregon 97310-0520
(503) 378-8406
Fax: (503) 373-7327

Pennsylvania
Director, Bureau of Children's
 Services
Office of Mental Health
Department of Public Welfare
Post Office Box 2675
625 Health & Welfare Building
Harrisburg, Pennsylvania
 17105-2675
(717) 772-2764
Fax: (717) 787-5394

Puerto Rico
Assistant Secretariat of Mental
 Health
GPO Box 61
San Juan, Puerto Rico 00936
(809) 765-6833
Fax: (809) 781-6102

Rhode Island
Assistant Director
Division of Children's Mental
 Health Services
Department of Children,
 Youth & Families
610 Mt. Pleasant Avenue
Providence, Rhode Island
 02908
(401) 457-5432
Fax: (401) 457-5363

South Carolina
Director, Division of Children,
 Adolescents & Their
 Families
Department of Mental Health
2414 Bull Street, Box 485
Columbia, South Carolina
 29202
(803) 734-7859
Fax: (803) 734-7848

South Dakota
Program Specialist
Department of Human
 Services
Division of Mental Health
700 Governors Drive
Pierre, South Dakota 57501
(605) 773-5991
Fax: (605) 773-5483

Tennessee
Director, Office of Child &
 Adolescent Services
Department of Mental Health
 & Mental Retardation
706 Church Street, Doctor's
 Building
Nashville, Tennessee 37219
(615) 741-3708
Fax: (615) 741-0770

Texas
Assistant Deputy
 Commissioner for Children's
 Services
Department of Mental Health
 & Mental Retardation
Post Office Box 12668, Capitol
 Station
Austin, Texas 78711
(512) 465-4832
Fax: (512) 465-4723

Utah
Children's Specialist/CASSP
  Coordinator
Division of Mental Health
Department of Social Services
120 North, 200 West, 4th Floor
Post Office Box 45500
Salt Lake City, Utah 84145-0500
(801) 538-4270 or (801) 538-4275
Fax: (801) 538-4016

Vermont
Deputy Commissioner
Director of Children's Mental
  Health Unit
Department of Mental Health
  & Mental Retardation
103 South Main Street
Waterbury, Vermont 05671-1601
(802) 241-2650
Fax: (802) 241-3052

Virginia
Director
Child & Adolescent Mental
  Health
Department of Mental Health,
  Mental Retardation &
  Substance Abuse Services
Post Office Box 1797
Richmond, Virginia 23214
(804) 786-2991
Fax: (804) 371-0091

Virgin Islands
Director, Division of Mental
  Health, Alcoholism & Drug
  Dependency Services
Department of Health
Charles Harwood Memorial
  Hospital
Christiansted, St. Croix
U.S. Virgin Islands 00820
(809) 773-1311, ext. 30130
Fax: (809) 773-7900

Washington
Administrator
Child & Adolescent Services
Mental Health Division
Department of Social & Health
  Services
Mail Stop 5320
Olympia, Washington 98504
(206) 753-4421
Fax: (206) 653-2746

West Virginia
Director, Division of
  Children's Mental Health
  Services
Office of Behavioral Health
  Services
Department of Health &
  Human Resources
1900 Kanawha Boulevard
Building 6, Room 7173
Charleston, West Virginia 25305
(304) 558-0627
Fax: (304) 558-1008

Wisconsin
SED Coordinator
Bureau of Community Mental
  Health
Division of Community Services
Department of Health & Social
  Services
1 West Wilson Street, Room 433
Madison, Wisconsin 53707
(608) 266-6838
Fax: (608) 266-0036

Wyoming
Child & Adolescent Mental
  Health Specialist
Division of Behavioral Health
Department of Health
449 Hathaway Building
Cheyenne, Wyoming 82002
(307) 777-5637
Fax: (307) 777-5402

National Association of Community Health Centers

National Association of
    Community Health Centers
1330 New Hampshire Avenue,
    Northwest
Suite 122
Washington, D.C., 20036
(202) 659-8008

For information about services available from the National Association of Community Health Centers, see Chapter 3.

Community Mental Health Centers

For information about services available from Community Mental Health Centers, see Chapter 3.

Rural or Migrant Health Centers

For information about services available from Rural or Migrant Health Centers, see Chapter 3.

State Vocational Rehabilitation (VR) Programs

For information about State Vocational Rehabilitation Programs, see under "Education and Training of Children with Special Health Care Needs," pages 393–400.

Regional Centers for Independent Living

Centers for Independent Living *teach skills to young adults and adults with disabilities so that they may function more independently and fully in society.* Such Centers are usually *not* residential programs. Regional representatives for the regional Centers can refer you to the local Center in your state most suited to the needs of your youth. When you contact the local Center, ask what specific services are available and how your youth can become involved with one or more of their programs (see Chapter 5 for additional information).

Member-at-Large
Programs in Accessible Living
1012 South Kings Drive, G-2
Charlotte, North Carolina
  28283
(704) 375-3977 (Voice and TT)
Fax: (704) 375-5907 (FAX)

Member-at-Large
KARF
700 Southwest Jackson
Suite 212
Topeka, Kansas 66603
(913) 235-5103 (Voice)
Fax: (913) 345-0020

Member-at-Large
Independence Center of
  Northern Virginia, Inc.
2111 Wilson Boulevard
Suite 400 (Administration)
Suite 634 (Community Service)
Arlington, Virginia 22201
(703) 525-3268 (Voice and TT;
  administration)
(703) 525-3462 (Voice;
  community service)
Fax: (703) 525-6835
  (administration)
Fax: (703) 525-3585
  (community service)

Member-at-Large
Resources for Living
  Independently
One Winding Way
Suite 108
Philadelphia, Pennsylvania
  19131
(215) 581-0666 (Voice)
(215) 581-0664 (TT)
Fax: (215) 581-0665

Member-at-Large
Northeast Illinois Program,
  Inc.
130 Parker Street
Suite 20
Lawrence, Massachusetts
  01843
(508) 687-4288 (Voice and TT)
Fax: (508) 689-4488

Representative, Region 1
Boston CIL
95 Berkeley Street
Suite 206
Boston, Massachusetts 02116
(617) 338-6665 (Voice)
(617) 338-6662 (TT)
Fax: (617) 338-6661

Representative, Region 2
Capital District CIL
845 Central Avenue
Albany, New York 12206
(518) 459-6422 (Voice and TT)
Fax: (518) 459-7847

Representative, Region 4
Center for Accessible Living
981 South Third Street
Suite 102
Louisville, Kentucky 40203
(502) 589-6620 (Voice)
(502) 589-3980 (TT)

Representative, Region 5
SEWCIL
6222 West Capital Drive
Milwaukee, Wisconsin 53216
(414) 438-5622 (Voice)
(414) 438-5627 (TT)
Fax: (414) 438-5626

Representative, Region 6
Progressive Independence
121 North Porter
Norman, Oklahoma 73071
(405) 321-3203 (Voice and TT)
Fax: (405) 321-7601

Representative, Region 7
Topeka ILRC, Inc.
3258 South Topeka Boulevard
Topeka, Kansas 66611
(913) 267-7100 (Voice)
Fax: (913) 267-0201

Representative, Region 8
Center for People with
    Disabilities
948 North Street
Suite 7
Boulder, Colorado 80304
(303) 442-8662 (Voice)
Fax: (303) 442-0502

Representative, Region 9
ILRC, San Francisco
70 Tenth Street
San Francisco, California
    94103
(415) 863-0581 (Voice)
(415) 863-1367 (TT)
Fax: (415) 863-1290

Representative, Region 10
Access Alaska
3710 Woodland Drive
Suite 900
Anchorage, Alaska 99517
(907) 248-4777 (Voice and TT)
Fax: (907) 248-0639

NICL, Executive Director
2111 Wilson Boulevard
Suite 405
Arlington, Virginia 22201
(703) 525-3406 (Voice)
Fax: (703) 525-3408

Administrative Assistant
NICL
2111 Wilson Boulevard
Suite 405
Arlington, Virginia 22201
(703) 525-3406 (Voice)
Fax: (703) 525-3408

President's Assistant
Troy Resource CIL
Troy Atrium
Fourth Street & Broadway
Troy, New York 12180
(518) 274-1979 (Voice)
(518) 274-0216 (TT)
Fax: (518) 274-7944

**American Association
of University Affiliated Programs (UAPs)
for Persons with Developmental Disabilities**

8630 Fenton Street, Suite 410
Silver Spring, Maryland 20910
(301) 588-8252 (Voice)
(301) 588-3319 (TT)

For information about how University Affiliated Programs (UAPs)
can be helpful, see Chapter 3.

INFORMATION ABOUT SERVICES
FOR CHILDREN AND YOUTH WITH
SPECIAL HEALTH CARE NEEDS AND THEIR FAMILIES

Advocacy and Family Support Organizations

For information about advocacy and family support, see Chapter 3 and see under "Advocacy and Family Support for Children with Special Health Care Needs," page 368.

National Information Center
  for Children and Youth with
  Disabilities (NICHCY)
Post Office Box 1492
Washington, D.C., 20001
1-800-695-0285 (Voice and TT)
(See Chapter 3)

National Information
  Clearinghouse for Infants
  with Disabilities and Life-
  Threatening Conditions
Center for Developmental
  Disabilities
University of South Carolina
Benson Building, 1st Floor
Columbia, South Carolina
  29208
1-800-922-9234 (Voice and TT)
(803) 777-4435
(See Chapter 3)

Developmental Disabilities Planning Councils

For information about Developmental Disabilities Planning Councils, see under "Advocacy and Family Support for Children with Special Health Care Needs," page 378.

National Center for Youth
  with Disabilities
University of Minnesota
Box 721
420 Delaware Street, Southeast
Minneapolis, Minnesota
  55455-0392
1-800-333-6293 (Voice)
(612) 624-3939
(See Chapter 3)

National Disease- and Disability-Related Organizations

For information about national disease- and disability-related organizations, see Chapter 6 and Appendix 6A, and see under "Advocacy and Family Support for Children with Special Health Care Needs," pages 368–371.

National Center for Education and Maternal and Child Health
2000 15th Street North
Arlington, Virginia 22201-2617
(703) 524-7802
(See Chapter 3)

National Early Childhood Technical Assistance System (NEC*TAS)
CB #8040
500 Nations Bank Plaza
Chapel Hill, North Carolina 27599
(919) 962-2001
(See Chapter 3)

Child Find Services

For information about Child Find Services, see Chapters 2 and 5.

United Way and Other Community Information and Referral Services

For information about services provided by United Way and other community information and referral services, see Chapter 3.

24-Hour Crisis Services

For information about 24-hour crisis services, see Chapter 6.

LEGAL ASSISTANCE

Protection and Advocacy (P&A) Agencies in Each State

For information about services provided by Protection and Advocacy (P&A) agencies, see under "Advocacy and Family Support for Children with Special Health Care Needs," pages 371–378.

Judge David L. Bazelon Center for Mental Health Law

For information about services offered by the Judge David L. Bazelon Center for Mental Health Law, see under "Advocacy and Family Support for Children with Special Health Care Needs," page 371.

Legal Services Corporation
750 First Street, Northeast
11th Floor
Washington, D.C. 20002-4250
(202) 336-8880
(See Chapter 2)

Women's Legal Defense Fund
1875 Connecticut Avenue,
  Northwest
Suite 710
Washington, D.C. 20009
(202) 986-2600
(See Chapter 2)

MISCELLANEOUS USEFUL TELEPHONE NUMBERS

AbleNet
1-800-322-0956 (Voice)
Contact AbleNet for information about materials this company develops and markets to help persons with disabilities to use battery and electronically operated toys, appliances, and communication devices.

Apple Computers, Office for Special Education Material
1-800-732-3131 (Voice)
Contact Apple Computers, Office for Special Education Material, for referral to information from "Worldwide Computer Solutions" about computer use for individuals with disabilities.

Architectural and Transportation Barriers Compliance Board (ATBCB)
1-800-872-2253 (Voice); 1-800-728-5483 (TT)
Contact the Architectural and Transportation Barriers Compliance Board (ATBCB) with questions about the access of individuals with disabilities on public and private transportation systems.

AT&T Accessible Communications Products Center
1-800-233-1222 (Voice and TT)
Contact AT&T Accessible Communications Products Center for information about assistive listening devices.

Centers for Disease Control, National AIDS Hotline
1-800-342-2437 (Voice—English);
1-800-344-7432 (Voice—Spanish); 1-800-243-7889 (TT)
Contact Centers for Disease Control, National AIDS Hotline for information about human immunodeficiency virus (HIV) and acquired immunodeficiency syndrome (AIDS) referral for services, and/or support in your local community.

Center for Rehabilitation
1-800-726-9119
Contact the Center for Rehabilitation for information about products and services for individuals with disabilities, particular expertise in technical assistance, and accessibility (e.g., transfer bars, ramps).

Child Support Enforcement
(202) 624-8180
Contact Child Support Enforcement for referral to a local agency to help you to collect child support.

Children's Hospice International
1-800-242-4453
Contact Children's Hospice International for education and support in caring for a child with a terminal illness, referral to the nearest hospice, and help in setting up a hospice for children.

Capitol Hill Switchboard
(202) 244-2131
To contact any U.S. Congressperson or Senator, ask the Capitol Hill switchboard operator to connect you to his or her office.

Family Pharmaceuticals of America
1-800-922-3444
Contact Family Pharmaceuticals of America about its mail-order service for maintenance medication and claims to sell below retail prices in community pharmacies.

Federal Information Center (FIC)
Contact a Federal Information Center (FIC) for information about any federal government program, service, or regulation. A toll-free telephone number for each state that has an FIC is listed below:

Alabama
Birmingham, Mobile
1-800-366-2998

Arizona
Phoenix
1-800-359-3997

Alaska
Anchorage
1-800-729-8003

Arkansas
Little Rock
1-800-366-2998

California
Los Angeles, San Diego, San
  Francisco, Santa Ana
1-800-726-4995
Sacramento
(916) 973-1695

Colorado
Colorado Springs, Denver,
  Pueblo
1-800-359-3997

Connecticut
Hartford, New Haven
1-800-347-1997

Florida
Ft. Lauderdale, Jacksonville,
  Miami, Orlando, St.
  Petersburg, Tampa, West
  Palm Beach
1-800-347-1997

Georgia
Atlanta
1-800-347-1997

Hawaii
Honolulu
1-800-733-5996

Illinois
Chicago
1-800-366-2998

Indiana
Gary
1-800-366-2998
Indianapolis
1-800-347-1997

Iowa
All locations
1-800-735-8004

Kansas
All locations
1-800-735-8004

Kentucky
Louisville
1-800-347-1997

Louisiana
New Orleans
1-800-366-2998

Maryland
Baltimore
1-800-347-1997

Massachusetts
Boston
1-800-347-1997

Michigan
Detroit, Grand Rapids
1-800-347-1997

Minnesota
Minneapolis
1-800-366-2998

Missouri
St. Louis
1-800-366-2998
All other locations
1-800-735-8004

Nebraska
Omaha
1-800-366-2998
All other locations
1-800-735-8004

New Jersey
Newark, Trenton
1-800-347-1997

New Mexico
Albuquerque
1-800-359-3997

New York
Albany, Buffalo, New York,
Rochester, Syracuse
1-800-347-1997

North Carolina
Charlotte
1-800-347-1997

Ohio
Akron, Cincinnati, Cleveland,
  Columbus, Dayton, Toledo
1-800-347-1997

Oklahoma
Oklahoma City, Tulsa
1-800-366-2998

Oregon
Portland
1-800-726-4995

Pennsylvania
Philadelphia, Pittsburgh
1-800-347-1997

Rhode Island
Providence
1-800-347-1997

Tennessee
Chattanooga
1-800-347-1997
Memphis, Nashville
1-800-366-2998

Texas
Austin, Dallas, Fort Worth,
  Houston, San Antonio
1-800-366-2998

Utah
Salt Lake City
1-800-359-3997

Virginia
Norfolk, Richmond, Roanoke
1-800-347-1997

Washington
Seattle, Tacoma
1-800-726-4995

Wisconsin
Milwaukee
1-800-366-2998

Note: TT users in any state may call 1-800-326-2996. If your area is not listed here, you may call (301) 722-9098.

Hearing Aid Helpline
1-800-521-5347 (Voice); (313) 478-2610 (Voice in Michigan)
Contact the Hearing Aid Helpline for consumer information about hearing loss and assistive hearing devices. The Helpline can provide names of professionals in your area who can test your hearing and fit you for a hearing aid. It is sponsored by the International Hearing Society

Hearing Ear Dogs

1-800-869-6898 (Voice and TT)
Contact Hearing Ear Dogs for information about dogs trained to be the "ears" for people. Dogs are free of charge to those in need.

Job Accommodation Network

1-800-526-7234 (Voice and TT); 1-800-ADA-WORK
Contact the Job Accommodation Network for information and referral for persons with disabilities regarding equipment and job site modification that will enable them to work and to obtain information about PL 101-336, the Americans with Disabilities Act of 1990.

Long-Distance Operators for Calls Involving TextType (TT)

To reach a long-distance operator to make a TextType (TT) call, dial 00. Your company's operator can connect you with the necessary relay service to place the call.

National Child Abuse Hotline

1-800-422-4453
Contact the National Child Abuse Hotline to report a case of abuse or neglect, to talk with a crisis counselor, or to get a referral for help in your community for yourself or someone else.

National Library Service for the Blind and Physically Handicapped

1-800-424-8567 (Voice); 1-800-424-9100 TT—English);
1-800-345-8901 (TT—Spanish)
Contact the National Library Service for the Blind and Physically Handicapped for information about library materials available to these groups (e.g., books on tape, photocopy information through the mail).

National Literacy Hotline

1-800-228-8813 (Voice); 1-800-552-9097 (TT)
Contact the National Literacy Hotline for referral to local programs that can teach any adult in your family to read. Programs are generally free of charge.

National Rehabilitation Information Center (NARIC)

1-800-346-2742 (Voice and TT) (Spanish speaker on staff)
Contact the National Rehabilitation Information Center (NARIC) for information about disabilities and service programs, rehabilitation products, and technical devices. NARIC can do a computer search for you.

National Self-Help Clearinghouse
(212) 642-2944
Contact the National Self-Help Clearinghouse for referral to self-help and mutual support groups across the United States.

Parents Anonymous
1-800-421-0353
Contact Parents Anonymous for referral to self-help and support groups for parents who feel overwhelmed and want to learn new ways to cope.

Pediatric AIDS Clearinghouse
(310) 395-9051 (Voice)
Contact the Pediatric AIDS Clearinghouse for information about hospitals providing services to children with human immunodeficiency virus (HIV) and acquired immunodeficiency syndrome (AIDS), education of parents with child who has HIV or AIDS, and encouraging research about pediatric AIDS.

Practitioners Reporting Network
1-800-638-6725 (Voice)
Contact the Practitioner's Reporting Network to report a problem in the functioning of medical equipment or a problem with medication.

President Bill Clinton, the White House Switchboard
(202) 456-1111

Sex Information and Education Council of the United States (SIECUS)
(212) 819-9770
130 West 42nd Street
Suite 2500
New York, New York 10036-7901
Contact the Sex Information and Education Council of the United States (SIECUS) for bibliographies of books and journal articles about sexual development. It has published *Sexuality and the Developmentally Disabled* (1992).

Sibling Information Network
(203) 648-1205
Contact the Sibling Information Network for brothers and sisters of persons with disabilities and information about how to start a sibling group.

Social Security Hotline
1-800-772-1213 (Voice); 1-800-325-0778 (TT)

Supplemental Security Income (SSI)
1-800-772-1213 (Voice); 1-800-325-0778 (TT); 1-800-392-0812 (TT in Missouri)

Texas Respite Resource Network
(210) 228-2794
Contact the Texas Respite Resource Network, Santa Rosa Children's Hospital, for referral to public and private respite programs across the United States.

United Way of America
(703) 836-7100
Contact United Way of America for referral to one of more than 450 United Way Information and Referral (I&R) services in local communities. There is at least one United Way I&R service in each state.

Glossary

ACCH   *See* Association for the Care of Children's Health.

"Adjusted gross income" (AGI)   An individual's or family's total income after a few "adjustments" are made (e.g., deduction for health insurance premium for self-employed individual and his or her family, 50% of required self-employment taxes). AGI is the basis on which a number of other deductions are determined (e.g., medical deductions, which must exceed 7.5% of AGI to be taken).

Admitting privileges   The right granted to a doctor to admit patients to a particular hospital.

Advocacy   Any activity done to help a person or group to get something the person or group needs or wants.

Advocate   A person who helps another person or group get something the person or group wants. An individual can be his or her own advocate.

AFDC   *See* Aid to Families with Dependent Children.

AFDC "need standard"   A standard each state uses in determining both a dependent child's eligibility for Aid to Families with Dependent Children and his or her level of benefit.

AGI   *See* "Adjusted gross income."

Agricultural Extension Service   An agency of the U.S. government that can help families with budgeting and money management. It has offices in each state and can be reached through your county government (see Chapter 9). Also known as *Cooperative Extension Service.*

Aid to Families with Dependent Children (AFDC)   A federal and state cash assistance program designed primarily for young and dependent children of single-parent or selected two-parent, low-income families; eligibility and available benefits vary by state. Applications are made at county Departments of Human Resources or Departments of Social Services (see Chapter 7).

Appealing a rejected health insurance claim   The process of requesting that a health insurance company reconsider making payment on a claim it refused (see Chapter 6).

Association for the Care of Children's Health (ACCH)   A national association of health professionals and parents who advocate for children with chronic illnesses who are in hospitals or community programs. This organization is a good source of information about chronic illnesses affecting children, in-hospital education, child development, and other programs of benefit to hospitalized children.

"At risk of developmental delay"   A phrase that describes children who have a high risk of delay in some area of their development because of conditions experienced *in utero,* at birth, or in infancy (e.g., exposure to alcohol or drugs in the uterus, low birthweight, lack of adequate nutrition or health care).

"Auxiliary aids and services"   A phrase found in PL 101-336, the Americans with Disabilities Act of 1990. It refers to the need for retail stores, schools, restaurants, public transportation, and so forth to provide reasonable assistance to individuals with disabilities so that they may have access to services in these places. Examples are lifts on buses, doors that open with electronic eyes, and wheelchair access to restrooms.

"Basic coverage plans"   Health insurance plans that generally provide limited coverage according to a scheduled rate of reimbursement that is often below the actual fee charged for care. Each hospital admission may be subject to a deductible (which can be waived), and you may be charged a small "co-payment" for each day of hospital care. Preventative care (e.g., routine physical examinations) are not covered at all (see Chapter 6).

(Judge David L.) Bazelon Center for Mental Health Law   A national legal advocacy organization that generally acts on behalf of groups of individuals, including children, who have emotional, behavior, or mental disorders. Their interest is in protecting the civil rights of these individuals and in helping to ensure their access to both public and private services and benefit programs, including public education and cash assistance (see Chapters 2 and 3).

Behavior management   One technique used to help an individual change his or her behavior in some desired way. To bring about such changes, daily routines are often varied, and rewards for desired behaviors may be given.

Bill collectors   Individuals who write or call debtors in an attempt to obtain payment for a particular unpaid bill. Businesses to whom you owe money (e.g., a hospital) hire collection agencies who employ bill collectors for this purpose. Collection agencies are paid part of the money they collect from you as their collection fee. Bill collectors and collection agencies are regulated by the Federal Trade Commission, which enforces all federal laws regulating debt collection practices. To limit their ability to embarrass or threaten you into paying debts you owe, state governments regulate the practices of bill collectors as well (see Chapter 9).

Blue Cross and Blue Shield "Caring" Programs   Private, non-profit programs arranged to help pay for children's medical care. A priority is helping children with chronic illnesses or disabilities whose families work but still cannot afford much of the care their children require. There are 25 "Caring" Programs in the United States at this time (see Chapter 6).

CAAs   *See* Community Action Agencies.

Care coordination   *See* Service coordination.

Case management   *See* Service coordination.

"Categorically needy"   An "optional eligibility" group under the Medicaid program in which each state can decide whether to cover individuals and if so, to what extent. Children in the "categorically needy" group include: 1) infants up to age 1 and pregnant women not covered under "required eligibility" groups, if their family's income is less than 185% of the federal poverty level (each state sets the income percentage below the federal poverty level at which individuals are eligible); 2) children younger than 21 years of age who meet income and resources limits for participation in Aid to Families with Dependent Children (AFDC) but are not otherwise eligible; 3) children receiving care under Medicaid's home- and community-based waiver programs; 4) children receiving state Supplemental Security Income Payments; and 5) children qualified under Medicaid's "medically needy" program (see Chapter 5).

CCC   *See* Consumer Credit Counseling Service.

CCEOs   *See* Community Action Agencies.

CDF   *See* Children's Defense Fund.

CHAMPUS   *See* Civilian Health and Medical Program of the Uniformed Services.

CHAMPUS "cost share"   The amount an individual eligible for CHAMPUS's General Program or Program for the Handicapped must pay as their share of the cost of benefits. The exact amount is based on the pay grade of the individual's active duty sponsor and can take the form of a co-payment, deductible, or monthly fee.

CHAMPUS General Program A CHAMPUS program that shares the cost of health care from civilian doctors and hospitals with families in the military services of the U.S. Active-duty military persons are *not* covered by this program. CHAMPUS's General Program operates independently of CHAMPUS's Program for the Handicapped (see Chapter 5).

CHAMPUS Handbook A book that contains the policies of the CHAMPUS Program including both the CHAMPUS General Program and the CHAMPUS Program for the Handicapped. It provides details about forms to use for different kinds of claims and how to complete each claim. It is available at each base or post hospital or other medical facility, or by writing to CHAMPUS, Aurora, Colorado 80045-6900.

CHAMPUS HBA *See* CHAMPUS Health Benefits Advisor.

CHAMPUS Health Benefits Advisor (HBA) An employee of CHAMPUS, whose responsibility it is to help individuals and families understand and use the CHAMPUS General Program and the CHAMPUS Program for the Handicapped. He or she provides assistance in clarifying procedures and explaining forms that must be completed for reimbursements. The HBA is often the person who negotiates with the CHAMPUS authorities to select coverage for a child. The base or post medical facility can provide the name and telephone number of its HBA.

CHAMPUS "Non-availability of Service Statement" A statement that must be obtained from your nearest military hospital to have CHAMPUS cover care in any non-military hospital (see Chapter 5).

CHAMPUS PFH *See* CHAMPUS Program for the Handicapped.

CHAMPUS Program for the Handicapped (PFH) A program that supplements CHAMPUS's General Program for eligible individuals. It provides health-related care for individuals with "moderate" or "severe" mental retardation, with a major physical disability, or with a combination of both (see Chapter 5).

Charitable contributions Cash or goods donated to a non-profit organization as charity. You must "itemize" your income taxes (i.e., file the "long form") to take advantage of this particular income tax deduction, and you must save your receipts for both the donations of cash and goods (see Chapter 8).

CHC program *See* Community Health Center program.

Child and Dependent Care expenses A federal income tax credit is available to any individual who is working or looking for work and pays someone 19 years or older to provide care for: 1) their child younger than 13 years of age, or 2) their dependent or spouse who is unable to care for him- or herself. A couple may file for this credit only if both of them are working or looking for work. "Looking for work" is defined by the IRS by a successful job search resulting in some earnings for the tax year in which the credit is to be claimed. A number of states offer some income tax credit for child and dependent care expenses (see Chapter 8).

"Child Find" Program One of the mandated services under PL 94-142, the Education for All Handicapped Children Act of 1975. This provision mandates that all states set up a system to identify as early as possible children with disabilities and to refer them to appropriate services. States must maintain a directory of services and have a widely publicized way for individuals to reach "Child Find" services. Many states have set up statewide toll-free telephone numbers for the referral of children and to find out how to get an evaluation for a child (see Chapter 2).

Children's Defense Fund (CDF)   A nonprofit advocacy organization for the health and welfare of children and families whose income is at or near the poverty level. One of CDF's priorities is helping to ensure that all children receive needed immunizations and other needed health care. CDF is based in Washington, D.C. (see Chapter 3).

Children's Special Health Care Needs (CSHCN) Programs   Programs for children with chronic illnesses and/or disabilities that used to be called Crippled Children's Services. The programs are operated by states under the federally funded Maternal and Child health programs. Eligibility for services and the extent of services offered vary greatly from state to state (see Chapter 5).

Chronic illness   A condition that is persistent or intermittent and causes disruption in an individual's life or functioning (e.g., hospital or home confinement, lost days from school or work, limitations in physical activity, dietary restrictions).

Church-sponsored "ministries"   Places individuals can go to meet emergency needs for shelter, food, clothing, medication, and so forth. Staff and volunteers working for "ministries" will either meet needs directly or arrange for another organization to do so. They can also make references to sources for ongoing assistance (see Chapter 6).

Civic organizations   Groups of volunteers organized to provide services to their communities (see Chapter 6).

Civilian Health and Medical Program of the Uniformed Services (CHAMPUS)   A program to help pay for health care from civilian doctors and hospitals for families in the U.S. military service. Families of all seven Uniformed Services are eligible for CHAMPUS as long as they are dependents of active-duty or retired military personnel, or widows or divorcees of military personnel. *CHAMPUS does not cover active-duty military personnel.*

CMHCs   *See* Community Mental Health Centers.

Collection agencies   Organizations who make money collecting outstanding debts owed to others. Their practices are regulated by both the federal and state governments. Their employees are called bill collectors (see Chapter 9).

Community Action Agencies (CAAs)   (Also known as County Commissions for Economic Opportunity [CCEOs].) Organizations that conduct and administer a number of government programs including Head Start, the U.S. Department of Agriculture (USDA) surplus food program, and job training and development. They also provide other services, including emergency financial assistance for food, housing, utility bills, and prescription medications (see Chapter 5).

Community Health Center (CHC) program   A program funded primarily by the federal government to bring a variety of outpatient health care services to rural and urban communities. Fees are based on the individual's or family's ability to pay (see Chapter 5).

Community Mental Health Centers (CMHCs)   Organizations that offer a variety of services for individuals with emotional, behavior, or mental disorders. Services offered are usually both outpatient and inpatient, and fees are based on the individual's or family's ability to pay (see Chapter 5).

Community Supported Living Arrangements (CSLA) Option to Medicaid, 1990   Amendments to the federal Medicaid law that allow individuals with chronic illnesses or disabilities who do not live in institutions to receive Medicaid coverage. This is a demonstration program that, as of 1993, is operating in eight states: California,

Colorado, Florida, Illinois, Maryland, Michigan, Rhode Island, and Wisconsin. Each of these states can decide, however, how many individuals it will fund under this demonstration program.

Complaint procedure   The particular procedure specified in a law or program for challenging a decision or complaining that a provision of a law was not followed.

Consumer Credit Counseling Service (CCC)   A nonprofit organization set up to help individuals and families to manage debt and credit problems (see Chapter 10).

Consumer Credit Protection Act Amendments, 1977   A federal law that, along with the Fair Debt Collection Practices Act Amendments of 1986, regulates the practices of bill collectors, limiting their ability to annoy you. The role of the Federal Trade Commission in overseeing them and your rights to sue a bill collector who has violated these laws are also described in this law (see Chapter 9).

"Conversion privilege"   The right of all individuals covered by a health insurance policy to change from a group policy to their own individual policy when: 1) children exceed the age or conditions under which they may be carried as dependents under their parent's or parents' health insurance policy; or 2) the individual sponsoring their insurance coverage him- or herself or their parent[s] is no longer employed by the group offering the insurance or is no longer a member of an association offering these benefits. *In the first case of dependent children, dependents of any age that are not capable of supporting themselves due to illness or disability can remain on their parent or parents' policy indefinitely* (see Chapter 6). In the second case, the federal government requires that all employers allow employees to "continue" their existing health insurance coverage for as long as 18 months after employment is terminated (with the former employee picking up the full cost of the insurance). Dependents of former employees can "continue" such coverage for as long as 36 months. At the end of those periods, the individuals would have the option to "convert" their existing group policy to an individual or family policy at private market rates.

Cooperative Extension Service   *See* Agricultural Extension Service.

"Co-payments"   The cost an insured individual pays (beyond the premium) as part of his or her share for health insurance coverage. A typical "co-payment" in a major medical plan is 20% of "usual and customary rates" (UCR).

"Covered services"   All services for which a health insurance company has stated (in a written agreement or contract) that it will pay its share of the cost.

County Commissions for Economic Opportunity (CCEOs)   *See* Community Action Agencies.

County Department of Human Resources   A county government agency in charge of administering many human service programs, including Aid to Families with Dependent Children, Food Stamps, and in some cases Medicaid. They also maintain offices of emergency assistance, which can help families obtain shelter, food, payment for utilities, rent deposits, rent, and prescription medications on an emergency or intermittent basis (see Chapter 5).

County Department of Social Services   *See* County Department of Human Resources.

Credits   Items for which a family's income tax bill is reduced dollar for dollar, up to the limits of the allowance (e.g., Credit for Child and Dependent Care expenses). For example, if you have allowable Child and Dependent Care expenses of $1,000 and you were allowed to take 20% of your expenses (based on the chart of income levels for this credit in particular), you would recover $200 of your expenses (see Chapter 8).

Crippled Children's Services   *See* Children's Special Health Care Needs Programs.

Crisis service   Most communities maintain some kind of crisis service, often a telephone crisis number. Some are operated 24 hours per day. These services can be helpful in locating services and emergency funds for a number of items, including prescription medications and medical supplies (see Chapter 6).

CSHCN Programs   *See* Children's Special Health Care Needs Programs.

CSLA Option to Medicaid, 1990   *See* Community Supported Living Arrangements Option to Medicaid, 1990.

DECs   *See* Developmental Evaluation Centers.

"Deductibles"   The cost an insured individual must pay *before* the health insurance policy will reimburse an insured individual or a provider for covered services. An example would be a $100 deductible per year on a "major medical" plan.

Deductions   A reduction of an income tax bill by a percentage of the cost of the item you are claiming. This percentage would be the rate or tax bracket at which you pay taxes (e.g., 21%). Your tax bracket is based on the amount of your total income; individuals with higher incomes pay in a higher bracket. An example is that if you had an eligible "medical deduction" of $500 and you were in the 21% tax bracket, you would recover 21% of your $500 deduction, or $105 (see Chapter 8).

"Dependent Care" coverage   Health insurance coverage available to children who are in school and no older than 23–24 years of age (depending on the particular insurance company). At that time, dependent children have the option of "converting" their coverage to their own individual health insurance policies. *In the case of children who are not able to support themselves economically due to illness or disability, it is recommended that they remain on their parent's or parents' policy as dependents indefinitely.* This is permitted by most state insurance laws, as long as the families notify the insurance company of the intention to do this *before* the dependent children reach the age at which they would not otherwise be allowed to remain on the policy (see Chapter 6).

Developmental Disabilities Planning Councils Councils created by federal and state laws to help ensure planned, coordinated services for individuals with severe developmental disabilities that are expected to be long-lasting. The councils are mandated to play a major role in helping individuals to become integrated into the general community and in establishing information on "recommended practices" to do so, and to analyze different state agencies' roles in assisting the independence of individuals with disabilities. At least half of the council membership is required to be persons with developmental disabilities.

Developmental Evaluation Centers (DECs) Diagnostic centers for children with developmental disabilities. They are usually staffed by a variety of professional specialties (e.g., pediatricians, child psychologists, social workers, educators). The service component is most often funded by state government. In many DECs, staff work closely with nearby universities.

"Developmentally delayed" A term used to describe children whose development is slower than most other children their age, as measured by standardized tests. Delay can be in one or more areas (e.g., cognitive development, physical development, communication development [speech and language], social or emotional development, skills).

Disability   A condition that may limit an individual's daily activity or functioning or that may require that the individual receive special services others do not need to attend school or work, or to care for children or a home. An example would be a deaf person who requires the assistance of a hearing person who signs to attend college. A child may be born with a disability or acquire it through an illness or accident.

Disability law   Any piece of legislation that relates to the rights or needs of individuals with disabilities or benefits available to them because of their condition (see Chapter 2).

Disease-related or disability-related organizations   Groups composed mostly of individuals with a particular disease and their family members and advocates. These organizations educate the public about the needs of their members who have disabilities or chronic illnesses and advocate for the interests of such members in both the public and private arenas.

Early Education for Children with Disabilities Program Projects (EEPCD)   Federally funded projects that provide outreach, demonstrations, technical assistance, and research institutes concerning early education of children with developmental disabilities.

Early intervention services (Part H)   A term generally used to describe a variety of services for children experiencing "developmental delay" in one or more areas or children with a diagnosed physical or mental condition that has a "high probability of resulting in developmental delay" (20 U.S.C. 1472 conveyed by NEC★TAS). Some states, at their option, serve children "at risk of delay." Children participating in this program can be from birth through 2 years of age. (Services can be given to selected 3-year-olds who will not be eligible for preschool services until the next school year.)

Services may be provided in the child's home or in the community and must include, at a minimum, assistive technology services devices, audiology, family training and counseling, health services, diagnostic or evaluative medical services, nursing services, nutrition services, occupational therapy, physical therapy, psychological services, service coordination, social work services, special instructions to families, speech-language pathology services, transportation to and from services, and vision services (34 CFR 303.12(d) conveyed by NEC⋆TAS).

Part H programs included in the Individuals with Disabilities Education Act (IDEA) are solely concerned with the provision of early intervention services. States define which children have developmental delays or have conditions with a "high probability of resulting in developmental delay" (see Chapters 2, 3 and 5).

Early and Periodic Screening, Diagnosis, and Treatment (EPSDT) Program   A special program under Medicaid that provides for the regular and routine screening of all children who receive Medicaid, to detect any developmental problem as early as possible and to seek appropriate treatment. A recent court order has made it easier for children who receive Medicaid to undergo such screenings, and to receive any "medically necessary" care at public expense whether or not such a service is included in a state's Medicaid plan (see Chapter 5).

Earned income   Income that comes from wages or self-employment.

Earned Income Tax Credit (EIC)   A federal income tax "credit" available to individuals or families who work, have an "adjusted gross income" less than $21,250 (in 1991; this amount increases each year), and have at least one child living with them. There are two potential credits available the EIC program: 1) the basic credit based on the number of children living with the taxpayer, and 2) the extra credit for a child born that tax year (see Chapter 8).

Education for All Handicapped Children Act of 1975 (PL 94-142) This federal law made concrete Section 504's (of PL 93-112, the Rehabilitation Act of 1973) mandate to educate children with disabilities at public expense. It required that all children 6 through 21 years old in primary or secondary school, meeting a state's definition of "disabled," receive a free, appropriate public education in the "least restrictive environment" (LRE). Any support services necessary for a child to "benefit from public education" (e.g., transportation) were also to be provided by school systems. According to this law, eligible children must have individualized education programs (IEPs), which are prepared for them annually by an appropriate group with full participation by the parent(s) and which detail all services the children will receive (see Chapter 2).

Education of the Handicapped Act Amendments of 1990 (PL 101-476) IDEA represents the culmination of 15 years of educational law relating to children with developmental delays, as defined specifically by each state for its children. Included in IDEA are mandates to provide services to preschool children (3 through 5 years of age), and primary and secondary school children (6 through 21 years of age) and strong inducements to provide services to infants and toddlers (birth through 2 years of age), including those with an established risk of delay. School-age children must be provided annual individualized education programs (IEPs). Families of infants and toddlers receiving early intervention services must be provided individualized family service plans (IFSPs) (see Chapters 2 and 5).

EEPCD *See* Early Education for Children with Disabilities Program Projects.

EIC *See* Earned Income Tax Credit.

Eligibility determination The process by which a child and/or family is considered for participation in a service or other benefit program.

Emergency Assistance Programs Cash or other benefits available through the county Department of Human Resources/Social Services or church ministries to help pay for utility bills, rent deposits, and/or prescription medications (see Chapter 6).

Entitlement A legally based cash or service benefit that is due any individual with the characteristics a program was designed to serve (e.g., Social Security payments to individuals over 65, Supplemental Security Income [SSI] cash payments to individuals with disabilities who meet other program requirements). In most cases, qualifying individuals must still apply for such entitlements and be found eligible.

EPSDT *See* Early and Periodic Screening, Diagnosis, and Treatment Program.

"Evidence of insurability" Proof required of some individuals to demonstrate to health insurance companies that their participation would not cost the company too much money. The test of this is an applicant's answers to a health history and health practice survey, and in some cases a physical examination (done at the company's expense). Health insurance companies use actuarial tables, which show the probability of a person to need a certain level of care, with the questionnaire and examination used to make a decision about whether to insure.

Exceptional Family Members Program A program in the military to provide information and support to military families with a member who has a chronic illness or disability. Such a group may carry a different name from one base or post to another (see Chapter 5).

Exclusions from coverage   Services that do *not* qualify for reimbursement by a public or private health insurance plan. Examples might be eyeglasses or weight reduction programs.

Exemptions   Amounts removed from one's income for tax consideration because of expenses expected to have been incurred in connection with these items. For example, a couple filing a joint federal income tax return gets an exemption for each individual living in their home for the majority of the year (including the taxpayers). The "personal exemption," which in 1992 was $2,150 per person, serves to exclude some of your income from taxation. Individuals or couples with an adjusted gross income (AGI) of more than $75,000 must take a smaller amount for "personal exemptions" based on their AGI amount (see Chapter 8).

Fair Debt Collection Practices Act Amendments of 1986 (PL 99-361) *See* Consumer Credit Protection Act Amendments of 1977.

Family and Medical Leave Act of 1993 (PL 103-3)   Law designed to protect the job security, seniority, and continued health insurance coverage of workers who need to take leave due to: 1) the birth or adoption of a child, 2) a serious illness of the individual, or 3) the serious illness of a family member. Under this law, workers are entitled to as many as 12 weeks of unpaid leave for any of these reasons. There are certain worker qualifications and employer exemptions; however, this law should assist families with children who have chronic illnesses or disabilities at birth and during health crises throughout their lives (see Chapter 2).

Family monthly budget   Any formal plan a family uses to meet the upcoming month's expenses with expected income. It might also include an expense for "savings" (see Chapter 9).

Family monthly expense record   A written form to record actual expenses for a month and compare them with budgeted expenses. As such, it is a tool to help match income with expenses and cut expenses where needed (see Chapter 9).

Family support groups   Formal and informal groups to assist families, emotionally or otherwise, who are going through particularly taxing experiences (e.g., homelessness, divorce, single parenting, the birth and rearing of a child with a chronic illness or disability). Family support groups have developed throughout the United States since the 1960s.

Federal Trade Commission (FTC) regional offices   Staff at the 10 regional offices of the FTC are responsible for monitoring the behavior of bill collectors and collection agencies to see that they comply with federal law in this area (see Chapter 10).

Federation for Children with Special Needs   A parent-founded and run organization assisting families whose children have a variety of special needs, including chronic illnesses and disabilities. The organization is based in Boston, Massachusetts, but is able and willing to match a child or family's needs with the most appropriate local resources in their home community (see Appendix B).

Federation of Families for Children's Mental Health   A national organization composed of parents of children and youth with emotional, behavior, or mental disorders. The organization is based in Alexandria, Virginia, but is willing to be a resource to families across the country (see Chapter 11).

"Fee-for-service" plans   Health insurance plans for which payment for service is separated from service delivery. The insured can receive covered services anytime, for any reason, and at one hospital or clinic or another.

Each time a service is given, a fee is charged and is paid (up to the "usual and customary rate") by the insurance company (see Chapter 6).

"Filing date" The date when an individual's application for Supplemental Security Income (SSI) is considered to have been made. The date of the first telephone call to SSI to request an application or the first visit to the Social Security Administration (SSA) field office to get an application for SSI can be considered the "filing date" *as long as a completed application for SSI is submitted within 60 days of the first inquiry with the Social Security Administration.* Although "eligibility determination" can take as long as 3 months, if your child is accepted by the SSI Program, payments will be made retroactively from the "filing date" to the present and subsequently on a monthly basis (see Chapter 7).

Food Stamp Program A federal program to help families with low incomes purchase food. The program is run by the U.S. Department of Agriculture but administered most often by county Departments of Human Resources of Departments of Social Services (see Chapter 7).

Foster/specialized home care An alternative living situation for a child with a chronic illness or disability. When the child's parents are unable to care for him or her, the child can be placed in another home arranged specifically for the care of children with special health care needs.

"Free, appropriate public education" A term that originated in Section 504 of the Rehabilitation Act of 1973 (PL 93-112) and was carried into all laws dealing with the education of children with disabilities in public schools. It describes the now legal requirement that children with disabilities be educated at public expense in a setting that is most conducive to their development, and fullest integration possible with children who do not have disabilities.

FTC   *See* Federal Trade Commission regional offices.

GA   *See* General Assistance Programs.

GA–Medical   *See* General Assistance–Medical Programs.

General Assistance–Medical Programs (GA–Medical)   A medical benefits program that accompanies most GA programs of cash assistance. GA–Medical programs pay for selected medical care and supplies (see Chapter 5).

General Assistance (GA) Programs   State and/or local programs of cash assistance for individuals with low incomes. They are designed to help individuals who are not eligible for Aid to Families with Dependent Children or Supplemental Security Income and families who are waiting to be enrolled in another income subsidy program. As of 1990, 45 states and the District of Columbia had GA programs (see Chapters 5 and 7).

Group home   An alternative living situation for children, young adults, and adults with special health care needs that are either physical or emotional and behavioral. Between 4 and 10 individuals supervised by trained staff share the costs of a small home as their primary residence (see Chapter 3).

Guardian   An individual with legal custody of a child who is not his or her biological or adoptive child. A guardian is generally appointed by a court to advocate for a child's interests when that child's parents are not available to do so.

Handicapped Children's Protection Act of 1986 (PL 99-372)   A law that allows a child's parents or guardians to be reimbursed for their "reasonable legal costs" *when they win* in an administrative hearing or court case (see Chapter 2).

Head Start   A federally funded preschool education program for children whose families have low incomes. Its purpose is to improve the skills of children from disadvantaged backgrounds and to offer other services and support to the children and their families. *Of the enroll-ment in each Head Start, 10% must be children with disabilities, which makes it easier for such children to obtain this service* (see Chapter 3).

Health Departments/Public Health Departments (county and area) Departments that provide a range of health care services to any citizen requesting this help who lives in the county or area they serve. Their services tend to emphasize preventative care (e.g., immuniza-tions, well-baby care, teen pregnancy clinics, teen mother and baby clinics, adolescent health clinics). Some Health Departments see sick children. All refer them to other treatment centers if they cannot provide the care themselves. Health Departments can conduct full or partial screenings for the Early and Periodic Screening, Diagnosis, and Treatment (EPSDT) program in Medicaid. Many are equipped with a representative of the county's Department of Social Services to take applications for Medicaid and Aid to Families with De-pendent Children (AFDC). Many health departments also provide assistance with transportation to and from clinics and reduced costs for prescription medications. Fees for services are based on an individual or family's ability to pay (see Chapter 4).

Health maintenance organization (HMO) A health insur-ance plan that links payment for medical care to the receipt of services in a particular setting. Coverage for health care is pre-paid, based on an annual fee per person. Care must be received in a given location, from a choice of given doctors and hospitals. There is an emphasis on preventative services. Each plan member chooses a "pri-mary care" physician who coordinates all of his or her care and controls access to specialists (see Chapter 6).

HEATH (Higher Education and Adult Training for Individu-als with Disabilities) Resource Center A federally

from birth through 2 years old with developmental delays or with an established risk of developmental delay. Although not required to do so, some states also elect to serve children at risk of developmental delay, and those services would also be administered by that state's lead agency. The lead agency for this program at the federal level is the U.S. Department of Education (see Chapters 2, 3, and 5).

Least restrictive environment (LRE)   The mandate in all education law regarding children with developmental delays that they be educated in the least restrictive environment possible. This means they should be as fully included as possible with children who do not have developmental delays. It also means that the educational environment of children with developmental delays must not inhibit them physically or otherwise in ways that would adversely affect their learning and/or development.

Legal Aid   *See* Legal Services Corporation.

Legal Services Corporation (Legal Aid)   Organizations that provide a full range of free or low-cost legal services to those who cannot afford a private attorney. Fees are based on an individual's or family's ability to pay. At least one legal aid office exists in communities of 100,000 or more individuals. *Some legal aid offices specialize in advocacy for children and other individuals with chronic illnesses or disabilities* (see Chapter 11).

Life skills training   Training for individuals in ways to manage their everyday lives (e.g., cooking, cleaning a room or apartment, personal hygiene, planning out a day, looking for a job or meaningful activity, managing money, shopping). This training is available in a number of places for young adults with disabilities (e.g., in schools, Independent Living Centers, Vocational Rehabilitation Programs) (see Chapter 3).

"Lifetime limitation" This term describes the overall maximum benefit that is available to each person insured in a "major medical" health insurance plan. The amount is commonly $500,000 or $1,000,000. Larger companies have the capacity to reinstate part or all of an insured individual's "lifetime limitation." Often this is done when an insured person's recent history has few claims under the policy (see Chapter 6).

"List of Impairments" A list developed by the Social Security Administration to use as a reference in deciding if a child is automatically medically eligible for the Supplemental Security Income (SSI) cash assistance program. Conditions on the "List of Impairments" for children include 66 childhood diseases and disorders divided into 13 categories or body systems (Clark & Manes, 1992). They include the following: organic mental disorders, mental retardation, mood disorders, Down syndrome, catastrophic congenital abnormalities, human immunodeficiency virus (HIV), and fetal alcohol syndrome (see Chapter 7).

Local education agency or school district A term that refers to the most local unit of a state's educational system. It would provide policy and guidance to a particular school's principal in addition to that school's board.

"Long Form" The federal income tax reporting forms to be filed by people who itemize their income tax deductions or have complex income tax returns.

LRE *See* Least restrictive environment.

"Major medical" plans An insurance policy that makes less use of limited reimbursement for specific types of services (except for psychiatric care) than a "basic coverage" plan. The "major medical" plan offers an overall "lifetime limitation" on total reimbursements under the plan. Similar to "basic coverage" plans, they make use of deductibles and co-payments to limit their expenses and discourage overutilization of services.

"Managed care" plans   A number of ways health care delivery and payment for health care can be organized to offer comprehensive health care services while controlling the cost of such services. This is done, among other ways, by controlling access to expensive services and bargaining with health care providers to lower their fees in exchange for a predictable source of patients. The most common form of a "managed care" plan is a health maintenance organization (HMO). Other ways include "preferred provider organizations" (PPOs) and "point of service" (POS) programs.

Maternal and Child Health Services block grant   A large amount of federal money given to each state to pay for a variety of kinds of maternal and child health services in accordance with federal guidelines. One such program is the Children's Special Health Care Needs (CSHCN) Program, which in some states funds a majority of the disease- or disability-related care for children who need such services and whose families have low incomes. *States were recently required by the federal government to spend at least 30% of their Maternal and Child Health block grant monies on their CSHCN Programs.*

Medicaid   A public health insurance program available to certain individuals and families with low incomes. It is financed jointly by the federal and state governments. All states have some kind of Medicaid program, although both eligibility standards and some benefits vary by state. There is no charge for the care, except for small co-payments in some cases to discourage overuse of particular services (see Chapter 5).

Medicaid—"basic services"   Services under the Medicaid program that are required to be offered by all states to all participants in the Medicaid program. These include: 1) inpatient hospital services, 2) outpatient hospital services, 3) physician services on both an inpatient and outpatient basis, 4) services in rural health clinics, 5) laboratory and x-ray services not provided by a hospital or rural health clinic, 6) care in skilled nursing facilities for individuals 21 years and older, 7) home health care, 8) family planning care and supplies, 9) services of a nurse midwife, and 10) services under the Early and Periodic Screening, Diagnosis and Treatment (EPSDT) program, to screen and treat children for developmental delays. With the exception of EPSDT, states can set limits on the extent and length of benefits offered (see Chapter 5).

Medicaid—"optional eligibility groups"   Certain groups for which Medicaid coverage is at the discretion of each state. Among others, these "optional eligibility groups" include: 1) "categorically needy" individuals, 2) "medically needy" individuals, and 3) those covered under TEFRA 134 (see also "Medicaid" and Chapter 5).

Medicaid—"optional services"   Services a state *may* provide under the Medicaid program, including: 1) prescription medications; 2) over-the-counter medications; 3) services in clinics including community health centers, community mental health centers, and school-based clinics; 4) services in emergency rooms of hospitals; 5) transportation to and from medical care; 6) dental care for those not in the Early and Periodic Screening, Diagnosis, and Treatment (EPSDT) program; 7) services in a skilled nursing facility for children younger than 21; 8) services in an inpatient psychiatric hospital for children younger than 21; 9) personal care services for individuals who need help with the basic activities of daily living; and 10) outpatient rehabilitative services to reduce a disability or improve functioning (see Chapter 5).

Medicaid—"required eligibility groups"   Groups that must be covered by a state's Medicaid program. The coverage of other groups is decided by each state. "Required eligibility groups" include: 1) any child of a recipient of Aid to Families with Dependent Children (AFDC) for which the AFDC recipient has custody; 2) a child or individual receiving Supplemental Security Income (SSI); 3) any child under 6 years old whose family income does not exceed 133% of the federal poverty level ($11,890 for a family of three in 1993); 4) a child from a two-parent family with low income and limited resources; 5) any child born after September 30, 1983 whose family's income does exceed 100% of the federal poverty level; 6) all children receiving adoption assistance or foster care in programs under Title IV-E of the Social Security Act; and 7) all children who have special circumstances making them part of a "protected group." An example would be a child who loses his or her cash assistance for a short time period (see Chapter 5).

Medicaid "waiver" programs   The federal Medicaid program will allow state Medicaid programs to apply for one of several "waivers," permitting the state to relax the rules governing the Medicaid program. This usually arises when the state can offer a service in a less expensive way that is desired by a child's family. An example of this is a 2176 waiver designed for children who require intensive home- or community-based care to avoid institutionalization. A state must apply for and obtain a waiver before it can offer an alternative service to a child. If a state is granted a "waiver" by the federal Medicaid agency, the state can limit how many children it will serve under that "waiver" program (see Chapter 5).

"Medically necessary services"   Services that will be paid for by public or private health insurance because they are certified as "medically necessary" by a doctor, or services that are found to be needed to treat a child found to have one or more developmental delays on a screening under Medicaid's Early and Periodic Screening, Diagnosis, and Treatment (EPSDT) program (see Chapter 5).

"Medically needy" An "optional eligibility" group under the Medicaid program. Each state can decide whether to cover individuals who are "medically needy" and if so, to what extent. Children in the "medically needy" category include those children who are otherwise eligible and their families who have incomes above 133⅓% of the maximum income level in their state to receive Aid to Families with Dependent Children (AFDC). They must also have *incurred* (not paid) enough medical expenses that, if paid, would reduce their incomes to a level that would qualify them under the "categorically needy" program. In some states, children can become eligible for Medicaid if their families make monthly cash payments to the state for the difference between their family income (less medical expenses) and the level allowed for Medicaid eligibility (see Chapter 4).

Medicare A federal public health insurance program for older Americans and certain individuals with disabilities (e.g., children and individuals of all ages who have permanent kidney failure). Medicare consists of two parts: 1) Part A for coverage of inpatient hospital care, care in a skilled nursing facility, or hospice care; and 2) an optional Part B for the services of physicians and other professionals, outpatient hospital services, medical supplies, and select self-administered drugs. Currently, Medicare does *not* cover most prescription medications (see Chapter 4).

Medicare Handbook The book that describes the federal government's Medicare program. It is available free of charge from the Social Security Administration (1-800-772-1213; 1-800-325-0778 [TT]) and contains program eligibility standards, a listing of covered services and benefits, and information about how and where to apply for Medicare.

Migrant/rural health clinics Health care clinics that are generally located in sparsely settled areas and provide routine health care for area residents.

Model programs Programs that demonstrate a new concept in service delivery or care. Once tried and proven useful, such programs serve as "models" on which others can base their service or care programs.

National Early Childhood Technical Assistance System (NEC★TAS) An organization based at the University of North Carolina that was created by the Education of the Handicapped Act Amendments of 1986 to provide technical assistance to state agencies and programs to help them implement the provisions of IDEA. NEC★TAS also fields information requests from parents of children with special needs and professionals working with this population of children. NEC★TAS can be reached at (919) 962-2001.

National Information Center for Children and Youth with Disabilities (NICHCY) A national information clearinghouse on childhood chronic illness and disability, programs serving these populations, related government laws and policies, parent support groups, advocacy organizations, and so forth. The organization with the current contract to provide these services is located in Washington, D.C., and can be reached at (202) 884-8200 (Voice and TT). If you are calling long-distance, ask the person you speak with to call you back so NICHCY can pay for the call. They are willing to do this.

National Parent Network on Disability (NPND) A national parent-run organization based in Alexandria, Virginia. It provides information for other parents about chronic illnesses and disabilities affecting children, and treatment and service programs available for these children and their families. Like the Federation for Children with Special Needs in Boston and the Federation of Families for Children's Mental Health, NPND is also a source of information about laws and government policies affecting children with chronic illnesses, disabilities, or other special needs. NPND can also refer families to support groups in or near their home community.

NEC★TAS *See* National Early Childhood Technical Assistance System.

NICHCY *See* National Information Center for Children and Youth with Disabilities.

NPND *See* National Parent Network on Disability.

OBRA *See* Omnibus Budget Reconciliation Act of 1989.

Occupational therapy (OT) Therapy given to individuals that emphasizes rehabilitation of physical movement above the waist, fine motor skills, or the activities of daily living (e.g., getting out of bed, getting to the toilet, dressing, eating breakfast).

Omnibus Budget Reconciliation Act (OBRA) A law, generally enacted once a year, that contains multiple pieces of legislation, often including changes in the Medicaid program. For example, OBRA of 1981, Section 2176, contained a new home- and community-based waiver program in Medicaid.

"Open enrollment period" A time period, usually 30 days each year or the first 30 days of an employee's employment, when individuals in a group insurance plan can join a plan or change from one plan to another without giving "evidence of insurability" (see also "evidence of insurability").

"Out-of-pocket expenses" The actual cost a taxpayer incurs for a medical expense (e.g., after any health insurance payments are made). On federal and state income tax returns, deductions are only allowed for out-of-pocket expenses that exceed a certain percent of adjusted gross income (AGI).

OT *See* Occupational therapy.

P&A organizations   *See* Protection and Advocacy organizations.

Parent advocacy groups   Groups of parents who have children with special health care needs. Among other reasons, parents in these groups have come together to advocate with agency administrators, government officials, and the public for the services and civil rights of their children and families.

Parent Training and Information (PTI) Centers   A national network of centers designed to help parents with children with special health care needs to find out about educational and related services their children are entitled to, and to help families feel more comfortable negotiating with school officials, teachers, and health care providers to get these services for their children (see Chapter 5).

Part B Programs   Educational and related services offered to children from 3 through 21 years old who fall into certain categories that define them as having a disability according to the Individuals with Disabilities Education Act (IDEA), and therefore require special education and related services (IDEA, 1991 and 33 U.S.C. 1401 conveyed by NEC★TAS).

Under Part B of IDEA, preschool programs serve children from 3 through 5 years of age. School-age programs serve children and youth from age 6 through 21.

Categories of disability that qualify a child or youth for Part B services include autism, deaf-blindness, deafness, hearing impairment, mental retardation, multiple disabilities, orthopedic impairment, other health impairment, serious emotional disturbance, specific learning disability, speech-language impairment, traumatic brain injury, or visual impairment including blindness (34 CFR part 300, section 300.7). Three states; Connecticut, Massachusetts, and South Dakota, do not use these categories. Some states use either "categorical" or "functional criteria" for determining eligibility in the preschool program. In these cases, children that are determined by standardized testing to have a "developmental delay" are admitted.

Required services under both preschool and school-age programs include assistive technology services and devices, audiology, counseling services, early identification, medical services for evaluation, occupational therapy, parent counseling and training, physical therapy, psychological services, recreation, rehabilitation counseling services, school health services, social work services, speech pathology, transportation, special education, and related services (34 CFR 303.12(d) as conveyed by NEC★TAS).

In both Part B programs, the school system must, with full participation of a child's parents, develop an annual individualized education program (IEP) for each child and an individualized family service plan (IFSP) for a child's family. States define specifically which children are considered "children with disabilities" (see Chapters 2, 3 and 5).

Part H   *See* Early intervention services.

Part H Programs   *See* Early intervention services.

Payment plans   Arrangements made with professionals, clinics, or hospital billing offices to pay over time the part of the bill owed *out of the family's own pocket.* This does not include the portion of the bill that expected to be covered by private or public health insurance, only the share owed after those policies or programs pay their part (see Chapter 10).

"Permanently and totally disabled"   A term that generally refers to an individual who has been or is expected to be ill or have a disability for at least 12 months. Individuals meeting this definition of "permanently and totally disabled" are eligible to take additional federal and state income tax deductions, exemptions, and/or credits (see Chapter 8).

Physical therapy (PT)   Therapy given to an individual to rehabilitate large muscle functioning or muscle functioning below the waist.

PL 94-142   *See* Education for All Handicapped Children Act of 1975.

PL 101-476   *See* Education of the Handicapped Act Amendments of 1990.

"Point-of-service" (POS) program   An insurance plan in which the concepts of a "health maintenance organization" (HMO), a "preferred provider organization," and a "fee-for-service" health care plan are combined. Insured persons are offered higher reimbursement and lower co-payments if they see certain physicians. When using these selected physicians, the insured individuals must use a "primary care physician" to coordinate care and direct referrals to specialists. If insured individuals choose to seek care from other physicians outside of the network and pay more for the cost of their services, they may choose any health care provider for any service and can refer themselves to specialists.

POS   *See* "Point-of service" program.

PPO   *See* Preferred provider organization.

"Pre-existing condition" exclusion clauses   Portions of an insurance policy that refer to health conditions for which an insurance company may reject an applicant for coverage or limit reimbursement to an insured person, for one or more service relating to an illness or disability the insured has or had in the past. This limitation can remain in force for as long as 2 years. When applicants apply for health insurance during an open enrollment period, there are *no* exclusions for pre-existing conditions (*see also* "open enrollment period").

Preferred provider organization (PPO)   A "managed care" health insurance plan in which insured individuals are given more favorable reimbursements if they use specified health care providers or if they use a particular hospital for inpatient care (see Chapter 6).

"Premiums"   Fees collected monthly, quarterly, or annually that give an eligible individual or family access to a health insurance program. An employer may share the cost of the health insurance "premium" with an insured individual, and "premiums" can often be deducted from an employee's pay on a "pre-tax" basis, saving the insured some money.

Preschool services or programs   *See* Part B Programs.

"Presumptive eligibility"   The situation in which an individual is presumed to be eligible for a service or a benefit program based on his or her obvious characteristics. In the SSI Program, children with at least 1 of 12 severe impairments who meet all other eligibility requirements (e.g., family income, resource limitations) are presumed to be eligible for SSI and can begin receiving payments immediately. Payments can continue until medical eligibility is more formally established or for as long as 6 months (see Chapter 7).

Primary care doctor   A term that can refer to two different things. First, pediatricians, family practice doctors, and internists are often referred to as primary care doctors, as they are often the first doctors seen when there is a problem. Second, the term *primary care doctor* is used to describe the person who has primary responsibility for an individual's health care and coordinates all other care he or she receives, including the care of any specialist.

"Primary" health insurance policy   The policy that pays portions of an individual's medical or related bills for covered services *first*, at the rate agreed upon in the policy.

Private health insurance   Health insurance an individual can obtain; 1) as a benefit of employment; 2) through membership in a union, nonprofit, or professional association; 3) as an individual if found medically insurable; or 4) through a "risk-pool" if it exists in an individual's state.

Private health insurance "certificate"   The written description of benefits provided in the health insurance plan that provides coverage to an individual or family as well as the conditions that must be met to receive those benefits. The "certificate" is often thought of as the policy, but it is a summary of the policy and is issued most often by the employer or association that has a contractual relationship with an insurance company to provide health insurance coverage for its employees or group members. *To get the most medical benefit for the least out-of-pocket cost, the parents of children with chronic illnesses or disabilities should become extremely familiar with the health insurance plans covering their children.*

Procedural safeguards   Procedures that must be followed by law to help protect an individual's and family's rights to confidentiality, access to information, full participation in a deliberative process, or appeal of an undesired decision. "Procedural safeguards" are generally written into a law (e.g., the Individuals with Disabilities Education Act [IDEA], which has an entire section devoted to "procedural safeguards").

Protection and Advocacy (P&A) organizations   Independent agencies created by federal developmental disabilities law to provide legal assistance, information, referral, and advocacy services to individuals with developmental disabilities or mental illness living in institutions or in the community. P&As are staffed primarily by lawyers and social workers (see Chapter 2).

Psychologist A professional trained in human development and human behavior. A child psychologist works solely with children and their families in a number of areas, depending on the focus of the professional's training and the work environment. Examples of jobs a psychologist might do include developmental testing of a child, assessment of a child's social interaction in school, and counseling of a child or a family. A psychologist may work alone, as part of a group private practice, or as part of a multidisciplinary team in a public or private clinic setting. Professional psychologists generally have at least a master's degree, representing 2 years of work and some practical experience after college. Many psychologists have doctoral (Ph.D.) degrees.

PT *See* Physical therapy.

PTI *See* Parent Training and Information Centers.

Public hospitals Hospitals that are financed largely by government funds and are open to the public for service.

"Reasonable accommodation" The requirement in PL 101-336, the Americans with Disabilities Act of 1991 that both public and private agencies and businesses must make reasonable efforts to assist individuals with disabilities to use their services and facilities. An example of this would be the requirement that all new buses put into service have lifts to accommodate wheelchairs (see Chapter 2).

Referral sources Individuals or organizations that refer others for services, or places where there are things or resources an individual needs and to which that individual can be referred for help.

Related aids and services A term similar to "auxiliary aids and services," except that it is used specifically in the context of the school system. It refers to any assistance or special services required to enable children with developmental delays to remain in and benefit from public education. The term was first used in Section 504 of PL 93-112, the Rehabilitation Act of 1973, when "appropriate education" for this child population was defined to include the receipt of "auxiliary aids and services" or "necessary support services" in addition to regular classes and special education classes.

"Resources"   A term used by the Supplemental Security Income (SSI) Program and other benefit programs such as Aid to Families with Dependent Children (AFDC) to describe things a child or family owns (e.g., furniture, a bank account, property). The SSI Program and AFDC limit the amount of resources a child or family can own to be eligible for benefits; however, not all resources are counted in determining eligibility (see Chapter 7).

Respite care   Programs to relieve the primary caregivers of an individual who requires intensive and extensive daily care. This can be due to a physical or mental illness. For children, respite care workers either come to the family home or, if possible, children are taken to facilities where they are cared for and supervised by trained workers for as little as a few hours to as long as a few weeks. Both public and private organizations sponsor respite care programs.

"Risk pool" for health insurance coverage   A way some states have developed to offer health insurance coverage to individuals who are otherwise "medically uninsurable." Individuals who join a "risk pool" are offered "fee-for-service" health insurance at rates just above the private market rate. Deductibles and co-payments are higher, coverage in a "risk pool" is often less comprehensive, and there are usually "pre-existing condition clauses" that exclude coverage of certain care for a defined period of time (generally not exceeding 2 years) (see Chapter 6).

Rural/migrant health clinics *See* "Migrant/rural health clinics."

School-age services Educational services provided to "children with disabilities" who are 6 through 21 years old (*see also* Part B Programs).

"Secondary" health insurance policy A health insurance policy that pays on an individual's professional or hospital bills for covered services only *after* a "primary" health insurance policy has paid its agreed-upon share. At that time, the "secondary" policy pays its agreed-upon share of the remaining balance of bills for covered services.

Section 504 of PL 93-112, the Rehabilitation Act of 1973 A section of the Rehabilitation Act of 1973 that deals with individuals or agencies who receive any federal grant monies. In Section 504, such individuals and agencies must provide equal opportunity to individuals with disabilities in all aspects of an organization's operations. Additionally, discrimination against individuals with disabilities is prohibited, both in hiring of workers for the organization and in delivery of the organization's services. Section 504 is also important because it paved the way for more extensive civil rights legislation for children with disabilities. Section 504 states that no child with a disability should be excluded from an appropriate and publicly funded education in any school system receiving federal funds (see Chapter 2).

Self-advocacy The process of asking for the items or services needed for one by oneself. It may involve, for example, speaking in person to a program or agency administrator, writing a letter to the school board or to members of Congress, or speaking at public meetings.

"Self-insured" An option large companies have for providing health insurance to their employees. Companies may choose to pay for employees' health care costs rather than buying a policy underwritten by an insurance company (e.g., Prudential, Blue Cross and Blue Shield). Self-insured plans may buy some health insurance coverage for "catastrophic illness" or serious, long-term health problems.

Service coordination   The process by which an individual's medical and related care is planned and coordinated, making use of all required services in the most efficient way possible. Some states and Medicaid still use the term *case management.*

Sheltered workshops   Supervised work settings in which individuals with physical or mental disabilities carry out routine tasks for modest pay. Examples are stuffing envelopes and packing boxes.

"Short Form"   Federal income tax reporting forms to be filed by a taxpayer who does *not* itemize income tax deductions and has a short and simple income tax return.

Sliding scale fee system   A fee system in which individuals are charged for services based on their ability to pay. Individuals or families earning more money pay more for the same service.

Social Security Administration (SSA)   A large federal government agency that administers a number of health and social service program. Included are the Medicare program, the Medicaid programs, the Supplemental Security Income (SSI) Program, and Title V programs offering a variety of kinds of maternal and child health services, including the Children's Special Health Care Needs (CSHCN) Program for children with chronic illnesses or developmental disabilities.

Social welfare organizations, private   A large number of private community organizations whose goals are to supplement the role of government in meeting the service of individuals in a particular community. The agencies can range from the local chapter of the American Red Cross to a Lutheran Social Services agency to the local 24-hour crisis service. Most are nonprofit organizations. Some are church-sponsored (e.g., Salvation Army). Others are free-standing (e.g., an area women's center) and receive their operating funds from United Way or private fund raising. Most social welfare organizations are open to all, unless otherwise specified.

Social worker   A human services professional trained to help individuals, groups, or communities solve interpersonal or group problems, or to meet an individual's or community's need for resources (e.g., income, housing, food, social services, employment opportunities). Social workers may work alone or in a group in private practice. Their emphasis is often psychotherapy. Other social workers work in public or private agencies in the community. Professional social workers have at least a college education. Many have master's degrees (M.S.W.), representing 2 years of work and some practical experience beyond college. A few have a doctoral degree (D.S.W. or Ph.D.), which tends to emphasize research and teaching in some aspect of the human behavior, human services, or public policy field.

Special Education Director   An individual who is responsible for overseeing the implementation of any federal and state programs affecting the education of children with chronic illnesses or disabilities who meet the federal and state criteria for service. Each state has a Special Education Director in their State Department of Education.

"Special Programs Office" of a hospital   The office in most major hospitals where individuals can seek financial assistance to pay for their medical care. In such an office, there is usually a staff person who can take applications for Medicaid, the SSI Program, and other benefit or grant programs. The child's doctor, clinic coordinator, or any social worker in the hospital should know how to reach such an office.

Special services   Services a child with a developmental delay needs in addition to those offered in a regular classroom to children without delays. These might include special tutoring or a separate class on one or more subjects for a number of children with developmental delays as examples. The trend today, however, is to include all children to the furthest extent possible. *Some states may call these special education services.*

Special Supplemental Food Program for Women, Infants, and Children (WIC)   A federally funded program to provide vouchers for the purchase of selected food items to: 1) pregnant women, 2) women who have recently delivered babies, 3) breastfeeding women, and 4) infants and children up to 5 years of age. Potential recipients must also be found to be lacking proper nutrition that could endanger the health of an unborn child, an infant, or a young child (see Chapter 7).

SSA   *See* Social Security Administration.

SSI   *See* Supplemental Security Income Program.

State Department of Education   The state agency responsible for administering all public education funds and programs in a state. This includes funds and programs to implement federal and state laws regarding the public education and provision of support services to children with chronic illnesses and disabilities who meet federal and state criteria for service. Some of these functions are delegated to local education agencies (see Chapter 5).

State Department of Insurance   The state agency, which may carry a different name in a particular state, responsible for overseeing the operation of all private insurance companies in a state, including health insurance companies. State Departments of Insurance usually maintain a Consumer Affairs Division to field complaints from the public about unpaid claims consumers feel should be paid or other violations of the contract a health insurance company has with an insured individual (see Chapter 6 and Appendix B, which lists each State's Department of Insurance).

State Department of Revenue   The state agency, which may carry a different name in a particular state, that is responsible for collecting revenue for a state. This agency administers collection of a state's personal income tax, if the state has one. It is important that parents of children with chronic illnesses and disabilities who pay personal income taxes in a state stay in contact with these agencies. *Your state's revenue-collecting agency can keep you up to date on state income tax deductions, exemptions, and credits that may be available to your family because of your child's condition* (see Chapter 8 and Appendix B, which lists each state's Department of Revenue or revenue-collecting agency).

State Medicaid agency   The state agency that develops and administers a particular state's Medicaid program, in conjunction with both the federal Medicaid program in the Social Security Administration (SSA) and local Medicaid agencies in a state (see Appendix B, which lists each state's Medicaid agency).

State Office of Developmental Disabilities   The state agency or department, which may carry a different name in a particular state, that is responsible for administering a state's community and institutional services to individuals with developmental disabilities. This includes children, and can include children with chronic illnesses, mental retardation, and emotional, behavior, or mental disorders. Sometimes services for children with these differing conditions are split between two state agencies (see Appendix B, which lists each state's Office of Developmental Disabilities).

State Office of Maternal and Child Health   The state office, usually located within a State Department of Health and/or a State Department of Human Services, that is responsible for administering all Title V programs, including the Children's Special Health Care Needs (CSHCN) Program (see Appendix B, which lists each state's Title V Office or Office of Maternal and Child Health).

State Office of Mental Health   A state's Office of Mental Health may be free-standing within the state's Department of Health and/or Department of Human Services, or may be combined with the state's Office of Developmental Disabilities or Office of Alcohol and Drug Abuse Programs. In any case, this office is responsible for administering a state's mental health service programs, including those for children. Many such programs are in the community.

State Office of Mental Retardation   *See* State Office of Developmental Disabilities.

State Supplemental Payments (to Supplemental Security Income)   As of 1994, 44 states supplemented the federal Supplemental Security Income (SSI) payment to program participants with subsidies of their own (see Chapter 7).

State Vocational Rehabilitation Agency   A state agency that administers all public vocational rehabilitation funds and programs in a state, including federal funds and program directives coming to a state from the federal government (see Appendix B).

"Standard" tax deductions   The amount the Internal Revenue Service (IRS) allows a taxpayer who does not itemize income tax deductions to subtract from his or her adjusted gross income (AGI) before computing income taxes. In 1992, the IRS allowed a standard deduction of $3,400 for single taxpayers, $5,000 for head-of-household taxpayers, $5,700 for married taxpayers filing jointly, and $2,850 for married taxpayers filing separately. *Individuals or couples with deductions exceeding these amounts should itemize deductions to recover more of their actual expenses* (see Chapter 8).

"Stop-loss clause"   A provision in a health insurance policy that allows the insured to limit out-of-pocket expenses. After spending a certain amount in a year on health care (e.g., $1,000), the health insurance company pays 100% of the costs of all covered services.

Supervised apartments   An alternative living situation for young adults and adults with chronic illnesses or disabilities (physical or emotional/behavior). Such individuals may be able to live alone or with roommates sharing their activities and chores together. A trained professional does not live with them, but stays in contact with them on a regular basis for both supervision and assistance (see Chapter 3).

Supplemental Security Income (SSI) Program   A federally funded and administered cash assistance program for older adults and individuals who are blind or have disabilities. In 1992, such a child or adult received as much as to $422 per month in assistance, regardless of the county or state in which he or she lived. In addition, 44 states (as of 1994) supplement federal SSI payments each month. Enrollment in the SSI Program brings the additional benefit of automatic eligibility for the Medicaid program (see Chapter 7).

Supported employment   A situation in which young adults or adults with chronic illnesses or disabilities are coached and/or supported in their jobs on a regular basis. This allows many individuals with disabilities to maintain jobs that they otherwise could not.

Surplus Food Distribution programs   A program in which food not needed by the U.S. government is distributed from time to time in most states under a Surplus Food Distribution Program of the U.S. Department of Agriculture. Community Action Agencies/County Commissions for Economic Opportunities are most often responsible for local distribution (see Chapter 7).

TAPP   *See* Technical Assistance for Parents Programs.

Technical Assistance for Parents Programs (TAPP)   Programs operated by Parent Training and Information (PTI) Centers. TAPPs offer peer-supported technical assistance to develop the leadership capabilities of PTIs, which serve all families in need.

"Third-party administrator" (TPA)   One way a health insurance plan can be administered; in this case, an employer, union, or nonprofit association contracts with an outside organization to run its health insurance plan.

Title V Programs   Programs legislated in Title V of the Social Security Act. A number of programs are funded by Title V; all concern maternal and child health. One of the most widely known relating to children with chronic illness or disability is the Children's Special Health Care Needs (CSHCN) Program (*see also* Children's Special Health Care Needs [CSHCN] Program).

TPA   *See* Third-party administrator.

UAPs   *See* University Affiliated Programs.

UCR   *See* "Usual and customary rate."

"Undue hardship"   PL 101-336, the Americans with Disabilities Act of 1991 states that public *and* private businesses must make "reasonable accommodations" so that individuals with disabilities have access to, and can make use of, their facilities. The one exception to this is for businesses for which such accommodation would cause extreme or "undue hardship" due to significant difficulty or expense for the size and type of business. In general, a larger employer is expected to make accommodations requiring more effort and expense than a smaller employer (see Chapter 2).

Unearned income Income from gifts of money, investments, child support payments, and payments from most public assistance programs.

University Affiliated Programs (UAPs) Programs affiliated with major universities and hospitals in every state. Their purpose is to conduct research, professional training, service delivery, and information dissemination to help support the independence, productivity, and inclusion in the community of individuals developmental disabilities.

"Usual and customary rate" (UCR) The rate on which a health insurance company bases its reimbursement for a covered service. This rate is supposed to be tied into measures of prevailing rates in a particular geographic area. As an example, if a doctor bills the family $123 for a covered service (and the annual deductible has been met), the insurance company will only pay 80% of the UCR for that service, which might only be $100. The family may be responsible for the full balance of the doctor's bill.

Vocational Rehabilitation (VR) Services A federal and state jointly funded program to help eligible individuals with disabilities to clarify their employment goals, develop skills, and become employed. *Young adults enrolled in VR Services can receive reimbursement for approved health care needed to reach their employment goals or stay employed* (see Chapter 5).

VR Services *See* Vocational Rehabilitation Services.

"Waiting period" The time period during which an employee is *not* eligible for employer-provided health insurance coverage.

WIC *See* Special Supplemental Food Program for Women, Infants, and Children.

"With a high probability of developmental delay" In early intervention program policy, this term refers to children with Down syndrome, seizure disorders, chromosomal disorders, genetic or birth disorders, severe sensory impairments, inborn errors of metabolism, or fetal alcohol syndrome. Currently, all states provide some referral, assessment, and treatment services to these children.

***Zebley* court decision, 1990** *Zebley v. Sullivan* (then Secretary of the Department of Health and Human Services) made it easier for children with chronic illnesses and disabilities to receive Supplemental Security Income (SSI) cash assistance. This was particularly so for children with emotional, behavior, and mental disorders. As a result of the court case: 1) the SSI Program was made available to thousands of children who would not previously be determined eligible for benefits; and 2) the SSI Program was required to reconsider the applications of more than 450,000 children whose applications had been denied before January 1, 1980 (see Chapter 7).

Bibliography

Adams, P.F., & Benson, V. (1990). Current estimates from the National Health Survey 1989. In *Vital Health Statistics 1990(10)*. Washington, DC: National Center for Health Statistics, U.S. Department of Health and Human Services.

Aetna Casualty and Surety Co. (1992). *The managed care solution.* Hartford, CT: Author.

Agosta, J., Bradley, V., & Knoll, J. (1992). *Toward positive family policy: Components of a comprehensive family support system.* Cambridge, MA: Human Services Research Institute.

Air Carrier's Access Act of 1986, PL 99-435. (October 2, 1986). Title 49, U.S.C. Appendix 1374, subsec. c: *U.S. Code Congressional and Administrative News, 1,* 100 Stat, 1080.

Alabama Department of Revenue, Income Tax Division (1991a). *Form 40: Alabama income tax forms and instructions.* Montgomery, AL: Author.

Alabama Department of Revenue, Income Tax Division (1991b). *Form 40A: Alabama income tax forms and instructions.* Montgomery, AL: Author.

Alliance of Genetic Support Groups. (1992). *Health insurance resource guide.* Chevy Chase, MD: Author.

Americans with Disabilities Act of 1990 (ADA), PL 101-336. (July 26, 1990). Title 42, U.S.C. 12101 et seq., Title 47

U.S.C. 152, 221, 225, 611. *U.S. Code Congressional and Administrative News, 1,* 104 Stat, 327–384.

Ames, P. (1990). The legal rights of people with disabilities. *The Deaf-Blind American, 29*(2), 14–18.

Anderson, B. (1987). *Becoming informed about your child's special health needs.* Boston, MA: Collaboration Among Parents and Health Professionals (CAPP) Project, National Parent Resource Center.

"Annual income tax guide." (1993, February). *Exceptional Parent, 23*(2), 38, 40, 62.

Arizona Department of Revenue. (1991). *State of Arizona 140: Resident personal income tax.* Phoenix, AZ: Author.

Arthritis Foundation. (1989). *Guide to Social Security Disability Insurance for people with arthritis.* Atlanta, GA: Author.

Arthritis Foundation. (1991). *Arthritis information: Health, life, and disability insurance for people with arthritis.* Atlanta, GA: Author.

Association for the Care of Children's Health. (1991). *Annual report.* Washington, DC: Author.

Association for the Care of Children's Health. (1993). *The national center for family-centered care.* Washington, DC: Author.

Asthma and Allergy Foundation of America. (1991). *1991 annual report.* Washington, DC: Author.

Beck, M. (1992, October 19). Painful remedies. *Newsweek,* p. 31.

Beckett, J. (1989). *Health care financing: A guide for families.* Iowa City: National Maternal and Child Health Resource Center, The University of Iowa School of Law.

Belcher, J.R., & Palley, H.A. (1991). The prospects for national health insurance reform. *Social Work in Health Care, 15*(3), 101–119.

Bensing, J. (1991). Doctor–patient communication and the quality of care. *Social Science and Medicine, 32*(11), 1301–1310.

Biro, P., & Daulton, D. (1991). *State planning document concerning three related federal initiatives.* Chapel Hill, NC: National Early Childhood Technical Assistance System.

Blue Cross of Western Pennsylvania and Pennsylvania Blue Shield Caring Program for Children. (1992). *Caring for children with special health care needs* (video). Pittsburgh, PA: Author.

Boettjer, J.W. (Ed.). (1991). *Masonic philanthropies: A tradition of caring.* Lexington, MA and Washington, DC: The Supreme Councils, 33, N.M.J. and S.J.

Bradley, V.J., Knoll, J., & Agosta, J.M. (Eds.). (1992). *Emerging issues in family support.* Washington, DC: American Association on Mental Retardation.

Brill, J., & Hartman, R.C. (1989). *Financial aid for students with disabilities.* Washington, DC: U.S. Government Printing Office.

Bureau of Taxation. (1991). *Maine 1991 individual income tax booklet: Long form 1040ME.* Augusta, ME: Author.

Butler, J., Singer, J., Palfrey, J., & Walker, D. (1987). Health insurance coverage and physician use among children with disabilities: Findings from probability samples in five metropolitan areas. *Pediatrics, 79*(1), 89–98.

Butler, P.A. (1988). *Too poor to be sick.* Washington, DC: American Public Health Association.

Callahan, D. (1990). Rationing medical progress. *New England Journal of Medicine, 332*(25), 1810–1813.

Carroll Publishing Company. *State executive directory, March–June, 1992.* Washington, DC: Author.

CH.A.D.D. (1990). *Children with attention deficit disorders.* Plantation, FL: Author.

CHAMPUS. (1990). *CHAMPUS handbook.* Washington, DC: U.S. Government Printing Office.

Children's Defense Fund. (1992). Legislative year in review. *CDF Reports, 14*(1), 1–5.

Children's Defense Fund. (1993a). Family and Medical Leave Act becomes law. *CDF Reports, 14*(3), 17.

Children's Defense Fund. (1993b). Special report: Health care reform. *CDF Reports, 14*(5), 6–8.

Civil Rights Act of 1991, PL 102-166. (November 21, 1991). Title 18, U.S.C. 241 et seq., 372, 2384, Title 28, U.S.C. 1343, 1443, 1446, Title 42, U.S.C. 1991 et seq.: *U.S. Code Congressional and Administrative News, 1,* 100 Stat, 1071–1100.

Clark, J. (1992, July). What to do if you lose your group coverage. *Kiplingers Personal Finance Magazine,* 74–77.

Clark, J., & Manes, J. (1992). *The advocate's guide to SSI for children: A manual for working with the laws, regulations, policies and procedures governing children's eligibility for Supplemental Security Income.* Washington, DC: Mental Health Law Project.

Cleary, P.D., Edgman-Levitan, S., Roberts, M., Moloney, T.W., McMullen, W., Walker, J.D., & Delbanco, T.L. (1991). Patients evaluate their hospital care: A national survey. *Health Affairs, 10*(4), 254–267.

Cleft Palate Foundation. (1989). *Cleft lip and cleft palate.* Pittsburgh, PA: Author.

Collaboration Among Parents and Health Professionals (CAPP) Project, National Parent Resource Center. (1991). *Resources for locating existing parent groups (and families).* Boston, MA: Author.

Committee on Ways and Means, U.S. House of Representatives. (1992). *Overview of entitlement programs: 1992 green book.* Washington, DC: U.S. Government Printing Office.

Commonwealth of Kentucky, Revenue Cabinet. (1992). *1991 Kentucky individual income tax forms 740.* Frankfort, KY: Author.

Commonwealth of Kentucky, Revenue Cabinet. (1990). *Tax facts.* Frankfort, KY: Author.

Commonwealth of Massachusetts, Department of Revenue. (1992). *Form 1, 1991 Massachusetts resident income tax form: All schedules and instructions.* Boston, MA: Author.

Commonwealth of Pennsylvania, Department of Revenue, Bureau of Individual Taxes. (1991). *1991 Pennsylvania individual income tax forms and instructions.* Harrisburg, PA: Author.

Commonwealth of Virginia, Department of Taxation. (1991). *Instructions for preparing resident forms 760 and 760S Virginia individual income tax returns for 1991.* Richmond, VA: Author.

Communicating for Agriculture. (1992). *Comprehensive health insurance for high-risk individuals: A state-by-state analysis.* Bloomington, MN: Author.

Comptroller of the Treasury, Income Tax Division. (1991). *Maryland tax returns for full-year and part-year resident individuals, 1991.* Annapolis, MD: Author.

Congressional Almanac Quarterly. Washington, DC: CQ, Inc.

Congressional Quarterly Weekly Report. Washington, DC: CQ, Inc.

Congressional Research Service. (1993). *Medicaid source book: Background data and analysis.* Washington, DC: Author.

Consortium of Family Organizations. (1990). *Implementation of P.L. 99-457: Parent/professional partnership in early intervention.* Washington, DC: Author.

Consumer Credit Protection Act Amendments of 1977 (Fair Debt Collection Practices Act), PL 95-109. (September 20, 1977). Title 15, U.S.C. 1692 et seq., Title 18, U.S.C. 891 et seq.: *U.S. Code Congressional and Administrative News, 1,* 91 Stat, 874–883.

Consumer Reports. (1992, August). Health care crisis: Are HMOs the answer? *Consumer Reports,* 519–531.

Consumer Reports. (1992, July). Wasted health care dollars. *Consumer Reports,* 435–448.

Crosser, M.D. (1992). Guest editorial: 1991 news from Washington. *Mental Retardation, 30*(1), iii–vii.

Cutler, B.C. (1993). *You, your child, and "special" education: A guide to making the system work.* Baltimore: Paul H. Brookes Publishing Co.

Cystic Fibrosis Foundation. (1990). *Annual report 1990.* Bethesda, MD: Author.

Department of Administration, Division of Taxation. (1991). *Synopsis of Rhode Island tax system.* Providence, RI: Author.

Department of Finance and Revenue, District of Columbia. (1991). *1991 District of Columbia individual income tax.* Washington, DC: Author.

Department of Tax and Revenue, Revenue Division. (1991). *West Virginia personal income tax resident forms and instructions.* Charleston, WV: Author.

Department of the Treasury, Internal Revenue Service. (1991a). *1991 1040 forms and instructions.* Washington, DC: Author.

Department of the Treasury, Internal Revenue Service. (1991b). *1991 1040A forms and instructions.* Washington, DC: Author.

Department of the Treasury, Internal Revenue Service. (1991c). *Instructions for form 1040EZ 1991.* Washington, DC: Author.

Department of the Treasury, Internal Revenue Service. (1991d). *Publication 502: Medical and dental expenses.* Washington, DC: Author.

Department of the Treasury, Internal Revenue Service. (1991e). *Publication 503: Child and dependent care expenses.* Washington, DC: Author.

Department of the Treasury, Internal Revenue Service. (1991f). *Publication 526: Charitable contributions.* Washington, DC: Author.

Department of the Treasury, Internal Revenue Service. (1991g). *Publication 535: Business expenses.* Washington, DC: Author.

Department of the Treasury, Internal Revenue Service. (1991h). *Publication 596: Earned income credit.* Washington, DC: Author.

Department of the Treasury, Internal Revenue Service. (1991i). *Publication 907: Tax information for persons with handicaps or disabilities.* Washington, DC: Author.

Developmental Disabilities Assistance and Bill of Rights Act of 1975, PL 94-103. (October 4, 1975). Title 42, U.S.C. 6001 et seq.: *U.S. Code Congressional and Administrative News, 1,* 486–507.

Dietrich, S.L. (1991). *Comprehensive care for people with hemophilia.* New York: The National Hemophilia Foundation.

Division of Revenue, State of Delaware. (1991). *1991 Delaware resident individual income tax return.* Washington, DC: Author.

Duchnowski, A., & Friedman, R.M. (1990). Children's mental health: Challenges for the nineties. *Journal of Mental Health Administration, 17*(1), 1–12.

Early Intervention Advocacy Network. (1990). *Guide to the Part H law and regulations.* Washington, DC: The Mental Health Law Project.

Early Intervention Advocacy Network. (1991). *The Part H-EPSDT connection.* Washington, DC: The Mental Health Law Project.

EDLAW, Inc. (Eds.). (1992). *Individuals with disabilities education act (IDEA, as amended by Public Law 102-119).* Potomac, MD: Editor.

Education for All Handicapped Children Act of 1975, PL 94-142. (November 29, 1975). Title 20, U.S.C. 1232, 1401, 1405, 1406, 1411 et seq., 1453. *U.S. Code Congressional and Administrative News, 1,* 89 Stat, 773–796.

Education of the Handicapped Act Amendments of 1983, PL 98-199. (December 2, 1983). Title 20, U.S.C. 1400 et seq., 1471 et seq.: *U.S. Code Congressional and Administrative News, 1,* 97 Stat, 1357–1376.

Education of the Handicapped Act Amendments of 1986, PL 99-457. (October 8, 1986). Title 20, U.S.C. 1401 et seq.,

1471 et seq.: *U.S. Code Congressional and Administrative News, 1,* 100 Stat, 1145–1177.

Esanu, W.H., Dickman, B., Zuckerman, E.M., Pollet, M.N., & the Editors of Consumer Reports Books. (1992). *Consumer reports books guide to income tax preparation.* Yonkers, New York: Consumer Reports Books, Consumers Union.

Extension Service, U.S. Department of Agriculture. (1992). *Commitment to change.* Washington, DC: Author.

Fair Debt Collection Practices Act of 1977 (Consumer Credit Protection Act Amendments), PL 95-109. (September 20, 1977). Title 15, U.S.C. 1692 et seq., Title 18, U.S.C. 891 et seq.: *U.S. Code Congressional and Administrative News, 1,* 91 Stat, 874–883.

Fair Debt Collection Practices Act Amendments of 1986, PL 99-361. (July 9, 1986). Title 15, U.S.C. 1692 et seq.: *U.S. Code Congressional and Administrative News, 1,* 100 Stat, 768.

Fair Housing Act Amendments of 1988, PL 100-430. (September 13, 1988). Title 28, U.S.C. 2341, 2342, Title 42, U.S.C. 3601 notes, 3602, 3602 notes, 3604 et seq., 3610 et seq., 3614a., 3615 et seq., 3631. *U.S. Code Congressional and Administrative News, 2,* 102 Stat, 1619–1636.

Family and Medical Leave Act of 1993, PL 103-3. (February 5, 1993). Title 2, U.S.C. 60m, 60n, Title 5, U.S.C. 6381 et seq., Title 29, U.S.C. 2601 et seq., 2631 et seq., 2651 et seq.: *U.S. Code Congressional and Administrative News, 1,* 107 Stat, 6–29.

Federal Trade Commission. (1988). Solving credit problems. *Facts for consumers.* Washington, DC: Author.

Federal Trade Commission. (1991). Fair debt collection. *Facts for consumers.* Washington, DC: Author.

Federal Trade Commission, Associated Credit Bureaus, Inc., National Foundation for Consumer Credit, & U.S. Office of Consumer Affairs. (1992). *Building a better credit record: What to do, what to avoid.* Washington, DC: Authors.

Federal Trade Commission & National Association of Attorneys General. (1991). *How to spot credit repair scams and correct your credit history yourself.* Washington, DC: Authors.

Federation of Families for Children's Mental Health. (1992). Our mission. *Claiming Children, 1*(4), 3.

Fitzpatrick, R. (1991). Surveys of patient satisfaction: I—Important general considerations. *British Medical Journal, 302,* 887–889.

Florida Department of Revenue, Division of Taxpayer Assistance. (1991). *Tax guide.* Tallahassee, FL: Author.

Food and Nutrition Service, U.S. Department of Agriculture. (1988). *Benefit targeting in the supplemental food programs.* Washington, DC: Author.

Food and Nutrition Service, U.S. Department of Agriculture. (1990a). *The food distribution programs.* Washington, DC: Author.

Food and Nutrition Service, U.S. Department of Agriculture. (1990b). *The temporary emergency food assistance program.* Washington, DC: Author.

Food and Nutrition Service, U.S. Department of Agriculture. (1992). *Food program facts.* Washington, DC: Author.

Fox, H., & Newacheck, P.W. (1990). Special private health insurance of chronically ill children. *Pediatrics, 85*(1), 50–57.

Freedman, S.A. (1988). *Power brokering at the state level for child health care.* Gainesville: Institute for Child Health Policy, University of Florida.

Friedman, E. (1990). Medicare and Medicaid at 25. *Hospitals,* 38–54.

Friedman, R.M. (1990, August 5). *Children's and Communities' Mental Health Services Improvement Act of 1990.* Tampa: Research and Training Center for Children's Mental Health, Department of Epidemiology and Policy Analysis, Florida Mental Health Institute, University of South Florida.

Friedman, R.M. (1991). *Community-based systems of care: A new research opportunity and challenge.* Tampa: Research and Training Center for Children's Mental Health, Department of Epidemiology and Policy Analysis, Florida Mental Health Institute, University of South Florida.

Fuchs, B.C. (1993). *CRS issue brief: Health care reform: Mandated employer-provided coverage.* Washington, DC: Congressional Research Service, Education and Public Welfare Division, The Library of Congress.

Fuchs, B.C., & Merlis, M. (1993a). *CRS issue brief: Health care reform: Tax system approaches.* Washington, DC: Congressional Research Service, Education and Public Welfare Division, The Library of Congress.

Fuchs, B.C., & Merlis, M. (1993b). *CRS report for Congress: Health care reform: President Clinton's Health Security Act.* Washington, DC: Congressional Research Service, Education and Public Welfare Division, The Library of Congress.

Fuchs, V.R. (1991). National health insurance revisited. *Health Affairs, 10*(4), 7–17.

Gorin, S., & Moniz, C. (1992). The national health care crisis: An analysis of proposed solutions. *Health and Social Work, 17*(1), 37–44.

Gortmacher, S.L. (1985). Demography of chronic childhood diseases. In N. Hobbs & J.M. Perrin (Eds.), *Issues in the care of children with chronic illness: A sourcebook on problems, services, and policies.* San Francisco: Jossey-Bass.

Gortmacher, S.L., & Sappenfield, W. (1984). Chronic childhood disorders: Prevalence and impact. *Pediatric Clinics of North America, 31*(1), 3–18.

Great Lakes Hemophilia. (1992). *Health insurance options for persons with hemophilia and HIV/ARC/AIDS.* Milwaukee, WI: Author.

Griss, B. (1988). Measuring the health insurance needs of persons with disabilities and persons with chronic illness. *Access to Health Care, 1*(1–2), 1–64.

Griss, B. (1989). Strategies for adapting the private and public health insurance systems to the health-related needs of persons with disabilities or chronic illness. *Access to Health Care, 1*(3–4), 1–90.

Hall, J., & Dornan, M.C. (1988). What patients like about their medical care and how often they are asked: A meta-analysis of the satisfaction literature. *Social Science and Medicine, 27*(9), 935–939.

Handicapped Children Protection Act of 1986, PL 99-372. (August 5, 1986). Title 20, U.S.C. 1415 et seq.: *U.S. Code Congressional and Administrative News, 1,* 100 Stat, 796–798.

Hanft, B.E. (1991). Impact of federal policy on pediatric health and education programs. In W. Dunn (Ed.), *Pediatric occupational therapy: Facilitating effective service delivery* (pp. 273–284). Thorofare, NJ: Slack.

Harris, L., & Associates. (1986). *Disabled Americans' self perceptions: Bringing disabled Americans into the mainstream.* New York: Author.

Hazel, R., Barber, P.A., Roberts, S., Behr, S.K., Helmstetter, E., & Guess, D. (1988). *A community approach to an integrated service system for children with special needs.* Baltimore, MD: Paul H. Brookes Publishing Co.

Health Insurance Association of America. (1989). *The consumer's guide to health insurance.* Washington, DC: Author.

Health Insurance Association of America. (1990). *Providing employee health benefits: How firms differ.* Washington, DC: Author.

Health Insurance Association of America. (1991). *The consumer's guide to long-term care insurance.* Washington, DC: Author.

Health Insurance Association of America. (1992a). *Group life and health insurance, Part A*. Washington, DC: Author.

Health Insurance Association of America. (1992b). *Group life and health insurance, Part B*. Washington, DC: Author.

Health Insurance Association of America. (1992c). *Group life and health insurance, Part C*. Washington, DC: Author.

HEATH Resource Center. (1989). *Vocational rehabilitation services: A postsecondary student consumer's guide*. Washington, DC: American Council on Education.

HEATH Resource Center. (1991). *Resource directory*. Washington, DC: The American Council on Education.

HEATH Resource Center. (1993). *Financial aid for students with disabilities*. Washington, DC: The American Council on Education.

Hebbler, K.M., Smith, B.J., & Black, T.L. (1991). Federal early childhood special education policy: A model for the improvement of services for children with disabilities. *Exceptional Children, 58*(2), 104–112.

Heiser, N., & Smolkin, S. (1993). *Characteristics of Food Stamp households*. Washington, DC: Food and Nutrition Service, U.S. Department of Agriculture.

Hill, I.T., & Breyel, J.M. (1991). *Caring for kids*. Washington, DC: Center for Policy Research, National Governors' Association.

Holohan, J., & Zedlewski, S. (1991). Expanding Medicaid to cover uninsured Americans. *Health Affairs, 10*(1), 45–61.

Horne, R. (Ed.). (1990). *A parent's guide: Assessing programs for infants, toddlers, and preschoolers with disabilities*. Washington, DC: National Information Center for Children and Youth with Disabilities.

Horowitz, S.M., & Stein, R.E.K. (1990). Health maintenance organizations vs. indemnity insurance for children with chronic illness. *American Journal of Diseases of Childhood, 144*, 581–586.

Idaho State Tax Commission. (1991). *1991 Idaho individual income tax booklet: Forms 40, 40EZ, and 43 instructions.* Boise, ID: Author.

Illinois Department of Revenue. (1991). *1991 IL-1040 instructions: General information.* Springfield, IL: Author.

Indiana Department of Revenue. (1991). *1991 Indiana individual income tax booklet with Forms IT-9 and IT-40ES.* Indianapolis, IN: Author.

Individuals with Disabilities Education Act of 1990 (IDEA), PL 101-476. (October 30, 1990). Title 20. U.S.C. 1401 et seq., 1471 et seq.: *U.S. Code Congressional and Administrative News, 1,* 105 Stat, 1145–1177.

Individuals with Disabilities Education Act Amendments of 1991, PL 102-119. (October 7, 1991). Title 20, U.S.C. 1401 et seq.: *U.S. Code Congressional and Administrative News, 1,* 105 Stat, 587–608.

Inlander, C.B., & Weiner, E. (1993). *Take this book to the hospital with you.* Allentown, PA: People's Medical Society.

Interstate Research Associates, Inc. (1990a). *A parent's guide: Doctors, disabilities, and the family.* Washington, DC: National Information Center for Children and Youth with Disabilities.

Interstate Research Associates, Inc. (1990b). *A parent's guide: To accessing programs for infants, toddlers, and preschoolers with disabilities.* Washington, DC: National Information Center for Children and Youth with Disabilities.

Interstate Research Associates, Inc. (1991). *A parent's guide: To accessing parent groups, community services, and to keeping records.* Washington, DC: National Information Center for Children and Youth with Disabilities.

Ireys, H.T., & Nelson, R.P. (1992). New federal policies for children with special health care needs: Imperatives for pediatricians. *Pediatrics, 90,* 321–327.

Jacobs, P., & McDermott, S. (1989). Family caregiver costs of chronically ill and handicapped children: Method and literature review. *Public Health Reports, 104*(2), 158–163.

Jewish Board of Family and Children's Services. (1992). *Celebrating a century of caring.* New York: Author.

Jones, N.L. (1991). Essential requirements of the act: A short history. *The Milbank Quarterly, 69*(Suppl. 1/2), 25–54.

Kansas Department of Revenue. (1991). *1991 Kansas individual income tax booklet.* Topeka, KS: Author.

Katz-Leavy, J.W., Lourie, I.S., Stroul, B.A., & Zeigler-Dendy, C. (1992). *Individualized services in a system of care.* Washington, DC: CASSP Technical Assistance Center, Center for Child Health and Mental Health Policy, Georgetown University Child Development Center.

Knights of Columbus. (1991). *These men they call knights.* New Haven, CT: Author.

LaPlante, M.P. The demographics of disability. *The Millbank Quarterly, 69*(Supp. 1/2), 55–77.

Larson, G., & Kahn, J.A. (1990). *How to get care for a child with special health needs.* St. Paul, MN: Life Line Press.

Laudicina, S.S., & Lipson, D.J. (1988). *Medicaid and poor children: State variations in eligibility and service coverage.* Washington, DC: Intergovernmental Health Policy Project, George Washington University.

Legal Services Corporation. (1993). *Program directory.* Washington, DC: Author.

Leukemia Society of America. (1991a). *1991 annual report.* New York: Author.

Leukemia Society of America. (1991b). *Patient-aid program.* New York: Author.

Lewin/ICF, Bell, J., & Associates. (1990). *State and local general assistance programs: Issues and changes.* Washington, DC: Authors.

Lewin, L.S., & Lewin, M.E. (1987). Financing charity care in an era of competition. *Health Affairs, 6*(1), 47–60.

Martin, D.A. (1992). Children in peril: A mandate for change in health care policies for low-income children. *Family and Community Health, 15*(1), 75–90.

Mayer, J.D. (1986). International perspectives on the health care crisis in the United States. *Social Science and Medicine, 23*(10), 1059–1065.

McManus, M.A. (1988). *Understanding your health insurance options.* Washington, DC: McManus Health Policy, Inc.

Medicare Q&A. (1991). Washington, DC: U.S. Government Printing Office.

Mental Health Law Project. (1992). *SSI: New opportunities for children with disabilities.* Washington, DC: Author.

Merlis, M. (1993a). *CRS issue brief: Health care reform: Managed competition.* Washington, DC: Congressional Research Service, Education and Public Welfare Division, The Library of Congress.

Merlis, M. (1993b). *CRS issue brief: Health insurance.* Washington, DC: Congressional Research Service, Education and Public Welfare Division, The Library of Congress.

Minnesota Department of Revenue. (1991). *1991 Minnesota individual income tax: Forms and instructions.* St. Paul, MN: Author.

Mississippi State Tax Commission, Bureau of Revenue. (1991). *Mississippi resident individual income tax forms.* Jackson, MS: Author.

Missouri Department of Revenue. (1991). *Missouri individual income tax: Forms and instructions.* Jefferson City, MO: Author.

Moore, C. (1990). *A reader's guide for parents of children with mental, physical, or emotional disabilities.* Rockville, MD: Woodbine House.

Montana Department of Revenue, Income Tax Division. (1991). *1991 Montana individual income tax booklet.* Helena, MT: Author.

Morgenthau, T. (1993, September 20). The Clinton solution. *Newsweek,* pp. 30–35.

Moynihan, J.D., Jr. (1991). Revising the health care system: Over 2,000 opinion leaders speak out. *Statistical Bulletin,* 72(3), 2–9.

Muscular Dystrophy Association. (1990). *MDA services for patient, family and community.* Tucson, AZ: Author.

Muscular Dystrophy Association. (1991). *1991 fact sheet.* Tucson, AZ: Author.

National Advisory Mental Health Council. (1991). Child and adolescent mental disorders. In *Mental illness in America: A series of public hearings* (pp. 17–25). Arlington, VA: The National Alliance for the Mentally Ill.

National Alliance for the Mentally Ill. (1990). *NAMI and you: Partners in hope in the decade of the brain.* Arlington, VA: Author.

National Association of the Deaf. (1992). *National Association of the Deaf.* Silver Spring, MD: Author.

National Association for Sickle Cell Disease, Inc. (1991). *Help!: A guide to sickle cell disease programs and services.* Los Angeles, CA: Author.

National Commission on Children. (1991). *Beyond rhetoric: A new American agenda for children and families.* Washington, DC: Author.

National Early Childhood Technical Assistance System. (1992). *Overview, infants and toddlers with disabilities program of Individuals with Disabilities Education Act (IDEA).* Chapel Hill, NC: Author.

National Easter Seal Society. (1991). *Shaping the future for people with disabilities.* Chicago, IL: Author.

National Flotation Health Care Foundation. (1990). *The National Flotation Health Care Foundation.* Los Angeles, CA: Author.

National Foundation for Consumer Credit. (1991a). *How consumer credit counseling services can assist you.* Silver Spring, MD: Author.

National Foundation for Consumer Credit. (1991b). *Using credit.* Silver Spring, MD: Author.

National Governor's Association. (1992). State coverage of pregnant women and children—January, 1992. *MCH update.* Washington, DC: Health Programs, Center for Policy Research, Author.

National Governor's Center for Policy Research. (1990). *Medicaid home- and community-based waivers as of July 1, 1990.* Washington, DC: Author.

National Health Policy Seminar. (1990). Toward a health care financing strategy for the nation. *Bulletin of the New York Academy of Medicine, 66*(4), 284–292.

Nebraska Department of Revenue. (1991). *1991 Nebraska individual income tax booklet, including: Form 1040N, Schedules I, II, and III, Form DPR, Form 4136N.* Lincoln, NE: Author.

Newacheck, P.W. (1989). Adolescents with special health needs: Prevalence, severity, and access to health services. *Pediatrics, 84*(5), 872–881.

Newacheck, P.W., & McManus, M.A. (1988). Financing health care for disabled children. *Pediatrics, 81*(3), 385–394.

Newacheck, P.W., McManus, M., & Fox, H.B. (1991). Prevalence and impact of chronic illness among adolescents. *American Journal of Diseases of Childhood, 145,* 1367–1373.

Newacheck, P.W., & Taylor, W.R. (1992). Children and chronic illness: Prevalence, severity, and impact. *American Journal of Public Health, 82*(3), 364–371.

New England Serve, Regional Task Force on Health Care Financing. (November, 1993). *Assessing the adequacy of national health care reform proposals: An analysis of the American Health Security Act of 1993* (Draft). Boston, MA: Author.

New York State Department of Taxation and Finance. (1991). *Resident income tax return IT-201-P packet.* New York: Author.

North Carolina Department of Revenue. (1991). *North Carolina 1991.* Raleigh, NC: Author.

Ohio Department of Taxation. (1991). *1991 Ohio income tax return and instructions.* Columbus, OH: Author.

Oklahoma Tax Commission, Income Tax Division. (1991). *1991 Oklahoma individual income tax forms and instructions.* Oklahoma City, OK: Author.

Omenn, G.S. (1987). Lessons from a fourteen-state study of Medicaid. *Health Affairs, 6*(1), 118–122.

Omnibus Budget Reconciliation Act of 1993 (OBRA), PL 103-66. (August 10, 1993). Title 5, U.S.C. 13601. *U.S. Code Congressional and Administrative News, 7,* 107 Stat, 612–613.

Omnibus Budget Reconciliation Act of 1981 (OBRA), PL 97-35. (August 13, 1981). Title 5, U.S.C. 2176. *U.S. Code Congressional and Administrative News, 1,* 95 Stat, 812–813.

Omnibus Budget Reconciliation Act of 1989 (OBRA), PL 101-329. (December 19, 1989). Title 5, U.S.C. 6403. *U.S. Code Congressional and Administrative News, 2,* 103 Stat, 2262–2264.

Omnibus Budget Reconciliation Act of 1990 (OBRA), PL 101-508. (November 5, 1990). Title 5, U.S.C. 4712. *U.S. Code Congressional and Administrative News, 2,* 104 Stat, 1388-187–1388-190.

Oregon Department of Revenue. (1991). *1991 Oregon individual income tax return and instructions: full-year resident form 40 and form 40S.* Salem, OR: Author.

Owen, M.J. (1991). What has the Social Security Administration done for you lately? Maybe more than you know. *Exceptional Parent, 4,* 40–42.

Palfrey, J.S., Mervis, R.C., & Butler, J.A. (1978). New directions in the evaluation and education of handicapped children. *New England Journal of Medicine, 298*(15), 819–824.

Passel, P. (1993, March 21). The dangers of declaring war on doctors. *New York Times,* p. 5.

Pathfinder International Diabetes Center. (1990). The new MCH Block Grant amendments: Challenges and opportunities for the Title V community. *Child Link, 2*(4), 1–2.

Pattee, S. (1990). *Tax deductions.* Bethesda, MD: Cystic Fibrosis Foundation.

Pauly, M.V., Danzon, P., Feldstein, P., & Hoff, J. (1992). A plan for "responsible national health insurance." *Health Affairs, 10*(1), 5–25.

Perrin, E.C., Newacheck, P., Pless, B.I., Drotar, D., Gortmaker, S.I., Leventhal, J., Perrin, J.M., Stein, R.E.K., Walker, D., & Weitzman, M. (1991). Issues involved in the definition and classification of chronic health conditions. *Pediatrics, 91*(4), 787–793.

Perrin, E.C., Sayer, A.G., & Willett, J.B. (1991). Sticks and stones may break my bones . . . Reasoning about illness causality and body functioning in children who have a chronic illness. *Pediatrics, 88*(3), 608–619.

Perrin, J.M., & Ireys, H.T. (1984). The organization of services for chronically ill children and their families. *Pediatric Clinics of North America, 31*(1), 235–257.

Perrin, J.M., Shayne, M.W., & Bloom, S.K. (1993). *The chronically ill child.* New York: Oxford University Press.

Protective Order of Elks of the United States of America. (1991). *Elks National Foundation: Annual report for fiscal year 1990–91.* Chicago, IL: Author.

Rehabilitation Act of 1973, PL 93-112. (September 26, 1973). Title 20, U.S.C. 1475, Title 29, U.S.C. 701 et seq., 702, 706, 720, 732, 741, 750, 761, 762, 771, 772, 774 et seq., 783, 792. *U.S. Code Congressional and Administrative News, 1,* 87 Stat, 409–454.

Rehabilitation Act of 1992, PL 102-569. (October 29, 1992). Title 20, U.S.C. 1475, Title 29, U.S.C. 701 et seq., 702, 706, 720, 732, 741, 750, 761, 762, 771, 772, 774 et seq., 783, 792. *U.S. Code Congressional and Administrative News, 3,* 106 Stat, 4344–4488.

Rich, S. (1993, November 2). What about you? *Washington Post Health,* p. 12. Washington, DC: The Library of Congress, Congressional Research Service.

Ripley, S. (1990). National Information Center for Children and Youth with Handicaps. *Exceptional Parent, 6,* 52–54.

Ripley, S., & Rewers, C. (1991). *A parent's guide to accessing parent groups, community services, and to keeping records.* Washington DC: The National Information Center for Children and Youth with Disabilities.

Robert Wood Johnson Foundation. (1992). *State limitations in health care financing reform.* Princeton, NJ: Author.

Rockefeller, J. (1992). Health care reform: Prospects and progress. *Academic Medicine, 67*(3), 141–145.

Rosenfeld, L. (1990). *Medically fragile children and their families: Special problems, special needs.* Hillsborough, NC: Orange County Department of Social Services.

Rosenfeld, L. (1993). Health insurance: Special health care needs. *Child Times of Alabama, III*(VII), 18–19.

Rosenfeld, L., Worley, G., & Lipscomb, J. (1987). *Saving money and getting help: Advice for families of children with spina bifida and other health problems.* Durham, NC: Spina Bifida Association of North Carolina and Duke University.

Rourk, J.D. (1984). Funding health services for children. *American Journal of Occupational Therapy, 38*(5), 313–319.

Ruritan National. (1990). *This is Ruritan.* Dublin, VA: Author.

Schlesinger, M. (1986). On the limits of expanding health care reform: Chronic care in prepaid settings. *The Milbank Quarterly, 64*(2), 189–215.

Schwartz, J., & Hager, M. (1992, December 14). Start the revolution with me. *Newsweek,* p. 58.

Self Help for Hard of Hearing People, Inc. (1992). *Resources for hearing impaired adults.* Bethesda, MD: Author.

Sex Information and Education Council of the United States. (1992). *Sexuality and the developmentally disabled.* New York: Author.

Shackelford, J. (1993). State/jurisdiction eligibility definitions for Part H. *NEC★TAS Notes, 5,* 1–13.

Shepard's acts and cases by popular names—Federal and state (4th ed.). (1992). Colorado Springs, CO: Shepard/McGraw Hill.

Shrine of North America and Shriners Hospitals for Crippled Children. (1990). *The story of Shriners Hospitals.* Tampa, FL: Author.

Social Security Administration. (1991). *Disability.* Washington, DC: U.S. Government Printing Office.

Social Security Administration. (1992). *SSI: Supplemental security income.* Washington, DC: U.S. Government Printing Office.

Spina Bifida Association of America. (1991). ADA in the workplace. *Insights into Spina Bifida,* 10.

St. Jude Children's Research Hospital. (1991). *ALSAC St. Jude Children's Research Hospital annual report.* Memphis, TN: Author.

Stark, S.L. (1989). *Health insurance made easy . . . finally.* Shawnee Mission, KS: Stark Publishing.

Starr, P. (1982). *The social transformation of American medicine.* New York: Basic Books.

State Department of Education, Division of Rehabilitation Services. (1992). *Adult vocational rehabilitation service: It's working.* Montgomery, AL: Author.

State of Arkansas, State Income Tax. (1991). *Arkansas 1991 individual income tax booklet.* Little Rock, AR: Author.

State of California, Franchise Tax Board. (1991). *California 1991 resident income tax booklet: Forms and instructions.* Sacramento, CA: Author.

State of Colorado, Department of Revenue. (1991a). *Colorado 1991 income tax: 104-long form, forms and instructions.* Denver, CO: Author.

State of Colorado, Department of Revenue. (1991b). *1991 Colorado property tax/rent/heat rebate: Form 104 PTC and instructions.* Denver, CO: Author.

State of Connecticut, Department of Revenue Services. (1991). *CT-1040/CT-1040EZ: Connecticut resident income tax forms and instructions.* Hartford, CT: Author.

State of Georgia, Department of Revenue, Income Tax Division. (1991). *Georgia income tax: Forms 500 EZ and 500 for 1991.* Atlanta, GA: Author.

State of Hawaii, Department of Taxation. (1991). *1991 Form N-12: Hawaii resident income tax forms and instructions.* Honolulu, HI: Author.

State of Iowa, Department of Revenue. (1991). *1991 IA 1040: IA schedules A and B, IA 126, IA 130.* Des Moines, IA: Author.

State of Louisiana, Department of Revenue and Taxation. (1991). *1991 Louisiana income tax return.* Baton Rouge, LA: Author.

State of Michigan, Department of Treasury. (1991). *1991 Michigan income tax returns and homestead property tax credit claims.* Lansing, MI: Author.

State of New Jersey, Department of the Treasury, Division of Taxation. (1991). *New Jersey gross income tax resident return NJ-1040 and homestead property tax rebate application, HR-1040.* Newark, NJ: Author.

State of North Dakota, Office of State Tax Commissioner. (1991). *North Dakota individual income tax form 37-S and form 37.* Bismarck, ND: Author.

State of South Carolina, South Carolina Tax Commission. (1991). *1991 resident personal income tax returns.* Columbia, SC: Author.

State of Vermont, Department of Taxes. (1991). *1991 Vermont income tax return.* Montpelier, VT: Author.

State of Wisconsin, Department of Revenue. (1991a). *Wisconsin income tax form 1 and instructions.* Madison, WI: Author.

State of Wisconsin, Department of Revenue. (1991b). *Wisconsin income tax form 1A and WI-Z and instructions.* Madison, WI: Author.

State of Wisconsin, Department of Revenue. (1991c). *Wisconsin income tax form 1NPR and instructions.* Madison, WI: Author.

Statistical Abstracts of the United States. (1992). Washington, DC: U.S. Government Printing Office.

Stout, H. (1993, March 11). Medical maze: Health-care experts devising Clinton plan face sticky questions. *The Wall Street Journal,* p. 1.

Stout, N.L., & Davie, A. (1989). *Vocational rehabilitation services: A postsecondary student consumer's guide.* Washington, DC: U.S. Government Printing Office.

Sullivan v. Zebley. (1990). 4 93 U.S. 521.

Support Dogs, Inc. (1990). *Support Dogs, Inc.: Opening doors to independence.* St. Louis, MO: Author.

Supreme Council, Grottoes of North America, M-O-V-P-E-R. (1989). *Dentistry for the handicapped.* Columbus, OH: Author.

Talbott, J.A. (1985). An insurance executive looks at changing patterns of health care. *Hospital and Community Psychiatry, 36*(2), 160–164.

Tavani, C. (1991). Report on a seminar on financing and service delivery issues in caring for the medically underserved. *Public Health Reports, 106*(1), 19–23.

Taxation and Revenue Department. (1991a). *1991 New Mexico personal income tax PIT-1 long form packet.* Santa Fe, NM: Author.

Taxation and Revenue Department. (1991b). *1991 New Mexico personal income tax PIT-B form packet.* Santa Fe, NM: Author.

Taxation and Revenue Department. (1991c). *1991 New Mexico personal income tax PIT-1A short form packet.* Santa Fe, NM: Author.

Tax Equity and Fiscal Responsibility Act of 1982 (TEFRA), PL 97-248. (September 3, 1982). Title 42, U.S.C. 134. *U.S. Code Congressional and Administrative News,* 1, 96 Stat, 375.

Technology-Related Assistance for Individuals with Disabilities Act of 1988 ("Tech Act"), PL 100-407. (August 19, 1988). Title 42, U.S.C. 2201, 2203, 2211 et seq., 2231, 2241 et seq., 2251 et seq., 2261, 2271. *U.S. Code Congressional and Administrative News,* 1, 102 Stat, 1044–1065.

Tennessee Department of Revenue. (1991). *State of Tennessee 1991 income tax forms.* Nashville, TN: Author.

Tetrick, A.P. (1989). *Medical insurance policy scrutiny: Guidelines for families with a chronic disease.* Worcester, MA: New England Hemophilia Center.

The Arc. (1992). *Introduction to The Arc.* Arlington, TX: Author.

Travelers Aid International. (1991). *Travelers Aid International: 1990–1991 annual report.* Washington, DC: Author.

Trohanis, P. (1992). *A brief introduction of the Individuals with Disabilities Education Act (IDEA) Amendments of 1991, P.L. 102-119 (formerly P.L. 99-457).* Chapel Hill, NC: National Early Childhood Technical Assistance System (NEC★TAS).

United Cerebral Palsy Association, Inc. (1991). *Every minute of the day . . . one person at a time: 1991 annual report.* New York: Author.

United Methodist Association of Health and Welfare Ministries. (1991). *1991 annual report: Preparing leadership for change.* Dayton, OH: Author.

United Way of America. (1992). *Directory of United Way affiliated information and referral services.* Alexandria, VA: Author.

United Way of America. (1992). *Where to call for help: A nationwide directory of United Way information and referral services.* Alexandria, VA: Author.

University of Alabama at Birmingham. (1992). Benevolent fund comes through in tough times. *Report, XVI*(18,1).

U.S. Advisory Commission on Intergovernmental Relations. (1991a). State individual income taxes: Table 18: Summary of personal exemptions, standard deductions, and deductibility of federal income taxes, 1991. *State Tax Guide.* Chicago, IL: Commerce Clearing House.

U.S. Advisory Commission on Intergovernmental Relations. (1991b). Table 21: State individual income taxes, itemized deductions, 1991. *State Tax Reporter.* Chicago, IL: Commerce Clearing House.

U.S. Department of Agriculture. (1992). *Food program facts.* Washington, DC: Author.

U.S. Department of Education. (1992). *Annual report to the President and to the Congress, fiscal year 1991, on federal activities related to the Rehabilitation Act of 1973 as amended.* Washington, DC: Author.

U.S. Department of Health and Human Services, Administration for Children and Families, Office of Family Assistance. (1990). *Quarterly Public Assistance Statistics: Fiscal Year 1990.* Washington, DC: Author.

U.S. Department of Health and Human Services, Administration for Children and Families, Office of Family Assistance. (1992). *Characteristics of state plans for Aid to Families with Dependent Children.* Washington, DC: Author.

U.S. Department of Health and Human Services, Health Care Financing Administration. (1991). *Medicare Q and A.* Washington, DC: U.S. Government Printing Office.

U.S. Department of Health and Human Services, Health Care Financing Administration. (1992). *Medicare coverage of kidney dialysis and kidney transplant services.* Washington, DC: U.S. Government Printing Office.

U.S. Department of Health and Human Services, Health Care Financing Administration Intergovernmental Affairs Office, Medicaid Bureau. (1992). *Medicaid services state by state* (HCFA Pub. No. 02155-93). Washington, DC: Author.

U.S. Department of Health and Human Services, Public Health Service, Health Resources and Services Administration. (1992). *FREE hospital care, nursing home care, and care provided in other types of health facilities under the Hill-Burton Program.* Washington, DC: Author.

U.S. Department of Health and Human Services, Social Security Administration. (1991). *Medicare.* Washington, DC: U.S. Government Printing Office.

U.S. Department of Labor, Pension and Welfare Benefits Administration. (1990). *Health benefits under the Consolidated Omnibus Budget Reconciliation Act.* Washington, DC: Author.

U.S. General Accounting Office. (1988). *Briefing report to the Committee on Labor and Human Resources, U.S. Senate, Health insurance "risk pools" for the medically uninsurable.* Washington, DC: Author.

U.S. Office of Consumer Affairs. (1992). *Consumer resource handbook.* Washington, DC: Author.

U.S. Senate. (1989, August 30). *The Americans with Disabilities Act of 1989: Report from the Committee on Labor and Human Resources.* Washington, DC: U.S. Government Printing Office.

U.S. Statutes at Large. Washington, DC: U.S. Government Printing Office.

Utah State Tax Commission. (1991). *1991 Utah booklet L individual income tax forms and instructions.* Salt Lake City, UT: Author.

Venture Clubs of the Americas. (1990). *Venture clubs of the Americas: A service organization for young professional women.* Philadelphia, PA: Author.

Vohs, J. (1988). *What families need to know about case management.* Boston, MA: Federation for Children with Special Needs.

Voting Accessibility for the Elderly and Handicapped Act, PL 98-435. (September 28, 1984). Title 42, U.S.C. 1973 et seq.: *U.S. Code Congressional and Administrative News, 1,* 98 Stat, 1678–1680.

Waid, M.O. (1991). *Medicaid: A brief summary of Title XIX of the Social Security Act.* Baltimore, MD: Health Care Financing Administration.

Washington Post Company. (1993, December 2). "Basic benefits you would get." *Washington Post Health.* p. 7. Washington, DC: The Library of Congress, Congressional Research Service.

Wells, N. (1989). *Understanding Medicaid coverage.* Boston, MA: Collaboration Among Parents and Health Professionals (CAPP) Project/National Parent Resource Center.

Wells, N. (1989). *Information on federal and state initiatives in health care financing and resources for further information.* Boston, MA: Collaboration Among Parents and Health Professionals (CAPP) Project/National Parent Resource Center.

Wells, N., & Anderson, B. (1988). *Health care financing: Issues, options, and strategies.* Boston, MA: Collaboration Among Parents and Health Professionals (CAPP) Project/National Parent Resource Center.

West, J. (1991a). Introduction—Implementing the act: Where we begin. *Milbank Quarterly, 60*(Supp. 1/2), xi–xxxi.

West, J. (1991b). The social and policy context of the act. *Milbank Quarterly, 69*(Supp. 1/2), 3–24.

Wilensky, G..R. (1987). Viable strategies for dealing with the uninsured. *Health Affairs, 6*(1), 33–46.

Williams, B., Simpson, J., & Bergman, A. (1991). Special report: Agencies issue ADA final regs. *United Cerebral Palsy Associations Special Report*, 1–11.

Worley, G., Rosenfeld, L., & Lipscomb, J. (1991). Financial counseling for families of children with chronic disabilities. *Developmental Medicine and Child Neurology, 33*, 679–689.

Index

Page numbers followed by "f" indicate figures; those followed by "t" indicate tables.

AbleNet, 471
Access to public and private facilities, 26–30
ACCH, *see* Association for the Care of Children's Health
Accidental injuries, 3
Activities and recreation services, 76
ADA, *see* Americans with Disabilities Act of 1990
Advocacy services, 6, 77–78, 104, 312, 368–378
  advocacy and *advocate* defined, 479
  Developmental Disabilities (DD) Planning Councils, 90, 378
  disease- and disability-related organizations, 48, 368–371
  need for continuation of, 339–340
  parent advocacy groups, 82–84, 512
  Parent Training and Information (PTI) Centers, 12, 13, 19–20, 45, 84–85, 124, 378, 512
  Protection and Advocacy (P & A) Agencies, 13, 34, 45, 77, 371–378, 470, 512, 516
  results of, 337–339
  role in health care reform, 346
  self-advocacy, 519
  Technical Assistance to Parents Programs (TAPPs), 20

AFDC, *see* Aid to Families with Dependent Children
Agricultural Extension Service, 9, 311, 379, 479–480
Aid Association for Lutherans, 223–224
Aid to Families with Dependent Children (AFDC), 9, 63, 110, 238, 256–258, 341, 415, 479, 480
  applying for, 258
  benefits available under, 256–257
  eligibility for, 257–258
  funding for, 256
  "need standard" for, 479
AIDS Hotline, 471
Air Carrier's Access Act of 1986, 34
American Association of University Affiliated Programs for Persons with Developmental Disabilities, 468
American Council of the Blind, 207–208, 368
American Foundation for the Blind, 208, 368
American Friends Service Committee, 224
American Health Security Act, 340–343
American Heart Association, 208, 368

American Juvenile Arthritis Organization, 208–209, 368
American Lung Association, 209, 368
American Lupus Society, 209, 368
American Red Cross, 224–225
American Society for Deaf Children, 210, 369
Americans with Disabilities Act (ADA) of 1990, 27–30, 68
  definition of person with disability, 27
    mental impairment, 28
    physical impairment, 27–28
  provisions on employment, 28–29
  provisions on public accommodations and services offered by private entities, 29
  provisions on public services, 29
  provisions on telecommunications, 29–30
  "reasonable accommodation" provision of, 517
  "undue hardship" provision of, 30, 526–527
Antidiscrimination laws, 35–37
Apple Computers, Office for Special Education Material, 471
Architectural and Transportation Barriers Compliance Board, 471
Assertiveness, 7, 331
Association for the Care of Children's Health (ACCH), 88–89, 368, 479, 480
Association of Jewish Family and Children's Agencies, Inc., 225
Association of Junior Leagues International, Inc., 225
Asthma, 3
Asthma and Allergy Foundation of America, 210, 369
AT&T Accessible Communications Products Center, 471
Autism, 3, 14
Autism Society of America, 211, 369

Auxiliary aids and services, 29, 102, 480–481
Availability of services, 1–2

Baptist Church, 202
Basic coverage plans, 171–172, 481
Becoming informed, 329–330
  about community services, 48, 94
  about laws and regulations, 12–15
  sources for, 6–7, 48, 78–91
Behavior management, 481
Bill collectors, 9, 99, 314–315, 481
Birth disorders, 21
Blindness, 3, 40
Blue Cross and Blue Shield, 8, 61, 165, 196
Budgeting, 9, 307–312, 495
Burns, 3

CAAs, see Community Action Agencies
Candlelighters Childhood Cancer Foundation, 211, 369
CAP, see Client Assistance Programs
Capitol Hill Switchboard, 472
Care coordination, see Service coordination
Caring Programs for Children, 195–196, 412–415, 482
Case management, see Service coordination
Categorically Needy Program of Medicaid, 108, 112, 482
Catholic Charities, U.S.A., 202–203, 226
CCCS, see Consumer Credit Counseling Service
CCEOs, see County Commissions for Economic Opportunity
Center for Rehabilitation, 472
Centers for Disease Control, National AIDS Hotline, 471
Centers for Independent Living, 466–468
Cerebral palsy, 3, 40

CH.A.D.D., *see* Children and Adults with Attention Deficit Disorders

CHAMPUS, *see* Civilian Health and Medical Program of the Uniformed Services

Charitable contributions, 270–271, 484

CHCs, *see* Community Health Centers

Child and Dependent Care expenses, 256–257
  federal tax credit for, 272, 484

Child Find, 17, 22, 26, 58, 101–102, 470, 484–485

Child Support Enforcement, 472

Children and Adults with Attention Deficit Disorders (CH.A.D.D.), 211–212, 369

Children's Defense Fund, 485

Children's Hospice International, 472

Children's Special Health Care Needs (CSHCN) Program, 51, 52, 62, 86, 108, 126–129, 485, 489
  eligibility for, 128–129
  funding for, 126–127
  learning about, 129
  services offered in, 127–128
  state agencies for, 436–442, 452

Chromosomal disorders, 21

Chronic illness or disability
  definitions of, 485, 491
  jobs that accompany care of child with, 5–8
  number of children with, 2

Church-sponsored ministries, 201–205, 251–252, 311, 413, 485

Civic organizations, 192, 199–200, 223–235, 413, 485

Civil Rights Act of 1991, 41

Civilian Health and Medical Program of the Uniformed Services (CHAMPUS), 4, 62, 108, 133–143, 450, 482, 485–486
  appealing decisions of, 142–143
  cost for participation in, 137–139
    inpatient services, 138–139
    outpatient services, 137–138
  cost share under, 482–483
  eligibility for, 133–134
  Exceptional Family Members Program, 137, 494
  filing claims under, 139
  General Program of, 483
  Handbook for, 483
  Health Benefits Advisor (HBA) for, 483
  non-availability of service statement for, 483
  Program for the Handicapped, 134, 139–142, 483–484
    applying for, 140–141
    costs to enroll in, 142
    eligibility for, 140–141
    filing claims under, 141–142
  services covered under, 134–136
  services not covered under, 136–137

Civitan World Headquarters, 226

Cleft Palate Foundation, 212, 369

Client Assistance Programs (CAP), 400–406

Clinton, President Bill, 476
  health care reform proposal, 340–343

CMHCs, *see* Community Mental Health Centers

Collection agencies, 9, 99

College education, 68–69, 500

Communicating for Agriculture, 193, 451

Community Action Agencies (CAAs), 62, 109, 157–158, 260–261, 406–413, 482

Community Health Centers (CHCs), 109, 155–156

Community Mental Health Centers (CMHCs), 76, 109, 155–157, 466, 486

Community Service Block Grant Agencies, 406–413

Community Supported Living Arrangements (CSLA), 34, 72, 486–487, 489

Complaint procedure, 487
Congressional Almanac Quarterly,
    13
*Congressional Quarterly Weekly
    Report*, 13
Consumer Credit Counseling Ser-
    vice (CCCS), 9, 311, 482,
    487
Consumer Credit Protection Act
    Amendments, 314, 477
Cooperative Extension Service,
    311, 488
Coordination of services, *see* Ser-
    vice coordination
Costs of health care, 4–5
    arranging payment plans for,
        186, 313, 330–331, 513
    assistance paying for, 60–63; *see
        also* Paying for medical care
    income tax deductions for
        federal, 265–269
        state, 275–277, 281–306
    insurance coverage for, 4, 60–61,
        164–195
    knowing in advance about, 97,
        98
    negotiating fees for, 8, 61, 185,
        313
    out-of-pocket, 4–5, 185–186,
        511
    ways to pay for, 8; *see also* Pay-
        ing for medical care
Council for Health and Human
    Service Ministries, 226–227
Counseling services, 6, 59–60
County Commissions for Econom-
    ic Opportunity (CCEOs), 62,
    109, 157–158, 260–261,
    406–413, 482, 488
Court rulings, 13
Credit reports, 312
Crippled Children's Program, *see*
    Children's Special Health
    Care Needs Program
Crisis services, 24, 255, 470, 489
Crohn's and Colitis Foundation of
    America, Inc., 212, 369
CSHCN, *see* Children's Special
    Health Care Needs Pro-
    gram

CSLA, *see* Community Supported
    Living Arrangements
Cystic Fibrosis Foundation, 213,
    369

DD Planning Councils, *see* Devel-
    opmental Disabilities Plan-
    ning Councils
Deafness, 3, 40
Debt management, 307–315, 379;
    see also Financial assis-
    tance; Paying for medical
    care
    arranging payment plans, 186,
        313, 330–331, 513
    budgeting and spending care-
        fully, 307–312, 495–496
    sample budget, 308*f*
    sample expense record,
        309*f*–310*f*
    services to help with, 311–312
    dealing with bill collectors, 9,
        99, 314–315, 481
    enrolling in public assistance
        programs, 313
    examining options for, 330–331
    negotiating with health care pro-
        viders, 8, 61, 185, 313
    seeking appropriate services at
        lowest cost, 312
    seeking help from private organi-
        zations, 314
DECs, *see* Developmental Evalua-
    tion Centers
Delivery of services, 47
Department of Developmental
    Disabilities, 87
Department of Labor, 191, 451
Department of Mental Health,
    87–88
Departments of Developmental
    Disabilities, 452–458,
    523–524
Departments of Education, 522
Departments of Human Re-
    sources/Social Services, 252,
    488
Departments of Insurance, 101,
    188, 423–429, 522–523

Departments of Mental Health, Children and Youth Services, 458–465, 524
Departments of Revenue, 264, 277, 279, 418–423, 523
Developmental delay
children at risk for, 21–22, 64, 480
children with high probability of, 21, 528
definition of, 490
education for children with, 20–23, 64–65
Developmental Disabilities Assistance and Bill of Rights Act of 1975, 34
Developmental Disabilities (DD) Planning Councils, 90, 378, 469, 490
Developmental Evaluation Centers (DECs), 489, 490
Developmental screenings, 53–54, 118–119, 120*f*–121*f*
Developmental services, 54–55
Diabetes, 2, 3, 40
Diagnosis and evaluation, 50–54
developmental, 53–54
emotional and behavioral, 52
physical, 50–51
Disability
definition of, 491
identification of children with, 17, 26, 57–58, 101–102
"permanently and totally disabled," 275, 513–514
Disability law, 491
Discrimination, 7
laws against, 35–37
Disease- and disability-related organizations, 48, 85–86, 196–198, 207–222, 255, 368–371, 469–470, 491
Down syndrome, 3, 21, 40

Early and Periodic Screening, Diagnosis, and Treatment (EPSDT) Program, 30–32, 51, 62, 108, 113, 118–119, 120*f*–121*f*, 338, 340, 492, 494

Early Education Programs for Children with Disabilities (EEPCD), 25, 491, 493
Early Intervention Program for Infants and Toddlers with Disabilities, 21
Early intervention services, 20–23, 64–65, 131–132, 491–492
lead agencies for administration of, 65, 380–386, 503–504
state central directory of, 23, 65
see also Part B programs; Part H programs
Earned Income Credit (EIC), 273–275, 492–493
Education for All Handicapped Children Act of 1975, 16–19, 493
Education of the Handicapped Act Amendments
of 1983, 16, 19–20
of 1986, 16, 20–24
of 1990, 17, 24, 493; *see also* Individuals with Disabilities Education Act (IDEA)
Education services, 64–70, 129–132
early intervention programs, 20–23, 64–65, 131–132, 491–492; *see also* Part H programs
Head Start, 67, 498–499
higher education, 68–70, 500
home teaching, 3, 67–68, 500
in-hospital teaching, 68, 502
laws and regulations on, 16–26, 64
problems getting compliance with, 103–104
least restrictive environment for, 130, 504
for life skills/job training and placement, 73–74, 504
local education agencies, 129–132, 505
Part B programs (3 through 5, 6 through 21), 20, 65–66, 108, 132
Part H programs (birth through 3), 20–23, 64–65, 86–87, 108, 131–132

Education services—*continued*
  lead agencies for, 380–386,
    503–504
  preschool programs, 18, 20,
    65–66; *see also* Part B pro-
    grams
  related aids and services,
    517–518
  school-age services, 66–67, 519
  special services, 522
  waiting lists for, 103
  what to expect from teachers,
    principal, and school dis-
    trict, 101–104
  auxiliary aids and services,
    102, 480–481
  free, appropriate public educa-
    tion, 102, 130, 498
  identification of children with
    disabilities, 101–102
  individualized education pro-
    gram (IEP), 15, 18–19, 25,
    66, 101, 102, 501
  individualized family service
    plan (IFSP), 15, 22–25, 65,
    66, 101, 102, 501
EEPCD, *see* Early Education Pro-
    grams for Children with
    Disabilities
EIC, *see* Earned Income Credit
Eligibility determination, 494; *see
    also specific programs*
Elks National Foundation, 227
Emergency assistance programs,
    62, 64, 109, 152–153, 237,
    250–255, 494
  crisis services, 24, 255, 470
  disease- and disability-related
    organizations, 196–198,
    207–222, 255, 368–371,
    469–470
  General Assistance (GA) pro-
    grams, 64, 253–254, 416
  kinds of help available under,
    152, 250–251
  local Departments of Human Re-
    sources/Social Services, 252
  ministries and churches,
    201–205, 251–252, 413
  requesting help from, 152–153

Emotional, behavior, and mental
    disorders, 3
  diagnosis and evaluation of, 52
  intervention and treatment ser-
    vices for, 55–56
  Community Mental Health
    Centers (CMHCs), 76,
    156–157
Employment
  Americans with Disabilities Act
    (ADA) provisions on, 28
  difficulty gaining access to,
    28–29
  Family and Medical Leave Act of
    1993 and, 41–42, 495
  health insurance available
    through, 164–166, 180–182
  health insurance coverage after
    termination of, 190–192
  income of persons with disabil-
    ities, 28–29
  job security protection, 41–42
  in sheltered workshops, 520
  supported, 525
  vocational rehabilitation (VR)
    services, 36–37, 45, 63,
    69–70, 74–76
Empowerment, 6
Entitlement, 16–35, 494; *see also*
    Legal rights
Epilepsy Foundation of America,
    213, 369
Episcopal Church, 203
EPSDT Program, *see* Early and Pe-
    riodic Screening, Diagnosis,
    and Treatment Program
Evidence of insurability, 173–174,
    192, 494
Exceptional Parent, 277

Fair Debt Collection Practices Act
    Amendments of 1986, 314,
    495
Fair Housing Act Amendments of
    1988, 34
Family
  counseling services for, 59–60
  information to keep readily
    available about, 323–324

involvement in health care, 3–4
jobs that accompany care of
   child by, 5–8
"natural helpers" and, 10
privacy of, 58
role in health care reform, 346
support groups for, 6, 496
uncertainties of, 5
Family and Medical Leave Act of
   1993, 41–42, 495
Family Pharmaceuticals of America, 472
Family Voices, 84, 368
FCSN, *see* Federation for Children
   with Special Needs
Federal Information Center (FIC),
   472–474
Federal laws, 12
obtaining copies of, 12, 35
summaries of, 13, 344
see also Legal rights
Federal Trade Commission (FTC),
   315, 379, 496
Federation for Children with Special Needs (FCSN), 33,
   82–83, 123, 368, 496
Federation of Families for Children's Mental Health, 83,
   123, 214, 368, 369, 496
Fee-for-service plans, 167, 168*t*,
   170–174, 496–497
advantages and disadvantages of,
   177–178
basic coverage plans, 171–172,
   481
costs of, 177–178
"evidence of insurability" and
   "pre-existing condition" exclusion clauses, 173–174,
   177, 494, 514
major medical plans, 172–173,
   505
Fetal alcohol syndrome, 21
FIC, *see* Federal Information Center
Financial assistance, 4, 7, 9,
   405–424
for college students with disabilities, 68
for medical care, 60–63; *see also*
   Paying for medical care

private sources of help, 61–62,
   163–206
public sources of help, 62–63,
   107–162
requirements for receiving,
   107–108
for other necessities of life,
   63–64
other sources of help, 237–261
   Aid to Families with Dependent Children (AFDC), 63,
      256–258
   emergency and temporary
      cash assistance, 152–153,
      250–255
   food distribution programs, 63,
      260–261, 416–418
   Food Stamp Program, 63, 259
   Special Supplemental Food
      Program for Women, Infants, and Children (WIC),
      63, 259–260
   Supplemental Security Income
      (SSI), 38–41, 238–250
for transportation services,
   58–59
see also Debt management
504 Accommodation Plan, 17
Food and Nutrition Service,
   416–417
Food distribution programs, 9, 63,
   238, 260–261, 416–418,
   525–526
Food Stamp Program, 9, 63, 238,
   259, 497
Foster homes, 70–71, 497
Free, appropriate public education,
   102, 130, 497
FTC, *see* Federal Trade Commission
Fund-raising groups, 199–200

GA programs, *see* General Assistance programs
General Assistance—Medical
   (GA–Medical) programs, 62,
   109, 149–151, 416, 498
applying for coverage under, 151
eligibility for, 150
services covered under, 150–151

General Assistance (GA) programs, 64, 253–254, 416, 498
  additional benefits of, 254
  applying for, 254
  cash available from, 253
  eligibility for, 254
  states without, 253
Genetic disorders, 21
Getting what you need, 327–335
Goals of book, 8–10
Grief, 5–6
Grottoes of North America, 199, 228
Group homes, 71, 498
Guardians, 498

Handicapped Children's Protection Act of 1986, 37, 498
Head injury, 3, 40
Head Injury Foundation, 6
Head Start, 67, 498–499
Health care, 54
  cost of, 4–5, 107
  evaluating quality of, 94
  family involvement in, 3–4
  paying for, 60–63; see also Paying for medical care
  preventative and routine services for, 56–57
  special needs for, 2–3
  see also Costs of health care
Health care reform, 109, 163–164, 171, 279, 340–345
  Clinton proposal for, 340–343
  evaluating proposals for, 343–345
  other proposals for, 343
  role of families and advocates in, 346
Health departments, 499
Health insurance, 3, 4, 8, 60–61, 164–195
  after job termination or resignation, 190–192
  appealing claims denied by company, 100, 188–190, 480
  available through employment, 164–166, 180–182
  "certificate" of, 167, 184, 516
  under Clinton health care reform proposal, 341–343
  co-payments with, 164, 172, 488
  comparison of options for, 177–180
  concerns for family of child with chronic illness or disability, 180–188
  conversion privilege for, 183, 191–192, 487–488
  coverage for adult children with disabilities, 182–183, 490
  covered services under, 488
  deciding between available plans for, 167–170, 168t-170t
  deductibles and, 489
  dependent care coverage under, 489–490
  exclusions from coverage under, 164, 495
  extent of coverage by, 165
  fee-for-service plans, 167, 168t, 170–174
  filing claims, 100
  individual versus family coverage, 180–181, 500–501
  lack of, 4, 154
  lifetime limitations on coverage, 183–184, 505
  making full use of policy, 166
  managed care plans, 167, 169t-170t, 174–177, 506
  for newborn infant, 180–181, 500–501
  obtained through unions, professional associations, fraternal organizations, and civic organizations, 192
  obtaining reimbursement, 101
  open enrollment period for, 174, 511
  payment for medically necessary services, 508–509
  payment of "usual and customary rates (UCR)," 164, 172, 527
  premiums for, 515
    income tax deduction for, 266, 269–270
    payroll deductions for, 181

primary and secondary policies, 100, 515, 519
private, 164–195, 516
"risk pools," 193–195, 518
self-insured plans, 165, 519–520
small group plans, 193
sources of, 163, 192–195
specialized individual plans, 194–195
state Departments of Insurance, 101, 188, 423–429, 522–523
"stop-loss clause" for, 525
third-party administrator (TPA) for, 526
waiting period for, 527
what to expect from company or plan, 99–101
Health maintenance organizations (HMOs), 165, 169*t*, 174–176, 499, 500
advantages of, 178–179
costs of, 179
relationship with primary care physician in, 187
see also Managed care plans
Hearing Aid Helpline, 474
Hearing Ear Dogs, 475
HEATH (Higher Education and Adult Training for People with Disabilities) Resource Center, 68–69, 81–82, 417, 499–500
Higher Education and Adult Training for People with Disabilities, *see* HEATH Resource Center
Hill-Burton Free Care Program, 109, 161–162
Hill-Burton hotline, 161–162, 412
HIV, *see* human immunodeficiency virus
HMOs, *see* Health maintenance organizations
Home- and Community-Based Care 2176 Waivers, 32–33, 108, 114, 116–118, 329, 508
Home- and community-based family-centered care, 500
Home-based teaching, 3, 67–68, 500

Hospitals
admitting privileges for, 479
education services for children in, 68, 502
paying bills from, 98–99
public, 154–155, 517
services available at, 154
using for routine health care, 155
Special Programs Office of, 521–522
what to expect from employees of, 97–99
business office personnel, 98–99
hospital staff, 98
Housing and residential services, 70–73
Community Supported Living Arrangements (CSLA), 34, 72, 486–487, 489
foster homes and specialized home care, 70–71, 497
group homes, 71, 498
other residential placements, 72–73
supervised apartments, 72, 525
Human immunodeficiency virus (HIV) infection, 40

ICCs, *see* Interagency Coordinating Councils
IDEA, *see* Individuals with Disabilities Education Act
Identification of children with disabilities, 17, 26, 57–58, 101–102
IEP, *see* Individualized education program
IFSP, *see* Individualized family service plan
IFA, *see* Individualized functional assessment
IWRP, *see* Individualized written rehabilitation plan
Immunizations, 153
Inborn errors of metabolism, 21
Inclusion in community, 500

Income
  adjusted gross (AGI), 266, 479
  earned, 492
  unearned, 527
Income tax, *see* Tax savings
Independent Living Centers, 74,
  500
Individualized education program
  (IEP), 15, 18–19, 25, 66, 101,
  102, 130, 501
Individualized family service plan
  (IFSP), 15, 22–25, 65, 66,
  101, 102, 501
Individualized functional assessment (IFA), 501
Individualized written rehabilitation plan (IWRP), 501–502
Individuals with Disabilities Education Act (IDEA), 14, 15,
  24–26, 57, 84, 101, 129–132
  definition of children with dis-
    abilities, 24
  obtaining information about pro-
    visions of, 131, 132
  Part B programs (3 through 5, 6
    through 21) under, 20,
    65–66, 108, 132
  Part H programs (birth through
    3) under, 20–23, 64–65,
    86–87, 108, 131–132
Individuals with Disabilities Education Act (IDEA) Amendments of 1991, 14, 17
Infant stimulation, 502
Information and referral (I&R) services, 6–7, 48, 78–91, 95,
  502, 517
  clearinghouses, 79–82, 502
    HEATH Resource Center,
      68–69, 81–82, 417, 499–500
    National Center for Education
      and Maternal and Child
      Health, 80, 470
    National Center for Youth
      with Disabilities (NCYD),
      81
    National Information Center
      for Children and Youth with
      Disabilities (NICHCY),
      79–80, 85–86, 469, 510

    National Information Clear-
      inghouse (NIC) for Infants
      with Disabilities and
      Life-Threatening Condi-
      tions, 80–81, 469
  disease- and disability-related or-
    ganizations, 48, 85–86,
    196–198, 207–222, 255,
    368–371, 469–470, 491
  national parent organizations,
    82–84
    Family Voices, 84, 368
    Federation for Children with
      Special Needs (FCSN), 33,
      82–83, 123, 368, 496
    Federation of Families for
      Children's Mental Health,
      83, 123, 214, 368, 369, 496
    National Parent Network on
      Disability (NPND), 83–84,
      123, 368, 510–511
  other organizations, 88–91
    Association for the Care of
      Children's Health (ACCH),
      88–89, 368, 480
    Developmental Disabilities
      (DD) Planning Councils,
      90–91, 378, 469, 490
    NEC*TAS, 89, 470, 510
    University Affiliated Programs
      (UAPs), 49, 51, 52, 89–90,
      468, 527
  Parent Training and Information
    (PTIs) Centers, 12, 13, 19,
    84–85, 104, 124, 378, 393, 512
  state government offices, 86–88,
    87
Intensive care nursery, 2, 6
Interagency Coordinating Councils
  (ICCs), 22, 502–503
Internal Revenue Service (IRS),
  264, 268–269, 272, 275, 278,
  417; *see also* Tax savings
International Association of Lions
  Clubs, 228–229
International Sunshine Society,
  229
I&R services, *see* Information and
  referral services
IRS, *see* Internal Revenue Service

Jewish organizations, 203–204, 225
Job Accommodation Network, 475
Job training, *see* Vocational Rehabilitation (VR) services
Jobs, *see* Employment
Judge David L. Bazelon Center for Mental Health Law, 38, 45, 77, 249, 367, 371, 470–471, 481
Judges' opinions, 13
Juvenile Diabetes Foundation International, 214, 369

Katie Beckett Waiver Program, 114, 328–329; *see also* Medicaid Optional eligibility groups
Kidney Commissions, 148
Kidney dialysis and transplant services under Medicare, 8, 40, 62, 108, 143–149, 503
  obtaining information about, 148–149
  Part A coverage, 143, 144*t*, 146
  Part B coverage, 145*t*, 146–147
  services not covered, 148
Kiwanis International, 229
Knights of Columbus, 229–230

Learning Disability Association of America, 214, 369
Least restrictive environment (LRE), 130, 504, 505
Legal Aid, *see* Legal Services Corporation
Legal rights, 11–45
  access to miscellaneous services, rights, and choices, 34–35
  antidiscrimination in education and hiring, 35–37
    PL 93-112 and, 35–36
    PL 102-569 and, 36–37
  becoming informed about laws and regulations, 12–15
    federal laws, 12–13
    judges' opinions or court rulings, 13
    state laws, 13

entitlement to full and appropriate services, 16–35
  expanded services for screening, diagnosis, and treatment under Medicaid, 30–32
    PL 101-239, 31–32
  full access to all public and private facilities, 26–30
    PL 101-336, 26–30
  payment of legal costs to family who wins court case on bases of discrimination, 37
  permission to sue for damages in cases of discrimination, bias, or harassment, 41
  protection of job security, 42–43
  public education, 16–26
    PL 94-142, 17–19
    PL 98-199, 19–20
    PL 99-457, 20–24
    PL 101-476, 24–26
    problems getting compliance with, 103–104
  reimbursement for home- and community-based services under Medicaid, 32–33
    PL 97-35, 32–33
  service development and coordination, 34
    PL 94-103, 34
  summary of, 42–45
  Supplemental Security Income (SSI) cash benefits, 38–41
Legal services, 76–77, 470–471
  for denied insurance claims, 189–190
  for denied Supplemental Security Income (SSI), 249
Legal Services Corporation (Legal Aid), 77, 104, 189, 249, 471, 504
Letter writing, 347–365
  data to include in letter, 349
  keeping copies of letters, 348
  reasons for, 347–348
  sample letters, 350–365
Leukemia Society of America, 215, 369

Life skills/job training and placement services, 73–76, 504
Independent Living Centers, 74
in public schools, 73–74
vocational rehabilitation (VR)
services, 36–37, 45, 63,
69–70, 74–76, 158–161, 527
Life-threatening problems, 49
LRE, *see* Least restrictive environment
Lupus Foundation of America, 215,
370
Lutheran Church, 204, 223–224

Major medical plans, 172–173, 505
lifetime limitations on, 183–184,
505
Managed care plans, 164, 167,
169*t*-170*t*, 174–177, 506
advantages of, 178–179
methods of cost control by,
174–175
service coordination in, 175–176
March of Dimes Birth Defects
Foundation, 215–216, 370
Maternal and Child Health (MCH)
Services block grants, 506
Medicaid, 4, 8, 9, 62, 108,
109–126, 506–509
acceptance by health care providers, 110
co-payments for services under,
110
denied application for, 126
eligibility for, 110–114,
328
Categorically Needy Program,
108, 112, 482
Medically Needy Program,
108, 112–113, 509
optional eligibility groups,
111–114, 507
Optional Services, 115–116,
117*t*, 507
required eligibility groups,
110–111, 507–508
required Basic Services,
114–115
funding for, 109

how and where to apply for,
122–124
information needed to complete
application for, 124–125
services available under,
114–121
Early and Periodic Screening,
Diagnosis, and Treatment
(EPSDT) Program, 30–32,
62, 108, 114, 118–119,
120*f*–121*f*, 338, 340, 492,
494
federally mandated basic services, 114–115, 506–507
limits on, 115
Optional Services, 115–116,
117*t*, 507
Waiver programs, 32–33, 108,
114, 116–118, 329, 508
state agencies for administration
of, 429–435, 523
time to notification about acceptance for, 126
transportation services provided
under, 58
Medicaid Amendments of 1981,
32–33
Medical assistance, *see* General
Assistance—Medical
(GA–Medical) programs
Medical evaluation, 50–51
Medically Needy Program of Medicaid, 108, 112–113, 509
Medicare, 509
coverage of kidney dialysis and
transplantation, 8, 40, 62,
108, 143–149, 503
obtaining information about,
148–149
Part A coverage, 143, 144*t*, 146
Part B coverage, 145*t*, 146–147
services not covered, 148
Handbook for, 509–510
Medications, 115
Mental Health Law Project, *see*
Judge David L. Bazelon Cen-
ter for Mental Health Law
Mobility aids, 2–3
Model programs, 510
Money Management Centers, 311

Muscular dystrophy, 40
Muscular Dystrophy Association,
    Inc., 216, 370

NARIC, *see* National Rehabilita-
    tion Information Center
National AIDS Hotline, 471
National Alliance for the Mentally
    Ill, Children and Adolescent
    Network, 216–217, 255, 370
National Association for Sickle
    Cell Disease, Inc., 217, 370
National Association for the Visu-
    ally Handicapped, 217–218,
    370
National Association of Commu-
    nity Health Centers, 156,
    466
National Association of Develop-
    mental Disabilities (DD)
    Planning Councils, 378
National Association of the Deaf,
    217, 370
National Center for Education and
    Maternal and Child Health,
    80, 470
National Center for Family-
    Centered Care, 88–89
National Center for Youth with
    Disabilities (NCYD), 81
National Child Abuse Hotline,
    475
National Coalition of Hispanic
    Health and Human Services
    Organizations, 230
National Down Syndrome Con-
    gress, 218, 370
National Down Syndrome Society,
    218, 370
National Early Childhood Techni-
    cal Assistance System
    (NEC•TAS), 89, 470, 510,
    511
National Easter Seal Society, 6,
    218–219, 255, 370
National Flotation Health Care
    Foundation, 230–231
National Fragile X Foundation,
    219, 370

National Head Injury Foundation,
    220, 370
National Hemophilia Foundation,
    220, 371
National Information Center for
    Children and Youth with
    Disabilities (NICHCY),
    79–80, 85–86, 469, 510, 511
National Information Clearing-
    house (NIC) for Infants with
    Disabilities and Life-
    Threatening Conditions,
    80–81, 469
National Kidney Foundation,
    220–221, 371
National Library Service for the
    Blind and Physically Hand-
    icapped, 475
National Literacy Hotline, 475
National Mental Health Associa-
    tion, 371
National Organization for Rare
    Disorders, Inc., 221, 371
National Parent Network on Dis-
    ability (NPND), 83–84, 123,
    368, 510–511
National Rehabilitation Informa-
    tion Center (NARIC), 475
National School Breakfast and
    School Lunch Program, 260
National Self-Help Clearinghouse,
    476
National Spinal Cord Injury Asso-
    ciation, 221, 371
"Natural helpers," 10
NCYD, *see* National Center for
    Youth with Disabilities
NEC•TAS, *see* National Early
    Childhood Technical Assis-
    tance System
New Eyes for the Needy, 231
NICHCY, *see* National Informa-
    tion Center for Children and
    Youth with Disabilities
NPND, *see* National Parent Net-
    work on Disability

OBRA, *see* Omnibus Budget Rec-
    onciliation Act

Obtaining services, 47–48, 47–91
  becoming informed about, 48
  immediately, 49
  sample letters for, 347–365
  sources of referral to help,
    78–91; *see also* Informa-
    tion and referral (I&R) ser-
    vices
  tasks required for, 47–48
  tips for getting what you need,
    327–335
  types of services, 50–78
    activities and recreation, 76
    advocacy services, 77–78
    assistance paying for medical
      care, 61
    assistance paying for other ne-
      cessities of life, 63–64
    counseling and support for
      child and family members,
      59–60
    diagnosis and evaluation of
      emotional and behavior
      problems, 52
    educational services, 64–70
    housing and residential ser-
      vices, 70–73
    interdisciplinary evaluation of
      development, 53–54, 503
    intervention and treatment for
      child's emotional or behav-
      ior problem, 55–56
    intervention and treatment for
      child's medical condition, 54
    legal services, 76–77
    life skills/job training and
      placement, 73–76
    other areas of need, 345
    physical diagnosis and evalua-
      tion, 50–51
    preventative and routine
      health care services, 56–57
    respite care, 60
    service coordination, 57–58
    services to improve or main-
      tain child's developmental
      level, 54–55
    transportation, 58–59
Occupational therapy (OT), 511

Offices of Maternal and Child
    Health (MCH), 442–450,
    452, 524
Omnibus Budget Reconciliation
    Act (OBRA), 511
  of 1989, 30–32
  of 1990, 34
Order of the Eastern Star, 227–228
OT, *see* Occupational therapy
Outpatient clinic settings, 95–97

P&A agencies, *see* Protection and
    Advocacy agencies
Pacer Center, 124, 378
Paperwork organization, 317–325
  how and where to store records,
    319, 324, 325
  information to keep readily
    available about child,
    319–320
  information to keep readily
    available about family,
    323–324
  keeping copies of letters,
    348
  key contacts for child's care,
    320, 321*f*–322*f*
  reasons to be organized, 317–319
  receipts for tax-deductible ex-
    penses, 266–268
Parent Training and Information
    (PTI) Centers, 12, 13, 19, 45,
    84–85, 104, 124, 378, 393,
    512, 516
Parents Anonymous, 476
Part B programs (3 through 5, 6
    through 21), 20, 65–66, 108,
    132, 512–513
  lead agencies for, 386–393
Part H programs (birth through 3),
    20–23, 64–65, 86–87, 108,
    131–132, 491–492, 513
  lead agencies for, 380–386,
    503–504
Paying for medical care, 61–63
  federal income tax deductions
    for, 265–269

private sources of help, 60–61,
163–206
Caring Programs for Children,
195–196, 413–416
civic, social welfare, and religious organizations,
198–205, 223–235
disease- and disability-related
organizations, 196–198,
207–222, 368–371,
469–470
health insurance, 164–195
public sources of help, 62–63,
107–162
Children's Special Health Care
Needs (CSHCN) Program,
126–129
Civilian Health and Medical
Program of the Uniformed
Services (CHAMPUS),
133–143
Community Action Agencies
(CAAs) or County Commis-
sions for Economic Oppor-
tunity (CCEOs), 157–158
Community Health and Men-
tal Health Centers, 155–157
county or area public health
departments, 153–154
emergency assistance pro-
grams, 152–153
General Assistance—Medical
(GA–Medical) Program,
149–151
Hill-Burton Free Care Program, 161–162
Medicaid, 109–126
Medicare's coverage of kidney
dialysis and transplantation,
8, 40, 62, 108, 143–149, 503
public hospitals, 154–155
requirements for receiving,
107–108
Rural and Migrant Health
Clinics, 157
state Departments of Education and local education
agencies, 129–132
types of, 108–109

Vocational Rehabilitation (VR)
programs, 158–161
Pediatric AIDS Clearinghouse, 476
Pediatricians, 56–57, 95–97
"Permanently and totally dis-
abled," 275, 513–514
Persistence, 328–329
Physical activity limitations, 2
Physical diagnosis and evaluation
services, 50–51
Physical therapy (PT), 514, 517
PL 93-112, *see* Rehabilitation Act
of 1973
PL 94-103, *see* Developmental Dis-
abilities Assistance and Bill
of Rights Act of 1975
PL 94-142, *see* Education for All
Handicapped Children Act
of 1975
PL 97-35, *see* Medicaid Amend-
ments of 1981
PL 98-199, *see* Education of the
Handicapped Act Amend-
ments of 1983
PL 98-435, *see* Voting Accessibility
for Elderly and Handicapped
Act of 1984
PL 99-361, *see* Fair Debt Collec-
tion Practices Act Amend-
ments of 1986
PL 99-372, *see* Handicapped Chil-
dren's Protection Act of
1986
PL 99-435, *see* Air Carrier's Access
Act of 1986
PL 99-457, *see* Education of the
Handicapped Act Amend-
ments of 1986
PL 100-407, *see* Technology-
Related Assistance for Indi-
viduals with Disabilities Act
of 1988
PL 100-430, *see* Fair Housing Act
Amendments of 1988
PL 101-239, *see* Omnibus Budget
Reconciliation Act (OBRA)
of 1989
PL 101-336, *see* Americans with Dis-
abilities Act (ADA) of 1990

PL 101-476, *see* Education of the Handicapped Act Amendments of 1990; Individuals with Disabilities Education Act (IDEA)

PL 101-508, *see* Omnibus Budget Reconciliation Act of 1990

PL 102-119, *see* Individuals with Disabilities Education Act (IDEA) Amendments

PL 102-166, *see* Civil Rights Act of 1991

PL 102-569, *see* Rehabilitation Act Amendments of 1992

PL 103-3, *see* Family and Medical Leave Act of 1993

Point-of-service (POS) plans, 170t, 174, 176–177, 514
   advantages of, 179
   see also Managed care plans

Poor Relief, *see* General Assistance—Medical (GA–Medical) programs

POS, *see* Point-of-service plans

Poverty level, federal, 111

PPOs, *see* Preferred provider organizations

Practitioners Reporting Network, 476

Pre-existing conditions, 173–174, 177, 341, 514

Preferred provider organizations (PPOs), 165, 170t, 174, 176, 515.
   advantages of, 179
   see also Managed care plans

Presbyterian Church, 204

Preschool education services, 18, 20, 64–66; *see also* Part B programs
   Head Start, 67, 498–499

Preventative health care services, 56–57

Primary care doctors, 187, 515

Problem solving, 330–335

Procedural safeguards, 526

Professional associations, 192

Professionals, 10
   dealing with, 93–105

obtaining information from, 50
   what to expect from hospital employees, 97–99
   what to expect from insurance company, 99–101
   what to expect from teachers, principal, and school district, 101–104
   what to expect in outpatient clinic settings, 95–97

Program for Kidney Dialysis and Kidney Transplantation, 8, 62, 503

Protected groups, 111

Protection and Advocacy (P&A) agencies, 13, 34, 45, 77, 371–378, 470, 512, 516

Psychologists, 517

PT, *see* Physical therapy

PTI Centers, *see* Parent Training and Information Centers

Public health departments, 153–154, 499
   locations of, 154
   services provided by, 153–154

Public Health Service, 191, 451

Public Law, *see specific PL number*

Quality of services, 94

Recreation services, 76

Rehabilitation Act of 1973, 35–36
   Section 504, 16, 17, 27, 29, 36, 339, 519

Rehabilitation Act Amendments of 1992, 37, 75

Religious organizations, 201–205, 251–252, 413

Resource contacts, 367–477
   advocacy and family support, 368–378
      Developmental Disabilities (DD) Planning Councils, 378
      disease- and disability-related organizations, 368–371

Parent Training and Information (PTI) Centers, 378
Protection and Advocacy (P&A) agencies, 371–378
debt management, 379
  County Agricultural Extension Services, 379
  Federal Trade Commission (FTC) regional offices, 379
education and training, 380–406
  Client Assistance Programs (CAPs), 400–406
  Part B lead agencies, 386–393
  Part H lead agencies, 380–386, 503–504
  state Vocational Rehabilitation (VR) programs, 393–400
financial and related assistance, 405–424
  Aid to Families with Dependent Children (AFDC), 416
  Caring Programs for Children, 412–415
  church ministries, 413
  civic and social welfare organizations, 413
  General Assistance (GA) and General Assistance—Medical (GA–Medical) Programs, 416
  health, social service, and religious organizations, 413
  HEATH Resource Center, 417
  Hill-Burton Hotline, 412
  Internal Revenue Service (IRS), 417
  regional offices of Food and Nutrition Service, 416–417
  state Community Service Block Grant Agencies, 406–413
  state Departments of Revenue, 418–423
health and related services, 452–468
  American Association of University Affiliated Programs for Persons with Developmental Disabilities, 468
  Children's Special Health Care Needs (CSHCN) programs, 452
  Community Mental Health Centers (CMHCs), 466
  National Association of Community Health Centers, 466
  Regional Centers for Independent Living, 466–468
  Rural or Migrant Health Centers, 466
  state Departments of Developmental Disabilities, 452–458
  state Departments of Mental Health, Children and Youth Services, 458–465
  state Offices of Maternal and Child Health (MCH), 452
  state Vocational Rehabilitation (VR) programs, 466
health insurance, 423–451
  Children's Special Health Care Needs (CSHCN) programs, 436–442
  Civilian Health and Medical Program of the Uniformed Services (CHAMPUS), 450
  Communicating for Agriculture, 451
  state Departments of Insurance, 423–429
  state Medicaid agencies, 429–435
  state Offices of Maternal and Child Health (MCH), 442–450
  U.S. Department of Labor, 451
  U.S. Public Health Service, 451
information about services for children and families, 469–470
  advocacy and family support organizations, 469
  Child Find, 470
  crisis services, 470
  Developmental Disabilities (DD) Planning Councils, 469

Resource contacts—*continued*
  national disease- and disabil-
    ity-related organizations,
    469–470
  United Way and other com-
    munity services, 470
  legal assistance, 470–471
    Judge David L. Bazelon Center
      for Mental Health Law,
      470–471
    Protection and Advocacy
      (P&A) Agencies, 470
  telephone numbers, 471–477
Resources, defined, 518
Respite care, 60, 518
"Risk pools," 193–195,
    519
Rudeness, 332–333
Rural and Migrant Health Clinics,
    109, 157, 466, 510, 519
Ruritan National, 231–232

Salvation Army, 232
School absences, 2
Schools, *see* Education services
Section 504, 16, 17, 27, 29, 36,
    339, 519
Seizure disorders, 3, 21
Sensory impairments, 21
Service coordination, 57–58, 97,
    175–176, 520
  increasing popularity of, 57
  laws on, 33–34
  in managed care plans, 175–176
Sex Information and Education
    Council of the United States
    (SIECUS), 476
Sheltered workshops, 520
*Shepard's Acts and Cases by Pop-
    ular Names—Federal and
    State,* 12
Shriners Hospitals for Crippled
    Children, 232
Sibling Information Network, 476
Siblings, 3
Sickle cell disease, 3
SIECUS, *see* Sex Information and
    Education Council of the
    United States

SKFB, *see* Soup Kitchens and Food
    Banks programs
Sliding scale fee system, 520
Small group insurance plans, 193
Social Security Administration
    (SSA), 520
Social Security Hotline, 477
Social welfare organizations,
    200–201, 413, 520–521
Social workers, 521
Soup Kitchens and Food Banks
    (SKFB) programs, 260, 413
Special education directors, *see*
    Part B Coordinators
Special Supplemental Food Pro-
    gram for Women, Infants,
    and Children (WIC), 63, 238,
    259–260, 522, 527
Specialized home care, 70–71, 497
Spina bifida, 3, 4
Spina Bifida Association of Ameri-
    ca, 222, 255, 371
SSA, *see* Social Security Adminis-
    tration
SSI, *see* Supplemental Security In-
    come
St. Jude Children's Research Hos-
    pital, 233
State government offices, 86–88
State laws, 13
Sullivan v. Zebley, 15, 38–39, 240,
    528
Supervised apartments, 72, 525
Supplemental Security Income
    (SSI), 4, 9, 15, 38–41, 63,
    110–111, 237, 238–250, 522,
    525
  appealing denial of benefits
    from, 248–250
  eligibility for, 238–242
    disability criteria, 38–39,
      239–241
    evaluating children for, 39–40,
      239–241
    income criteria, 41, 241–242
    limit on resources for, 242
    List of Impairments, 39–40,
      240, 505
    "presumptive," 40, 246–247,
      515

filing date for, 497
funding for, 238
how to apply for, 242–244, 406, 477
information needed to complete application for, 244–245
state supplements to, 238, 250, 524
time to hear about acceptance for, 245–248
Support Dogs for the Handicapped, Inc., 233
Support groups, 6, 330, 496
national parent organizations, 82–84, 512
Surplus Food Distribution programs, 9, 63, 238, 260–261, 416–418, 525–526

Taking time off, 8
Tax Equity and Fiscal Responsibility Act of 1982, Section 134 (TEFRA 134), 113–114
Tax savings, 7, 9, 263–306
on federal income tax, 264–275
charitable contributions, 270–271, 484
credit for Child and Dependent Care expenses, 272, 484
credit for the elderly or disabled, 275
deductions, exemptions, and credits defined, 265–266, 488–489, 495
deductions for medical and related care, 265–269
earned income credit (EIC), 273–275
exemptions, 271
itemizing deductions, 265, 503
"long form" and "short form," 265–266, 505, 520
self-employed health insurance deduction, 269–270
standard tax deductions, 266, 524–525
Internal Revenue Service (IRS) publication about, 264

on state income tax, 275–277, 281–306
suggestions for filing income tax returns, 277–278
Technical Assistance for Parents Programs (TAPPs), 20
Technology-Related Assistance for Individuals with Disabilities Act of 1988, 34
TEFAP, *see* Temporary Emergency Food Assistance Program
TEFRA 134, *see* Tax Equity and Fiscal Responsibility Act of 1982, Section 134
Telecommunications, 29–30
Telephone calls, 348
Telephone numbers, 471–477
Temporary Emergency Food Assistance Program (TEFAP), 260, 413
Texas Respite Resource Network, 477
TextType (TT) calls, 475
The Arc, 210, 369
Title V programs, 526
Transition to adult living, 20, 25, 69, 73–74
Transportation services and payments, 58–59, 257
income tax deduction for mileage, 267–268, *269*
Traveler's Aid International, 233–234
TT, *see* TextType calls
2176 Waivers, 32–33, 108, 114, 116–118, 329, 508

UAPs, *see* University Affiliated Programs
Unemployment, 28–29
Uniformed Service Organization World Headquarters, 234–235
Unions, 192
United Cerebral Palsy Association, 222, 371
United Methodist Church, 204–205
Association of Health and Welfare Ministries, 234

United Way of America, 200, 311, 312, 470, 477
University Affiliated Programs (UAPs), 49, 51, 52, 89–90, 468, 527
University benevolent funds, 200
U.S. Code Congressional and Administrative News, 12

Venture Clubs of the Americas, 235
Vocational Rehabilitation (VR) services, 36–37, 45, 63, 69–70, 74–76, 109, 158–161, 527
  applying for, 161
  community agencies providing, 75–76
  eligibility for, 75, 158–159
  funding for, 160–161

state contacts for, 69–70, 393–400, 466
  termination of, 160
  types of, 159–160
Volunteers of America, National Headquarters, 235
Voting Accessibility for Elderly and Handicapped Act of 1984, 34
VR services, *see* Vocational Rehabilitation services

Wage losses, 5
White House switchboard, 476
Women's centers, 311–312
Women's Legal Defense Fund, 43, 471

Zebley court decision, 15, 38–39, 240, 528